Nazorean

Nazorean

How a Jewish Wisdom Sect
Gave Birth to the Church

KEM LUTHER

WIPF & STOCK · Eugene, Oregon

NAZOREAN
How a Jewish Wisdom Sect Gave Birth to the Church

Wipf & Stock
An Imprint of Wipf and Stock Publishers
199 W. 8th Ave., Suite 3
Eugene, OR 97401

www.wipfandstock.com

PAPERBACK ISBN: 979-8-3852-2597-2
HARDCOVER ISBN: 979-8-3852-2598-9
EBOOK ISBN: 979-8-3852-2599-6

07/30/24

For Ilyas and Faiz

The multitude of the wise is the salvation of the world.

—WISDOM OF SOLOMON 6:24

Contents

Preface		ix
Abbreviations		xi
1	Spiritualities	1
2	Sects and Strings of Pearls	24
3	Wisdom and Sages	51
4	Wisdom in Matthew	79
5	Brother James	125
6	Nazoreans and Therapeutae	139
7	John the Nazorean	161
8	*Psalms of Solomon* and Acts	224
9	Nazoreans Elsewhere	243
10	Misapplied Metaphors	252
Appendix		259
Bibliography		275
Name Index		285
Ancient Document Index		289

Preface

WRITING HISTORY, SAID THE philosopher and historian R. G. Collingwood, is weaving "a web of imaginative construction."[1] The efforts of the historian and the novelist, he points out, do not differ in their attention to imagination—both use it to construct their stories. Where they differ is that the historian's narrative, guided by a zeal for the real, molds itself around interpretations of evidence.

In this book, I construct five of Collingwood's imaginative webs. They are interrelated takes on topics touching on Jewish sects and the Bible's wisdom tradition. The heart of what I want to cover is in the last two webs, the fourth (chapter 6) and the fifth (chapters 7–9). The fourth web paints a picture of the Nazoreans, a poorly documented sect that evolved into Christian Judaism. The fifth web is about a split in this sectarian movement, a division that is reflected in the most primitive documents of Christianity. These two webs, since they take the study of the historical Jesus in an unusual direction, may be somewhat controversial. If they are, please put this down to my tilt toward the imaginative side of the web-making task.

To weave these two difficult webs, I start by constructing three less controversial webs on which they can be suspended. The first of these foundational webs (chapter 2) is a story about several Jewish sectarian movements. I explore how second-temple Jewish sects contested the scriptural interpretations of mainline Judaism. The second web (chapter 3) reviews the wisdom tradition in the Hebrew Scriptures and in the Christian books that expanded this part of the Bible. This OT[2] heritage of wisdom shaped the way that many Jews in the late Second Temple period understood their relationship to God and the cosmos. The third

1. Collingwood, *Idea of History*, 244. His discussion of the webs is on 242–6.

2. I will designate these expanded Scriptures as "OT." For an explanation of this term, see the section in the Appendixes on "The problem with 'Old Testament.'"

web (chapters 4 and 5) extends the OT wisdom tradition into the field of NT studies, looking at how the Gospel of Matthew and the Epistle of James bear the imprint of a wisdom heritage.

Translations in the text of this book, unless otherwise noted, are by the author. There are a few places where the numbering of chapters and verses in the Masoretic Hebrew text differs from that found in most English translations. In these cases, I have cited the English numbering. Where the numbering of the Psalms differs in Catholic and Protestant Bibles, I have adopted the Protestant/Hebrew sequence. Note also that I have followed the common shorthand of referring to "the author of the Gospel of John" simply as "John" and applying the analogous convention to the other three gospels. I use these conventions without any suggestion that Matthew, Mark, Luke, and John are the names of the persons who wrote their gospels.

The bibliography at the end is a list of articles and books cited in this study. A bibliography the size of this book would only make a small dent in the literature that is relevant to the topics in biblical studies covered in this text.

I hardly know where to begin in thanking those who helped bring this book to life. The constant support of my wife and family throughout the long process has been essential. Early versions of the manuscript were read by Ian, David, Jeanne, and Philip. The less tangible—but no less real—support given by the friends with whom I share my Christian journey has also been important. Work on this text has reminded me, almost daily, of interactions with outstanding teachers in the first half of my life. Of all those who stepped into that role, I remember best those who modeled the attitudes of curiosity and learning that they hoped to find in their students.

Abbreviations

Ag. Ap.	*Against Apion*
Ant.	*Jewish Antiquities*
ASR	*American Sociological Review*
BBS	*Behavioral and Brain Sciences*
Bek.	*Bekhorot*
CBQ	*Catholic Biblical Quarterly*
CBR	*Currents in Biblical Research*
Cherubim	*On the Cherubim*
Contempl. Life	*On the Contemplative Life*
Vir. ill.	*De viris illustribus*
ET	*Expository Times*
Flight	*On Flight and Finding*
Good Person	*That Every Good Person is Free*
Haer.	*Adversus haereses*
Hist.	*Ecclesiastical History*
HTR	*Harvard Theological Review*
JBL	*Journal of Biblical Literature*
JECS	*Journal of Early Christian Studies*
JEH	*Journal of Ecclesiastical History*
JSHJ	*Journal for the Study of the Historical Jesus*
JSNT	*Journal for the Study of the New Testament*
JSP	*Journal for the Study of the Pseudepigrapha*

Life	*Life of Flavius Josephus*
Neot.	*Neotestamentica*
NETS	*New English Translation of the Septuagint*
NovT	*Novum Testamentum*
NTS	*New Testament Studies*
Orig. Princ.	*De principiis*
Pan.	*Panarion (The Refutation of All Heresies)*
SR	*Studies in Religion*

1

Spiritualities

OF ALL THE AREAS of human intellectual endeavour, the most distorted by tainted perspectives is the study of the Bible. Interpretations of the life of Jesus are the most susceptible to personal bias.[1] True objectivity, says Elisabeth Schüssler Fiorenza, "can only be approached by reflecting critically on and naming one's theoretical presuppositions."[2] I'll begin my imaginative webs, then, by bringing the imaginer into the picture.

A few decades ago, religious and psychological writers began to use the plural term "spiritualities" to describe how we orient ourselves toward matters of faith. I have come to think of my own journey as a transition through three of these. Each new spirituality, when I stepped into it, distanced me from its predecessor. The distances have now become so great that I no longer feel like the same person that lived the first two stages. I still possess his name, his debts, some of his memories, perhaps a few molecules of his body, but not much more.

SPIRITUALITY ONE

For most persons with an attachment to a faith tradition, their spiritual lives are shaped in the family home. In my case, this formation, if it happened, was subtle. I was born on a Nebraska ranch to parents that had no active connection to a church. Both had grown up in families with

---

1. "There is no venture more tainted by personal history than writing a life of Jesus" (Schweitzer, *Reimarus*, 4).
2. Schüssler Fiorenza, *In Memory of Her*, xvii.

strong Protestant traditions, but they had abandoned these traditions long before I was born.

One of these interrupted faith traditions came from the family of my father. My father's mother had died at age eighteen while my father was still a toddler, so my dad's earliest years were spent with grandparents. Reports say that these grandparents were faithful members of a denomination known as the Church of God. Earlier in their lives, family histories say, they may have been Free Will Baptists. The exposure of my dad to these church traditions, however, was brief. As soon as he was old enough, my father married and set up his own household, and when he did, he left behind any identification with his grandparent's religious beliefs and practices. Whatever my father may have learned about his family's religious tradition, he did not pass it along to his son.

My mother was also born into a church-oriented community. Her grandfather was a minister in a Missouri branch of the Dunkers, a church that is part of the German Baptist Brethren. The man must have been an important figure in that denomination—he has an entry in the *Brethren Encyclopedia*. Her father, a preacher's kid, appears to have been a participating member of the Dunker church, at least when he was young. In his twenties, though, my grandfather married a Baptist woman, and this may have started his withdrawal from the Dunkers. When my grandparents were in their forties, they traded their business in Missouri for a farm in the Nebraska Sandhills. The move marked the end of my grandfather's involvement in churches. My grandfather's wife, my maternal grandmother, continued to identify as a Christian and occasionally played the organ for a small church in their remote Sandhills town. None of their seven children, however, carried into their adult lives any sense of belonging to a church.

By the time I came into the picture, my father had three grown children from an earlier marriage. These older half siblings, who formed the extended family in my early years, also had no attachment to a church. In my earliest years, then, I knew no more about religion and the Christian church than what I heard on the radio or read in books.

This changed in the last years of grade school. While my immediate kin had abandoned any public expressions of faith, my wider family, my dad's siblings and aunts and uncles, kept up their connections with a variety of churches. Several of them, I later learned, were part of the Salvation Army. I have pictures of them in their Army uniforms, with their polished brass buttons and their red-banded caps and bonnets. An aunt of mine, a member of a local church, began to pick me up on Sunday mornings and take me to church with her. The church was an Evangelical United Brethren congregation, part of a denomination that is now included in the United Methodist Church. For several years, from perhaps the age of nine or ten, I was part of the Sunday school in that church. I also attended the worship service after Sunday school, even though it was a service that made almost no accommodation to children—I spent most of the services daydreaming. When I became a teen, I joined the church's young adult group. I was also, for a year or so, a member of the church choir.[3]

From this early exposure to mainline Protestantism in rural Nebraska, I emerged, against all odds, with what is sometimes called a "faith formation." I wish I could tell you how this formation altered my behavior and beliefs, but I can't—much of it has gone from memory. In a letter that Sigmund Freud wrote to Karl Abraham in 1924, he mentioned a paper he had written almost fifty years earlier: "To feel that I am the same person as the author of [that paper] is a strong demand on the unity of the self. But it appears to be the case."[4] Like Freud and his forgotten paper, I would also be pressed to tell you what the connection is between me and the boy that I was. The faith formation that I received, however, seems to have sunk deep. The tune of an old hymn, the smell and echo of a church sanctuary, a thumbed Bible, the feel of a shellacked wooden pew—all of these can still awaken in me a sense of belonging and childhood.

God says to Pascal in the *Pensées*, "You would not seek me if you had not found me."[5] But what had I found in these early experiences? I might have replicated my parent's church experience—early exposure and adult indifference—if another influence had not intervened. That influence was education. I was attuned from my earliest years to the larger intellectual world. I do not know why. My parents, my much-older siblings, and my many aunts and uncles and cousins had almost no interest in this dimension of life. Few of them had attended high school. If there were educated professionals among them—doctors, scientists, lawyers, or teachers—I had no contact with them.

This other influence in my life first expressed itself, when I entered high school, in an interest in science and math. As I picked up the basic tools of science, I absorbed along with them a perspective that was inimical to religion. I found in the sciences a grand scheme of nature that was

3. A testimony to inclusiveness over quality.

4. Freud and Abraham, *Briefwechsel*, 779. Letter dated September 21, 1924.

5. Pascal, *Pensées*, 604. In Sellier's numbering, this is part of pensée 751.

silent on the issues of God and immortality. The designs of the divine were replaced, in the stories of science, by random events. The point of view that I had received from my earlier exposure to the church started to look, when seen from the perspective of science, like an elaborate set of myths. Dividing the world between science and religion, between knowledge and faith, seemed to heap all the truth on the side of science.

I was unhappy with this split, but I was not ready to compromise my new intellectual journey. When I began to voice my concerns about the incompatibility of science and religion, I had trouble finding people who could see the problem. I talked about it with leaders in my church. They suggested that the facts of science could be accepted without question. Religion, they said, could fill in where science left off. I was not satisfied with this approach. It seemed to be a shaky foundation for a life of faith. A God-of-the-gaps, as John A.T. Robinson points out in *Honest to God*, "is constantly pushed further and further back as the tide of secular studies advances."[6] With enough expansion of scientific knowledge, faith could shrink to nothing.

The only other person who had anything to say about my problem was one of my high school classmates, the son of a minister at a local evangelical church. This friend introduced me to his father. In discussions with my friend and his father, I encountered an approach to Christianity that was outside of my experience with the church. It was a kind of rationalism that accepted science's ground rules for deciding what was true and what was not. Where faith and science disagreed, however, this brand of religion was ready to challenge science. The theory of evolution, for example, was simply wrong if it said that God did not directly create species. The many stories in the Bible that seemed like fables—angels visiting people and demons possessing them, God destroying the world with a flood—were facts on the same level as the facts of science.

I could not at first accept these claims. But my friend's approach did address the problem that was bothering me—that the assumptions made by a scientific understanding of the world seemed to take away all its magic and value. I wanted to know more. Was it possible that a religious view of the world could push back against science instead of accepting the crumbs it left under the table? My evangelical friend and his father were passing along ideas to me that they had picked up in their own faith journeys, but they did not know enough detail about these ideas

6. Robinson, *Honest to God*, 37.

to convince me that they were right. They pointed me, though, to some of the literature written by evangelicals with science backgrounds. I read these books and corresponded with some of the authors. And I started attending my friend's church.

I make this sound as though I was on a strictly intellectual journey. I wasn't. Arthur Koestler, describing his own conversion to communism in the thirties, points out that faith isn't acquired by reason. We do not "enter the womb of a church as a result of logical persuasion."[7] Much of what was happening to me can't be explained in syllogisms. I was, after all, a hormone-ridden teen at the time of my evangelical conversion. By the social standards of the day, I wasn't the sort of kid a parent would worry about—no gang memberships, no heavy drinking or other drugs, no rap sheet. But I still had a sense of moral failure, especially when I measured myself against the standards that I had learned from my early church experiences. I had some sexual adventures and sadistic fantasies that seemed unchristian. I was bothered by my pride and occasional outbursts of anger. I had weight problems and couldn't stick to diets. These failures left me with a deep sense of guilt. If God existed, I thought, God wouldn't be pleased with me.

The message I was hearing at the evangelical church that I had begun to attend spoke to this sense of failure. The remedy it prescribed was being saved. Salvation involved owning up to my sins, confessing them to God (not, thankfully, to another person), and asking for forgiveness. The act would be followed by erasure of these bad marks and the bestowal of an inner power that would let me do what I knew was right. This kind of salvation was something that I desperately wanted. It seemed like it might restore my childhood sense of God's presence. To take such a step would mean, of course, that I accepted there was some reality to religious belief, so the moral and the intellectual moves were connected. I agonized for some weeks over what to do. Finally, in the spring of my junior year of high school, my desire outweighed my reluctance—I bent my knee and became evangelical Christian.

SPIRITUALITY TWO

Taking this step transformed my life. Augustine prayed at his own conversion that he had begun "to unwill what I wanted and to will what you

---

7. Koestler, *The God that Failed*, 25.

wanted."[8] I had no idea where my new outlook would lead—giving up my own plans for my life was part of what the move meant. As Koestler notes, for the new believer, "the whole universe falls into pattern like the stray pieces of a jig-saw puzzle assembled by magic at one stroke."[9] The poet Stephen Spender, also talking about his conversion to communism, compared his own framework switch to finding "the sum of all sums."[10] The intermediate calculations leading to this sum didn't have to make sense—any objection they raised would eventually cancel out of the equation. Not all my intellectual problems were resolved by my conversion, but I hoped that, further along in my new life, that the pieces would somehow click into place, that the sums would add up.

The most immediate outcome of my conversion was a change in my college plans. As a result of some state tests, I had been given a scholarship to the University of Nebraska. My friend, the pastor's son, was planning to attend a bible college in Chicago to prepare for the ministry. I wondered whether I should also attend the same college. While I had no plans to become a minister, there was much about my leap into this new life that I wanted to understand. I decided to decline the university scholarship and enrol in the three-year program at Moody Bible Institute.

I stayed at Moody for all three years of the program. My experiences there were varied and complex—I could write chapters about them. Let me sum them up, however, with just four impressions—three about what I learned at Moody and one about what I didn't learn but should have.

First, I realized at Moody that *the Evangelicalism I had embraced was much less unified than I thought*. I believed that by choosing to become an evangelical Christian, I had made the hardest and most important choice of my life. Instead, I found myself having to decide what sort of evangelical I was. A variety of institutions, spiritual styles, and doctrinal beliefs all competed for my attention. With no objective means of comparing them, all I could do was reach inside myself and see what fit best with my own interests and skills. This, though, was the same self that I had put aside to become a Christian, now sneaking in the back door. My desire to participate in a larger intellectual world, the impulse that had led me to a scientific framework that discouraged religious ideas, became a lodestone in deciding where my Christian journey should go. But this time I

8. A literal translation of Augustine's metrical "nolle quod volebam et velle quod volebas" (Augustine, *Confessions*, 9.1.1.).

9. Koestler, *The God that Failed*, 32.

10. Spender, *The God that Failed*, 255.

didn't want to re-enter the sciences—I knew too well the call of that siren. I decided that I would tackle the humanities. By the time I left Moody, I was already making plans to enter university teaching, perhaps in philosophy. I had big questions, and philosophy, though it did not always provide answers, at least affirmed that big questions were worth asking.

The second turn I took at Moody centered on *my emotional and spiritual life*. The broader public thinks that Evangelicalism is a set of ideas. Those who are around it for a while soon realize that experience trumps doctrine. The goal of the evangelical is to live wrapped up in a spirituality. The spirituality that was most widely practiced at Moody included a combination of constant thankfulness, interior dialogue with Jesus, regular devotional reading of the Bible, concern for the spiritual state of non-evangelicals, willingness to submit to external authority, and acceptance of opposition as a test of faith. This may sound like a lot of balls to juggle at once, but keep in mind that this list is just an unpacking of what evangelicals themselves perceive as a unified spiritual personality. Nor is this a program that individuals are forced to implement by their own efforts—spiritualities are *group* practices and attitudes. Those who are in the groove know intuitively when others are part of the same program. By the same token, those who are *not* members of the group often recognize that evangelicals share something that they aren't part of. In the years after I was at Moody, a reporter who was not an evangelical wrote an article on the school for *Time Magazine*. He puzzled over the handshakes that he received from Moody students. When I read that article, I realized, for the first time, that the spirituality we shared at Moody included a specific way of greeting other people. The magazine writer had no access to the spirituality itself, but he recognized that something outside of his perception was at work.

I did my best, the first year I was at Moody, to live inside this evangelical spirituality. In the fall of my second year, however, just when I was getting the hang of it, I received a body blow that took me out of the game. Before I went to Moody, a new woman had come into our church fellowship. She did not have an evangelical background, so she went through the same stages of conversion that I did. I started to spend a lot of time with her. We soon fell in love. She was a year behind me in high school, so in the next year, my first year at Moody, she stayed in Nebraska, finishing her senior year. The separation was painful, but we wrote constantly to each other and longed for school vacations when we could rekindle our relationship. She left home to attend the University of Nebraska, and I began my second year at Moody. That fall, while returning to her home on a school break, the car she was driving was struck by a drunk driver. As soon as I got word of the accident, I flew back to Nebraska, arriving in time to spend a few silent minutes with her before she died.

After the funeral, I returned to Moody. I was in a bad place, numb in body and spirit. A more seasoned evangelical might have found some comfort in evangelical spirituality. For me, though, any attempt to practice the spirituality called to mind the deepest loss I had ever known. I was thrown back on attitudes that predated my conversion. I should probably have left Moody at that point, but I was in no state to make any decision about my life. I just coasted. But I knew, from that point on, that my own program was branching. Parts of me were transitioning into a different spirituality. It would be a while before I was ready to shake off all the tatters of the evangelical cocoon, but the change had begun. I was losing the handshake.

The third turn I took in my years at Moody Bible Institute was a smaller event, but one with a long reach. It concerns the changes in *how I read the Bible*. In my last year at Moody, when the numbness waned and I began to see color and sense feelings again, I started dating. I soon met the woman who would become my lifetime companion. But it wasn't just my social and emotional life that awakened during that last year at Moody. I had acquired, by then, some of the tools that I needed to approach the text of the Bible on my own. I could work directly with Greek and Hebrew sources, and I was starting to get some sense of the historical background of the documents in the Bible. I began to spend more time in the library working on my own questions, less time with classes and assignments. The Moody library was heavily slanted toward an evangelical understanding of the Bible, but I found enough books and articles from other perspectives to set me on the way toward a broader approach to the text of the Bible.

Every Jewish and Christian community, says the Jewish scholar James Kugel, comes to their sacred texts with the expectation that the words contain a message from God given under conditions of divine inspiration. As such, the texts can contain no contradictions—the disparate parts must have, at some deeper level, an inner harmony.[11] Evangelicals take a unique tack on this assumption. Most of them believe that this inspiration has caused the Bible to be a perfect historical record of exactly

---

11. Kugel, *How to Read*, 15.

what God wants readers to know about the events described. The Bible therefore contains no factual errors or inconsistencies, either in religion or science.[12] Evangelicals go to great trouble to explain how apparent inconsistencies in this error-free text are surface disagreements. Some of their workarounds are clever.[13] Anyone who finds claims of an inerrant text to be preposterous should spend some time reading these explanations. I found it impossible to come up with an inconsistency that could not be explained. Ask evangelicals why none of the four gospels agree about the wording of the titulus, the three-language plaque affixed to the cross of Jesus that described Jesus as the "King of the Jews," and you discover that each gospel was translating a different language or that each gospel was abbreviating a longer inscription. Ask whether Jesus ate the Passover meal and was crucified on the next day, as the Synoptic Gospels say, or whether he was crucified on the Day of Preparation that ended with the Passover meal, as the Gospel of John says, and you learn that different calendars were being used. Ask why Matthew and Luke do not agree on Jesus's genealogy, and you discover that Luke has Mary's ancestral line and Matthew has Joseph's. And on it goes. After a while, of course, the explanations began to look like a long string of special pleadings. But I could find no smoking gun, no single passage that could not be explained using evangelical assumptions about an inerrant text.

After many months of this back and forth—months that stretched into the period after I finished the program at Moody—I began to consider larger questions about what historical records are and how they are interpreted as history. This was when I first understood that the sort of pristine historical record assumed by the inerrant approach did not—could not—exist. History was both the question brought to the records and the answer the records gave to the question. Evangelical beliefs about inerrancy, by removing the views of the human authors from the equation, take away the very questions that give meaning to historical narrative. In trying to test contradictions in the evangelical understanding of the biblical text, I was chasing a phantom.

12. The Chicago Statement on Biblical Inerrancy, widely available on the internet and in print, is the evangelical standard. It was signed by more than 200 church leaders in 1978. "We affirm that Scripture in its entirety is inerrant, being free from all falsehood, fraud, or deceit. We deny that Biblical infallibility and inerrancy are limited to spiritual, religious, or redemptive themes, exclusive of assertions in the fields of history and science" (Chicago Statement, Article XII).

13. On some of the strategies employed to maintain an inerrant text, see Rezetko, "Introducing *Misusing Scripture*," 31–3.

I can't reconstruct the exact process that I went through to arrive at this broader understanding of how history works. Later, when I was studying philosophy, I would associate this approach with the works of R.G. Collingwood.[14] During the writing of history, Collingwood points out in his books, we do not read the story directly off the data—our histories, when we write them, are always answers to the questions we have brought. A historical fact, then, is both the answer to the question *and* the question itself. When the questions we bring are those of a community, the answers gain a feeling of objectivity. This feeling of objectivity, when it forgets its subjective source, can masquerade as something it is not.

Before I leave these years that I spent at Moody and how I changed while I was there, let me mention something that I didn't learn when I was there but should have. My thinking in those days was still highly analytic. Given a focused problem, I would worry the question, like a dog on a bone, until some resolution appeared. But that same intensity made me miss obvious facts when the subject was slightly out of focus. Hovering in the background, both at the time of my evangelical conversion and in the years that I was at Moody, was the issue of how I defined the movement that I was part of. Historians sometimes call this movement "neo-Evangelicalism." We didn't call it that—I and my friends thought of ourselves as simply "evangelicals." We used that term instead of "fundamentalists." Fundamentalists, we thought, were old-line, anti-intellectual, unenlightened believers. On a point-by-point basis, we realized, evangelicals weren't all that different from fundamentalists. The rebranding flagged a change in attitude rather than belief. Evangelicals, the people at Moody would have said, were more ready to engage secular culture than the fundamentalists were. Evangelicals wanted to be separate from the world but not in a way that took them out of the world. They liked to accept the assumptions of secular society and show how they could lead, rationally and inevitably, to their own evangelical perspective.

---

14. My first acquaintance with the works of Collingwood came through my study of the idealist tradition in philosophy. Later I would learn that some branches of biblical studies also trafficked in Collingwood's ideas about historical knowledge. For a review of his influence in biblical studies, see Ryan, "Jesus at the Crossroads." Collingwood, says Ryan, is "a forerunner of postmodern historiography" who operates by "connecting the evidence with robust threads of historical imagination" (Ryan, "Jesus," 69). The lack of attention to Collingwood's historiographic principles, Ryan suggests, indicates "the degree to which New Testament studies have developed in relative isolation from other historical disciplines" (Ryan, "Jesus," 88).

You would think that I and my friends at Moody, in calling ourselves evangelicals, would have had a clear idea what an evangelical was.
But the truth was that we didn't know how to draw a circle that encompassed evangelicals and left everyone else outside. Groups are always
defined more by what they are not than by what they are. Protestants,
for example, are not Roman Catholics. The opposition is even coded in
the name—they protest. The essence of evangelical/fundamentalist self-
definition stemmed from a disagreement in the nineteenth century about
how to apply historical-critical studies to the text of the Bible. Those who
disagreed with evangelicals, the explanation went, were modernists. The
definition of evangelical became a story about nested concentric circles.
Evangelicals were Christians, not pagans or atheists. Evangelicals were
Protestants, not Catholics. Evangelicals were not modernists.

But who were the modernists that those of us in this innermost
circle were supposed to disagree with? I was told that they were usually
found in mainline denominations, groups such as Methodists, Presby-
terians, and Lutherans. The students at Moody, I could see, were usually
not from these types of churches. They came from independent churches,
or from churches that had organized themselves into small denominations, or from several types of Baptist churches, or from English Brethren circles. A few Moody students, however, belonged to the mainline
denominations, so modernism, whatever it was, must have been more
a feature of the leadership in these mainline denominations than of the
rank-and-file.

No one that I knew at Moody, however, felt that all those remaining in the circle after excluding the modernists were true evangelicals.
There were other groups that had to be moved outside. The Mormons, for
example. And all the Jehovah's Witnesses and Christian Scientists. The
way to exclude them, according to what I learned at Moody, was to define
them as cults. I was confused, though, about what made a cult a cult—
the issues seemed to differ from one cult to another. But the church, I
learned, had a long history of excising heterodox groups, some of them
with significant followings, so putting a few tens of millions of Christians
outside of the evangelical circle did not seem as odd as it should have.

What I didn't consider in those years, however, were the Christians
who belonged to the groups that were neither modernists nor evangelicals nor Catholics nor cults. My friends and I didn't give much thought,
for example, to the many holiness groups, such as Wesleyan Methodists and Nazarenes. Or the groups that belonged to the adventist sects,

such as the Church of God and the Seventh Day Adventists. Or the peace
churches, such as the Mennonites and German Baptist Brethren. Or the
Salvation Army folks. Or the enormous number of Pentecostal sects. The
Christians in these groups, we knew, were not noted modernists. Some
people from these backgrounds had even found their way to Moody. But
they didn't seem like they were pure-wool evangelicals either. To explicitly exclude them, however, would mean making prominent issues out
of minor differences, so it seemed best to ignore these groups. While I'm
not happy that I accepted the party line about Catholics and cults, I can
appreciate why I didn't make an issue of it when I was at Moody. It came
with the territory. What I can't understand, though, is why my friends and
I did not see this herd of elephants in the room—this multitude of simple
Christians that were not defined by the war against modernism. My own
relatives and ancestors were part of these ignored groups. I should have
spoken up for them.

After my time at Moody, I spent a year at Cornell in New York acquiring the background in humanities that I probably should have had
before my intense exposure to the text of the Bible. I then transferred to
Loyola University in Chicago to do an undergraduate degree in classics.
I think of these educational experiences as my second immersion into
the broader secular world, but this was not a time of complete isolation
from religious issues. In these years, my wife and I attended an inner-city
church that was located on the border between an impoverished black
community in Cabrini-Green, the hippie scene in Chicago's Old Town,
and the *Playboy* lifestyle on Clark Street. The people who attended La-
Salle Street Church were usually marginalized evangelicals. Most were
not as ready to step out of their backgrounds as I was—especially if they
were cradle evangelicals. One issue we all agreed on, though, was that
the practice of the Christian faith could not be isolated from the pressing
social and political issues of the day. Black liberation, the war in Vietnam,
rock music, alternate lifestyles, gender equality, therapy groups—whatever was capturing the attention of the American public found its way
into our little church in one form or another. Ironically, the church was
located just a few blocks north of the Moody Bible Institute campus. On
Sundays, I would stand on the steps of the church and watch the students
from the institute march past the front door of the church on their way to
worship at Moody Church a few blocks north—the women with skirts to
their knees, the men with no facial hair. They were a visible reminder of
what I was leaving. But no one at LaSalle could tell me where I was going.

I was divided between involvement in this cutting-edge church and immersion in the non-church world of my Loyola studies. But not even my classes at Loyola were thoroughly secular. Loyola was founded as a Jesuit school. Over the years, Jesuits had dominated the university's philosophy department. In the years before I attended Loyola, however, rigid Thomistic thinking was losing its hold on Catholics. New faculty hires into Loyola's philosophy department were often attracted to existentialism, phenomenology, and other breaking philosophical trends. To make room for these different views, several of the older Jesuits were moved out of philosophy and into the classics, where they could finish out their teaching careers drilling students in the Latin and Greek they knew so well. As a result of this role-shifting, most of my classical language courses at Loyola were taught by men in clerical collars. Old men in collars. But I didn't mind—they loved their languages and taught me to love them too. My time at Loyola was, now that I think about it, my first real exposure to Catholics. My teachers no doubt inculcated their Jesuit attitudes into their lessons, but in those years, I didn't know enough about old-line Thomism to recognize the indoctrination, and by the time I had studied and rejected a more potent brand of Thomism, I had forgotten whatever subtexts I may have picked up during my Loyola lessons. All I remember are the language studies.

I had planned to bridge from a study of the classics into a graduate program in philosophy. But political events forced a detour. This was the early seventies and the war in Vietnam was entering its most intense phase. The draft had dogged my steps since high school. Like many other young Americans, I felt that the war was wrongheaded and immoral, and I did what I could to avoid being drawn into it. Being enrolled in a college had provided a convenient deferment. Now that deferment was ending. Draft exceptions were still in place, however, for ministerial students. An evangelical seminary just north of Chicago had added a master's degree in philosophy of religion to its regular ministerial degrees. Banking on the fact that my draft board would consider any seminary-based program deferable, I enrolled in the MA program.

If it had been a typical evangelical seminary, I probably would not have extended my studies there. The school had undergone a massive expansion, however, quadrupling its student body in just few years. The enlarged institution included students who were part of the more radical and exploratory strains of Evangelicalism. Some of the instructors brought in by the new dean also represented this outlook. While the seminary's teachers did not deviate—publicly, at least—from the creeds and practices of the more conservative denomination that had founded and still funded the seminary, many of them emphasized parts of the heritage that the denomination did not consider important. During my time at the seminary, I felt free to continue my intellectual explorations. In the years after I left the seminary, the denomination panicked and re-asserted control. Several of the faculty left and the more radical students were kicked out.

The seminary gave me my first teaching experience—my background in classics had landed me a job teaching introductory Greek courses. I found that I enjoyed the lectern end of the classroom. I was also able to do intense work on philosophy texts in my seminary years. When I finally transferred to a secular graduate program, I was probably more familiar with the range of standard philosophy texts than many of my fellow students.

But what was happening *inside* me in these years of transition, the years between when I began to exit evangelical spirituality and the years before I took up my third spirituality? I find it difficult to bring this period of my life into focus. When I made the transition into Evangelicalism, the switch happened overnight. But entry into the third spirituality was a long process. It crept up on me. I can find traces of this transition in four of my interactions, one with a writer, one with liturgy, one with politics, and one with a question.

Somewhere in the years at Moody and Loyola and the seminary, I began to read the works of C.S. Lewis. This famous writer had died when I was still in high school, but Lewis's reputation continued to grow in the sixties and seventies, especially among young evangelicals. He was an Oxford and Cambridge scholar of Medieval and Renaissance literature. Raised in the established church in Northern Ireland, he embraced a form of atheism as a teen—at about the same age when my own thoughts turned in that direction. Lewis's skepticism was reinforced by horrific experiences in the WWI trenches. By the time he was thirty, however, he had converted to a traditional form of Christianity. The conversion brought him back to the Anglican communion.

Lewis struggled with what this conversion meant and how he could describe it to others. He first attempted a John-Bunyan-like allegory (*Pilgrim's Regress*)—a natural choice for a scholar of medieval English allegories, but a disastrous one for reaching a wide audience. He next experimented with fantasy fiction (his so-called "space trilogy"). Again, the medium failed the message—the books did not sell well until Lewis became famous for his later works. When the BBC appealed to him to give a series of radio talks during WWII, Lewis began to translate his experiences with the church into a series of small nonfiction books on Christian essentials. In these books, Lewis blended philosophy and the theology of a basic ("mere" was the term he used) Christianity. These small books catapulted him to fame as a defender of Christian orthodoxy. The Narnia books for children that he wrote in the fifties expanded his reputation.

On my first encounter with Lewis, I was attracted by his apologetic works. I also enjoyed the fact that Lewis defended the historical doctrines of Christianity without adopting all the social and political distinctions made by evangelicals—Lewis drank beer, smoked a pipe, read mostly secular literature, and had nothing to say about evangelical hot topics such as inerrancy and eschatology. By his Anglican demeanor, Lewis was helping me to move away from a wholesale identification with American evangelicals. When I first read Lewis, however, I had only a barebones understanding of the philosophy behind the theology and apologetics in Lewis's works. Once I began to acquire some philosophical chops, I realized that Lewis's mere Christianity was not, by any measuring-stick, mere philosophy. Lewis underpinned his theological arguments with an abstruse Platonism that was similar to the philosophical framework that captivated Renaissance thinkers. Many of his arguments only worked when readers stood on the same philosophical platform. The more I studied modern philosophy, the less sense it made to me to hitch the Christian message to such old workhorses. I continued, however, to read books by and about Lewis, eventually substituting an interest in the personal life of Lewis for my earlier attention to Lewis's philosophy and theology. The later autobiographical works of Lewis, *Surprised by Joy* and *A Grief Observed*, became some of my favourite books in the seventies.

The second trace I can follow in these transitional years wanders through my experience of Christian liturgy. My life, as a child, had been liturgically dense. I was surrounded by the mysteries of faith and the symbols that represented them. Methodists are not renowned for their liturgical flair, but those who come to it with no background can find themselves, as I did, in a penumbra of symbols, practices, words, and art. My later move into the evangelical fold became a stripping of the altars. Evangelicals applied the yardstick of rational meaning to every dimension of their spiritual experience. Religious activities with no immediate interpretations were considered idolatries and pagan holdovers. As I moved out of the evangelical framework, a measure of this earlier experience of mystery began to return to my life. I found that I could let symbols be symbols without having to ground them. I could feel a deep consciousness flowing through the symbols and bypassing my mind. When asked what was happening to me, I would often talk about being on a liturgical journey, from low church to high church. Many once-evangelicals in my age cohort, I found, were on this same journey. Some made their way into Roman Catholicism, Eastern Orthodoxy, and high Anglicanism. I didn't—in these years, I was prepared to acknowledge mystery but not yet ready to enter it. Still, I attached great significance to the small steps toward a more historical forms of worship that were happening at LaSalle Street Church, and after leaving Chicago, I would seek out churches that had retained a measure of the Christian liturgical heritage.

The third movement I can trace in these years of transition is posed against a backdrop of politics and social justice. At first, I was not political. I grew up in the Age of Eisenhower, that long period when most Americans were not loud liberals or loud conservatives. When the political ruckus of the sixties happened, in the presidential elections of 1960 and 1964, I didn't find myself passionate about the political dialogue. I brought this same indifference into my evangelical experience. At first, I thought that evangelicals around me were also apolitical. When asked about their political orientation, they would insist that these distinctions were not important. Their kingdom was not of this earth.

As time went on, however, I began to notice that profound political commitments were often masked by this rhetoric of indifference. When political issues were discussed and political choices were made, evangelicals tended to side with conservative forces. For me, feeling around to see where I fit into the political scene, this became a problem. I found myself more sympathetic to strains of progressive political thought. The tendency for evangelicals to appeal important questions to the Bible made me wonder, when it came to political questions, whether evangelicals and I were reading the same text. The overall thrust of the ethical teachings in the Scriptures seemed to be that Christians should have a special concern for those on the social margins.

In this quest for a Christian understanding of social justice, I was not alone. A vanguard of evangelicals was marching in the same direction. At the seminary, I found myself interacting with a group that started a magazine, the one that became the left-leaning *Sojourners*. Evangelical women around me began to accept feminist critiques. Blacks who identified as evangelicals testified to the latent racism they found in their colleagues. Prominent evangelical politicians took antiwar stances. It was perhaps because of these progressive movements in the late sixties and early seventies that I delayed my final exit from evangelical circles. There was, for a few brief years, something commentators thought of as the "young evangelicals" or the "evangelical left." I was naïve enough—I was still in my twenties when all of this was happening—to think that the larger body of American evangelicals would welcome new voices into their discussions. In the mid-seventies, as the evangelical community began to clamp down on its dissidents, I gave up the few ties that still bound me to the movement. When Moody Bible Institute dismissed a faculty member because the man's wife had made statements that sounded vaguely feminist, I stuck my Moody diploma in an envelope and sent it back to the school.

I can detect a fourth trace of my transition into a new spirituality in a pair of conflicting answers that I gave to a question. In the early seventies, I was part of a church discussion group. The people at LaSalle Street Church called these "cell groups."[15] One evening, when the people in my cell group were talking about the goal of religious life, I said that the goal was "to grow in our knowledge of God." I thought, in my sad pride, that this was a clever response. A few years later, recalling this discussion, I was struck by how partial and biased my answer was. The act of knowing positions the knower in a framework that stands opposite and separate to what is known. This separation can't be overcome by more knowledge—increasing knowledge only increases the separation. The real goal of religious life, I came to realize, is reducing this separation. It was not just a knowledge of God that I was seeking, but union with God. And the way to reach it was not knowledge, but love. Setting these two responses to the question side by side made it clear to me, if I hadn't realized it before, that I had left behind any attachment to Evangelicalism. Even when I was moving away from it, I had been letting my experience with Evangelicalism define the horizon of my questions. Now an unexpected and subterranean flood swept me into unknown territory. I was seeking answers to new questions.

By the time I was in the middle of my graduate study of philosophy at the University of Chicago, I had embraced and left behind two distinct

---

15. Not the best choice for a name, it turned out. In the reactionary eighties, some of our phones were tapped.

Christian spiritualities. The first was the uncomplicated faith of my childhood—a kind of "God's in his heaven—All's right with the world!" feeling.[16] Simple and naïve but bred in the bone. Engagement with an adult world began to strip this from me in my teens. An attempt to re-capture this simple faith led me, in my late teens, to adopt an evangelical spirituality. Within a few years, I knew that this was not for me—I could not stretch the evangelical garment to cover all that I was and was becom-ing. I would begin to enter, by the end of the seventies, a third spirituality.

SPIRITUALITY THREE

Writing about my first two spiritualities has been difficult. Not only be-cause my memory is faulty, but also because I do not easily speak about my own inner life. If describing these earlier spiritualities was hard, how-ever, they are nothing compared with the difficulties that I face in ex-plaining this third spirituality. The problem is that I'm still in it. To reduce it to a few talking points, I would need to stand outside of it. Still, I must give some account of it, since this spirituality is the strongest influence on what I am writing about in this book.

First, let me express surprise that there is anything to write about. How easy it would have been to have let my childhood faith fall by the way. Thomas Merton, reflecting on a similar period in his own life, his pass-ing experience of English-schoolboy Anglicanism, notes that "practically everybody does go through such a phase, and for the majority of them, that is all it is, a phase and nothing more."[17] I could also have walked away from my short exposure to evangelical spirituality and adopted a secular distrust of all religion. Instead, I found myself pursued and overtaken by Francis Thompson's hound of heaven.

In the modern world, we tend to think of belief as private and per-sonal. But no matter how private our beliefs, there is a public dimen-sion to them. Faith always has a reference community. Even when we are absent from these communities, we still picture ourselves traveling through our inner worlds arm and arm with other people. My two earlier spiritual personalities had mainline Protestantism and American Evan-gelicalism as their reference communities. The reference community for

---

16. Browning, *Poems*, 40. Pippa's song from the poem "Pippa Passes."

17. Merton, *Seven Storey Mountain*, 65.

the spirituality that blossomed in my later life has made Christian mystics my traveling companions.

As my experience with this new spirituality broadened, I began to read books by mystics and books about mysticism. One of my earliest fascinations was with the seventeenth- and eighteenth-century pietists. I was drawn to them, I think, because they were a bridge between medieval mystical traditions and evangelical spirituality. Thomas Merton's works, first his *Seven Storey Mountain*, later his other books, introduced me to the Catholic mystical traditions. Books by the English author Evelyn Underhill provided a panoramic view of Christian mysticism and encouraged me to learn more about the medieval mystics. For several years I was caught up in the study of St. Francis. Simone Weil was another obsession. I subscribed to the Paulist Press Classics of Western Spirituality series and read many of the sixty volumes of it that are still on my shelves. In these books and authors, I found both a mental compass and corporal practices that helped me enter the experience of mystic spirituality.

Mystic spirituality is described in different ways by different writers. Some of them emphasize the universal perspective of this spirituality and note that elements of it emerge in all religious traditions. This is the "Perennial Philosophy" that Aldous Huxley describes in his works, his "Highest Common Factor."[18] My own study and experience focused more on the Christian expressions of this spirituality. Tracking down the mystic elements within the larger landscape of the church, it turns out, requires some work. While mystic insights occur and reoccur over the long history of the church, mystics have always lived on the margins of mainline Christianity. Sometimes Christian traditions welcome them into the mix, sometimes the traditions circle the wagons and leave them outside. Richard Rohr calls the mystics "eccentrics"—at the margins where they live, their small weight is multiplied by centrifugal forces at play in the dance of faith.[19] Their large influence on the church is not measured by their numbers.

For me, the essential insight of Christian mystics, the one that sets their spirituality apart from other types of Christian spirituality, is this: within the mystic perspective, the divine, the human, and even the world itself all exist in a dynamic and unified continuum. No experience of any section of this continuum can permanently ignore the rest of it.

18. Huxley, *The Perennial Philosophy*, vii.
19. Richard Rohr, *Universal Christ*, 1.

This insight can find itself at odds with Christian teachings that highlight dualisms—a God out there set against humanity over here, heaven above and hell below, sin earlier and salvation later, bishops and clergy in charge and laity obeying, men as leaders and women as followers, and so on. Not only do the mystics of the Church see the whole, they also insert as much of the whole as they can into every experience—they cannot despair without feeling hope, they cannot have faith without doubt, they cannot be lonely without being loved. I delved into the writings of the mystics and, as the young Edna St. Vincent Millay wrote, "Infinity / Came down and settled over me."[20] The whole continuum of life became the playground of my mind and spirit. I began to learn, by taking baby steps, how to enter this playground through the gates of the many dualisms that ruled my life.

While I was studying mystic spirituality, my professional life continued on its own track. I finished the PhD at the University of Chicago and spent several years teaching philosophy in an American university. My head and my heart were not completely disconnected during this time, though. I had started my study of philosophy by reading the American and English linguistic analysts, but I found little in these writers that could throw light on my inner journey. The language analysts operated within the same set of assumptions about physical reality and verification that were employed by the sciences and by the Evangelicalism that I had abandoned. The analysts were skilled in the use of critical tools, and I was glad to acquire some of these tools. The more I read philosophy, though, the more I became aware that there were other philosophical traditions with alternate assumptions about the nature of knowledge. I found myself attracted to the idealist traditions that dominated Continental philosophy. By this time, I had acquired some of the language tools I needed to engage Continental philosophy. Since the fountainhead of the Continental idealist tradition was Hegel, I decided to write my dissertation on him.

Looking back, my choice of the texts of Hegel as a topic of study and writing at the University of Chicago was not the smartest move. Chicago, founded on the American pragmatism of John Dewey and others, had slid with almost no resistance into the analytic camp that dominated English-language philosophy in the middle of the twentieth century. Most of the faculty there in the seventies were not enthusiastic about the

20. Millay, *Collected Poems*, 4. From her early poem "Renascence."

kind of philosophy being done in Europe. I had finished all the degree requirements except the dissertation, however, so the only concern about shifting my studies to the European tradition was putting together a thesis committee that would be sympathetic enough to give me a hearing. I was able to assemble such a committee because the University's philosophy department, attempting to prove that it was open to all types of philosophy, appointed to its faculty the French philosopher Paul Ricoeur. Ricoeur was on campus because he had an engagement, for three months of every year, with the University's divinity school. I cobbled together a committee consisting of Ricouer and a couple of the more broad-minded profs and launched into the study of Hegel and Continental philosophy.

Somewhere in the decade that I worked intensively on the texts of Hegel, I became—if I was not already—a philosophical idealist. The word "idealism" can mean a lot of things in philosophy. At a minimum, an idealist rejects the all-too-common assumption that the world is ultimately made up of small, unconscious, indivisible particles that somehow give rise to consciousness. Idealists believe, in contrast, that reality must, from the bottom up, have components that we associate with consciousness. The physical world treated by classical mechanics, which leaves little room for the conscious observer, is considered by idealists to be an illusion projected onto the screens of our consciousness. Instead of mind being an emergent property of matter, the physical world is treated as an emergent property of consciousness.

There is much more I could say about idealism, but I won't take it further here. Other writers explain the issues better than I could.[21] What is more to the point here is that my switch to an idealist perspective had a practical result. I realized that I could, at long last, follow my earlier bent toward the sciences without subscribing to a materialist worldview. This opened the door for me to return to the sciences.

Armed with my new perspective, I came to see science as a rule-guided game that could throw light into dark corners, but only when

21. In the seventies, when I began to look seriously at idealism, there were few contemporary English philosophers taking that position. "Idealism," like "Communism," had become a scare word. George Musser is not far off the mark when he says that "most modern philosophers, not to mention physicists, detest idealism; it strikes them as mystical to assume that reality is all in our heads" (Musser, *Putting Ourselves*, 173). Some thinkers working on what was called "the sociology of scientific knowledge" in those years, however, were laying the foundation for modern idealism without using the term. Since the seventies, the situation has improved a bit. Among the most accessible of the current English writers on idealism, for those who want to look into it further, are Susan Schneider, Robert Merrihew Adams, and Bernado Kastrup.

those corners were the ones defined by the assumptions of the sciences. As Werner Heisenberg says, science does not describe and explain nature itself, but "nature as exposed to our method of questioning."[22] About the larger picture—the unity of life and the ordering of experience—science, as I now understood it, had little to say. In mid-career I left my university position in philosophy, moved to Canada (my wife's home country), and began to teach mathematics and computer science. I did the same sequence of degrees in computer science that I had done in philosophy, specializing in computational linguistics. I even started to write another dissertation. This time, though, I didn't finish the degree. I was interrupted by a career change.

The change was triggered by a sabbatical break that I took from my teaching. The purpose of the break was to complete my graduate studies in computer science. An undiagnosed illness that went on for several months, however, made it impossible to keep up with my program. During that forced break, not wanting to be idle in the few hours of each day that I could stay awake, I wrote a book. One book led to another, and I eventually left my second academic post to take up a final career as a writer. Over the last thirty years, my books have taken me on a Cook's tour of human thought. They have ranged over topics such as genealogy, social history, linguistics, and natural history. Yet somehow, in all this scrabbling and scribbling, I wrote almost nothing about my lifelong interest in the Bible, religion, or spirituality. Until now.

I should mention one last personal event in my journey. This step seems to have little bearing on the assumptions I bring to my understanding of religion and the text of the Bible, but it may. I'm thinking about my current church affiliation. My wife and I have lived in many places, and wherever we have moved, we have joined local Christian congregations. The variety of churches that we have been part of has enriched our lives. Besides the independent church on the north side of downtown Chicago that I mentioned earlier, we have been members of a Reformed congregation, a Mennonite group, and two Anglican churches. In addition, my wife, who is a musician, has been an employee in a United Church and a Christian Science congregation. She has also been a volunteer member of choirs connected with a Baptist church and a Presbyterian school.

While this may seem like a denominational smorgasbord, the variety is perhaps not all that great—these are all Protestant or semi-Protestant

22. Heisenberg, *Physics and Philosophy*, 75.

churches. About twenty years ago, the menu changed. My wife, on her own journey through the mystical life, decided that she wanted to become a Roman Catholic. Many of the mystical writers that she had been reading were Catholics and she wanted to know more about their ecclesiastical context. She took this step, and a year later I joined her.

We picked an odd time to come into the Catholic community. Many Catholics were headed in the other direction. In recent decades, the institution has been rocked by waves that would have swamped a smaller boat. The issue most often in the news, of course, is that of abuser priests and the bishops who have shielded them. Problems less in the news, however, may be even more intractable. Entrenched gender roles in the Catholic communion have sidelined women and silenced their voices. The movement for change launched by the Second Vatican Council has steadily eroded. Liturgical reform seems to have stopped or reversed. The loss of vocations has left in its wake a top-heavy and distant hierarchy. These problems have made it difficult for us to relate to the institution at large. Most of our Catholic experiences have been with the orders that have preserved some of the church's long mystical traditions, such as the Benedictines, Franciscans, and Jesuits. As I write this, we worship with a community formed around a house of Franciscan brothers.

I don't know what this connection with the Catholic Church means for the studies in this book. I mention it because I don't want readers to think that I am concealing it. I just acknowledge that it is there and that it has opened a few doors—for both my wife and me—into the church's long tradition of mystic spiritualities.

This, then, is the imaginer behind the five "webs of imaginative construction" in this book. Buried somewhere in my journey—a trek through three different spiritualities and the rocky landscape of North American religion in the second half of the twentieth century—are the questions to which the webs in this book try to provide answers. The first web I will weave casts its threads and nodes around an issue—sectarianism—that has never been far from my thoughts. The sects that emerged in late Second Temple Judaism built the houses that first-century Christians moved into.

2

Sects and Strings of Pearls

PEOPLE WHO READ THE Tanak[1] for the first time as adults have an advantage. They often notice what those of us who grow up with dissociated Bible stories overlook—that there is a central narrative, a plot, that runs through the whole text. Even though the Hebrew Scriptures are a collection of individual books (from twenty-four to thirty-nine, depending on how they are divided), and the books fall into many different literary categories (history, poetry, prophecies, fiction, and more), and the parts were written over a long period (a half-millennium, give or take), they all contribute to the telling of a single story. That story is how God created the world and people mishandled it, leading God to select one specific tribe, the Jews, and make an exemplary nation out of them. God chose them while they were a small band of nomads, brought them into a sedentary agricultural setting (Egypt) where they could thrive and multiply, authorized the new multitude to conquer and occupy a land of its own (Israel), and provided them with written codes and with political leaders—judges at first and later kings—to rule over them. God authorized the kings to build a temple. Finally, as punishment for ignoring the favors given to them, God wrenched them from their land and returned them to it, without restoring their political sovereignty.

The need to narrate a central story creates a tension between the texts drawn into the Tanak and the uses to which they are put. We might compare the compilation of the Tanak to the crafting of a pearl necklace.

---

1. For an explanation of the term "Tanak," see the section in the Appendixes on "The Problem with 'Old Testament.'"

Every pearl that ends up in the necklace has its own history, but the messy life of each pearl is not like the position they later occupy in the jewelry. To enter the new setting, the pearls go through a process of harvesting, selection, and modification. The modifications for pearls might include polishing, having holes drilled through them, and threading on a string. In the same way, the various books of the Tanak have this double history. They are often selected and modified for a different purpose than the ones that brought them into existence. That purpose is the role they play in the central narrative.

Most biblical scholars focus on a 250-year period as the era when the books of the Tanak were collected and shaped around this core narrative. The period begins with the Babylonian captivity, which started when the First Temple was destroyed and Jewish leadership was deported to Babylonia. The deportations were completed about 580 BCE. The period includes the restoration under the Persians, during which some Jewish communities returned to Israel and the Second Temple was built. The returned exiles were governed as the Persian province of Jehud until conquered by the troops of the Greek Alexander in the late fourth century BCE.

The events described in Nehemiah 8–9 may point to the act of pearl stringing in this period. When the people who had returned to Jerusalem after the captivity gathered to celebrate Sukkot, the Feast of Tabernacles, the scribe Ezra addressed the people and read Torah to them. In the sermon in Nehemiah 9, which is put in the mouth of the Levites, we find a version of the core narrative. The writer of these chapters presents it as a summary of an already existing Tanak, but what we have in these chapters may be the narrative being used to string the Tanak together. Many of the bits that were strung, of course, had been assembled out of smaller collections. Some sections of the Pentateuch, the Torah of the Tanak, may have been drawn together prior to the captivity.

The product of this textual pearl-stringing was soon promoted to the level of Scripture and honored as a fixed reference text for Jewish religion. But "fixed," at least for the next few centuries, didn't mean "untouchable" or "unchanging." The addition of small bits and a smoothing of the narrative was still possible. The Book of Daniel, parts of which scholars date to the second century BCE, was probably added last. Not only was the selection of books in transition—the text itself was not stable. One of the major finds to come out of the discovery of the Dead Sea Scrolls, which date to the first three centuries BCE, was that the text of the Tanak was still fluid during the late Second Temple period, with multiple and competing textual traditions. The stabilization of the Tanak text, which led to the Masoretic version that replaced all other textual traditions, appears to have happened in the century after the fall of Jerusalem in 70 CE.

The newly collected books of the Tanak provided continuity to the Jewish faith. When the Jews returned to their land after the Babylonian captivity, they were a small group in regular contact with larger cultures and languages. Pressures to assimilate would come, over the next few centuries, from Greeks, Parthians, Romans, Egyptians, and Syrians. The Tanak, with its deep-time monotheism, gave the Jewish people an edge over the relatively young and pluralistic religions of their neighbors. The Jewish historian Josephus, in a first-century CE polemic work directed against an Egyptian writer, based part of his argument on the antiquity and unity of the Tanak. The scriptures were held in such high regard by the Jewish people, he pointed out, that they would not add or subtract or change anything in them. They were "a record of all time" that contained "the very decrees of God," unlike the written records of the peoples around them that were contained in "many different books that disagreed and conflicted."[2]

It would be easy to assume, anchored by such a reference point, that disagreements about what it meant to be a Jew in the Second Temple period would have been small. But a text by itself could not unite a nation caught up in the rip tides of foreign cultures that surged through the Middle East. In the last half of the Second Temple period, several attempts were made to restring the pearls of the core narrative. Three of them stand out—the revisions of Enochic, Essene, and early Christian Judaism. In this chapter, we'll review these three sectarian[3] movements and see how each of them handled the reference point established by the Jewish Scriptures.

ENOCHIC JUDAISM

European scholars were largely unaware, until a couple of centuries ago, of one of the earliest attempts to reinterpret the core narrative of Judaism.

---

2. Josephus, *Ag. Ap.* 1.8.

3. The application of sociology to biblical studies has led to several ways of understanding the meaning of "sect." For the purposes of this book, I'll take a broad approach to defining "sect." Any movement in the Second Temple period is a sect when it distances itself from the Jewish religious authority centered around the temple and its cult and provides an alternative to the mainline interpretation of the Tanak.

The Greek deuterocanonical books were well known to scholars because of their use in the Roman Catholic tradition. A few other books, often lumped together as pseudepigrapha, were known because of their incorporation into the various manuscripts of the Septuagint, the standard Greek version of the OT produced in the late Second Temple period. But scholars in the West lost track of some of the other books that were treasured by ancient branches of the Church. The Egyptian, Ethiopian, and Eritrean Orthodox Churches included some of these texts in their Bibles.

One of these forgotten texts was a Ge'ez version of the *Book of Enoch* (also called *1 Enoch*). Western adventurers brought back copies of this work from Egypt in the eighteenth century. While students of the Bible had known bits and pieces of it, mostly from Greek sources, they had not been able to read the whole work. By the early nineteenth century, translations of the *Book of Enoch* from Ge'ez sources had been published in the various European languages. Scholars, though, were not sure how old this book was. They knew it only as a Christian-era document. Behind the Ge'ez and Greek texts, scholars thought, there must be Aramaic or Hebrew antecedents, but there was no firm proof of the age of the document. Once fragments of Aramaic and Hebrew versions of the *Book of Enoch* turned up in the caves at Qumran and confirmed the age of certain parts of the text, Biblical scholars began to take renewed interest in it.

The *Book of Enoch*, it was soon apparent, was not one book but several—perhaps five—that had been written between the third century BCE and first century CE. What tied the books together was the figure of Enoch, the antediluvian patriarch who was the grandfather of Noah. The books relate his journey to heaven and back. Enoch recounts, while on his heavenly sojourn, his experiences, visions, and prophecies.

The tales about Enoch appear to be a riff on a short passage found in Genesis 5:21–25. The passage tells us that Enoch sired his son Methuselah when he was sixty-five and then, 300 years later, he "walked with God, and was not, because God took him." Among the long lives attributed to the patriarchs, a span of only 365 years would have been considered a life cut short, so early interpreters understood this phrase to refer, not to Enoch's death, but to his assumption into heaven while he was still alive. These brief verses in Genesis, thought some scholars, triggered the creation of an extensive story cycle around Enoch and his post-assumption life. Other scholars, however, suggested that the dependencies between the *Book of Enoch* and the Genesis passage might flow in the other direction. Parts of the story cycle, they surmised, may have predated the Genesis passage, and the author of Genesis was making a quick head nod toward the cycle.

The *Book of Enoch* is a long book, about the size of Isaiah. One of the oldest sections of Enoch, known as "The Book of the Watchers," provides a cosmological background to the tale of Enoch. It connects the Enoch cycle with a few verses in the next chapter of Genesis (6:1–7) that tell how the "sons of God" took the "daughters of humans" as wives, giving rise to a race of giants. The Genesis story then segues into a description of human wickedness and God's resolve to wipe out everyone except Noah and his family. The Genesis text seems to link the rise in wickedness with the unnatural union of angels and humans. The *Book of Enoch* adds significant detail to this barebones tale. A race of rebel angels, led by the angel archrebels Samyaza and Asael, come to earth and beget a race of giant half-breeds who kill and cannibalize the inhabitants of the world. These fallen angels teach men and women dangerous crafts, such as the forging of weapons and the use of cosmetics. God responds to these evil acts by sending his good angels to bind the rebels and imprison them until the day of judgment. The offspring of the rebels, the giants, are slain, and the spirits of the giants become evil spirits that wander the earth. Enoch comes into the story when he is summoned to heaven and sent to the imprisoned angels to ask them to repent. He helps them draft a petition for their release, which God rejects. Acting as the messenger for the petition, however, gives Enoch a chance to tour the precincts of the upper world. Good angels, who are his companions on the tour, are at hand to answer his questions, and Enoch reports to his readers what he sees and hears.

In another old section of the *Book of Enoch*, sometimes called "The Astronomical Book," one of Enoch's angelic interpreters reveals to him a calendric system based on the solar year. A section of the *Book of Enoch* called "The Dream Visions" unrolls an elaborate allegory in which animals act out the history of the world from the flood to the days of the Maccabees. A fourth section of the *Book of Enoch* is cast as a letter from Enoch to the generations that will follow him. In one part of the letter, he summarizes the flow of human history as a sequence of ten weeks that begins with the patriarchs and culminates in a final judgment and a new heaven. In a final section of the *Book of Enoch*, known as the "Book of Parables" or the "Similitudes," a supernatural messiah, the "son of man," oversees apocalyptic events in which the righteous dead are raised, the fallen angels are condemned, and Enoch learns further secrets about heaven and earth.

We don't know nearly as much as we would like about this remarkable collection. Perhaps the most troubling gap in our understanding concerns the community behind the book. The sections of the *Book of Enoch*, written over many centuries, are not the compositions of one or two inventive writers—a durable community must have been the source of the text. But the histories we have from the Second Temple period do not pinpoint a faction that maps onto the text. We know, mostly through the writings of Josephus, about partisan groups that we can identify as Pharisees, Sadducees, Essenes, and Sicarii. We also hear about a few smaller, transient sects. Scholars have tried to align the community behind the *Book of Enoch* with one of the known groups. The Essenes seem to be the best candidates—multiple copies of almost all the sections of the *Book of Enoch* have been found in the scrolls that the Essenes left behind in the caves at Qumran. Aspects of Essene theology, such as their belief in predestination, their confidence in the soul's afterlife, and their interest in angels, fit well with themes in the *Book of Enoch*. But not everything we know about the Essenes lines up with the *Book of Enoch*. One of the most popular theories that connects the *Book of Enoch* with the Essenes describes the Enochians as a pre-Essene movement that split, with one group becoming the Essenes described by historians (and perhaps further splitting into the urban Essenes and the stricter community at Qumran) and the other group feeding into the early Christian movement, contributing its apocalyptic themes and its focus on evil spirits. The small Epistle of Jude is the most explicit NT witness to the impact of this stream of Enochic Judaism on Christian Judaism.

Identifying the historic Enochian community is not the issue here. We are more interested in the relationship of this community to the Tanak. We want to look at the way it restrings the pearls. The writers of the *Book of Enoch* inherited the Hebrew Scriptures, but they had a story to tell that was different from the one that was used to weave together the texts that ended up in the Tanak. We hear nothing in the *Book of Enoch*, for example, about the Garden of Eden and willful human failure. This is replaced by a story of an angelic rebellion in which the humans are passive victims. Nor do we hear about God revealing the law through Moses. Instead, God reveals divine plans through conversations with a patriarch who was the ancestor of all living humans, not just the Jews. In the *Book of Enoch*, the divine presence does not confront people in a temple—God is in heaven, presiding over a royal court. That said, we shouldn't make a major case out of aspects of the Jewish faith that are missing from the

Book of Enoch. Parts of the community may have had a relationship with traditional Judaism that is not reflected in the text.

Whenever I read the *Book of Enoch* and think about the community behind it, my thoughts bend toward the work of Bryan R. Wilson, a sociologist of religion at Oxford in the last half of the twentieth century. My first teaching job, after my graduate study at the University of Chicago, was at Eastern Mennonite University in Harrisonburg, Virginia. I was the only philosopher on campus, so I taught all the philosophy courses offered by the school. There was no philosophy minor or major—all the students in my courses were from other fields of study. They were taking my courses either out of personal interest or to meet distribution requirements. I soon learned that the standard academic approach to philosophy could not hold the attention of such students. For the philosophy of religion course, I decided to tap into Wilson's work on church-sect typology. The students in my classes, mostly Mennonites, had grown up in religious groups that were partially alienated from the Protestant mainstream, so they had a native interest in sectarian expressions of faith. In addition to making the classes interesting to the students, Wilson's typology also helped me to sort out some of my own experiences.

Underlying the Wilson classification of sects is the more fundamental distinction between church and sect. Something like this distinction seems to be going on in Second Temple Judaism. While some scholars talk about the "Judaisms" of the Second Temple period and downplay attempts to identify a core Judaism that the various sects departed from, it seems to me that there *is* a default Judaism—it is the faith and practice of the group that put together the first string of Tanak pearls. This core Judaism would correspond to the church in Wilson's church/sect distinction. The core Judaism of the Second Temple period, however, was never dominant in the way that the church was in societies and states around the Mediterranean and in Northern Europe. The strength of a core religion is inseparable from the strength of political entities that protect it, and the Jewish governments in this period were extraordinarily weak. This weakness can make the core narrative of Second Temple Judaism difficult to trace in certain periods.

If core Judaism corresponds to the church, the peripheral Judaisms that arose during the Second Temple period take on the role of Wilson's sects. As a sect, Enochic Judaism fits best into the type that Wilson calls a "gnostic" or "manipulationist" sect. Gnostic groups do not tend to form countercultural movements that withdraw from mainstream society. For the most part, they share mainstream values and goals. However, they also claim to have a special knowledge, an esoteric teaching that complements received Scripture. Membership in such gnostic groups is limited to those possessing this knowledge.

The Christian sect that Wilson cites for the gnostic category is Christian Science, a group widely known for its award-winning magazine (*Christian Science Monitor*), its worldwide reading rooms, its supplementary Scriptures (Mary Baker Eddy's *Science and Health with Key to the Scriptures*), and its outsized influence among opinion-shapers. For all its reputation, however, there are relatively few Christian Scientists—perhaps around 50,000 today. The word "gnostic" in Wilson's name also hints that the same sect category would fit the second-century CE Christian Gnostics, another group whose numbers were probably much smaller than their impact. Gnosticism's strong dualism and its cultivation of secret knowledge remind us of the Enochians.

While I've had some contact with Christian Science, it has not been enough to give me a living picture of one of Wilson's gnostic sects. To ground this sect type in my own experience, I have to reach outside of religion and think about the role that science plays in contemporary public discourse. Science presents itself as the guardian of a knowledge that is only fully accessible to its initiates. Scientists set aside personal passions and values to seek salvation in a knowledge-based community. These are fundamental gnostic perspectives. In twenty-first-century Western societies, however, science has become such a pervasive point of view that we no longer think of it as a sectarian alternative to social life. It has risen to the status of church in Wilson's typology. But there was a time in my own life, when I was still a teen and deeply embedded in the values of family and rural community, that science was an attractive alternative, a gnostic sect, that offered me a way of salvation.

If we think of Enochic Judaism, then, as a sort of early Jewish version of Christian Science or Gnosticism or modern science, we may not be far off the mark. We strain to find documentary traces of their community, but this may be because they did not physically separate from mainstream Judaism and because their numbers were small. The only footprint they left—a deep one—was a vast cosmology that marked the trail for later Jewish sects.

We can see a closer connection between the *Book of Enoch* and the texts of the Tanak in a related work. The *Book of Jubilees*, also written in Hebrew/Aramaic but preserved in its entirety only in the Geʿez of the

Ethiopian church, blends the cosmology of the *Book of Enoch* with stories from the books of Genesis and Exodus. *Jubilees* begins and ends with Moses on Mount Sinai receiving the law. While on the mountain, Moses talks with a figure called the "Angel of the Presence." The *Book of Jubilees* claims to be a record of this conversation.

This angel, a member of the highest order of angels, imparts to Moses the contents of what is written in heavenly books. The revelation includes the law which Moses inscribed on tablets, but it also consists of many of the stories that we find in Genesis about the patriarchs. As the angel tells the stories, however, it does not recite the tales just as we have them in Genesis. Some are abbreviated and some are expanded with new materials. The author of *Jubilees* is concerned that the plots of the Genesis stories and the motivations of the actors in the tales are not always clear, so many passages supply these stories with more plausible narrative lines. In telling us about Abraham's sacrifice of Isaac, for example, the angel introduces a third character, a leader of the rebel angels who has been allowed to remain on earth with a small army of evil spirits. This fallen angel becomes the one who tries to get Abraham to offer a human sacrifice, a literary move that distances God from the awkward position of asking Abraham to murder his child. The move also transfers the story into the universe described in the *Book of Enoch*. Other Genesis stories that are retold in *Jubilees* make special accommodation to the 364-day solar calendar favoured by the Enochians. The major Jewish festivals are either pushed up into the heavenly realm or back into the days of the patriarchs, suggesting that God's plans for Israel are a subset of larger plans for the world.[4]

The *Book of Jubilees* is just a single author's take on how the new core narrative conveyed in the *Book of Enoch* might lead to new perspectives on the Tanak. We have no way of knowing how other branches of Enochic Judaism might have gone about the task. *Jubilees* does make it clear, though, that the reframed cosmology in the *Book of Enoch* and the core narrative around which the Tanak was built were not either/or choices for many Second Temple Jews. For sectarian Jews, the scriptural reference point of Judaism, though fixed, could be interpreted in more than one way.

---

4. A curious corollary of this transfer of Jewish customs into the larger universe is the belief expressed in *Jubilees* that the highest orders of angels were created circumcised.

ESSENE SECTARIANS

We find another restringing of the Tanak pearls in the Essene sect of Judaism. Unlike the Enochians, the Essenes left behind documentary evidence that talks about the sect itself. Two kinds of sources give us information about them. One stream of data comes from first-century Greek and Latin writers who described the group. The other stream comes from Khirbet Qumran, an ancient settlement on the cliffs above the western side of the Dead Sea. Beginning in the late forties, scrolls and scroll fragments—the now-famous Dead Sea Scrolls—were found in caves near the ruins of the settlement. Archeological data from Khirbet Qumran and the contents of the cave scrolls become relevant to our understanding of the Essenes when we make two assumptions. The first is that the people who lived in the settlement in the first century BCE and the first century CE were in fact a settlement of the Essenes described by the Greek and Latin authors. The second assumption is that the scrolls in the caves were the library of this group. The great majority of scholars who have studied the scrolls and the settlement have been willing to make both assumptions.

A few nearly complete scrolls were recovered from the Qumran caves, but most of the scrolls are represented by small fragments. Assembling and comparing these fragments suggests that there may have once been at least 800–900 documents in the caves. Many of these scrolls were Tanak texts. Others were documents that may have come from non-Essene sources, such as the *Book of Jubilees* and the *Book of Enoch* mentioned above. A significant number of the reconstructed documents, however, appear to have originated in the Essene community itself.

Before discussing what we can learn about the Essenes from the cave documents, let's review what outside writers say about the sect. Our most extensive and reliable source is the Jewish historian Josephus. He claims to have spent part of his youth with three Jewish groups, the Sadducees, the Pharisees, and the Essenes. In his writings, he describes these as three "philosophies" or "sects" or "parties." No matter which Greek word he uses, or which English words we use to translate them, what Josephus seems to be saying is that the three divisions of Judaism represented exclusive allegiances. Each had a distinct approach to what it meant to be Jewish in the Second Temple period. If you belonged to one of these groups, you didn't belong to another.[5]

5. In this book, because I'm using "sect" in the sense employed in the church-sect typologies, I'll reserve the word "sect" for groups that more clearly fit into the sectarian

Josephus describes the Essenes in more detail than the Pharisees or Sadducees. The Essenes were, according to him, a largely celibate sect that expanded by bringing children into the society and teaching them Essene ways.[6] Essenes lived in communities that shared assets and elected their administrators. They met before sunrise to pray and then went out to work at individual jobs—mostly farming work—throughout the morning. Around noon, they convened for a special meal. Before eating, they would immerse themselves in water and don garments of white linen. Prayers would be offered at both ends of the meal. After the meal, they would put on their work clothes and return to their jobs. At the evening meal, they sometimes allowed visitors to join the community for a guided discussion. Visitors who wanted to become part of Essene communities took vows of good behavior and obedience, pledging honesty to those in the community and agreeing to not reveal certain doctrines and practices. Members who broke these vows would be expelled from the core community for periods of time. As long as they were part of an Essene cell, members kept strict Sabbaths and avoided ritual pollution.

Josephus records several Essene customs. They had, he says, a special interest in healing and medicines. They refused to rub olive oil on their bodies, and they would spit only to the left. Their latrine customs were notable—initiates into the community were given trowels to dig deep holes for their excrement and skirts to wrap around themselves to keep away prying eyes when they were over the hole. Frugal to extremes, they would wear their clothes and shoes until they were frayed and worn out.

Our main interest here, though, is not their peculiar community habits, but in how their beliefs and practices related to the wider Jewish traditions of the Second Temple period. On this issue, Josephus leaves us with unanswered questions. One point on which he does contrast the beliefs of the three factions is the matter of the afterlife. The Sadducees, he reports, did not believe in life after death. The Pharisees believed in soul survival and an eventual resurrection of bodies from the dead. The Essenes held that, though their bodies perished, souls were immortal,

---

side of the church-sect division. The Pharisees and the Sadducees, which have more resemblance to the church side of the dichotomy, I'll call "groups," "movements," or "factions" of Judaism.

6. Some of the Essenes, Josephus notes, rejected celibacy in favor of family life. The descriptions he gives of Essene customs seem to have more relevance to the celibate Essenes, but some features may apply to both.

and that at death good souls went to a place of happiness and bad souls to regions of punishment. Josephus's second point of contrast among the factions centers around the issue of free will. Sadducees, he says, held that human actions were free and undetermined. The Pharisees accepted that some actions were free, but they believed that others were determined. The Essenes were strict determinists—God selected, before the creation of the world, those who would follow him and those who would not. Josephus also hints at a third contrast, the difference in the factions' understanding of the role of the temple. Both Sadducees and Pharisees were active in the temple sacrifices. Essenes, even though they sent freewill offerings to the temple, did not bring animal sacrifices, regarding their own worship as a more suitable atonement for their sins. The Sadducees and Pharisees must have felt keenly this departure from consensus—Josephus says that they banned the Essenes from the temple.

But what was the attitude of the Essenes toward the Hebrew Scriptures? We learn from Josephus that the Sadducees were strict constructionists. Only the Tanak held the commands of God. The Pharisees, in contrast, accepted the traditions of the fathers, a body of oral tradition that the rabbis, the later successors of the Pharisees, would designate as a second Torah. On the Essene use of the Tanak, however, Josephus is silent. He does mention that certain Essenes who were trained in the writings of their prophets could foretell the future. This suggests that their community had members who gave themselves to study of the Scripture, which in turn implies some perspective on how Scripture could be interpreted and used. But Josephus does not tell us anything else about this important aspect of Essene belief. The first-century Alexandrian philosopher Philo, in his description of the Essenes, does throw one ray of light on this question. He tells how the Essenes sat together on the Sabbath and discussed passages that had been read from books. He added that "most of their philosophical study is carried on through old-fashioned allegory."[7]

Philo recognized a nonstandard form of biblical interpretation, allegory (*symbolon*), among the Essenes, but he doesn't explain how it worked. To see how the Essenes handled the Tanak, we must turn to our second stream of data, the sectarian writings found in the caves at Qumran. When the documents in the Dead Sea caves were first uncovered, scholars made the assumption that almost all the non-Biblical scrolls

---

7. Philo, *Good Person* 82.

represented the beliefs of the Essenes. Time and further study of these documents have erased this assumption. The library documents, we now think, reflect the reading habits of the movement as well as their in-house textual productions. The collection of texts from the Dead Sea caves "can be viewed loosely as a partisan library, within which hermeneutic control was presumably exercised by a minority of sectarian documents."[8]

If we are going to look at the use of the Tanak within the community at Qumran, then, we must divide the non-Biblical documents into two groups: those that were read with profit by the Essenes and those that represent the actual beliefs and practices of the Qumran sectarians. But which documents are sectarian productions? We can't go by the frequency of the works found in the caves. Many copies of *Jubilees*, for example, were found at Qumran, but *Jubilees* is unlikely to have been composed by the Qumran sectarians. The best rule for dividing the Dead Sea documents seems to be vocabulary. The sectarian documents contain special terms that were not used by other Jewish groups. Certain words and phrases were dog whistles to the Qumran faithful.

By pulling together the views expressed in these language-selected sectarian documents, we get a glimpse into the inner life of the Essene sect at Qumran. The documents show, as Philo suggested, that the Essenes engaged in a unique interpretation of the Tanak. We get hints of this interpretation in the sectarian constitutions. These constitutions, found in two large documents and several smaller fragments of documents, resemble what later church writers would call "manuals of discipline." Like these later manuals, the Essene documents contain a blend of history, beliefs, and community rules. One of these manuals is known as the *Damascus Document*.[9] The Dead Sea Scrolls also yielded a second lengthy manual, now commonly called the *Community Rule*. The practices described in the *Community Rule* do not agree in all points with those in the *Damascus Document*, leading scholars to believe that they represent different stages of the Qumran community. Or perhaps different sections of the Essene movement.

---

8. Jonathon Campbell, "Qumran sectarian writings," 798.

9. The *Damascus Document* was familiar to scholars before the Dead Sea Scrolls were discovered. Solomon Schechter found a copy in a storeroom attached to the Ben Ezra Synagogue in Old Cairo at the end of the nineteenth century and published it as "Fragments of a Zadokite Work." Schechter's manuscript was a medieval copy of an older work, and scholars speculated that it may have derived from some pre-Christian Jewish communities. When several large sections of this document turned up in the caves at Qumran, the link between the Damascus Document and Essenes was established.

The large *Community Rule* scroll mentions the study of the Tanak (1QS VI, 6–8). The scroll says that whenever ten community members are gathered in one place—a number that seems to have been the sectarian equivalent of a quorum—someone was supposed to be engaged in the study of the Tanak day and night, with members of the community taking turns filling this role. In addition, all the members had to gather "for a third of every night of the year" to read from their holy books, pray, and interpret Scripture.

The *Community Rule* confirms the engagement of the scroll community with the Tanak. But how did these gathered sectarians interpret the Tanak? We find some hint of this in an oath that members took on admission to the community and probably renewed at regular ceremonies (1QS V, 8–10). In this oath, the applicant promises to "return to the law of Moses according to all that he commanded, with whole heart and whole soul [attending to] the revelation from it [given] to the sons of Zadok, the priests keeping the covenant and seeking his will." These words suggest a special hermeneutical method, one that was exclusive to the community members, who called themselves the "sons of Zadok."

We learn more about this community and its exclusive revelations in the *Damascus Document*. At a time when Israel had turned away from God, the document says, a remnant was preserved that took root 390 years after the Babylonian Captivity. This would place the foundation of the community somewhere late in the third to early in the second century BCE. For the first twenty years after the foundation, the *Damascus Document* tells us, members of the community groped their way like blind people. Then God "raised up for them a teacher of righteousness to guide them" (CD-A I, 5–11). The new community listened to God and "dug a well" (CD-A VI, 3). The well, the writers go on to explain, was the Law—in particular, the community's new perspective on it. The tool that the group used to dig the well was the "seeker of the law" (CD-A VI, 7), an alias for the leader known as the "teacher of righteousness" (CD-A I, 11). God revealed to the members of the new planting, and not to the Jewish religious authorities, "hidden matters, in which all Israel had gone wrong," including mistakes about the Sabbath and the festivals (CD-A III, 14).

We can gather more details about how this revelation affected the Qumran perspectives on the Tanak in several of the sectarian commentaries on Tanak texts. The most complete of these commentaries found at Qumran is the one on Habakkuk. The author of the commentary cites verses from prophecies of Habakkuk and then gives the *pesher*, the interpretation of the verse. One of these verses is Habakkuk 1:5, which reads, "Look among the nations, and see and be truly amazed—for the Lord is doing a deed in your days. You would not believe it if it was told."[10] The Qumran commentator says that the verse refers to the "traitors with the man of the lie" who do not believe in what "the teacher of righteousness" spoke "from the mouth of God." The teacher "had interpreted all the words of God's servants the prophets, through whom God declares all the things that will come upon the last generation" (1QpHab II, 1–9).

We might be tempted to say that the commentator has provided a contemporary application of a Scripture verse found in Habakkuk. There is, however, more going on in this commentary than simply drawing broad applications of old words. The commentator is claiming that his interpretation is what God meant to say through Habakkuk. A piece of Scripture written more than half a millennium before the days of the commentator was not correctly understood by any of its readers until its meaning was revealed to the teachers of this sectarian community.

This updating of scriptural meaning is more dramatically displayed in other *pesharim*. A Dead Sea Scroll fragment that is a commentary on Psalm 37, for example, employs the peculiar hermeneutic of the sect to interpret the verse from Psalm 37:10, "Yet a little while and the wicked will not exist; you will examine his place and it will not be there." The commentator says the passage means that "at the end of forty years . . . not a wicked person will be found on the earth" (4Q171 II, 7–8). The specific duration, forty years, is probably a reference to a belief in the Essene community (mentioned in the Damascus document, CD-B XX, 14–15) that the defeat of their enemies would come forty years after the death of the "unique teacher," another name for the teacher of righteousness. It is difficult to explain how the commentator could get "forty years" out of "yet a little while" without appealing to some kind of direct revelation about the true meaning of the verse.

Reading through the various *pesharim* that have been preserved at Qumran reinforces this sense of privileged sectarian access to special revelation. For the Essenes, the Scriptures were only partly understood by earlier prophets and writers. Because they were empowered by the same "spirit of holiness" that had inspired the earlier writings of the prophets (1QS VIII, 15–16), the Essene interpreters were poised to comprehend them fully. Prophecy became a script for their own experiences.

---

10. The translation is from the Masoretic text. Most of the verse is missing from the Qumran fragment.

And what a script it was. Several religious groups in the Middle East adopted a novel way of relating to their social contexts during the third century BCE. In the communities that were friendly to this new point of view, we find an emphasis on dreams and visions, a fascination with angels, and a sense that the end of the world was at hand, an end that would culminate in a final judgment of the living and the dead. Many of the groups that adopted these views—often referred to as "apocalyptic" perspectives—were also attracted to a deterministic framework that featured cosmic struggles between good and evil. These same communities tended to minimize their contact with the outside world, expecting its violent overthrow rather than its reform.

At Qumran, this apocalyptic withdrawal is probably what led to the separation from the Jewish temple and its sacrifices. The sectarians anticipated a soon-approaching age that would be instituted on earth by the Holy Spirit. This Spirit was already at work in the Qumran community. What they foresaw was the arrival of a time when sins would be expiated by lovingkindness "without the flesh of burnt offerings and without the fat of sacrifice." The "perfection of the way," not the blood of animals, would be "as acceptable as a pleasant freewill offering" (1QS IX, 4–5). This belief discouraged the Qumran community from participating, for the interim, in temple worship.[11] They were also put off by the failure of the temple authorities to adopt a solar calendar containing a fixed number of weeks. From the point of view adopted by the Qumran Essenes, the lunar calendar in use at the temple caused the festivals to be celebrated too early or too late. Dozens of fragments from the sectarian Qumran literature are part of an extensive polemic in favor of their date calculations.

In terms of Bryan Wilson's typology, these apocalyptic communities would belong to the "adventist" (also called "revolutionist") sect type.[12]

---

11. The full set of Essene beliefs about the temple sacrifices is hard to discern. Eileen Schuller notes that "prayer was not meant to replace ultimately the sacrificial system." It was a substitute "in the present 'time of Belial'" (Schuller, *The Dead Sea Scrolls*, 61).

12. Bryan Wilson's sect types are ideal types. Many sectarian movements share aspects of different types, especially ones that lie outside of the Protestant home field of Wilson's typology. I mention this here because one attempt to fit the Essene movement into Wilson's sect types classifies it as introversionist/pietist. Eyal Regev recognizes that the apocalyptic themes of the adventist type are also found in Qumran, but he also finds evidence for the wisdom and mystical themes of the Wilson's introversionist type and tries to show that, of the two options, "introversion was the predominate one" (Regev, *Sectarianism in Qumran*, 69). It characterized the earliest stages of the Essene movement, and adventist apocalyptic themes evolved later in the sect's history. I would flip Regev's analysis—for me, adventist themes predominate in the Essene subculture and

Christian adventist sects, says Wilson, regard the established church as enemies of God and focus on "the coming overturn of the present world order" and the transition to a heaven-sent rule. To be part of this new rule, members of the sect must maintain "doctrinal and moral rectitude."[13] In their study of the Bible, adventist sects give special prominence to the apocalyptic and prophetic books. Christ is often pictured by the Christian adventist groups as a divine commander as well as a Savior. The Qumran sectarians also looked for future military leaders with divine powers.

The most typical and prominent of the Christian adventist sects, according to Wilson, are the Jehovah's Witnesses. I've had almost no exposure to the Jehovah's Witnesses, beyond a few door knocks and proffered *Watchtower* magazines, but my experience with Evangelicalism put me into contact with groups that fit the adventist sect type. The Qumran sectarians remind me of these evangelical groups. The way the authors of the sectarian scrolls reject the temple worship of their contemporaries, the way they stress a special system of reading prophetic literature so that it becomes a script for their own times, the way that they enforce adherence to a detailed set of purity rules—all of these make me feel that I know this sect from the inside. I travelled, for a few years, with a sectarian movement that rejected the ancient liturgy of the Christian church, read all political events in the light of the dispensationalism described in their Scofield Bibles, and promoted a lifestyle without dancing, drinking, smoking, and movie-going.

EARLY CHRISTIAN JUDAISM

In Enochic Judaism, we find a restringing of the Tanak pearls that is motivated by a vision of the heavenly clash between good and evil. Under the influence of the Enochic vision, the author of the *Book of Jubilees* reinterpreted the early books of the Torah, lifting Jewish laws and customs into a heavenly framework that embraced all the tribes of the earth. The Qumran sectarians, in their reinterpretations, shaped the Tanak into a screed for a separatist community whose members would be the only ones to inherit the Tanak blessings promised to Israel.

---

introversionist themes are secondary. Later in this book I introduce another sectarian subgroup, the i-Nazoreans, that does fit better with Wilson's introversionist sect type.

13. Wilson, "Analysis," 6.

For our third take on Tanak revisioning, we turn to the early Christian church. Christianity moved from a strictly Jewish sect to a primarily non-Jewish movement in less than a half-century. Because of this rapid transition, historians tend to view the early days of Christianity as steps on the way to what it later became. In recent decades, the research agenda has broadened, and Christianity's Jewish matrix has become the focus of intense study. This research underlines the fact that Christianity was, in its early days, an alternative Judaism. As a Jewish sect, the primitive church had to work out, just as other Judaisms did, what its relationship was to core Judaism. It had to decide how to handle the Tanak.

We don't have to dig for documentation about how Christian Judaism reworked the Tanak. The Christian texts of the NT have—depending on how we count them—around 800 quotations and allusions to the Hebrew Scriptures. About a third of these are direct citations.[14] I learned to call the direct citations, when I first began to study the Bible, "Old Testament quotations in the New Testament." Referring to them as "quotations," however, can be misleading. I have quotations in this book from other authors. In using these quotations, I am not (usually) trying to reshape the way you view these authors. The point of my quotations is that I agree or disagree with what they have said. What we observe in the NT references to the Tanak is more complicated. The citations are a bold claim that the NT writers have some revealed insight into the meanings of these old texts—meanings that were somehow not available at the time the texts were written. "Interpretations" might be a better word than "quotations."

The tension between the way that moderns understand quoting and the way that referencing happens in NT citations troubled me in the years when I was hanging out with evangelicals. I tried at first to understand the NT interpretations of the Tanak in the way that quotations might be employed in a sermon. A homilist would read a biblical passage from the pulpit and then explain what the application of the passage was for the congregation. The minister might, for example, read the story about David and Bathsheba from 2 Samuel and say that this was a warning to couples in the flock not to engage in adultery. The pulpit warning would be considered an *application* of the passage. No one in the congregation hearing this reference would think that the writer of 2 Samuel told the story as an exclusive message for that church at that particular time. The

14. Fewer if we remove the citations—about thirty—that refer generically to the Scriptures without quoting a specific source. See Lanier, "As It Is Written."

meaning of a passage in its own context was separate from whatever applications might be drawn from it.

But this application model, when I focused it on many of the NT interpretations of the Tanak, didn't work well. Take as an example a passage in the infancy narratives of the Gospel of Matthew, one that we will study in more detail in chapter 4. Joseph, warned in a dream that Herod wants to kill the baby Jesus, flees with his wife and son to Egypt. After Herod dies, Joseph and his family return. The writer of Matthew goes on to say that the Egypt detour happened "in order that what was spoken by the Lord through the prophet might be fulfilled 'I have called my son from Egypt'" (2:15). The plausible Tanak source for this quotation is a passage in which God, speaking through the prophet Hosea, says, "When Israel was a young man, I loved him, and I called my son out of Egypt." Linking a statement made many centuries earlier about the wanderings of a whole nation to the specific movements of Jesus's family was not, by a long shot, the sort of common and literal meaning that evangelicals valued. Applications were supposed to flow in one direction only, from the source to the target. In this case, the target leans backwards and generates the meaning of the source.

Evangelicals had many explanations for this peculiar kind of referencing. At Moody, I found myself reading about foreshadowing, prefiguring, and OT types/NT antitypes. But these explanations did not speak to the central question, which was why we should be asked to read the NT literally and historically when the NT writers did not read their own OT in this way.

Richard B. Hays, in his book *Reading Backwards*, illustrates the tension I was feeling with a pointed question.[15] If you were asked, he says, to write a college paper on a passage from the Torah, and in the paper, you contended that the Passover story was really about Jesus, what sort of grade would you expect from your teacher? Even my instructors at Moody would have frowned on such a move. The standards of hermeneutics and history employed in current scholarship clash with how the writers of the NT referenced the Tanak.

As difficult as this hermeneutical problem was for me, the failure to meet even minimal standards of historical interpretation was not the worst problem with the way the Tanak was used by the NT writers. The hardest problems for me, in the days when I was among evangelicals,

15. Hays, *Reading Backwards*, 4.

were the misquotations. Translations were not inspired, we knew—only fringe evangelicals would exalt an English translation of the NT, even the cherished King James Version, over the Greek text it was translated from. In the case of the Tanak, it was the original Hebrew and Aramaic that were the words of God. But when NT authors quoted the Tanak, they didn't usually translate directly from Hebrew/Aramaic. The NT writers wrote in Greek and, because they knew the Hebrew Scriptures in Greek translations, quoted mostly from the translations.

The Greek translations that they used, which we call the Septuagint, were made in the three centuries before the Common Era. Miracle stories had grown up around how these translations came about. The miracles hinted that God had a hand in the translations. Setting the Greek texts side by side with their Hebrew and Aramaic sources, however, shows human hands at work. The Septuagint translators were massively inconsistent in their renderings. Sometimes they did literal translations, so literal that they were bad Greek. But sometimes they translated so loosely that the results looked like paraphrases. The book of Isaiah was the most popular NT go-to from the Tanak, and some sections of the Septuagint Isaiah translations were freewheeling.[16] The translators, moreover, had varying degrees of familiarity with Hebrew sources—even when they were being literal, they didn't always make the right choices when they turned their Hebrew texts into Greek.

Let me mention a couple of these misquotes. The Gospel of Matthew records that when Jesus made his dramatic entrance into the temple premises in the last week of his life, some children disturbed the crowd by shouting "Hosanna to the son of David." When his opponents called the actions of the children to Jesus's attention, he said, "Have you never read that 'from the mouth of babes and nurselings you have ordained praise'" (Matt 21:15–16). In this case, Jesus was quoting Psalm 8:2. But the Hebrew text reads "from the mouth of babes and nurselings you have ordained *strength.*" What Jesus says in Matthew comes from the Septuagint reading, which replaces the word "strength" with "praise." We don't know why the Septuagint has a different word at this point in the text. It may be that the Septuagint translators were looking at a non-Masoretic text. Or the translators may have misread the Hebrew text. Or they may

16. The translator may at times have been "uncertain about the frequently difficult text" and may even have "possessed a different Hebrew original." In addition, "he sometimes rendered by means of an interpretive and actualizing paraphrase rather than an exact translation" (Hengel and Bailey, "The Effective History," 120).

have translated loosely. In any case, they produced a translation that is at variance with our best Hebrew sources, and the author of Matthew puts the variant into the mouth of Jesus.

A second example. In Mark 7:5–8, when Jesus's opponents confront him about his failure to follow their rules on food purity, he challenges their motives. He starts off by saying "Isaiah prophesied correctly about you hypocrites" and then quotes what God says about Israel's hypocrisy in Isaiah 29:13. The passage that Jesus quotes follows closely the Septuagint reading of the verse. The Septuagint reading, however, is more of a paraphrase than a translation of the underlying Hebrew. In particular, the Hebrew source does not contain the clause, found in both the Septuagint and in Mark's quotation, "in vain do they worship me" (7:7). The added clause seems to be a summary comment that the Septuagint translator inserted into God's accusation.

These are only two of many dozens of examples in which an OT citation in the NT mishandles the Hebrew or Aramaic sources. When we add this misquotation issue to the other problem, the failed hermeneutic, we realize that more is going on in these NT interpretations of the Tanak than a simple citing of relevant prophecies.

Getting my head around this unusual use of the Tanak by the NT writers was a slow process. When I first encountered the problem, I saw only two solutions. One was the approach taken by the historical-critical schools. In this view, the NT authors were excused for their careless use of the Tanak by the primitive context in which they were operating. First century writers couldn't be expected to achieve standards of contextual meaning that would come along 1500 years later. As rustics at the fringe of the empire, they couldn't even be held to the standards set by classical Athenians writers such as Thucydides. Sloppy scholars but zealous believers, the early Christians had the bad habit of turning questionable connections to the Tanak into vehicles for their message. This solution, of course, was not popular among evangelicals.

The other solution, which made more sense to evangelicals, was that the disagreement between the interpretations of the NT authors and the contextual sense of the quoted Tanak readings were overblown. Far from being rustics and sloppy scholars, the NT writers were, under the direct guidance of the Holy Spirit, super-interpreters. Their citations did not misconstrue the meaning of the Tanak passages. Instead, they furnish "a uniquely valid and insightful commentary on the Hebrew Scriptures."[17]

That last line comes from the book *Old Testament Quotations in the New Testament*, whose lead author was Gleason Archer. He and one of his students put this book together for a 1981 meeting of the Evangelical Theological Society and later published it through Moody Press. I knew Archer. He taught at the seminary that I attended, and I took his Hebrew and OT courses when I was there. He had an amazing command of ancient languages and a Ph.D. from Harvard in classics. He was, however, a strait-laced fellow with rigid opinions about biblical inspiration and inerrancy. Still, I carried for him a sort of grudging respect. In those days I put a high value on Ivy League school traditions—higher than they warranted—and Archer was one of the ways I connected with them.

When we read through the detailed discussions of problematic OT quotations in Archer's book, we learn that the NT writers used Septuagint texts because the Septuagint was the Bible of their readers. Though the writers were aware of the Hebrew and Aramaic sources, they chose readings from the translations whenever they did not contradict the inspired text. And, of course, they had the Holy Spirit to direct them, ensuring that their paraphrases were accurate and inerrant. Archer does warn us, however, that "the NT authors were guided into interpretive techniques that Bible scholars today could hardly find justification for in their own treatment of Scripture."[18] For the Matthew 2:15 passage mentioned above, about Hosea predicting Jesus's trip to Egypt, Archer invokes a theory of types and antitypes. Jesus, he says, was "Israel represented and personified" and therefore had to "recapitulate, as it were, the career of his nation." Presumably this is one of the Spirit-guided interpretive techniques available to NT writers that are no longer available to us. We could not use the same reasoning to claim, for example, that the toddler Jesus must have been forced, like the Israelites, to make bricks for Egyptian monuments. Or that Jesus on his way back from Egypt found manna in the desert. The interpretative license provided by the Holy Spirit seems to have expired at the end of the apostolic era.

When the historical-critical and the evangelical approaches were the only two solutions to the citation problem, I was not happy with either one. Both solutions undercut the agency of the NT authors. The

17. Archer and Chirichigno, *Old Testament Quotations*, x.

18. Archer and Chirichigno, *Old Testament Quotations*, xxx.

critical approach turned them into untutored bumpkins. The evangelical approach didn't give them much credit either—the questionable interpretive work of the NT authors was managed behind the curtains by a puppet master who magically turned human choices into divine ones. No one seemed to care that the authors might have been making interpretive choices appropriate to their social context. Instead, they are frog-marched through a modern hermeneutic landscape.

My way out of this dilemma came many years later, after I had a chance to look more closely at the wider story of Second Temple Judaism. The NT authors, I came to understand, were doing what the Essenes had done before them and the Enochians had done before the Essenes—they were restringing the pearls of the Tanak. If the received reading of the Tanak found in the core narrative did not support what was being revealed to the sect, then the received reading needed to be reinterpreted. The sects who did this reinterpretation did not enforce the distinction between source and translation languages, nor did they elevate earlier revelations over later ones—the same God who had spoken to the prophets and patriarchs was speaking directly to members of the sect.

The Christian sect's new way of reading the Tanak, of restringing the pearls, is most visible in the gospels of Matthew and John, the two gospels with the deepest embedding in the Jewish matrix that gave rise to the Christian sect. They present, as Richard B. Hays notes, a "retrospective reinterpretation of Israel's traditions . . . in the light of the events of the cross and resurrection."[19] Of the approximately sixty direct quotations of the Tanak in Matthew, about ten of them are formula quotations, introduced by a phrase such as "[this event] took place to fulfill what had been spoken through the prophet." John also has formula quotations, some similar to Matthew's fulfillment formula, others that start off with the phrase, "as it is written." These formula quotations make strong claims about meaning and the Tanak. The authors of Matthew and John are not saying "what Jesus did might trigger a memory in some of our readers of the OT passage that goes like this." They are presenting a bold new reading of the Tanak, one that departs from the received interpretation. Matthew employs the new readings without apology. John doubles down on Matthew's claims by suggesting that Jesus appears in some form through the whole of the Tanak story, starting with his Logos presence at the creation. As John unfolds the story, notes Hays, "the great feasts

---

19. Hayes, *Reading Backwards*, 35.

of Israel's worship are newly seen, in retrospect, to be replete with signs and symbols of Jesus." Israel's redemption at the time of the Exodus from Egypt becomes "a vast figural matrix, a story in which the manna from heaven signifies Jesus' flesh."[20]

While the gospels of Matthew and John contain the most forthright reinterpretations of the Tanak, the most concise summary of this shift in perspective is perhaps in Luke. The author of Luke's gospel includes a post-resurrection story about two of Jesus's followers who, in the days following Jesus's death, were walking to a village a couple of hours away from Jerusalem (24:13–27). The risen Jesus falls in with them, but they fail to recognize him. When they tell him about the confusion that had seized the disciples in the wake of the Passover events, the stranger reprimands them for "not believing all that the prophets had spoken." Then, starting off from Moses and all the prophets, "he interprets for them the things concerning him that were in all the Scriptures." But he still doesn't tell them who he is. The revelation of his identity comes only after they reached the place where they were going. The two travelers persuade Jesus to stay for supper, and at supper, when he breaks bread and gives it to them, "their eyes are *opened*, and they recognize him." Jesus vanishes and they talk about how excited they were when he "*opened* the scriptures for us" while they were on the road. Returning to Jerusalem, they join his disciples and discover that they weren't the only ones having encounters with the resurrected Jesus. As they talk, Jesus appears again and tells them that "everything written in the law of Moses and in the Prophets and in the Psalms about him had to be fulfilled" and goes on to once again "*open* their mind to understand the Scriptures" (24:44–45). In the triple use of the verb "opened" in Luke's post-resurrection stories, we see the program for the new sectarian reading of the Tanak. This "opening" mentioned in Luke is the interpretation that shifts the Tanak narrative to a new plane. It breaks the old string of pearls and gives the NT authors a tool to restring them. Jesus himself becomes the string.

One of the most dramatic illustrations of this *opening*, this revisioning of Tanak texts to support the Christian message, occurs in the book of Acts. In the second chapter, Peter preaches a sermon to the Jews gathered for the Feast of Pentecost. To explain the charismatic gifts of tongues and the heavenly flames of fire that the people had just witnessed, Peter recounts what Jesus had done in his life and how God raised him from the

20. Hayes, *Reading Backwards*, 92.

dead after he was crucified. Peter then makes the dramatic claim that "it was impossible for him to be held by the agony of death" (2:24). To prove this impossibility, Peter lays out a sequence of logical steps that lead to this conclusion. He begins by quoting the end of Psalm 16, a Davidic Psalm. The psalmist predicts that God "will not abandon my soul in Hades" nor "allow your holy one to see corruption" (2:25–28). This prediction seems not to have been correct, Peter observes, because David died and the tomb where he was buried "is with us to this day" (2:29). This hangs the audience on the horns of a dilemma, since David, an acknowledged prophet, could not have made such a simple mistake. The resolution of this dilemma, says Peter, is that David was not speaking about himself. He was prophetically looking ahead to the resurrection of his descendant Jesus. It was Jesus's soul that was not abandoned and whose flesh did not see corruption (2:31–32).

This hermeneutical move in Acts becomes, in miniature, the early Christian program for handling the core narrative of Second Temple Judaism. The program takes apart the pearls of the Tanak and restrings them on a new narrative. As Peter explains to his audience, the new narrative makes a better setting for the pearls because it better explains the meaning of Tanak passages.

Investigating this new narrative will be a question for upcoming chapters, when we examine passages from NT books. We end this discussion by tying up one last thread. In the case of the Enochians and Essenes, I appealed to the typology of Bryan Wilson to help us understand the motivations behind the sect-oriented restringing of the Tanak. The Enochians fit into Wilson's gnostic type and the Essenes resemble his adventist type. In making these analogies, of course, we are extending Wilson's work beyond its original scope. We are transferring mainline Judaism into the role of the church and modeling the Judaisms that challenged the core narrative as Christian sect types. If we now ask which of Wilson's types fits Christian Judaism, our transfer of Wilson's Christian sects into a Second Temple frame leads us into a possible confusion. The Judaism of the early church, though presumably the faith of a Jewish sect, was fleeting. Within two or three generations, this sect of Judaism would become the mainline Christian church, a gatekeeper of its own traditions. The church would eventually encompass perspectives that ranged over the beliefs of many of its sectarian subsets. Those who try to classify the early Jewish church with Wilson's sect types, we discover to no surprise, place it in several different—and sometimes multiple—types.

But if we focus on that moment when Christianity was still a Judaism, there is one of Wilson's sect types that fits it rather well. This is one that he calls the "conversionist" type. Represented in the modern church by groups such as the Pentecostals and the Salvation Army, conversionist sects center their teaching and activity around evangelism. They set up a specific personal experience as a test of admission to the group, emphasizing individual sin and redemption. To encourage this experience, conversionist sects adopt a variety of revivalist techniques. The mainline group that they define themselves against is viewed with distrust, especially its professional clergy.

The Jewish sect that formed around the ministry of Jesus was closely connected to the work of John the Baptist. The Baptist's message—that Jews should repent and be baptized for the remission of sins because the reign of heaven was at hand—was the personal-experience doorway into his conversionist movement. John did not travel to address crowds, as a revival preacher might. They traveled to hear him at his baptismal sites. Because his message presented Jews with a path to salvation that did not begin with the priests and their temple service, John found himself at odds with the professional clergy.

To model the early church as a conversionist Jewish sect, however, seems simplistic, given that features of other sect types would emerge as the movement expanded. When we force the primitive church into a single category, we overlook the adventist themes that we see in Paul's letters and the Gospel of Matthew. We also overlook an important stream of Jewish thought that is not well modeled[21] in Wilson's sect typology—the wisdom tradition in Judaism and the early church, which we will take up in the next chapter. We need a better handle on the earliest expressions of Christian Judaism before we can begin to compare it—or parts of it—to other sects.

This, then, is the first of my five webs of imaginative construction. It is a picture of mainline Judaism and a core narrative built around texts that were eventually included in the Tanak. It is also a story about sectarian Judaisms offering alternate readings of the central texts. These sects, in my metaphor, have restrung the pearls of mainline Judaism—they have adopted novel textual interpretations that reflect their own community life.

---

21. It may be partially modeled by Wilson's introversionist sect type.

This restringing process has happened—and will happen—wherever religions incorporate texts, certain interpretations of these texts become normative, and groups arise to challenge the norm. The religions of the book, Judaism, Islam, and Christianity, are fertile sources for this sort of text-bending sectarianism. What sets apart these second-temple examples—the Enochians, the Essenes, and the Christian Jews—is not just that they are the first documented examples of this restringing. It is, instead, the outsized importance of texts in this second-temple cauldron of belief. Jews of this period had a strong sense of political sovereignty but lacked real independence. This led them to bank a large portion of their cultural identity in sacred texts, preserving it for a time when they regained a measure of sovereignty. Internal challengers to Jewish authority found it necessary, if they were to remain Jewish, to provide their own interpretations of these texts.

3

Wisdom and Sages

EVANGELICALS ARE PEOPLE OF one book. They study, memorize, and quote the Scriptures. Believers at my high school carried Bibles around with them as a testimony to their devotion, always taking care never to stack other books on top of them. Other Christian groups, I was told when I became part of an evangelical church, watered down the Word by introducing alternate sources of authority, such as tradition, liturgy, and personal experience.

Once I began to climb the ladder of liturgy into the more ritual Christian traditions, I assumed that I would be leaving behind this singular focus on the Bible. I was wrong. In the evangelical circles that I traveled in, we studied the Bible a lot, but our worship services did not include significant amounts of Scripture. The pastor might read a short bit of the Bible that was the text for the day then go on to exposit this text in his sermon. Sometimes that passage was the only public recitation of the Bible in the service. The more liturgical traditions, in contrast, had two- and three-year cycles of Scripture readings in their worship services. These readings covered extensive sections of the Bible. Evangelicals, I realized, were more attached to the *interpreted* word than the *read* word. Sermons in evangelical circles used up a half hour or more of a worship service to explain a one-minute reading. Homilies in liturgical churches were 10–15 minutes long, often taking up only double or triple the amount of time that the readings themselves occupied.[1]

---

1. A priest once asked me, "What's the difference between a sermon and a homily?" I replied, "I don't know, what?" "Fifteen minutes," he said.

We didn't read *all* the Bible in the liturgical cycles. Only about a quarter of the Bible was covered. After a few years of exposure to this cycle, I began to detect a bias in what was being included and what was being left out in the OT readings. I started searching for some documentation on this issue and came across a website maintained by a Jesuit scholar.[2] On this site, he analyzed the sources of the lectionary readings for the daily Mass. His charts showed that my impressions were not mistaken. There was a bias. For his analysis of the lectionary, the researcher had grouped the OT readings into six categories. He then computed how much of each section was covered in the lectionary cycle. The smallest section, Psalms, had the strongest coverage, and the largest section, the Historical Books, had the weakest coverage. In comparing the four sections between these two extremes, however, one number stood out. Only one-eighth of the verses in the wisdom literature were covered during the cycle. Seven-eighths of the section was liturgical dark matter.

Seeing these low numbers reminded me of my earliest encounter with the wisdom books of the Bible. After hooking up with the evangelicals, I took on the task of reading the Protestant Bible cover to cover. Like many people who had grown up on Bible stories, I was surprised at some of the wadding between the stories. I had been told nothing about the long and boring tables of ancestors, the bloody tales of battle and revenge that included rape and dismemberment, and the sexual escapades of some of the minor characters. I reasoned, though, that the gritty parts of the OT, even though they may have been a hard slog, at least made sound moral points. We learn from them that blood leads to more blood and that sexual desire is not the best life coach. What surprised me most in my read-through, however, was what I found when I reached the OT's wisdom books. They contained moral and religious perspectives that seemed inconsistent with messages in the rest of the Bible. The Song of Songs was—on the surface, at least—an erotic love poem with nothing in it about God or Law. The Book of Ecclesiastes promoted a go-for-the-gusto approach to life. Proverbs was a celebration of casuistry, a Polonius on steroids dishing out long strings of aphorisms. In the book of Job, the protagonist takes God to court for unethical behaviour. He loses, even though he has the better case, because God pulls rank. I remember wondering how books like these could have ended up as part of Scripture. Evangelicals had their explanations, of course, and I sought these out.

2. Just, "The Catholic Lectionary Website."

But the deeper issue—why there was something that needed to be explained—remained. The wisdom books didn't feel like they belonged in what I thought, at that time, the Bible was about.

The problems presented by the wisdom literature did not go away with my exit from the evangelical camp. These same problems were also at the root of the lectionary bias in the liturgical churches that I later attended. The issue of what to do with the wisdom books has also dogged academic literature. In surveys of the OT before 1950, it is difficult to find even a chapter devoted to them.[3] The academic pickings became better over the next few decades. I would be many years into my adult life, however, before I was able to delve into this secondary literature and to make some sense out of what was going on in the wisdom books.

To explain how my viewpoint on these books has changed, the place to begin is with the web that I wove in the previous chapter. When the Tanak was stitched together at the beginning of the Second Temple period, a core narrative guided the process. A summary of this narrative, I noted, is found in the Sukkot sermon of the Levites recorded in Nehemiah 9. The narrative itself, which begins with the story of Abraham and ends with subjugation to the Persians, leaves little room for the message of the wisdom books. The Levite speakers, however, preface their summary by blessing the Lord and saying "You yourself have made the heavens, the heaven of heavens and all their hosts, the earth and all that is upon it, the seas and all that is in them. You yourself give life to all of them, and the hosts of heaven worship you" (9:6). In this brief introduction, the core narrative is framed in a wider context. The God who became the guardian of Israel, it maintains, is not just a tribal God. It is the same God who created the whole world and who sustains all life. Stepping back into this larger frame transports us into the world occupied by the wisdom books. We see in this introductory passage an acknowledgement of the wisdom tradition, a recognition that the tranche of texts bearing witness to this tradition have a place in the Tanak.

In Jewish legend, the group who assembled the Tanak in the early years of the Second Temple period were known as the "Great Assembly." The hundred or so elders and prophets who were members of this assembly would no doubt have included some who would have been sages, key players in the wisdom tradition. The presence of these sages would account for the inclusion of wisdom texts in the Tanak. The sages'

---

3. Smend, "Interpretation of Wisdom," 257.

contribution provides a larger context, a framework within which the world-ordering God unfolds the more intimate events that make Israel the chosen people.

The addition of these framing texts to the Tanak, however, sets the stage for a conflict between the message of the wisdom books and the message of the core narrative. The wisdom books, especially the older ones, tell us about broad, faith-related issues that arise from an encounter with this universal God. The rest of the Tanak addresses the more specific issue of what it means to be this God's special people, convened and contracted under the Abrahamic, Mosaic, and Davidic covenants. The character of God viewed through the lens of the covenants can be quite different from the character of God seen outside the covenants. This difference was recognized soon after the Tanak was assembled. In the Babylonian Talmud, the writer observes that the authorities in the Mishnah and Talmud "wished to hide the Book of Ecclesiastes, because its words are self-contradictory." They didn't suppress it, though, giving as their reason that the book's "beginning is words of Torah, and its end is words of Torah."[4] Looking at a wisdom book from within the covenant narrative forced them to frame the book to fit the received narrative. What they failed to recognize was that the bracketing runs in the opposite direction—it is the broader wisdom perspective that frames the narrower covenant narrative.

In the rest of this chapter, I will weave my second imaginative web. In it, I will try to get a fix on the wisdom *community* and the forms that it took in the Second Temple period. Then we will look at some of the principal wisdom *themes*, including the personification of Wisdom threaded through the various books. First, though, some thoughts about the *terminology* of the wisdom books.

TERMINOLOGY

Wisdom literature takes its name from the frequent use of the word "wisdom" in the texts. In the Hebrew texts of the Tanak, this is almost always the Hebrew word *hokhmah*. In the Greek texts of the OT, *sophia* is used as a translation of *hokhmah*. Variations of the words, such as *hakham* and *sophos*, both meaning "wise" or "wise person," are also frequent.

---

4. Epstein and Slotki, *The Babylonian Talmud*, Shabbat 30b. I have cited the literal version of the translation.

Rendering these terms into English as "wisdom" and its cognates is not always satisfactory since the English words have only a partial overlap in meaning with the Hebrew and Greek terms. English speakers, for example, tend to contrast knowledge and wisdom, with knowledge being about matters of fact and wisdom being the wise use of knowledge. The Hebrew and Greek terms are more encompassing. The knowledge of the world that we gain through science—and the skills by which we manipulate this world—are also *hokhmah*. In some cases, even amoral shrewdness is referred to as *hokhmah*.[5]

Expanding our notion of wisdom to include different types of knowledge, however, does not resolve all the translation issues. The characteristics of knowledge in the ancient world differ from that of modern knowledge. We tend to think about knowledge as a dynamic and continually increasing body of information. At the time the Tanak was assembled, James Kugel notes, knowledge was "a fixed, utterly static set of facts, the unchanging rules that underlie all of reality as we know it." To have *hokhmah* was to understand these hidden rules, to "master all that had been discovered of life's underlying pattern."[6] This ancient view of wisdom had a long run—in Europe, it held on until the Enlightenment. Isaac Newton, surveying the regularities of natural systems, could call them the "laws of nature" because he thought of them as fixed rules emanating from a lawgiver. By the time we get to the nineteenth century, Newton's phrase seems archaic enough to be a metaphor. We want to write "laws," signalling with quotation marks our belief that the regularities of natural systems do not need to be traced back to divine fiat. We think of this change in how we look at knowledge as progress, and it may be, but conceptual gains always contain conceptual losses. What we gained in scientific credibility during the Enlightenment, we lost in our ability to position ourselves in the world occupied by the wisdom tradition. Modern people may disagree about certain facts of science, but a world in which the perspectives of Enlightenment science do not define what is knowable is, for many people, incomprehensible. We struggle to put ourselves into the conceptual frame of OT wisdom.

Besides making liberal use of the word "wisdom" and its cognates, many of the wisdom books share a common literary device. Four of the six wisdom books in the Christian OT—Proverbs, Ecclesiastes, the Song

5. See the list of morally ambiguous applications of *hokhmah* in McLaughlin, *An Introduction*, 4.

6. Kugel, *How to Read*, 506.

of Songs, and the Wisdom of Solomon—feature King Solomon in an authorial role. Solomon was the iconic *hakham*, the ultimate sage. The link between Solomon and wisdom is based on four stories from the book of 1 Kings. In the first story (3:5–15), the young Solomon, recently crowned king of Israel, has a dream in which God asks him what gift he would like to have. Instead of asking for a long life or riches, he asks for "a listening heart" to enable him to govern his people well. God, pleased with Solomon's humble request, gives him "a wise and discerning heart" and tells him that he would acquire a level of wisdom that no one possessed before him or would possess after him. Later in the same chapter, Solomon exercises this new gift to resolve a disagreement between two women about which of them was the mother of a living child and which was the mother of a dead child (3:16–28). When the people witnessed the astute judgment of Solomon, they were in awe at "the wisdom of God in him" (3:28).

The third story, found in the next chapter of 1 Kings (4:29–34), makes a direct connection between Solomon and the wisdom tradition. "God gave wisdom to Solomon and very great discernment," the writer says, "an expanse of mind like the sand on the seashore. The wisdom of Solomon was greater than the wisdom of all the people of the East and all the wisdom of Egypt." The wise Solomon left behind him a thousand *meshalim*, wise sayings. His collected discourses ranged over trees, herbs, animals, birds, reptiles, and fish.

The last tale about Solomon's wisdom is the legendary meeting between Solomon and the Queen of Sheba (10:1–13). She came to Solomon with gifts and put to him a series of hard questions. Solomon answered all her questions. Hearing the king speak and seeing his magnificent attire and retinue took her breath away. She said "the report I heard in my country about your words and wisdom is true. I did not believe the report until I came and saw it with my own eyes. Indeed, not even half was told to me."

We don't know in which direction this link between Solomon and the wisdom tradition runs. Did King Solomon initiate the wisdom tradition, or did the wisdom writers mold a legendary figure into their own image? The social and political context of early Israel suggests that Solomon could have had a role in introducing an international wisdom tradition into Israel, even if the specific wisdom works attributed to him were foisted on him by later sages. Solomon and his father, King David, have always been enigmatic figures. Archeologists fail to find the same physical evidence for the roles attributed to them by the Hebrew writings that they find for the later kings of Israel and Judah. And the Tanak stories we have about David and Solomon feel like they have marinated in folk traditions. But when we think about what it must have been like for tribal groups to have come together to set up a united regency, then an early king introducing wisdom scholarship and wisdom schools into the new nation makes sense. This move would have legitimated the new royal line in the eyes of surrounding nations, giving it the polish of civilization. Just as Solomon's foreign marriages tied the young nation into a network of international royal houses, Israel's newly minted sages provided the diplomatic channels that were essential for independence. Governments, we often forget, rely as much on the stories that are told about them as on their armies and weapons. A king who not only promoted the international science of the ancient world but was himself an exemplar of the science—this was exactly what the new nation needed to become a player on the world stage. The wisdom initiatives of King Solomon may be more than a legend.

WISDOM COMMUNITIES

We sometimes refer to the members of the group that looked back to Solomon as their founder as "sages." But did the sages form a unique social class? Did they have their own institutions? These are questions that have been widely debated in the scholarly literature over the last half century. The lack of clear references to groups of sages and to their institutions has polarized the debate. Some scholars maintain that there was no social caste of sages, just sporadic collections of wise people. Others argue that the schools of sages were more well-defined and enduring.

I'm inclined to view sages as a durable professional class, at least in certain periods of Jewish history. We can see something that looks like a specific social stratum of sages as far back as the first Jewish kingdom. Many of the sayings in the Book of Proverbs, for example, may reach back to this early period, and if we look at the virtues extolled in some of the book's maxims, a picture emerges of a professional class serving those who are in power. Judging by the advice proffered in Proverbs, this group is financially secure—they seem to have enough money to make loans and they manage households that include servants. Members of the group are encouraged to avoid lying and flattery, to decline bribes, to respect social hierarchies, to maintain good reputations, to be temperate at feasts, and to learn to pacify the wrath of kings. These are all qualities desirable in servants of a royal court. Sages probably occupied roles in the government as advisers, ministers of state, diplomats, scribes, and judges. They merged into the bureaucracy when governments were strong and withdrew into their caste identities when the kings were weak or antagonistic.

During the Babylonian Captivity and the early years of the Second Temple, the sages seem to have developed their own training institutions, adopting social roles that were independent of formal government. We get a glimpse of the third-century activity of these institutions in the postscript to Ecclesiastes (12:9–14). The writer, referring to the author of the previous chapters, says, "Beside being wise, the teacher taught the people knowledge, weighing and arranging many wise sayings." Learning, teaching, writing, and collecting, according to this author, were all part of the role of a sage. By the time we get to Ben Sira, who lived and worked during the first quarter of the second century BCE, we have some possible evidence for wisdom schools. The sage Ben Sira says, "Draw near to me, you uneducated, and lodge in my house of instruction. . . . Put your neck under the yoke and let your soul receive instruction" (Sir 51:23,26). The contents of Ben Sira's book support this institutional reading—his book seems like it could have been a manual used in the school. Besides the usual snippets of wisdom, the book contains passages on business practices, household management, legal obligations, the importance of travel, proper behavior at funerals, and table manners. His students probably came from families with a history of public service and when they graduated, they would have assumed similar roles.

Institutional roles in the nation of Israel in the years from the eighth to the second century BCE include king, prophet, and priest. To these we should add a fourth, the role of sage. We find an explicit reference to these roles in the Book of Jeremiah, probably a sixth-century BCE redaction of Jeremiah's seventh-century prophecies. At the time the book was written, the self-governance of Israel had been suspended and their kings had been demoted, but the author of Jeremiah recognizes the other three segments of Jewish leadership. He puts into the mouth of Jeremiah's enemies these words: "Come, let us make a plot against Jeremiah. For [if we do,] the Law will not stray from the priest, nor counsel from the wise (hakham), nor speech from the prophet" (18:18).

To image the roles played by these four social groups, we can turn to analogies with modern societies. The kings would correspond to our institutions of government. Priests were to Israel what the church, synagogue, mosque, or temple is to us. The Jewish *prophets* played a role much like our media—as a conscience-driven source of information that was independent of government. The *sages* did for Israel what our schools and universities now do, acting as repositories and distributors of certain kinds of community knowledge.

As purveyors of knowledge, the sages of Israel stood with their feet in two camps. On the one side, they were interpreters of the core narrative, joining the priests as teachers of Torah. On the other side, they were the doorway through which an international wisdom tradition made its way into the covenant community. We can detect the international exchange of shared wisdom ideas over a period of more than a millennium. Specific teachings in the wisdom books of the OT tap directly into this exchange.

An article published in 1924 by a German Egyptologist illustrates this exchange.[7] He points out that a word in Proverbs 22:20 that didn't seem to make sense in the context—a word that some interpreters amended to read "heretofore" and that the Septuagint translators rendered as "three days ago"—could, with one small change, become the word for "thirty," making the verse read, "Have I not written to you thirty sayings of counsels and knowledge?" This change connects the verse to an Egyptian document known as the *Instruction of Amenemope*. The Egyptian text, a papyrus scroll written in abridged hieroglyphics, was brought to the United Kingdom in 1888. It languished in the British Museum for nearly forty years before it was published in photofacsimile form with an accompanying translation. The scroll contains advice about the way to live. The advice is a potage of maxims and rules, as it is in the Book of Proverbs. There are thirty chapters of this wisdom advice in the *Instruction of Amenemope*, and at the end of the scroll the writer says, "Look to these thirty chapters; they inform, they educate."[8] Besides sharing the number thirty, about a dozen contiguous verses of Proverbs 22 have close correspondences to advice in the *Instruction of Amenemope*, and there are significant parallels in many other Proverbs passages. It is almost beyond debate that either the Egyptian *Instruction of Amenemope* was a source document for Proverbs or the *Instruction of Amenemope* and Proverbs shared a common source.

7. Erman, "Eine ägyptische Quelle."

8. van den Dungen, "The Instruction of Amen-em-apt."

WISDOM PERSPECTIVES

When O.S. Rankin called the wisdom books of the OT "the documents of Israel's humanism,"[9] he captured an important parallel. Both moderns and the ancient wisdom sages know what it means to leave generous space for a *human-sided interpretation of existence.* The sages were empirical observers of both natural events and human experiences. They collected their observations, cinched them together using reason, and deposited them in a sapiential tradition. While nationalistic perspectives—including Jewish covenantal theology—tended to treat people as members of social groupings, as small cogs in a larger mechanism, the wisdom tradition focused on autonomous individuals.

We also find suggestions of *a shared cosmology* in the teachings of the sages. Nailing this down to specific doctrines is difficult—we are dealing with perspectives that range over many centuries and through many cultures. Scholars who have tackled this problem have invoked fuzzy sets, prototype theory, and Wittgensteinian family resemblances to account for the diversity. One reasonably persistent subject in the wisdom tradition is natural theology. God, imaged as a creator rather than a redeemer, is seen as a source of universal truth and justice. Revelation primarily comes to us, not from the written Law, but through an order that God has imposed on creation. This order is mirrored in natural phenomena that range from the vast movements of heavenly bodies to the detailed habits of animals and insects. By careful attention, we can read this book of nature. The compilers of Proverbs advise the lazy person to "go to the ant, observe its ways and become wise" (6:6–8), not because the individual ant is wise, but because the wise system of nature set up by the Creator flows through the providence of the ant.

Wisdom is handed down the line of sages by means of *special rhetorical devices.* At the beginning of Proverbs, the compilers outline their intention to impart "wisdom and instruction" via *mashal* (saying) and *dibhrey hokhamim* (wise words), making use of both *melitzah* and *hidhah* (1:6). These last two words are hard to translate—many English versions render the first as "enigma" or "figure" and the second as "dark saying" or "riddle."

We can see these rhetorical techniques at work throughout the Book of Proverbs. One of the principal devices employed by the authors is, as the name of the book suggests, a kind of proverb. These sayings, though,

---

9. Rankin, *Israel's Wisdom Literature,* 3.

do not always correspond to what English speakers mean by "proverb," which is typically a pithy adage such as "haste makes waste" and "a stitch in time saves nine." The sayings that we find in the Book of Proverbs are more like tight packages of reasoned advice. In his book *Old Testament Wisdom*, James Crenshaw calls this kind of expression, "a short sentence founded upon long experience containing a truth."[10] A good example is found in Proverbs 26:17: "The passerby who meddles in someone else's argument is like a person grabbing the ears of a dog."[11]

In addition to these proverb-like sayings, several other saying formats are on display in the Book of Proverbs. We see examples of the argument from greater to lesser, *argumentum a fortiori*. "The underworld and the place of destruction are open before the Lord; how much more the hearts of humans" (15:11). We also see the reverse of this, the argument from lesser to greater, *argumentum a minore ad maius*. "There is one who disperses, and yet adds more, and there is one who holds back what is justly due and ends up poor" (11:24). Whole sections of the book contain antithetic parallels that contrast opposite behaviours. "An abomination to the Lord are those perverse in heart; his delight are the blameless in conduct" (11:20). Some proverbs make use of a "better than" structure. "A serving of vegetables where there is love is better than a fatted ox with hatred in it" (15:17). There are also beatitudes ("happy are") and curses ("woe to"). One device that seems to have been a favorite of the sages—a format that we do not use much in English speech—is the numerical list. "Three things are too wonderful for me, four things that I don't understand: the way of an eagle in the sky, the way of a snake over a rock, the way of a ship in the midst of the sea, and the way of a man with a maid" (30:18–19). Rhetorical and riddling questions also come into the mix. Many examples can be found in the Book of Job, such as "Call to mind, now, who has perished when innocent? Where has the upright been destroyed?" (4:7). Finally, we find a few allegories and parables. The allegorical comparison in Ecclesiastes 12:1–7 between the end of life and the decay of a homestead, the one that begins "Remember your Creator in the days of your youth," is one of the finest poetic passages in world literature. While some of these literary devices occur in other kinds of literature, particularly in prophetic writings, the mix and intensity of the rhetorical forms in the wisdom literature stand out.

---

10. Crenshaw, *Old Testament Wisdom*, 19.

11. Been there, done that. With the arguers, I mean. Not the dog.

The editors of Proverbs drew on an international fund of wisdom to construct a body of wisdom teachings for Israel. The same can be said for the other wisdom books in the OT. Ecclesiastes and the Wisdom of Solomon have connections to Greek philosophy. The Book of Job and the Song of Songs tap into the Persian philosophical traditions. But we shouldn't, in these cases, be looking for specific influences of foreign perspectives on Jewish tradition. What we are dealing with is a transnational philosophical movement that embraced thinkers in many traditions, including the Jewish tradition. The movement would have given rise, in varying times and places, to institutions of learning, bodies of literature, and professional convocations.

WISDOM AS PERSON

In Israel, the trek through wisdom traditions took three byways not found in the wider wisdom movement. Two of these byways I have already mentioned. First, Jewish sages nativized the wisdom tradition by shaping it around the King Solomon story cycles. Second, they used wisdom themes to bracket the central narrative of Jewish covenantal theology. In the third byway, they created a new player in the heavenly court to embody the role of wisdom.

In the OT texts, the new player is called "Wisdom." English speaking scholars have the habit of referring to this character as "Lady Wisdom," "Dame Wisdom," or "Woman Wisdom" and applying the English feminine pronouns "she/her/hers" to the character. The habit is based, in part at least, on the fact that the words for "wisdom" in Hebrew and Greek are in the feminine gender and that the Hebrew and Greek pronouns that refer to Wisdom are, by dint of syntactical agreement, also in the feminine. By itself, this grammatical fact does not justify the feminization of the Wisdom character—those who work in languages with gendered syntax are comfortable with dissonance between grammatical gender and actual gender. What we need to consider is not syntax, but the social roles that are ascribed to Wisdom. And in this case, the roles are mixed in gender. Sometimes the actions of Wisdom correspond to traditional feminine activities in the social world of Second Temple Judaism, sometimes to traditional masculine activities. The first-century Jewish thinker Philo, who adopted personified Wisdom into his cosmology, tended to use feminine metaphors for Wisdom. At times, though, he reverted to masculine analogies. In a rare moment of insight, Philo confesses, "We say, then, without heeding the difference in grammatical gender, that the daughter of God, Wisdom, is both male and father, sowing and begetting in souls learning, instruction, knowledge, sound sense, and good and praiseworthy actions."[12] Instead, then, of using a name that predisposes us to seek feminine analogies, such as Woman Wisdom, I will either capitalize the word "Wisdom" or use the phrase "Person Wisdom" when I refer to this wisdom literature persona. The pronouns of choice will be "it/its," though in certain contexts masculine or feminine pronouns will be the best option.

Passages that mention Person Wisdom can be found in almost every Wisdom Book in the OT. In fact, if we regard Wisdom as a female character, then the extent of her treatment would be larger than that of any other woman in the Bible.[13] Even cast in the role of a man, Wisdom would still rank among the top ten Biblical characters in terms of coverage. That a character so important in the Bible is so little known in comparison to other OT characters is probably because the literature in which Wisdom appears is so poorly known. Let's look briefly at some of the Person Wisdom passages in the OT.

The oldest reference to Wisdom may be a poem inserted into chapter 28 of Job. The poet is amazed how humans, by damming streams and channeling through rock, can bring to light the precious metals and jewels hidden in the earth. Wisdom, the poet goes on to say, is similarly hidden from sight. Unlike the treasures of the earth, however, Wisdom can't be recovered by human skills—only God knows where it can be found. In this early passage from Job, Wisdom is not yet imaged as a person. Wisdom does, however, have a role in this poem that is somewhat independent of both God and humans.

In the first nine chapters of the Book of Proverbs, Wisdom emerges as an independent personality. Representing an abstract quality as a person is *personification*. John Bunyan employs this literary trick in *Pilgrim's Progress*. When Pilgrim and his companion arrive at a silver mine called Lucre, for example, a fellow named Demas invites them to break off their journey to the Heavenly City and dig for treasure. Bunyan derives the name from the statement put in the mouth of Paul in 2 Timothy: "Demas has abandoned me, having loved the present world" (4:10). Demas, we

12. Philo, *Flight*, 52.
13. Cited by Fontaine, "Wisdom in Proverbs," 112–3.

would say, personifies the sin of greed. When we first hear about Wisdom in Proverbs 1–2, we might think that the writer is employing this kind of personification. "Wisdom cries out in the street; in the squares it raises its voice," says the writer. Wisdom, when it goes out into the public, asks, "How long, foolish ones, will you love being fools?" It offers two paths to the hearers. For the ones who listen, Wisdom promises security and understanding. For those who do not listen, the future holds disaster and distress.

The compiler of the Book of Proverbs returns to the story of Wisdom in chapter 8, repeating the tale of how Wisdom goes out into the highways and byways—this time to a high place in front of the gates of the town—and calls out again to those who are not wise. Wisdom's message in this chapter is less harsh, more carrot than stick. "Wisdom is better than jewels; nothing desirable compares to it." Wisdom says that "I love those who love me" and that "the one who seeks me earnestly will find me." But then the tale shifts, and Wisdom begins to talk about its past. "The Lord *acquired* me at the beginning of his way, before his works of old. From ancient times I was *poured out*, from the beginning, from the earliest time of the earth. When the deep did not exist, I was *brought forth*" (8:22–24). The three Hebrew verbs describing the generation/creation of Wisdom—the ones with translations in italics—can all be understood as aspects of reproduction. God, acting as both father and mother, gives birth to Wisdom, who shares the divine image. Person Wisdom then goes on to mention several events in the first chapter of Genesis and says that, before all this, "I was near to the Lord, as an *amon*, and I was delighting day by day, always playing in front of the Lord—playing in the world, the Lord's earth, and my delight was with humankind" (8:30–31). *Amon* is a rare Hebrew word. It may refer to Wisdom's role as an architect of creation, or it may be a way of saying that Wisdom was God's dear child. Both make sense in context. Later interpreters of the wisdom tradition tend to understand *amon* as "child."

The description of Wisdom in this chapter of Proverbs carries us beyond the usual meaning of personification. As an active agent with a cosmological role, it now has real substance. The writer invites us into a world before the world, into a time that precedes Genesis 1:1. Wisdom was then with God. It was fashioned by God and begotten by God. As God's companion, it played a part in creating the world.

In this encomium to Wisdom in Proverbs, we perhaps observe the influence of the international sapiential tradition on the Jewish religious framework. Since certain passages in Proverbs seem to cast Wisdom into feminine roles, some scholars speculate that the person of Wisdom was a vehicle to introduce female deities favored by the non-Jewish sages into the monotheistic, male-oriented Godhead of Judaism. I'll leave this as what it is—simple speculation. For our purposes, the significance of Wisdom lies not in its origin but in its use. Wisdom brackets Jewish cosmology and theology with a sapiential framework that is larger than the world of the Torah. The sage who initiates students into the practice of wisdom shows them a way of reaching God that bypasses the difficult ascent through Law and the patriarchs. Taking students to the court of heaven along an inner path of right thinking and right action, the sage lays aside the ups and downs of national politics that are closely connected to covenantal theology.

This revelation of Wisdom as a person throws light on the rest of the Book of Proverbs. What seemed to me, when I first encountered it, to be an indigestible mound of epigrams and advice, becomes a picture of a pilgrim sage probing and testing truths, seeking to find a way through an inner landscape and into the presence of God. We'll see where this takes the story of Person Wisdom when we come to the last century before the common era. But first, a visit with the sage Ben Sira.

The deuterocanonical book of Sirach is the longest wisdom book in the OT. It was composed in Hebrew in the first third of the second century CE by a Jerusalem sage and teacher known as Jesus/Joshua, son of Eleazar, the son of Sira. In the closing decades of the second century, the sage's grandson, while spending some time in Alexandria, Egypt, made a rather literal translation of his grandfather's work into Greek. The Greek version of the book found its way into Septuagint collections and via the Septuagint, into the Christian OT. The Hebrew version of the book, however, was not merged into the Tanak.[14] Since the early years of my Christian journey were spent among Protestants with low-church traditions, people whose Bibles contained only the Tanak in their OT, I missed out on Sirach when I first read through the wisdom books of the OT. My initial encounter with the text was in the reading cycle of a liturgical church. Only a small fraction of Sirach came within the compass of the lectionary cycle. I'm not sure when I first read the book front to back—it may be when trying to find Ben Sira's roster of saints. This is the list that

---

14. For many centuries, the Hebrew source text of Sirach appeared to have been lost. Manuscript discoveries in the last two hundred years have restored about two-thirds of Ben Sira's Hebrew version.

starts with the line, "Let us now praise famous men" (44:1).[15] I returned
to Sirach when I began to look more closely at the wisdom traditions of
the OT. From a more thorough study of it, I came away with two strong
impressions. The first was about the community behind wisdom thought.
Ben Sira was a teaching sage, and reading his book as classroom notes
makes us feel a part of the long wisdom tradition. Sirach begins and ends
his book with wisdom. Its first verse is "All wisdom is from the Lord and
is with him forever." In the prayer/psalm from the book's last chapter,
Ben Sira says to God, "I sought wisdom openly in my prayer; before the
temple I was continually asking for it, and I will never stop seeking it"
(51:13–14).

My second impression was that Ben Sira had too much ambition.
At the end of the book (50:27), Ben Sira signs his own work with the
line, "I, Jesus son of Eleazar, son of Sirach of Jerusalem, who poured out
wisdom from his heart, have written in this book instruction in understanding and knowledge." This is a rare case where the author of an OT
book puts himself forward as author—almost all of the other books are
either anonymous or pseudepigraphic. Nor is Ben Sira shy about claiming divine authority for his signed work. "I will make instruction shine as
the morning, and I will cast its beam into the distance," he says. "I pour
out instruction as prophecy and leave it behind for posterity" (24:32–33).
Ben Sira inserts himself into the line of prophets and recommends his
book for the official canon. He would fail to achieve this exalted status, at
least for the Jewish Bible he was targeting. Ironically, he may have failed
because he tried too hard. In the Second Temple period, the best way to
get a book recognized as authoritative was not to sign it and advertise
inspiration, but to claim it was authored by someone with an established
prophetic reputation, such as Moses, Solomon, or Daniel.

Two of the chapters of Ben Sira's book—chapters 1 and 24—link his
book of wisdom to the Person Wisdom cosmology. In the first chapter,
Ben Sira acknowledges, as Proverbs does, that God "created Wisdom before all things" (1:4). The Lord "saw it and took its measure and poured
it over all God's works" (1:9). We get more detail on this creative act in
24:3–4, when Ben Sira says that Wisdom "came forth from the mouth
of the Most High" and "covered the earth like a mist." At first, it "dwelt
in the heights" and its "throne was in the pillar of the cloud." Ben Sira's

---

15. This was an expression I knew better as a book title—writer James Agee and
photographer Walker Evans employed this name for their book of depression-era pho-
tographs of white cotton-picker families.

understanding of the role of Wisdom—up to this point, at least—is consistent with what we find in Proverbs. But then the tale takes a surprising turn. According to Ben Sira, Wisdom didn't stay in its heavenly home. It came down from its lofty position in the heights to interact with the nations. The Creator commanded Wisdom to let its "tent rest in Jacob" and its "inheritance be in Israel" (24:8). From then on, Wisdom "served in the holy tabernacle before the Lord" and its "sphere of authority was in Jerusalem" (24:10–11). Later in the chapter, Ben Sira becomes even more explicit. Wisdom, he says, is "the book of the covenant of the Most High God, the law that Moses commanded to us" (24:23).

Wisdom is Torah? While we would expect the wisdom tradition to take on new features in late Second Temple Judaism, putting an equal sign between the Person Wisdom and the Jewish Law creates some friction with the international and humanistic trends of the wisdom tradition. Ben Sira has appropriated Wisdom's cosmology to support the central narrative of Second Temple Jewish faith. Mishnaic Judaism would follow Ben Sira in this novel move.

When we examine the Gospel of John in chapter 7, we will see the Christian sect also trying to restrict Wisdom to a singular context. Before we let Person Wisdom commit itself to such specific roles, however, let's look at one last instalment in the wider humanistic story of Wisdom. This is found in a philosophical work written, scholars think, in Alexandria, Egypt, during the last century before the Common Era. The Wisdom of Solomon, the last Wisdom Book of the OT, is probably the only OT book authored in Greek. The composer was a writer who, though Jewish, was thoroughly trained in Greco-Roman rhetoric.

We call the book the Wisdom of Solomon because the writer, though he never says, "I am Solomon," channels the biblical Solomon when he speaks. The text of the book falls into two halves. The first half (chapters 1–11) uses wisdom as a theme and ends with a small set of encomia about the famous figures of the Tanak from Adam to Moses who were aided by Person Wisdom. The second half (chapters 12–19) segues into the events of the Exodus and the wilderness years and addresses God as the motive force. Like Ben Sira, the author of the Wisdom of Solomon finds connections between covenantal Jewish theology and wisdom motifs. Unlike Ben Sira, he does not equate Torah and Person Wisdom.

The Wisdom of Solomon takes up the story of Person Wisdom in chapters 6–11. When we first meet Wisdom, we find ourselves in the story begun in the Book of Proverbs. Wisdom is "shining and unfading and easily seen by those who love it" (6:12). The person who rises early to seek it finds Wisdom "sitting at the gates." Wisdom is not just passive, however. It "goes around seeking those worthy of it, graciously making itself known to them in their paths and meeting up with them in every thought" (6:16). After describing the joys and advantages of this encounter with Wisdom, the writer promises a big reveal: "I will explain what Wisdom is and how it came about. I won't hide from you the mysteries but will trace it out and bring knowledge of it into the open" (6:22). Concerned that his readers might question where this new information comes from, the author steps deeper into the role of Solomon. The king to whom God gave "an unerring knowledge of what exists, in order to see the structure of the world and the working of its parts" (7:17), is unlikely to be mistaken about the nature of Wisdom. Especially considering that "Wisdom, the artificer of all things" (7:22), taught Solomon what he knows.

The author starts the reveal with a list of twenty-one qualities of Wisdom. Here they are, taken from a recent translation of Wisdom of Solomon:

> For there is in [Wisdom] a spirit that is intelligent, holy, unique, of many parts, subtle, free-moving, lucid, unpolluted, distinct, invulnerable, loving the good, sharp, unhindered, beneficent, loving towards humanity, firm, unfailing, free from care, all-powerful, all-surveying, and penetrating all spirits that are intelligent, pure, most subtle (7:22–23, NETS).[16]

Just after this list, we find the most explicit description of the relationship between Wisdom and God in the wisdom corpus. Wisdom, we learn, is "the breath of the power of God," and "a pure emanation of the glory of the Almighty" (7:25). It is "a refulgence of everlasting light," "a flawless mirror of the working of God," and "an image of God's goodness" (7:26). The vocabulary of Middle Platonic and Stoic philosophy has been mined by the author of the Wisdom of Solomon to provide words to describe Person Wisdom.[17] This companion of God, while not giving up its prerogatives, stoops to cultivate intimate relationships with certain people: "In every generation Wisdom passes into holy souls and turns them into friends of God and prophets" (7:27).

---

16. The NETS translation of the Wisdom of Solomon is by Michael A. Knibb.

17. The Middle Platonism of Plutarch (late first century CE) can be matched to many of the ideas in the Wisdom of Solomon. See Barrier, "Middle Platonism."

Throughout this text we find overlapping uses of "Wisdom," "spirit of Wisdom," and "Holy Spirit." At one point, for example, Solomon asks God, "Who knows your counsel, unless you yourself have given Wisdom and have sent your Holy Spirit from on high?" (9:17). By the time we get to chapter 11 of the book, the creating and guiding acts associated with Wisdom have been folded into the activity of God or the Spirit of God. Wisdom is given a position in the Wisdom of Solomon so exalted that, when seen from a distance, the members of the heavenly court blur together.

These three OT wisdom books—Proverbs, Sirach, and the Wisdom of Solomon—show a development of the Wisdom persona. We begin with a personification of wisdom, hardly more than a metaphor, and end up with a full-fledged person with some mysterious relationship to the Godhead. No matter how exalted Wisdom's position, however, it continues to interact with creation, especially with individual people.

Those who are keeping score might notice that I left out passages about Wisdom that are found in the third chapter of the Book of Baruch, a second-century BCE work attributed to the scribe of Jeremiah and included in the deuterocanonical literature. I left them out because, while they illustrate how widespread the idea of Wisdom was in this period, they don't really add much to our understanding of who Wisdom was. Besides omitting Baruch, I also left out passages about Wisdom in works that did not end up in the OT. Two of these extra-canonical sources, though, are worth mentioning because they show how Jewish sages handled and expanded the role given to Wisdom by the OT books.

One of these sources is found in the section of the *Book of Enoch* known as "The Similitudes." This section of *Enoch* is considered a late addition to the *Enoch* collection, perhaps dating to the first century BCE or first century CE. In chapter 42, a short passage—perhaps a poem that has been inserted into the surrounding narrative—tells us that Wisdom, after searching for a place to live, finally found a home in the heavens. From there, it went out to dwell with humans (42:2), but its experience in the human world was not a happy one. Wisdom went back to its heavenly place and settled down among the angels. This is the only text that details a two-directional movement of Wisdom—going forth to dwell with people then returning to be with God.

A second source of interest for the study of Wisdom is the Jewish philosopher Philo, a thinker we will be visiting again in chapter 6. Philo flourished in Alexandria, Egypt, during the first half of the first century

CE. I call him a philosopher, and this is appropriate because in one sense all sages are philosophers (i.e., lovers of wisdom), and all the wisdom writings we have been looking at are a philosophical tradition. When we use the term "philosophy" in modern Western languages, however, we usually attach it to a wisdom tradition that arose in the Greek city-states in the fifth century BCE. By this Greek standard, what the wisdom writers of the OT did was theology or religion rather than philosophy. This is a distinction that will not bear much scrutiny, but we won't get far here if we start excavating our foundations. Even when we accept this narrow standard about what is real philosophy, however, Philo is still a philosopher—he employs both the Hellenistic and the Jewish wisdom tradition in his writings.

Philo's writings had almost no impact on Jewish thought in the millennium after his death. We have his writings today because of his influence on Christian theology. In the first, second, and third centuries CE, it was the church and not the synagogue that wanted to make its peace with the Greek philosophical tradition. Philo's integration of the Jewish and Greek traditions, Christian apologists found, gave them a starting point. Thanks to Christian copyists, more than two-thirds of the seventy-odd titles written by Philo have survived.[18]

Because Philo's works were filtered through the concerns of the Christian thinkers, we typically hear about only two of Philo's ideas—his concept of the Logos and his allegorical method of interpretation. This was true in my case—I emerged from my formal tutelage in Christianity with these two simple handles on Philo. Only later, when I had looked at his writings as works of ancient philosophy and at Philo himself as a late avatar of a wisdom sage, did I begin to appreciate the larger context of his work.

The treatment of the Person Wisdom in Philo is consistent with what we find in the Wisdom of Solomon.[19] Philo's descriptions of Wisdom, though, are more dependent on metaphor than passages from the Wisdom of Solomon are. In one place, for example, Philo says that God

18. Seland, "Why and How," 157. Not only Philo but almost all Jewish literature from the first centuries BCE and CE has been transmitted to us through Christian channels. This would include the works of Josephus, the Septuagint, almost all the pseudepigrapha, and all of the deuterocanonical books. See Kraft, "Multiform Jewish Heritage."

19. Many scholars posit an Alexandrian origin for the Wisdom of Solomon. If so, then it seems likely that Philo—another Jewish sage of Alexandria—would have known this work. Assuming, of course, that the Wisdom of Solomon was written before Philo died.

and knowledge entered into a "union" (not a coupling, Philo is careful to note, like human sex). This God-espoused knowledge is the pre-existent Person Wisdom—Philo even quotes the passage from Proverbs 8 that talks about Wisdom being present with God before creation. Wisdom, then, "receiving the seed of God, bore, when her labors had reached their end, the only and beloved perceptible son, the world."[20] While Philo's many metaphors give us vivid images of how Wisdom interacts with both the divine and human realms, assembling Philo's metaphors into a unified philosophical system is difficult. Like the author of the Wisdom of Solomon, Philo drew on an education that included Platonic and Stoic philosophical systems. Both authors, following the practice of earlier thinkers in the wisdom tradition, insert Jewish covenantal theology into a framework of international wisdom. The activities of Person Wisdom therefore face in two directions. On the one side, we find Wisdom, via philosophical reflection, becoming a part of the abstract emanation of the divine into human experience. On the other side, Wisdom takes on specific roles in relation to the nation of Israel. Neither author takes Ben Sira's bold step of equating Wisdom with Torah, but both find the best evidence of Wisdom's work in the Jewish story.

Philo goes beyond the author of the Wisdom of Solomon in one very specific way, however. Because he is more influenced by Stoic philosophy, Philo includes the Stoic Logos in his system. The Logos is the seminal reason that brings the universe into existence. It resides most fully in human thought. For some of the less religious Stoics, human reason *is* the divine, but neither Philo's Platonized philosophy nor his Jewish theology can accept a totally immanent Logos. Instead, Philo pictures the Logos as a demiurge, a being that can dirty its hands with matter and creation while still retaining the image of God. He agrees with the Stoics, however, that the most complete expression of the Logos is not in physical creation but in its interaction with the human mind—it makes people wise. This role for Logos sounds like the activity of Wisdom, and the roles played by Wisdom and Logos in Philo's system overlap. Scholarly attempts to tease apart the roles of Wisdom and the Logos in Philo's system have not met with much success. Several of Philo's metaphors for Wisdom, for example, are also applied to the Logos—such as being the express image of God, being light, being a mother, and being a river. Philo does, then, add an extracanonical chapter to the story of Wisdom, but he adds the

20. Philo, *Drunkenness*, 30.

chapter so late in the Jewish wisdom tradition that the chapter merges with the Christian wisdom story—the topic we begin to address in the next chapter.

WISDOM AND APOCALYPTIC

In its waning centuries, the Jewish wisdom tradition was rocked by a shift in popular Jewish religion. This change, captured by the term "apocalyptic," had its strongest effect on the sectarian alternatives that challenged Judaism's core narrative. The three eccentric movements that we looked at in the previous chapter—Enochic Judaism, Essene sectarianism, and Christian Judaism—all incorporated elements of the apocalyptic. Even mainline Judaism dallied with it. A key apocalyptic text, the Book of Daniel, became the final book received into the Hebrew canon.

The new perspective seems to have entered the Jewish milieu in the decades following the Hellenistic incursions into the Middle East in the late fourth century BCE. It was a diffused sentiment, not a definable movement with leaders and agendas. Scholars resort to terms such as "mood," "temper," and "impression" when they describe the apocalyptic shift. Although Hellenism may have triggered the shift, the ideas associated with the apocalyptic seem to have more in common with eastern influences—Babylonian and Persian—than with the western Greeks. But whatever their source, the new influences altered the universe in which the Jewish people lived. The three centuries after the political shakeup of Alexander the Great become, in the phrase used by Philip Jenkins, a "crucible era."[21] Many traditional religious ideas, cast into the melting pot, emerge from it transformed. Imagine, for a moment, the Jewish tribes wandering through a large movie studio. Leaving the stage set of Mosaic covenantal theology with its backdrops of Law and Sinai and tabernacles and temples, they walk onto a new set. The sceneries on the new set are vast historical panoramas painted with figures of angels and demons. Assistants come onto the new stage and hand out scripts marked "Secret—do not remove from studio." The sound effects on the old stage, the chanted psalms and murmur of temple sacrifices, switch to war trumpets and the screams of battle. Most of the people are frightened by the new set and hurry back to their old stage, but a few stay, modifying their

---

21. Jenkins, *Crucible of Faith.*

performances to fit the new milieu. Those who stay become the sectarians we discussed earlier.

The apocalyptic shift was accompanied by a new literature. We have already seen examples of it. In addition to the Book of Daniel, we have the large and thoroughly apocalyptic *Book of Enoch*. The sectarian writings of the Qumran Essenes employ apocalyptic themes. The NT Book of Revelation and certain passages in the gospels and epistles also belong to this genre. In addition to these better-known examples, numerous other works from the second century BCE to the second century CE can be assigned to the corpus—among them we could list the *Assumption of Moses*, the deuterocanonical 2 Esdras, and the *Testaments of the Twelve Patriarchs*. Taken together, these works constitute "a substantial written universe."[22] The rise and demise of the apocalyptic in the late Second Temple period is one of the most documented intellectual events in the Second Temple period.

Certain themes dominate the apocalyptic literature. First and foremost is the placement of the writers on a cosmic timeline. History in the core narrative of the Tanak is concerned with God's selection of the Jewish people. The story picks up with the call of Abraham and ends with Israel subjugated to surrounding nations. In the first chapters of Genesis, of course, we do find a slight nod toward a wider history, but the rest of the Genesis narrative fits within a limited time and place. In the extended timeline of the apocalyptic, the universe begins with a primal struggle between God and the forces of evil. We learn about the roles played in this drama by Satan, the good and bad angels (many of them mentioned by name), and demons. The supernatural world, once an amorphous other, resolves into a series of places that include a multitiered heavenly court and descending gradations of hell and punishment. When humans enter the cosmic story, they are pawns in the game, their fates directed by forces beyond their control. We are also given a vision of the endpoint of the cosmic timeline that includes the defeat of the enemies of God, the resurrection of the dead, and a final judgment in which humans are assigned, according to their deeds and allegiances, to either bliss or suffering.

The reaction of any reader to a story so vast would be "How do we know all this?" In response to this question, the apocalyptic authors provide us with various certificates of credibility. Famous characters—among them Enoch, Noah, Jacob, Daniel, Moses, and Ezra—receive and record

22. Jenkins, "The Crucible Era," 38.

visions and revelations. Some apocalyptic authors are carried into heaven and have conversations with interpreting angels. We learn about heavenly tablets on which the secrets of the world and the plan of the ages are recorded. The human intermediaries get glimpses of what is written on these tablets, and angels encourage them to reveal certain passages to their friends and families so that they will be handed down through the generations. In 2 Esdras, for example, five scribes take dictation for forty days and produce ninety-four books (14:42–47). Ezra is told to make twenty-four of them public, presumably the books of the Tanak, allowing both worthy and unworthy people to read them. Seventy books, however, are reserved for the wise. These secret books, we assume, contain the apocalyptic visions that embrace both the beginning and the end of the world.

To convey their secret revelations, apocalyptic writers make use of exotic symbols. "Over the course of the years," notes D.S. Russell, "a pattern of imagery and symbolism was evolved—indigenous and foreign, traditional and mythological—which became part of the apocalyptists' stock-in-trade."[23] The symbols include strange beasts, such as the fabled Behemoth and Leviathan, various dragons, and the chimeric creatures in the visions of Daniel. Ordinary animals also come into the story. Bulls, sheep, lambs, rams, lions, eagles, elephants, and camels stand in for humans and angels in apocalyptic recitations of world history. Friends and enemies are often designated with fixed circumlocutions in the apocalyptic texts, as we have seen in the Qumran sectarian literature with its "teacher of righteousness" and "man of the lie." Certain numbers take on special meanings, especially the digits three, four, seven, ten, twelve, forty, seventy, and their multiples. The use of these symbols underlines the esoteric nature of the apocalyptic revelations—only those who are in on the secrets know how to decode the symbols.

Two enduring ideas come into Jewish thought about the time of the apocalyptic shift. While these ideas merge with apocalyptic teaching and are nourished by it, we don't know whether their appearance is fully explained by the shift. The first is the idea of a messiah, or messiahs. These are individuals anointed (*mashiach* comes from the Hebrew word for anointing) for a special task. The task was often associated with important events in future timelines, such as the liberation of Israel from its enemies. In some of the apocalyptic writings, we find the rubric "son of man" applied to this messianic figure.

23. Russell, *Method and Message*, 122.

The second idea that emerges in this period is that of an afterlife. In earlier Jewish literature, death was either the end of existence or a transition into the realm of shades. Postexilic writings start to hint at an alternate destination after death, and by the third century BCE, the belief had become widespread that either the soul separated from its body at death and went to a supernatural realm or that both soul and body would be later reanimated to enjoy the bliss of heaven or the suffering of hell. The second-century Book of Daniel reflects this new belief: "Many of those who sleep in the dusty ground will awaken, some to everlasting life, some to disgrace and everlasting repulsion" (12:2). The book of 2 Maccabees, also written in the second century BCE, assumes this stance when it tells the story of seven brothers and their mother who were martyred for their devotion to the Jewish law. The mother tells her sons, "The Creator of the world will with mercy give breath and life back to you again" (7:23). Anticipation of this afterlife would have a profound impact on both apocalyptic and non-apocalyptic spiritualities.

What effect did the apocalyptic shift have on the wisdom tradition? Some biblical scholars in the first half of the twentieth century speculated that apocalypticism might have been an offshoot of the wisdom tradition. The Book of Daniel may have led them in this direction—the Daniel who has apocalyptic visions seems to be a professional sage, a wise man. But pairing wisdom and apocalyptic perspectives is an odd mating. The two perspectives represent different approaches to life. The wisdom tradition focuses on the observable world of nature, interpreted through wise sayings. The sage's attention is directed to present experience in a world that is inherently good. Fellow travellers are found in urbane and international wisdom communities. The apocalyptic writers, in contrast, orient their attention to a supernatural world. Rather than living in the present, they live for a time to come, rejecting the current and corrupt world and associating with groups—often rural groups—that withdraw from society. Their truths are revealed in dreams and visions, not in wise sayings.

For all this difference, however, there is a partial convergence of wisdom ideas and apocalyptic themes in the late Second Temple period. We can see this fusion in books such as the deuterocanonical 2 Esdras— toward the end of the book, apocalyptic passages give way to sections of sayings and beatitudes that seem to be lifted from a wisdom text. The final wisdom book of the OT, the Wisdom of Solomon, displays a mixture of wisdom tropes, apocalyptic themes, and belief in life after death. We see this most clearly in the extended argument between the ungodly and the persecuted saints (chapters 1, 2, 5). At the culmination of the debate, we have a glimpse of the righteous enjoying eternal life in the presence of the Most High (5:15–16). The unrighteous are not so fortunate—the Lord, girded with armour, hurls lightning, hailstones, and floods (5:17–23) against them. Ben Witherington refers to this somewhat artificial convergence of wisdom and apocalyptic traditions as "an arranged marriage."[24] Arranged or not, however, it is an actual union, and we can see the tensions of this marriage of wisdom and apocalypse at work in NT texts.

RETHINKING WISDOM

My first brush with the wisdom literature of the OT was brief, only enough to let me know that I was looking at something out of the ordinary. I found that I could read them devotionally, following a practice that evangelicals called "claiming verses," but I couldn't fit them into a systematic way of interpreting the Bible. As I dipped into them over the next couple of decades, the message of the wisdom books started to have more resonance. I was bringing to the text new questions.

In the years when I was studying and teaching philosophy, I began to look at the wisdom books with different eyes. These books, I realized, were attempts by philosophers to answer the pressing questions of their own age. In the works of the wisdom sages, I saw Jewish thinkers struggling to find a place where they could stand. They wrestled with abstractions, as all philosophers do, but they also tried to put words to their unique human experiences. The embattled Job, asking why the righteous suffered, refused to accept pious platitudes as answers. His own suffering became the yardstick for measuring the justice of God. The teacher who speaks in the Book of Ecclesiastes knew that fleeing existential depression was pointless—like all demons, it must be faced and named. The compiler of Proverbs devised an ethical system that could be defended without appeal to miraculous revelations. The author of the Song of Songs, searching for a way to unite with the divine, explored the metaphor of human love. Sirach sought a middle ground between the Torah and the wisdom of the sages, illustrating one with the other. The writer of the Wisdom of Solomon attempted to unite Greek philosophy with his experience of Judaism. The wisdom sages were, one and all, the philosophers of their

24. Witherington, *Jesus the Sage*, 384.

time and place. As a student of philosophy, I felt a common bond with them that reached across two millennia.

More than just my study of philosophy, however, was shifting the place from which I was approaching the wisdom literature. I was learning to respect the sages as thinkers, but I still wasn't trusting them as companions on my own spiritual journey. This only began to happen when I acquired more experience with the mystical traditions of Christianity. The poet and critic Kenneth Rexroth, whose works inspired the beat generation of the fifties and who eventually became part of the Catholic mystical movement, penned an article on Ecclesiastes in 1966. He found in Ecclesiastes, the Song of Songs, and some of the later folk tales (Ruth and Esther) "revelations more fundamental than those of Moses and the Prophets." These books, he noted, attracted Jewish and Christian readers whose journeys involved "mysticism, meditation, and contemplative prayer." Many of the important mystic theologians "turned to this literature because it opens channels into the deepest recesses of the interior life."[25] So it was with me. The sages added a philosophical component to the OT message, but they also brought with them a clearer vision of the mystical life, a vision that was hidden from me until it began to take up residence in my own life. I discovered that I was able to read the wisdom books devotionally, as I had done in my evangelical years. The difference was that, instead of latching onto a verse here and there, I could now confront the contexts in which the words were spoken. By walking with the sages through their anguishes, confusions, and insights, I was tilling the soil in which seeds of faith were planted.

To raise the wisdom books from their lectionary neglect, I have emphasized in this chapter the independence of the movement that they represent. I have also pitted them against other types of OT literature. But arraying Solomon and Moses against each other, as though they were in some kind of grudge match, misrepresents the role of wisdom literature in the Second Temple period. As James Kugel points out, the wisdom mentality wasn't just confined to the inclusion of a few wisdom books in the Tanak. Instead, it was a "*way of reading*, as much as the texts themselves, that Jews and Christians canonized as their Bible."[26] The wisdom books do much more than add a clutch of gnomic sayings to the Tanak.

---

25. Rexroth, *With Eye and Ear*, 114.
26. Kugel, *How to Read*, 671. Emphasis mine.

They license wisdom messages that are concealed in the histories, prophecies, legislation, and poetry of the Bible.

Several of the Psalms, for example, show the direct influence of the wisdom movement, and many more can be read from a wisdom stance. This is especially evident in psalms that are addressed to listeners rather than to God—we find the same kinds of advice in them that were proffered by the sages. Some of these psalms even share key vocabulary words with wisdom literature and make use of the themes and rhetoric of wisdom teaching. Roland Murphy, a scholar of wisdom literature, includes Psalms 1, 32, 34, 37, 49, 112, and 128 in the wisdom canon.[27]

Some passages in the writings of the prophets also call to mind the wisdom traditions. Isaiah, especially the second half of the book, edges into wisdom territory. The suffering servant passage in Isaiah 52–53, read by Christians as a prophecy about Jesus and by Jewish interpreters as an allegory of the Jewish nation, could be read as a parable about Person Wisdom. It begins with "See, my servant will *act wisely*" (52:13). At the end of the Isaiah passage, we learn that "by his *understanding* the righteous one, my servant, will make many righteous" (53:11). (In later chapters, I will explore a specific way—through a Jewish wisdom sect— that the servant of God in the Isaiah texts and the Person Wisdom of the wisdom texts might be linked.)

In addition to their influence on the Tanak, the wisdom schools spread their influence around the margins of biblical literature. In the previous chapter, we looked at the Dead Sea Scrolls. Given the extreme sectarian and apocalyptic stance taken by members of the Qumran group, we would not expect them to be sympathetic to viewpoints built on international scholarship. Even so, a few of the documents recovered from the Qumran caves make use of wisdom themes and techniques. In the texts grouped as 4QInstruction (4Q415–4Q417), we encounter teacher-to-student advice on some of the same topics covered in the Book of Proverbs.

When the Christian Jewish sect took shape late in the Second Temple period, it would also borrow from the wisdom heritage of its Second Temple matrix. This second imaginative web I have woven, about the influence of a durable wisdom tradition on the OT, provides a starting point for my third web, the story of how this wisdom tradition influenced the Christian Jewish movement.

---

27. Murphy, *Tree of Life*, 103.

4

Wisdom in Matthew

CHRISTIANITY, WHEN IT FIRST emerged, was a Jewish sect. We sometimes read about Jewish Christianity, but it is more appropriate to think of the early church as a form of Christian Judaism. It did not remain a Jewish sect, of course. In the two generations after the death of Jesus, a pair of forces transformed this sect into a different movement. The first was the inclusion in the sect of a large number of gentiles. These newcomers diluted the specifically Jewish aspects of the faith. The second was the dismantling of institutional Judaism. In the years between 68 and 70 CE, Roman armies destroyed much of Jerusalem and ended temple worship. Judaism would reinvent itself as Rabbinic Judaism over the next few decades, modeling itself around Pharisaic ideas and separating itself from Christian Judaism.

What was this brief phase of Christian Judaism like? The reports about this sect from non-Christian sources provide few insights into the movement. What we do have are the documents of the NT. These documents, however, were collected, edited, and propagated by an institution that was leaving its Jewish roots behind. Using these documents as sources for Christian Judaism requires critical interpretation. We need to separate later agendas from their historical sources.

When I was trying to think like an evangelical, the critical task was less daunting. The gospels and Acts—the historical books of the NT—were composed, we believed, by the people whose names were attached to them, and they were written as early as possible. This meant that Acts would have been written by Luke in the early 60s CE, just before Paul's death, and the gospel assigned to Luke a bit before that. Mark, also not an apostle, would presumably have written his gospel about the same time as Luke. The gospels by Matthew and John, because they carried names of apostles, were potentially much earlier—they could have been composed in the first decade or two after the crucifixion. The epistles of the NT, some of them ascribed to persons whose lives overlapped with that of Jesus, also tended to be given early dates. Pseudepigraphy was rejected outright—if a letter was wrong about its author, could it be right about anything else? Since the evangelical approach downplayed disagreements between the authors of the NT, Paul and the other letter writers were thought to reflect the same ideas and attitudes found in Jesus and the apostles. Under dating schemes and assumptions such as these, the Christian Judaism of the first half of the first century CE ends up looking a lot like the expanding Christian church of later decades.

When I surrendered these evangelical assumptions, I swung, like a pendulum, to the other extreme. I concluded that almost nothing could be extracted from the NT that would give us a reliable picture of the life of Jesus and the experience of the earliest church. All we could know from the available documents was the self-consciousness of the Christian church some fifty to one hundred years after the death of Jesus. Depictions of the earliest years of the church, I came to believe, said more about the persons drawing the pictures than they did about Jesus and his disciples.

A swinging pendulum does not stay at the peaks of its amplitude, however, and in recent decades I have found myself less of a skeptic. The scholarly exploration of the Jewish roots of Christianity that began in the sixties and seventies, spearheaded by postliberal Protestants such as E.P. Sanders, has provided us with tools to sift through the NT documents and find their earlier strata. The bump given to studies of Second Temple Judaism by the publication of the Dead Sea Scrolls and the Jewish pseudepigrapha has also contributed to our understanding of Jewish sectarian movements and the matrices that gave rise to them.

In this and the following chapters, I want to think about the Jesus movement in the light of the OT wisdom tradition. Expressions of this tradition—ones clear enough to recognize—are confined to certain NT documents. But if these wisdom-influenced writings are also texts that reflect the earliest stratum of the church, then the case for Jesus playing the role of a sage and for Christian Judaism being a wisdom sect is strengthened. I have come to believe that three NT documents—the gospels of Matthew and John and the Epistle of James—belong to this stratum. In this chapter, I will focus on the Gospel of Matthew.

ASSUMPTIONS ABOUT MATTHEW

Before we delve into the wisdom texts of Matthew, we need to consider the status of this gospel in NT critical studies. At any given time, there is usually a consensus among scholars about how the documents of the NT connect with one other and with the background events against which they were written. This consensus shifts from one generation of scholars to another, sometimes in small steps, sometimes in large leaps. Students whose ideas align with the shifting front have a huge advantage when they write about the NT—they don't have to state their assumptions. Those who are misaligned are less fortunate.

For the Gospel of Matthew, I'm out of step with the current critical consensus. So let me take a moment to review three of the assumptions I'm bringing to this study. These concern the nature of the community behind the Gospel of Matthew, its relationship to the other gospels, and the date of its composition.

First, I have come to believe that *the Gospel of Matthew is the product of a Jewish community*. Both the writer and his immediate community thought of themselves as practicing Jews. They respected the community markers of first-century CE Judaism, including circumcision, sabbath-keeping, and dietary purity. They were aware, of course, that they held additional beliefs that most Jews disagreed with and that these disagreements could be serious and divisive. Many of the stories in the Gospel of Matthew are about conflicts between the Jewish authorities and Jesus, conflicts that were no doubt echoed in the community's own experiences with the Jewish establishment in the decades after the crucifixion. These differences with their fellow religionists, however, did not set the Matthean sectarians outside the boundaries of the Jewish community. They may have thought of their beliefs, in fact, as more mainline than that of their opponents, as a "perfected or fulfilled Judaism brought to its goal by the long-awaited Christ."[1]

A quick readthrough of Matthew's text underlines its Jewish embedding. We might wonder, with some justification, how this could have been missed. But it was. Reading Matthew as the early church's transition

---

1. Hagner, "The *Sitz im Leben*," 48.

out of Judaism has deep roots in Christian scholarship. By the second century CE, the church had become a gentile organization and Christian Judaism was reduced to a marginalized and often vilified rump. Over the years, students of the Christian Scriptures latched onto hints in the gospels that the future of the faith lay with gentiles rather than Jews. The emergence of the critical tradition in late eighteenth-century Europe—a time and place of rampant antisemitism—only reinforced this trend. Not until the rise of interest in Jewish studies and Second Temple Judaism in the decades following World War II did the Gospel of Matthew begin to recover its early context.

My second assumption is that *Matthew contains, more than the other Synoptic Gospels, the earliest exemplars of stories about Jesus.* At one point, this assumption would have been an easy one to make. Before the late 1700s, the Gospel of Matthew held a pre-eminent place among the gospels. When Christian writers quoted sayings by Jesus and stories about Jesus, they favored Matthew's versions. They also believed that Matthew was the oldest of the gospels, a position that Augustine of Hippo argued in the fifth century.[2] Mark, in contrast, was the least cited and least used of the gospels. With the advent of higher criticism in the eighteenth century, this ancient tradition was flipped. Mark came to be seen as the first gospel to be written, with Matthew and Luke copying passages from Mark's gospel into their own works. Just after WWII, this approach to the relationships among the gospels began to be called "redaction criticism."

Redaction critics like to point out how the author of Matthew used and altered the text of Mark. Matthew's compiler would have used most of Mark—about 90% of Mark's verses have approximate parallels in Matthew. Matthew's gospel is a much longer book than Mark, though. Some 45% of Matthean verses have no equivalent in Mark. A bit more than half of these non-Marcan verses have parallels in Luke. The verses that are similar in Matthew and Luke could be a result of Matthew copying from Luke or Luke copying from Matthew. The approach favored by redaction critics, however, is to posit an earlier, lost text called "Q" (for the German word *Quelle*, meaning source) that both Matthew and Luke copied from. Once you put Q and Mark on Matthew's writing table, it becomes convenient to invent a further lost source, called "M," to account for the 20% of Matthew that has no parallel in Mark or Luke. The author of Matthew

---

2. Augustine, *Harmony of the Gospels* 1.3

becomes, from the redaction-critical perspective, a "tinkering editor" rather than an author.[3]

The gospels of Matthew, Mark, and Luke are known as the "Synoptic (literally, 'seeing together') Gospels," and the question we are discussing—how they are related to each other—is called the "synoptic problem." The view that Mark's gospel was written first came to be known as "Marcan priority" and the schema where Matthew copies from Mark and Q is dubbed the "two-source hypothesis." The older view, Matthean priority, has in recent decades gone by the name "two-gospel hypothesis" because in this scenario, the author of Mark would have had the gospels of Matthew and Luke in front of him. There are, as you might imagine, many variations on these two major approaches to the synoptic problem.[4]

At this point, scholarly consensus heavily favors Marcan priority and the two-source hypothesis. The grip of this consensus, however, has been loosened in recent decades by four trends in gospel research. One source of change has been the application of modern literary criticism to the study of the gospels. Literary criticism of the gospels emphasizes the integrity of the author's role and the way that the writer structures the text for the reader. To begin the study of a text with a comparison to the author's sources is, from a literary viewpoint, methodologically unsound.[5] Practitioners of literary criticism may still assume Marcan

3. The phrase is from MacDonald, "Imitations," 374.

4. These variations often invoke staged compositing, oral traditions, and liturgical uses. The synoptic problem becomes especially problematic when we impose on first-century CE practices our modern, post-printing standards about publishing and final editions. Matthew Larsen points out that "accidental publication, post publication revision and multiple authorized versions of the same text" were common in the period when the NT was put together. Publication was an amorphous social construct, with every new draft functioning "only provisionally and temporarily as a final draft." The modern mind, in contrast, associates the cluster of concepts around the words "author," "book," and "publication" with very different images. We think about a physical product, a bound book with hundreds or thousands of identical copies and a complex mechanism for multiple editions, but early composers and readers of gospel texts regarded the gospel "not as a book, but as a fluid constellation of texts." Books were not so much published as they were "textualized." Because of this conceptual difference between the ancient and modern constructs, scholars tend to "import anachronistic ideas of bookish finality and containment" (Larsen, "Accidental Publication," 376–9) when they think about the composition of the gospels. For a more in-depth discussion of these issues, see Larsen, *Gospels Before the Book.*

5. Bauer, *Structure of Matthew's Gospel,* 25. Narrative criticism does not do away with the need to address textual issues—it simply declines to *start* with them. Christopher Skinner notes that most of the narrative critics that he has interacted with "do not demonstrate by their work" that beginning with the narrative approach absolves

priority—most probably do—but they don't make this assumption a focus of synoptic research. A second source of change was a frontal assault,
beginning in the sixties, by advocates of Matthean priority.[6] These scholars established—if nothing else—that many of the traditional arguments
for Marcan priority assumed what they set out to prove. Though rebuffed
by mainline scholarship, these confrontations left behind pockets of students who were willing to contemplate Matthean priority. A third source
that has weakened Marcan priority and redaction criticism has been a
renewed interest in the contribution made to NT texts by the oral transmission of eyewitness events.[7] A fourth source of change has been the
recent emphasis on the Jewish context of Matthew. Gospels that take a
pro-gentile perspective, such as Mark and Luke, are more likely to be
dependent on a gospel that reflects the stance of the early Jewish church.

A looser grip, however, is still a grip, and Marcan priority is still
widely accepted.[8] The debate turns on subtle points. The question of
who the copyist was is not a simple one. Parallel passages that only make
sense in one direction of copying are rare to nonexistent—explanations
can be found, it seems, for even the most unlikely of copying choices. To
solve the problem, every difference in pairs of similar readings must be
looked at from both points of view, asking whether the overall scenario
makes more sense if the copying goes in one direction rather than the
other. Having spent more than half of a long life squinting at these copied
passages from both directions—on my shelves are three well-thumbed
Greek gospel synopses—I have concluded that Matthean priorists have
the better argument.[9]

---

them "from wrestling with difficult textual or historical issues" (Skinner, "Narrative
Readings," 429).

6. NT scholars who helped to revive the modern interest in the two-gospel hypothesis include Dom Bernard Orchard, William R. Farmer, and David L. Dungan.

7. Two of the most prominent voices appealing to oral influence on texts are those
of Richard Bauckham and James D.G. Dunn. See, for example, Bauckham, *Jesus and the
Eyewitnesses*, and Dunn, *Jesus Remembered*. Neither author relinquishes Marcan priority, but their approaches raise questions about traditional form-critical (their primary
target) and redaction-critical (a secondary target) interpretations of gospel texts.

8. David Wenham points out, "It is as though the Markan hypothesis has a stran-
glehold on scholarly thinking." When redaction critics refer to gospel dependencies,
"quite feasible alternatives are not even considered" (Wenham, "Matthean Priority," 74).

9. When I claim that Matthew's gospel has the most primitive versions of the
Synoptic stories, I mean that it has the most primitive *Greek* versions. There has been
speculation about early versions of Matthew in Hebrew or Aramaic. Much of this theo-
rizing hangs on a comment in the works of the fourth-century Eusebius of Caesarea.

The third assumption I'll make is that *the Gospel of Matthew reached something close to its current form somewhere between 40 CE and 60 CE*, probably closer to the later date. Again, this runs counter to the majority opinion in NT scholarship, which places the composition of our received version of Matthew in the last decades of the first century. This time, though, I find myself in a much more substantial minority than I do on the issue of Matthean priority. In the late eighteenth and early nineteenth centuries, when higher criticism began to be applied to the documents of the NT, large parts of the NT were thought to have been composed up to a century after the events described in the documents. Since then, we have witnessed a reverse date creep, with more and more of the NT documents being slotted in ever-earlier slices of time. And when one document's date moves, it tends to drag others with it, because most of our dating is relative rather than absolute. Austin Farrer once described the dating issue of one of the NT books in relation to the others as "a line of tipsy revelers walking home arm-in-arm," each kept in position by the others.[10]

In 1976, Bishop John A.T. Robinson, a NT scholar who up to that time had accepted the chronological systems of his academic colleagues, wrote a book in which he pointed out that modern beliefs about the dates of NT documents had almost no foundation.[11] Many of the earlier dates that were employed in the pre-critical period could be defended as readily—and in some cases more readily—than the dates assumed by critical schools. A significant feature for dating the gospels, Robinson noted, was the lack of awareness in the gospels about the destruction of Jerusalem in 70 CE. None of the four gospels mention it as a historical event. They do contain predictions about a forthcoming cataclysm that would affect Jerusalem, and these forecasts were once thought to be after-the-fact prophecies, but the predictions are so vague that they can be used to argue the opposite point. Christian documents written after 70 CE, Robinson notes, describe the events around the fall of Jerusalem much more explicitly than the predictions in the gospels.

He had access—as we no longer do—to a five-volume work by Papias, a bishop of Hierapolis in the early second century. Papias, says Eusebius, wrote that "Matthew made an orderly arrangement of the sayings in the Hebrew language, and each translated these as he was able" (Eusebius, *Hist.* 3.39.16). Exactly what this sentence means has been intensely debated. Even if there are Hebrew and Aramaic precursors to sections of Matthew, the Gospel of Matthew that we know is a Greek narrative produced by a person with competent Greek language skills.

10. Farrer, *Revelation of St. John*, 37.

11. Robinson, *Redating*.

One of these gospel prophecies, in fact, comes close to being the fabled smoking gun for early dating. This is the prediction near the end of the Gospel of Matthew about the "desolating sacrilege." As chapter 24 of Matthew begins, Jesus is leaving the temple area. His disciples point out to him some of the temple buildings. He is not impressed and remarks that "not one stone here will be left on another." The topic is dropped, but after the group leaves the temple and climbs the nearby Mount of Olives, the disciples ask Jesus when the destruction of the temple and other apocalyptic events will take place. He describes for them a coming time of wars and famines and earthquakes. This chaotic period will be followed by persecutions of the believers. Many will abandon the cause, but those who remain faithful will deliver the gospel to all nations. And then, says Jesus, "the end comes," and it arrives with a series of signs. The first of these signs will be "the abomination of desolation that was spoken through the prophet Daniel that will be standing in the holy place" (24:15). The gospel writer then does an aside—the only time in the whole book that the author of Matthew breaks the fourth wall—and comments "let the reader understand." The aside points to Daniel 9:26–27. In these verses the prophet Daniel says that the anointed one, the Messiah, "will be cut off" and the armies of "the prince who is to come" will destroy Jerusalem and the sanctuary, causing the sacrifices and offerings to cease and replacing them with "the abomination that desolates." In the context of Daniel's prophecy, the abomination is probably the pagan sacrifice that King Antiochus IV offered in the Jerusalem temple in 167 BCE. Jesus transposes this sign and the destruction of the city and temple to the end times. When the desecrating act happens, Jesus says, those in Judea should "flee to the mountains" and prepare for a time of great suffering. Then, "immediately after the suffering," the sun and moon are darkened, the stars fall from the heavens, and the Son of Man appears and gathers his people.

If we assume that the author of Matthew (and the author of the parallel passage in Mark) are exercising any kind of editorial supervision in reporting this prophecy of Jesus, then we have a clear difference between an author writing in 50–60 CE and one writing in 80–90 CE. The earlier Matthew would not have known about the 70 CE destruction of the Second Temple and the cessation of temple sacrifices. The catastrophe could be shuffled into the deck of end-time events without impugning Jesus's prophetic insight. A later Matthew, however, would know that the loss of the temple and its sacrifices had already happened and that it was not accompanied by the other end-time events. How likely is it that he would report this mistaken prophecy? And why would he bother to give Jesus's advice on how to respond at the appearance of the abomination ("flee to the mountains") if this event has already happened? These predictions "virtually exclude a post-70 date for either the Matthean or Marcan gospels."[12]

This problem has affected the dating of the gospels. Marcan priorists now commonly place the writing of the Gospel of Mark in the years just before the destruction of Jerusalem. The prophecy about the abomination of desolation is one of the main reasons for this. Matthew, though, still gets booted to later decades, with the explanation that the post-destruction prophecy in Matthew 24 was just the author copying the earlier passage in Mark. If, however, Matthew's gospel has retained the more primitive version (as I and some others believe), then the argument for a pre-70 CE Mark would apply with equal force to Matthew.

Such are the conclusions I have reached and the assumptions I will be making about the Gospel of Matthew in this chapter. Even if I had the time to write—and you had the patience to read—an extended set of arguments for these conclusions, nothing could be proved beyond doubt. That Matthew's gospel was composed in the 50s and 60s of the first century CE, that it was composed for a Christian Jewish community, and that it (or some pre-final draft of it) was the first Synoptic attempt to weave the circulating stories about what Jesus said and did into a unified biography—issues like these will always depend on a balance-of-evidence approach. We have no rabbits (or rabbis) to pull out of hats. If we did, the problems would have been solved long ago.

Whenever I think about the critical issues surrounding the Gospel of Matthew, I sense some irony. My current perspective on the text is perhaps nearer to where I was in my years as an evangelical than at any point in my later life. I haven't gotten to where I am, however, by returning to evangelical presuppositions about an immaculate text—I still think the documents of the Bible are historical works that can be handled in the way that we treat other historical works. My earlier pendulum-swing to the critical left reached a high arc, I believe, because of a dichotomy that was handed to me in my adolescent years, when I was told that I had to be either an evangelical or a modernist. At the time, of course, I didn't know exactly what a modernist was, but that didn't matter—carving the

12. Bernier, *Rethinking*, 47.

world into joints has never been dependent on clarity. Once I had bought into the evangelical/modernist dichotomy, it became a way of making sense of the world. When I no longer felt that I could be an evangelical, then I assumed that I must be a modernist. I suppose that I even wanted to be a good modernist, in the same way that I had wanted to be a good evangelical. Being a good modernist, however, meant divorcing my faith from a historical reading of the text. It was a divorce that never really took, and because it didn't take, I started to question the dichotomy that was driving the pendulum swing. Surrendering the dichotomy allowed me to consider ideas from both sides without committing to prepackaged frameworks.[13]

MATTHEW'S INTRODUCTION AND THE WISDOM TRADITION

With this all-too-short detour into some of the historical issues behind the Gospel of Matthew, we turn to the text itself. The first time I read the Gospel of Matthew cover to cover, I read it as a person who wanted to believe. I was seventeen years old, so I must have known a little bit about critical reading. I had no familiarity, though, with the historical context of NT documents. For me at that time, the text was as transparent as clean glass. I wanted to encounter the story, not the tellers of the story. And I did.

In one sense, the Gospel of Matthew is still the best place to meet the story in its purest form. The other three gospels reveal authors with more forward and distinct personalities, making it more difficult to forget that there is a speaker. The writer of John wants to pull you into his own narrative style and his mystical approach. Mark tries too hard to drop you into the middle of an action story and keep it moving. The writer of Luke assumes the authority of a well-read historian—as he tells us in the first paragraph of his gospel. Matthew, in contrast, seems more cobbled together, less edited.

We might start, then, by asking why the Gospel of Matthew is like this—that is, why no authorial presence, or at least not much of a presence, seems to emerge from the text. It could be, of course, that the

---

13. I'm putting a positive spin on this, of course. From a less favorable perspective, it could be said that I failed at both tasks, becoming neither a good evangelical nor a good modernist.

author was a skilled writer who knew how to hide himself in the text. More likely, though, he was the opposite—a humble writer (or perhaps more than one writer) who inherited a large amount of source material. He did what he could to turn these sources into a scroll that expressed the faith of his community. Establishing his own presence in the text was not a priority.

This person could, of course, be the Matthew who was a disciple of Jesus. In chapter 9 of the gospel, we hear about the call of this Matthew. He was a tax farmer, a Jew who served the Roman authorities by collecting customs and tribute. It was an occupation despised by the overtaxed Jews. Jesus sees Matthew sitting at his collection table and says to him, "Follow me" (9:9).[14] The next verse has Jesus and his disciples reclining at table in a house with tax collectors and ritually impure people—perhaps in Matthew's own house. As a tax collector, the disciple Matthew would surely have been literate and would have had a habit of recording events, making him a candidate for later authorship of a gospel.

I do not think, though, that this Matthew is the final author of the gospel that bears his name. The gospel lacks the personal touches that an eyewitness would bring to the text. A more likely scenario is that the disciple Matthew was responsible for collecting, and perhaps translating for Greek-speaking congregations, many of the teachings and deeds of Jesus. These may have circulated as "Matthew's collections." When the gospel writer (or writers) later assembled and edited these collections and stitched them into the first full-scale biography of Jesus, perhaps doing all this after Matthew's death, they might have described the gospel as a work based on a core of Matthew's materials. Later copyists, receiving this tradition, labeled their scrolls/codices as "according to Matthew." This is all a guess, of course. But it does go some way toward explaining the weak personal imprint in this gospel.

In this earliest amalgamation of stories into a biography of Jesus, we find footprints of the wisdom tradition of the OT that we looked at in the previous chapter. The first place we might look for signs of this are in the introductory materials, from the beginning of the gospel up to the middle of chapter 4. In these texts, occupying a bit under 10% of

---

14. The parallel passages in Luke 5:27 and Mark 2:14 record this person as "Levi" and "Levi the son of Alphaeus." Possibly Levi and Matthew are the same person, though it would be odd for a person to have two Jewish names. In the lists of the twelve disciples found in Matthew, Mark, and Luke, the name "Matthew" is listed, not Levi. The disciple in these lists that is the son of Alphaeus is Jacob/James, not Levi.

the book, we find a genealogy of Jesus, the story of Mary's pregnancy, the visit of the magi, the ministry of John the Baptist, and the temptation of Jesus in the wilderness. What the Matthean evangelist seems to be doing in these introductory materials is establishing the authority of Jesus, providing us with his credentials.

The genealogy in Matthew's first chapter (1:1–17) shows that Jesus was, through Joseph, both a descendant of Abraham (and thus could speak as a Jew) and a descendant of David (with a claim to the vacant throne of David). In the next part of the introduction, an angel of the Lord adds its authority to Jesus's credentials by revealing to Joseph that "what is conceived in Mary is from the Holy Spirit" (1:20).

Unlike the extended nativity story we find in the Gospel of Luke, the actual birth of Jesus gets little coverage in Matthew. All we learn is that Mary had the predicted son and that his parents called him "Jesus." From here the Gospel of Matthew transitions into the visit of the magi (2:1–12). These will be the next players to certify who Jesus is. They arrive in Jerusalem, having travelled from "the East," with a story about a "king of the Jews" being born. Magi were often court advisors in the countries of the Middle East. Their role in the birth narratives may be that of royal ambassadors.

After the visit of the magi, Matthew's gospel tells us no more about Jesus until he arrives, as an adult, at the place where John the Baptist has set up his evangelistic operations in "the wilderness of Judea," somewhere near the lower reaches of the Jordan River (3:1–17). John becomes Matthew's next witness to Jesus. John's support was not trivial—the Baptist was a celebrity, known throughout Israel. Even Josephus, born after John's death and writing at the end of the first century CE, knew about John's reputation. According to Josephus, John was so popular that Herod Antipas had him arrested, imprisoned, and then put to death because he feared that John might become the nucleus for a rebellion.[15]

The story of John in the introduction to Matthew's gospel culminates in the baptism of Jesus, an event that becomes a further attestation of who Jesus is. This time the testimony comes directly from God. As Jesus emerges from the water where he was baptized, he has a vision and hears a voice. Jesus, Matthew says, sees "the heavens opened" and "the spirit of God, as a dove, coming down and resting on him." The vision is accompanied by a "voice from heaven," a bat kol, saying, "This is my son, my beloved, with whom I am pleased" (3:17).

---

15. Josephus, *Ant.* 18.5.2.

With the authentications out of the way—the witness of Jesus's ancestral line, the revelations by angels, the testimony of the magi, the certification by John the Baptist, and finally the authority of the voice of God—Matthew is ready to set the public ministry of Jesus in motion. The reader of the gospel is in a privileged position. Before the public ministry of Jesus begins, we already know who Jesus is. He is the son of Abraham, the son of David, and the Son of God. What remains to be seen and what lends dramatic tension to the story is how the people and organizations that Jesus will encounter—who do not know what the reader knows—will handle this unusual person.

TRIALS AND TEMPTATIONS

Before launching into the ministry of Jesus, Matthew pauses to tell the story of Jesus's temptation by Satan (4:1–11). Jesus is led, after his baptism, "into the wilderness," where he fasts for forty days. After this, the devil tries to deflect him from his call to public ministry by making three tempting offers. The record of these temptations is strange, by any account. The church father Origen singled it out as an event that could not have literally happened.[16] Unlike the rest of Matthew, in which Jesus interacts with either his followers, his opponents, or the Roman government, we have no correlation—and no possible correlation—for the temptation events.

There are three ways that the temptation story, which is repeated in Luke (4:1–12) and summarized in Mark (1:12–13), could have been drafted and included in Matthew. One source for it could be Jesus himself—it could have happened to him, and he could have told the story to his followers. The second is that the author of Matthew could have invented it out of whole cloth and the other gospel writers copied it. The third is that this is a story that Jesus crafted as a symbolic discourse, but his hearers took it more literally than it was intended, transforming it into a specific event from his life.

This third option may be the best explanation. To see what Jesus might have meant by this tale at a symbolic level, we must first consider a parallel passage from Josephus, the writer that I mentioned earlier. At the beginning of his autobiography, Josephus says that he was born in the late 30s CE to a Jewish family with both royal and priestly roots. He was

16. Origen, *Orig. Princ.* 4.16.

raised and educated in Jerusalem and became such a prodigy in the study
of the law that by the time he was fourteen, Jewish leaders were asking for
his opinion. "When I was sixteen," he goes on to say, "I decided to try out
the sects among us. There are three of these: the Pharisees, the Sadducees,
and the Essenes." He went through "hard trials and many labors" with
these sects. He did this because, he observes, "I could only choose the
best practice if I experienced them all."[17]

The program of selection followed by Josephus may have been
pursued by other Jews taking up the study of Torah. Jesus was also a
prodigy in the Jewish Scriptures, if we can trust the passages in Luke's
gospel (2:41–51) about Jesus's experiences in the Jerusalem temple as a
twelve-year-old. Might Jesus have set himself, like Josephus, to study the
teachings of the three major sects? If so, we can read the temptation story
as an account of his internships.

For the first test, the tempter says to him, "If you are the Son of God,
command that these stones become bread." Jesus replies, "It is written,
'you shall not live by bread alone, but by every word that comes from the
mouth of God'" (Matt 4:3–4). The quotation that Jesus flings at the devil
is from Deuteronomy 8:3. In this Torah passage, Moses says to the Israelites that God fed them with the mysterious manna so that they would
realize that gifts coming directly from God (manna) are more important
than those derived from human effort (cultivated agricultural products).
This round of debate between Jesus and the devil could represent Jesus's
reaction to what he had learned about the teachings of the *Pharisees*. The
Pharisees interpreted the Scriptures through an oral law that was, they
believed, as old as the written law. Bread, a common metaphor for teaching and instruction, could stand in this exchange for the reinterpreted
Torah of the Pharisees. Jesus rejects this bread-alone approach for one
in which guidance about the interpretation of the law came, not through
the tradition of oral law, but through an immediate and personal connection with the Father. He tells the devil, in effect, that he values heavenly
manna (a direct and trusting relationship with God) more than earthly
bread (oral traditions).

In the second test, the devil takes Jesus to Jerusalem and sets him on
a tower of the temple. He says to him, "If you are the son of God, throw
yourself off, for it is written that 'he will give command about you to the
angels' and 'they will catch you up in their hands, so that you don't stub

17. Josephus, *Life* 2.

your foot against a stone'" (Matt 4:6). The devil is quoting Psalm 91:11–12 to Jesus. Jesus's reply to the devil (Matt 4:7) is another quotation from Deuteronomy (6:16): "Do not put the Lord your God to the test." This exchange may represent Jesus's encounter with the teachings of the *Essenes*. As Josephus notes in his description of this sect, the Essenes were, unlike the Pharisees and Sadducees, strict determinists, with a tendency toward fatalism. Jesus, as the Son of God, rejects such passivity. He is an active agent who has a give-and-take relationship with the Father. His obedience to God is not the blind obedience encouraged by the Essenes. Challenging God to send angels to break his fall is not a testimony to this kind of relationship but to a lack of it.

The third and last round tempts Jesus with earthly power. This time the devil takes him to a mountain and shows him all the nations of the earth. He offers them all to him if Jesus will worship him. Jesus counters this challenge (Matt 4:10) with a third quotation from Deuteronomy (6:13), which Jesus renders: "You will worship the Lord your God and give service to him alone." The word "alone" is not found in the Deuteronomy passage. Jesus adds it to the quotation, I think, to heighten the contrast between his choice and that of the *Sadducees*. The Sadducees, a relatively small sect, were entwined with the power structures of Roman and Jewish politics. They tended to be wealthy, to live in the best houses, and to occupy the most important political positions. The Sadducees believed that they served God with this lifestyle. Jesus's issue with them was that they didn't serve God *alone*—they also prostrated themselves before the authority of the world and its riches. As Jesus will point out in his first sermon in Matthew, "you cannot serve both God and wealth" (Matt 6:24).

Josephus, after his study of the teachings of the three sects, "enlisted with a holy man named Banus who passed his days in the desert, ate food that grew uncultivated on trees, and took cold-water baths to purify himself."[18] Banus seems to have been an ascetic in the mold of John the Baptist. Jesus will, in a similar way, follow up his own exploration of the Jewish sects by an association with John the Baptist and his populist movement. The paths of Josephus and Jesus, however, diverge at this point. Josephus decides to adopt the lifestyle of a Pharisee. Jesus rejects all three options. As I will suggest in coming chapters, he chooses a fourth option, a non-Essene sectarian stance.

18. Josephus, *Life* 2.

The writers of the Synoptic Gospels, it would appear, have taken the temptation story less symbolically than it was intended. They have transferred it to a literal and historical level. The reasons for this transferral may lie in the way that the Synoptics handle symbolism in Jesus's teachings. The synoptic writers favor one kind of *mashal*, the parable, as a teaching tool. Dozens of these are attributed to Jesus.

The parables of Jesus in the Synoptics fall into several subtypes. Some seem to be stories with a moral point—not all that different, perhaps, than one of Aesop's fables or a Grimm's fairy tale (but set in a more realistic landscape—Jesus was not a fan of talking animals and magic spells). A few of the parables, though, approach a type of symbolic discourse that we might call "allegory," a form in which the various players and events in the parable map in a more detailed way onto the referent of the story. But even these more allegorical parables fall short of what I would call "classic allegory." They are still third-person stories, where the speaker is not part of the action. In allegories such as *Pilgrim's Progress*, the narrator is present as the "I" of the story.

Compare the approach of the synoptic authors with what we find in the Gospel of John. John, though packed with symbolic discourse (as we will see in chapter 7), contains almost nothing that we would call a synoptic-like parable. The closest it comes is perhaps the allegorical story found in chapter 10, where Jesus says, "I am the door of the sheep" and "I am the good shepherd." The extended analogy in John's chapter makes a connection between the experiences of sheep and shepherds and the relationship of Jesus to his followers. If it is a parable, it is an allegorical parable, but with a different kind of allegory than we find in the synoptic parables—Jesus inserts himself into the John 10 story with an "I." When speakers enter the landscape of their symbolic discourses, every turn of the story can have some allegorical referent, some mapping from story to situation. This passage in John, with its "I" and its detailed mapping, is closer to classic allegory than the synoptic parables are.

If we step back and survey the types of symbolic discourse found in the OT, and especially in the wisdom literature, we find classic allegory. Consider the stories in Ezekiel where the prophet has a vision. The prophet himself is usually present in the story. In Ezekiel 37, for example, God brings Ezekiel into a valley full of desiccated bones and commands him to prophesy to the bones. When he does, the bones come together, flesh appears on them, and the enfleshed people come alive. We learn at the end of this vision that this allegory applies to the nation of Israel—that the Jewish people, metaphorically dead and skeletonized because they have been stripped of their homes and property, will once again return to their lands and flourish. Think also of the Song of Songs, a book of love poetry that both Jewish and Christian interpreters have read as an extended allegory about the love between God and God's faithful. The narrator uses the first-person throughout the piece. It is classic allegory.

We would expect that Jesus, then, if he truly understood himself as the heir of the wisdom tradition, would have included classic allegory in his wisdom toolkit. The absence of this symbol-type from the Synoptics should make us wonder whether some filtering has taken place, whether we are hearing the full range of symbolism in Jesus's teachings. This filtering, I suggest, may be the reason why the temptation passage in Matthew 4 has come down to us in a literal rather than a symbolic reading. The synoptic authors, confronted with a classic first-person allegory in the teachings of Jesus—one that told how he confronted and refuted competing schools of thought—failed to recognize a rhetorical vehicle that did not fit within the rather narrow symbolic range of their parables.

If an overly literal reading of an allegory is the source of the temptation story in Matthew, this still does not tell us where the raw material of the allegory came from. Could some personal experience of Jesus, not wholly unlike the story itself, have given rise to the allegorized story? I'm inclined to think that the story has longer legs, that it might have already been a symbolic discourse *before* Jesus retold it with himself as the actor. To explore this, however, requires that we first look at Jesus's sectarian background, which we will do in the last two imaginative webs. At the end of this book, I'll return to the question of how the temptation story might have developed from a sectarian polemic.

SERMON ON THE MOUNT

Matthew's construction of Jesus's life begins, after four chapters of introductory materials, with the Galilean ministry and the call of the first disciples. Jesus had hooked up with John the Baptist in Judea. To get Jesus into Galilee, the author of Matthew cites the arrest of John as the motivation. Once in Galilee, Jesus goes first to his hometown of Nazareth, then to Capernaum on the Sea of Galilee. At Capernaum he draws two sets of brothers into his ministry, Simon Peter and his brother Andrew and the brothers James and John, sons of Zebedee. From his base in Capernaum,

Jesus begins to conduct preaching and healing tours all through Galilee. He attracts large crowds. On one of these tours, Jesus climbs to the top of a hill, sits down in the circle of his disciples, and begins a talk.

The written presentation of this talk, which we call the "Sermon on the Mount," occupies chapters 5–7 of the Gospel of Matthew. It is the longest uninterrupted reproduction of Jesus's teaching in the Synoptic Gospels. Even so, it's not that long. The passage could have been read in a Matthean synagogue in less than a half hour—not far off the mark of many contemporary sermons. We should not, though, imagine that the text represents a single underlying verbal event. The sections of the Sermon on the Mount have no unifying theme, and there are no transitions between topical breaks.

Earlier, Matthew had summarized Jesus's message as "Repent, for the reign of God is at hand" (4:17). In this first homily, we have the expansion of the summary. The various sections are, as many have noted, the new laws of this impending reign of God. And they are laws, not just advice. Even the fact that the Sermon on the Mount was delivered from a mountain (probably a high hill) underlines the similarity between this passage and the Mosaic legislation.

I knew parts of the Sermon on the Mount from my earliest days in the church. I memorized its Beatitudes and Lord's Prayer. In Sunday School, I would have heard about the lilies of the field, the log in my own eye, the narrow gate, the house on the rock, the salt of the earth, and the closet of prayer. When I turned to the Bible as a young adult, looking at it through evangelical eyes and reading it as a larger whole, I found the Sermon on the Mount inspiring but also challenging. Deep down, I was somewhat unsettled by it. Under the influence of the evangelical emphasis on reading the NT through Paul's law-free approach, I didn't know what to make of the legal system encoded in the sermon. Jesus's summarization of the law later in the gospel, when he told the Pharisees that the two greatest commandments were, "Love the Lord your God with all your heart and with all your soul and with all your mind" and "Love your neighbor as yourself" (22:34–39), was more to my liking. Embedded in Protestantism, I would later realize, was a longstanding stereotype of Judaism as an inferior religion. One of the Protestant yardsticks for measuring religious superiority has been liberation from an immature reliance on codes of behaviour. It would take a few years before I recognized this bias and began to remove it from my view of the world. Recalibrating my reading of the Bible with this new understanding took even longer. I now see the Sermon as a carefully stitched sampler of what it meant for the early church to be both second-temple Jewish *and* followers of Christ.

For the purposes of this book and its focus on the wisdom tradition, two aspects of the Sermon on the Mount interest me. The first is how Christian Judaism positions itself with respect to the core narrative of Second Temple Judaism—the way, in terms of our earlier metaphor, that *it restrings the pearls of the OT.* In the second half of Matthew 5, we get our best look at what this restringing means. Jesus expresses his attitude toward the law and follows this with a series of contrasts between his own teaching and those of his opponents.

The passage that introduces these contrasts (5:17–20) is a pivot text. Either you accept what it says at face value, or you find ways of explaining why it doesn't mean what it seems to mean. Jesus starts this section with a strong statement of his attachment to Judaism, saying, "Don't think that I have come to tear down the law or the prophets." He adds the hyperbolic claim, "Truly I say to you, not one iota or stroke will ever pass from the law until heaven and earth pass away." As if this weren't clear enough, he doubles down by saying, "Whoever relaxes one of these commandments and teaches this to people shall be named as least in the reign of heaven, and whoever does and teaches them shall be named as great in the reign of heaven." Given these emphatic statements, it seems impossible that scholars could deny that the Matthean community was a law-observant sect of Judaism. "A stronger affirmation of the continuing validity of the Torah," Joel Marcus comments, "is hard to imagine."[19] And yet many students of the Bible have either reinterpreted or ignored this passage and emphasized statements in Matthew that have what they imagine is a more pro-gentile thrust. As mentioned above, I am assuming that the Gospel of Matthew is written by and for a law-observant sect of Christian Jews. For me, this bold claim in Matthew 5:17–20 needs no alternate reading. Jesus's program for his listeners is a renewed Judaism.

The author of Matthew may have led off this section of the Sermon on the Mount with his emphatic allegiance to the law because without it, the next part of this section could appear, in the eyes of some Jews, to loosen the grip of the law. Jesus and his community of Christian Jews have restrung the pearls—they have arrived at a reading of the core narrative that does not align with that of other Jewish sects. Before offering the next part of this section, in which Jesus will highlight some of the key

---

19. Marcus, "Enigma," 122.

differences, the writer wants his readers to know that the pearls, though restrung, are not lost. Jesus is not doing away with the law.

Jesus begins this exposition of differences (5:20–48) with a summary overview: "For I tell you that if your righteousness does not surpass that of the scribes and Pharisees, you will never enter the reign of heaven."[20] He then fleshes out this summary with five or six contrasts between his own understanding of the law and the teachings of the scribes and Pharisees. These contrasts, usually called the "Antitheses," all adhere to the similar format. They begin with some variation of "you have heard it said" and follow the phrase with either passages from the Tanak or popular interpretations of it. The Antitheses then continue with Jesus's emphatic "but *I* say to you" and add several sentences explaining why the initial quotations can't be taken at face value.

The Baptist theologian and ethicist Glen Stassen points out that calling these teachings "Antitheses" is not accurate.[21] The word "antithesis" implies two parts, but the passages are really triads. The initial statements of the triads are expressions of what Stassen calls *traditional piety*. The quotations expressing this piety may come from the Tanak, but what they point at is not the Tanak itself but a way of reading the Tanak.[22] Following these quotations, Jesus shows how the action mentioned in the traditional reading is just a larger piece of a *vicious cycle* whose outcome is the behavior in the quotation. Finally, Jesus discusses a *transforming initiative* that his listeners can take to break out of the cycle. In the first triad in Matthew 5:21–26, for example, the statement of traditional piety is "you shall not kill." The vicious cycle is the way everyday expressions of anger or disdain (such as saying, "You fool!") are the soil in which murderous actions take root. To break out of this cycle, Jesus advises his followers to search in themselves for the disagreements and attitudes that

20. The quoted sentence about the righteousness of the disciples exceeding that of the Pharisees in Matthew 5:20 is grouped in most translations with the affirmation of the Jewish law mentioned just before it. The sentence goes more naturally with the subsequent discussion of differences in the Antitheses.

21. See the discussion in Stassen, "The Fourteen Triads."

22. Because Jesus begins the Antitheses with the statement that the righteousness of his disciples must "go beyond that of the scribes and Pharisees" (5:20), some commentators suggest that the legal points contradicted by Jesus were the interpretations of the scribes and Pharisees that were at variance with a plain reading of the Tanak. This is probably not the case—some passages corrected by Jesus come directly from the Tanak. What Jesus is doing is just what every sectarian Jewish movement from the Second Temple period does—restringing the pearls of the Tanak by adapting and reinterpreting the received text and stories.

lead to anger and then to take action to eliminate them, such as trying to reconcile with a brother who has something against you. As the summary at the head of the Antitheses says, the ethical sensitivity of Jesus's followers had to go beyond the letter of the law. Some Tanak interpreters, we may suppose, had made accommodation for behavior that included anger and derisive speech, so long as that behavior did not lead to personal violence. Jesus calls attention to the psychological and spiritual unreality of drawing such lines in the sand. Better, he says, to address the issue where it begins—in the heart.

This triad pattern is followed in the remaining Antitheses (with, as Stassen notes, one omission and one inversion of the last two thirds of the triad). Viewed as triads, the Antitheses become, not contradictions of the covenantal law, but reinterpretations that get behind the wording and address the more fundamental issues that gave rise to the law. The new teaching, by removing the circumventions, upholds rather than undercuts the law.

At the end of the Sermon on the Mount, the author of the gospel observes that "the crowds were astonished at Jesus's teaching, for he was teaching them with authority, yet not in the way their scribes taught" (7:28–29). Not every hearer of what Jesus had to say in the Antitheses would have agreed that Jesus had a valid reading of the law, but many of them must have been open to his alternative interpretations. For those who were open, the question for them became one of trust—did they trust this teacher of the new law enough to adopt his interpretations and to become his followers? The writer of Matthew hoped that his fellow Jews would come to believe what he and his community already knew—that the new interpretations of Jesus were nothing less than the Word of God.

The second broad observation I will make about the Sermon on the Mount is about *how well it dovetails with the wisdom conventions of Second Temple Judaism*. The rhetorical figures found in the Sermon are the standard types we find in the wisdom literature. This is signaled at the beginning of the Sermon by the Beatitudes. The first eight of the Beatitudes begin with the phrase, "blessed is." Macarisms[23] such as this are found throughout the OT, but they are especially common in the Psalms and wisdom literature. Among those found in Proverbs is a macarism spoken by Person Wisdom. Wisdom says, "Blessed is the person who hears me, keeping watch at my gates day by day and guarding my

---

23. Called "macarisms" because the Greek word for "blessed" is *makarios.*

doorposts" (8:34). For the most part, OT macarisms are singletons that are followed by explanations and elaborations. This would suggest that the long string of them in Matthew's Beatitudes may be a collection of individual macarisms uttered on different occasions. When the Dead Sea Scrolls were discovered, however, we were surprised to find among its wisdom documents a damaged fragment (4QBeatitudes, 4Q525) with four consecutive macarisms following what looks like a fragment of a fifth. Even more interesting, these Dead Sea Scroll macarisms seem to be about the advantages of *hokhmah*, wisdom. The string of macarisms at the beginning of the Sermon on the Mount may be following an established pattern associated with wisdom literature.

The lead-in macarisms are only the first of several wisdom traces in the Sermon on the Mount. The whole tenor of the sermon places it in the wisdom tradition. We find many examples of the practical advice that characterizes Proverbs and other wisdom documents—instructions on how to pray, to fast, to control anger and sexual desire, to provide alms, to avoid hypocrisy and anxiety, and to manage wealth. Both the wisdom tradition and the Sermon on the Mount make connections between the plan of God coded in nature (the birds, flowers, and grass, for example, of Matt 6:25–33) and what this means for human conduct. The father-son motif of the wisdom tradition, with the instructor imparting wisdom to his students as a father to a son, is echoed in Jesus's frequent references to God as Father—the phrase "your Father" occurs some dozen times in the Sermon. Many of the standard rhetorical devices of the sages are sprinkled through the Sermon, including metaphors of all stripes ("you are the salt of the earth"), dialogic contrasts (the Antitheses), comparisons of wise and foolish behavior (houses built on sand or rock), major-minor transitions (giving your son a stone when he asks for bread), and analogies (throwing pearls before swine). The Sermon provides us with some takeaway proverbs, but Jesus also seems to be interacting with several pre-existing expressions of folk wisdom. If I were translating the Sermon, I'd be tempted to put quotation marks around phrases such as "If salt has lost its taste, how shall it be salted,"[24] "The eye is the lamp of the body," "No one can serve two masters," "Sufficient to the day is its

---

24. We may have evidence that this line was a folk idiom. A Talmud passage reads: "When salt is spoiling, with what does one salt it to preserve it? Rabbi Yehoshua said to them: With the placenta of a mule. They said to him: But is there a placenta of a mule? Rabbi Yehoshua said to them: And does salt spoil?" (*b. Bek.* 8b, William Davidson translation).

trouble," "Do not give what is holy to dogs,"[25] and "You will know them by their fruits." The Sermon, like other wisdom literature, either exegetes these folk sayings or uses them to shore up arguments. The sheer number of aphorisms in the Sermon and in other discourses attributed to Jesus in the NT gospels, says David Aune, "makes it certain that Jesus regarded himself and was regarded by his followers . . . as a Jewish sage and teacher of wisdom."[26]

It is also worth noting that only one historical character from the Tanak is mentioned in the Sermon on the Mount, and this figure is Solomon, the central player in wisdom texts. Jesus tells his followers to "consider the flowers of the field." The flowers do no work, yet God provides for them so well that "not even Solomon, for all his magnificence, was dressed like one of these" (6:28–29). This may seem like a passing mention, but the Solomon theme pops up again later in Matthew, when Jesus refers to himself as "greater than Solomon" (12:42). Although these are the only two places in Matthew, apart from the genealogy of the first chapter, where Solomon's name is used, Matthew has many of his characters addressing Jesus as "son of David." We tend to read this as a standard Messianic epithet, but the title "son of David" as a Messianic title is a late development, hardly earlier than the NT itself. When "son of David" is used in the OT, it almost always refers to Solomon, the immediate son of David, so we may have glancing references to Solomon hidden in these "son of David" addresses. It is interesting to note that both Proverbs and Ecclesiastes, wisdom books whose writers pose as Solomon, call him "son of David" in their initial verses, something Matthew also does in his first verse ("This is the genealogy of Jesus Christ, the son of David.")

MIRACLES AND MENTORING

I had a red-letter Bible when I was young. It had the words of Jesus printed in a red typeface. If I still had that Bible, flipping through the pages of Matthew would show that the words of Jesus are clumped into five sections of the book. Besides the Sermon on the Mount in chapters 5–7,

---

25. *Temurah*, a tractate of the Babylonian Talmud in the order *Kodashim*, takes up the question about whether animals dedicated for sacrifice that are subsequently found to be blemished can be redeemed and fed to dogs. The practice is controversial because (as the tractate assumes throughout) what is holy cannot be fed to dogs. This assumption was probably coded as a common adage.

26. Aune, "Oral Tradition," 240–1.

which we have just looked at, we have the instructions to Jesus's disciples in chapter 10 (sometimes called the "Mission Instructions"), his volley of parables in chapter 13, the discourse on church/synagogue discipline in chapter 18 (often called the "Community Regulations"), and the Little Apocalypse of chapters 24–25. The author of Matthew almost certainly had source documents in front of him in which the teachings of Jesus were topically clumped. He may have created these source documents himself, or he may have inherited them from others.

In addition to these teaching texts, the author would also have had stories about events in Jesus's life that he needed to include in his narrative biography. As best he could, he stitched these together with coarse chronological threads. These non-teaching materials, as we can see from chapters 8–9, include stories about Jesus's miracles and about the mentoring of his disciples. Both story lines have potential connections to the wisdom tradition of Second Temple Judaism.

Many of the miracles reported by Matthew are exorcisms, and in first-century Israel, magic and exorcistic rites were linked to Solomon, the titular head of the wisdom tradition.[27] Incantations used in these rites were thought to have been formulated by Solomon and passed down through the centuries. Some of the rites used the magic name of Solomon. When Matthew says that "they brought to Jesus many people who were demon-possessed, and he cast out the spirits with a word" (8:16), we have to wonder if that word might have been a Solomonic incantation.

While much of the literature describing Solomonic magic comes from after the time of Jesus, there are intriguing hints that a folk tradition was already in place by the first century CE. A fragmentary Qumran text from the first century BCE (11QApPsa, 11Q11) contains several psalms and incantations used in exorcisms, and one of the bits uses the name of Solomon. The historian Josephus, writing in the last decade of the first century and retelling the story of Solomon that we know from the books of Kings and Chronicles, adds that "God granted him to learn the skills to counteract demons, for the benefit and healing of people. He compiled spells for the relief of illnesses and left behind the formulas of exorcism by which those who bind the demons drive them out, never to return. Even today, this kind of healing is very powerful among us."[28] Josephus goes on to tell of a conjurer he knew, Eleazar, who could draw out demons from

27. A review of the role of Solomon in late antiquity exorcisms can be found in Torijano, "Solomon and Magic."

28. Josephus, *Ant.* 8.45–6a.

people's nostrils by holding under their noses a ring containing a root that Solomon had prescribed for exorcism. He knew that the demons had departed when they tipped over a cup of water that had been set at a distance from the person being healed.

Some of the miracles of Jesus we call "nature miracles." These are non-healing miracles that subvert the normal course of physical experience. Matthew has more of these than any other gospel. The first one is found in 8:23–27—a boat on the Sea of Galilee carrying Jesus and his disciples is caught in a storm and Jesus stills the storm with a command. Later we hear about Jesus multiplying loaves and fishes (14:13–21 and 15:32–39), walking on water (14:22–33), conjuring money from the mouth of a fish (17:24–27), and wilting a fig tree with a curse (21:18–22). Even these nature miracles may have a wisdom tie-in. The author of the Wisdom of Solomon, writing as Solomon, says "May God grant me to speak with judgment . . . , for it is he who gave me to know true knowledge of what exists, to know the unity of the world and the working of its elements . . . , the natures of animals . . . , the forces of spirits . . . , the varieties of plants and the powers of roots . . . . For Wisdom, the fashioner of all things, taught me" (7:15–22). Someone who knew the secrets of nature and who could use this knowledge to manipulate nature would have been filling the role of Wisdom's greatest student, Solomon.

By the time Matthew's readers have finished the Sermon on the Mount and started on Matthew 8, the author hasn't told them much about the disciples. Readers have learned that Jesus had a home base in Capernaum, a town on the north shore of the Sea of Galilee, and they know that four fishermen from there—Peter, Andrew, James, and John—signed on as disciples. Jesus seems not to have had his own house in Capernaum ("The Son of Man has nowhere to lay his head," 8:20), so he and his followers may have been staying in the Capernaum homes of his first disciples when he wasn't on the road. This is supported by a story in Matthew 8. Jesus enters Peter's Capernaum house, heals Peter's mother-in-law, and is still there in the evening when the sick and demon-possessed seek him out (8:14–16). After this, clues about a wider circle of disciples—and would-be disciples—begin to show up in Matthew's narrative. An anonymous scribe says that he wants to become a disciple, but Jesus discourages him (8:19–20). Another follower, described as a disciple, asks for a leave of absence (8:21–22). Matthew joins the group (9:9). The gospel hints that the size of Jesus's close-knit group is growing, but when the reader learns at the beginning of chapter 10 that twelve founding members are already on board, it comes as a surprise. Matthew seems to imply that there were just twelve at this point—when he commissions them, the text says that "he called his twelve disciples." The other synoptic authors suggest that Jesus selected these twelve out of a larger group of disciples.

Just before commissioning the twelve, says Matthew, Jesus carried out speaking and healing tours "in all the cities and villages, teaching in the synagogues, preaching the good news of the reign [of God], and healing every disease and infirmity." The people seemed to him to be "sheep without a shepherd." He told his disciples that "the harvest is great, but the workers are few" and asked them to pray for more workers (9:35–37). At the commissioning of the twelve disciples, Jesus "gave them authority over unclean spirits, so that they could cast them out and could heal every disease and infirmity" (10:1). The purpose of the commissioning seems to have been the extension of Jesus's public ministry. When the twelve disciples (which means "learners" or "students") are named, Matthew also calls them the twelve apostles (which means "ambassadors" or "those who are sent"). And Jesus does in fact send them out, charging them to avoid the towns where gentiles and Samaritans lived and to focus on "the lost sheep of the house of Israel" (10:5–6). The disciples are licensed to preach about the impending reign of God and to perform healings and exorcisms.

In the rest of chapter 10, Matthew reproduces a collection of Jesus's teachings that relate to discipleship and mission, framing the teaching as an address to the commissioned disciples. This section is the Mission Instructions, the second of Matthew's extended discourses. The six teachings that Matthew has inserted into chapter 10 are a muddled group. While each section has some relevance to the ministry of the disciples, it is hard to imagine some of these instructions being given to the disciples at this stage of the ministry. The most apropos teachings in this package are the first, the third, and the last. The other three seem anachronous or inappropriate.

The inconsistencies of this commissioning sermon aside, we do find an important wisdom motif in this section, and that is the sage as mentor for the next generation of sages. This was a feature of the early church that I overlooked when, as a new evangelical, I first took up a serious study of the Bible. Evangelicals emphasize the immediate relationship of every believer to Jesus. No Christian's faith, they say, is secondhand—God has no grandchildren. This view of what makes a person a Christian has both advantages and disadvantages. On the plus side, it fits well with the modern individualism that emerged from the Enlightenment. In addition, personal immediacy encourages believers to have an active inner life. On the negative side, the evangelical approach to belief has a flattening effect. The many structures in which we are embedded—families, tribes, societies—can lose their relevance to faith. Rejecting secondhand faith often means overlooking these important social structures.

In those early days, I viewed the role of the disciples through the lens of my own experiences. Like me, they had put their faith in Jesus as God. Like me, they struggled to live out this belief. I thought of them as Christian groupies whose main role was to serve as foils for dialogue and debate, much like the characters in Plato's Dialogues who interact with Socrates. This was a rather limited lens through which to view the disciples and their role. Even at that time, I had other lenses, if only I had used them. Besides being a new believer, I was also a new student—these were my first years of college. I was testing points of view, willing to change my mind if what I learned failed the test. I was enmeshed in a hierarchical system that encouraged me to both respect and challenge those who were higher on the educational ladder. I was also grounding myself in my culture's framework of literature. All of this could have been a place from which to view the role of the disciples. At that time, however, I considered my experiences as a student and learner to be sub-Christian—only the immediacy of my Christian identity was supposed to be important.

Somewhere along the line, as I emerged from the evangelical subculture, I began to think about the disciples as students in an educational program. Getting my head around the OT wisdom literature was an important step in seeing the disciples in this role. The wisdom tradition, as I mentioned earlier, is an early analogue to the modern educational system. Sages such as Ben Sira seem to have set up schools and curricula to deliver their knowledge and practices to other people. Jesus himself may have experienced this sort of wisdom mentoring before he began his own educational program. When Jesus launched his ministry of teaching and preaching and healing, then, collecting a group of disciples may not have been an afterthought—he may have understood that a large part of his public role would be setting up a school.

Hints about a wisdom school poke through the stories and teachings collected in Matthew. The Sermon on the Mount, Matthew says, was delivered to the disciples rather than to the crowds that followed him and them—Jesus went up the mountain to get away from the crowds, not to teach them.[29] The passages in the Sermon on the Mount, from the Beatitudes to the houses built on sand and rock, could be considered segments of the school's curriculum. Later, when Jesus calms the storm at sea that threatens to swamp the boat carrying him and the disciples (8:23–27), he uses the event as a field-trip lesson. ("Why are you afraid, short-on-faith ones?")

The chapter before the commissioning of the disciples shows us the school in action. Students and teacher are closely linked. When the Pharisees challenge Jesus's preference to eat with tax collectors (9:10–13), the Pharisees approach the disciples with their question. This lumps the students with their teacher. Immediately after this, the disciples of John the Baptist come to Jesus to ask why his disciples do not fast as they and the Pharisees do (9:14). This question assumes that the teacher is answerable for the practices of his students. This two-way association between teacher and students is a valid assumption when the goal of the student is to become a functional equivalent to the teacher. In the sermon delivered after the commissioning of the disciples, Jesus says that the "disciple is not above the teacher." It is sufficient for the learner to "become like his teacher." In the last section of this sermon, Jesus unites the teacher and the trained student by saying, "The one who receives you, receives me" (10:40). Reading these passages as classroom events in a wisdom school help us to imagine the context from which Matthew has selected his stories.

LITTLE WISDOM

We can pick out themes in chapters 8–10 of Matthew, such as exorcisms and discipling, that are consistent with a wisdom school movement. By themselves, these themes are just hints about an agenda. In chapters 11–13, however, we have a collection of stories and events that seem to be drawn directly from a wisdom playbook. Students of the NT have given this section various names. I'll call it the Little Wisdom section of the gospel.

For the content of Little Wisdom, Matthew may have been tapping into wisdom sources from the early days of the Christian Jewish sect. We do not have these sources, and they can't be reconstructed from the material at hand. Not everyone agrees with this, though. Some redaction

---

29. The idea that the Sermon on the Mount was also addressed to the crowds probably comes from Luke's shortened version in Luke 6:17–49, which takes place on a plain in the presence of his disciples and many other people.

critics roll their speculation about the sources of Little Wisdom into their theories about the Q source. In the Little Wisdom section, the authors of Matthew and Luke track together and Mark does not follow them, so the two-source hypothesis assigns these materials to the hypothesized Q. In the last decades of the twentieth century, several NT scholars tried to define Q as a wisdom document.[30]

The two-gospel hypothesis, which I am assuming in this book, places Matthew before Mark and Luke. This means that we have no surviving sources for Matthew. Any guesses about Matthew's sources must be based on internal hints in Matthew. The only exception to this would be if Mark or Luke, in sections where they parallel Matthew's text but have a significantly different reading, had some access to Matthew's sources. (Later in this chapter, I will examine one of these cases.)

Little Wisdom begins with the phrase "when Jesus had finished giving instructions to his twelve disciples" (11:1), the phrase that marks the end of Jesus's Mission Instructions. The first section of Little Wisdom is a long discussion (11:2–19) about an encounter between Jesus and the disciples of John the Baptist. John is in prison, and he hears about what Matthew calls "the works of the Christ." This is an unusual phrase. Matthew does not use the Greek word for "Messiah" much, and when he does, it usually has an article in front of it, so we should probably understand this reference—and most of Matthew's other "Christ" references—to be a way of referring to people's belief in a messiah.

John the Baptist has heard about Jesus's miracles, and they seem to be evidence that this is the person he had predicted would come after him, the one who would "baptize with the Holy Spirit and with fire" and inaugurate the judgments of the messianic age (3:11–12). He asks Jesus, via the followers he has sent, "Are you 'the coming one,' or should we wait for someone else?" (11:3) This is, of course, more than an academic question for John, who is imprisoned in Herod Antipas's fortress of Machaerus. He has little hope of escape unless someone can marshal enough political and military clout to overcome the fortress defenses. An angry messiah at the head of an army would have been more than welcome.

Jesus's reply to John's query is an exercise in subtlety. He begins by citing miracles from his public ministry. The blind receive their sight, the lame walk, the lepers are cleansed, the deaf hear, and the dead are

30. Interest in the Q-as-wisdom approach seems to have declined in recent decades, perhaps because scholars have become less confident about their ability to agree on what belongs to Q (or even whether there was a Q).

resuscitated. In the prophecies of Isaiah, these outcomes are linked to God's imminent judgment of the world. Fragments from a Qumran manuscript (4QMessAp, 4Q521), which also tick off many of these same events, associate them with the coming of a messiah. On the surface, then, Jesus appears to be giving a "Yes" answer to John's question. But it is a qualified "Yes." A simple "Yes" would have meant that Jesus accepted John's interpretation of what the messiah would do. The ambiguity leaves Jesus free to have an alternate interpretation of the messianic project.

The disciples of John depart, and Jesus turns to the crowd following him and speaks to them about John's role. He calls John "a prophet," but also "more than a prophet," since he was the messenger spoken of in the Book of Malachi, the one who "prepares the way" for the Lord to return to his temple and purify its sacrifices (11:9–10, quoting Mal 3:1). In this encomium to his predecessor, Jesus says that "among those born of women, no one has arisen who is greater than John the Baptist. But the least in the reign of heaven is greater than he" (11:11). The last sentence is meant to shock. In the space of those few words, Jesus has flipped the way his listeners think about John. From being the greatest, he becomes the least. This sort of contradiction, which is usually the setup for an explanation, is a wisdom trope, and the expected explanation follows. Jesus says, "And from the days of John the Baptist until now, the reign of heaven is assaulted by force and the assaulters violently seize it. For all the prophets and the law prophesied up until John" (11:12–13).

This explanation about the reign of God and violence has evoked many interpretations, both of how to read the sentences and of what they mean. For what it is worth, I offer one more interpretation, keeping in mind that this verse occurs at the beginning of a section of Matthew that has multiple allusions to wisdom themes. If John the Baptist is at once the greatest and the least, then there must be two ordering systems, two ways to measure the significance of John. In one ordering, he is the greatest, in the other, the least.

By providing two orders against which his hearers can rate the greatness of John the Baptist, Jesus invokes a standard wisdom device. A foundation of wisdom thinking, as we have seen, is the teaching of the two ways. We are confronted, the sages say, by the way of life and the way of death, the path of the wise and the path of the foolish. As the personified Wisdom in Proverbs expresses it, "the one who finds me finds life," and "all those who hate me love death" (8:35–36). For those familiar with wisdom teachings, turning the two ways into ranking systems is a simple move—some can be at one place on the spectrum of life, others can be another place on the spectrum of death. What Jesus says next, though, is novel. He separates the two ways along a time sequence. In the time before John the Baptist, the reign of God was a political goal achieved by armies and intrigue. Violent rulers brought their version of the reign into existence by force. To those who succeeded at this game of thrones, it seemed like the path of life, but it was actually the path of death. In the section of the timeline that begins with the mission of Jesus, a new way, the way of life, starts to parallel the way of death. The reign of God announced by Jesus belongs, not to rulers and armies, but to wisdom and life. The disciples gathered around Jesus are students in the school of this revised reign, living out the implications of its new laws.

The ministry of John the Baptist becomes the pivot point to this new reign. In Jesus's explanation, however, it isn't clear where John himself is on this timeline. The "until now" in Jesus's explanation could be exclusive (up to but not including) or inclusive (up to and including). This ambiguity returns us to Jesus's ambiguous "Yes" to the query by John's disciples. The Baptist seems to announce the same reign of God as Jesus. But John had fallen into an old way of understanding this reign. He assumed that "the coming one" would bring immediate judgment and a baptism of fire. Jesus, as a result, must tread a fine line in his replies to John's disciples. Only certain aspects of John's ministry—the call to national repentance, for example—can be rolled into the new reign. John, then, is both inside and outside this reign, both the greatest and the least. On the old timeline, which maps onto the way of death, he stands at the top of his peers. He is a prophet calling people to ethical behaviour and preparing them for a coming judgment. John, however, since he is not yet certain that Jesus is the one sent from God, hasn't even taken the first step into the way of life.

Jesus wraps up this initial section of Little Wisdom with a parable (11:16–19). He describes a group of children sitting in the marketplace playing a pair of games. In one game, the children imagine themselves at a joyous occasion, perhaps at a wedding. Some pretend to play instruments and encourage the others to dance. But the rest of the children are spoilsports—they won't join the happy game. In the second game, the children pretend to be at a sad event, such as a funeral. Some of them start the ululation of professional mourners. The others won't go along with this second make-believe either. The parable, says Jesus, applies to the receptions given to him and to John the Baptist. John called his followers to a life of fasting and mourning for sin. Jesus encouraged a lifestyle of celebration and joy. The two ways of the wisdom tradition are not represented in this parable by Jesus and John but by the ones who initiate the games and the ones who won't go along. The uncooperating children are offered multiple play options, games of sadness and games of joy, but because they are following the way of death, they reject them both. Lacking imagination, they are unable to acknowledge the reign of God in any of its manifestations. They won't climb the ladder to join John on the top rung of the old way, and they won't step onto the bottom rung of the ladder of the new way.

Jesus concludes this discourse about John the Baptist with the first explicit reference to wisdom in Matthew. He puts in Jesus's mouth the summary sentence, "Wisdom is justified by its works" (11:19).[31] The "works" that "justify (uphold) Wisdom" are the "works of the Christ" mentioned at the start of this passage about John the Baptist, the works that John heard about from his prison cell. The miracles that Jesus has performed, the author of Matthew is telling us, are witnesses to the presence of Wisdom. The fact that the Little Wisdom section of Matthew starts off with the question about Jesus's relationship to John the Baptist hints that the author of Matthew has started drawing on a wisdom source for this section of his gospel.

The next passage that ties Matthew's Little Wisdom section into a wisdom tradition is the famous discourse in 11:25–30 with the "take my yoke upon you" saying. The passage begins with a prayer. Jesus praises his Father for "hiding these things from the wise and intelligent" and "revealing them to infants." We aren't told what the things are that God has hidden from the wise. Unless the phrase is some vague back-reference to what has been mentioned earlier in the text, we may be dealing with

---

31. Matthew's wisdom episode about John the Baptist should be compared with the parallel passage in Luke 7:18–35. The two Gospels have versions of this discourse so similar that copying—one of the writers copying from the other or both copying from a common source—is the most likely explanation for their agreements. Either way, Luke seems to have misunderstood the meaning of his source. In the summary statement at the end, Luke reads "Wisdom is justified by all its children." In this Lukan reading, Jesus would not be summing up the whole discourse about John the Baptist. He would be reflecting on the parable he has just spoken about the children in the marketplace, saying that the reign of God announced by John and Jesus, both of whom are Wisdom's children, justifies/upholds the message of Wisdom. The Lukan reading does not preserve the ambiguity between the two public ministries. Instead, it proclaims that John and Jesus are *both* part of the Wisdom agenda. The author of Luke, it seems, has overlooked the balanced ambiguity of the passage and altered his source to make more immediate sense. Matthew's summation, "Wisdom is justified by its works," preserves the overall ambiguity.

a borrowing from a source that contained a now-lost referent for "these things." We are still in the realm of wisdom, as we can see by the mention of "the wise," but in this case the wise person is on the other end of the stick—God reveals the truth to "infants" rather than to "the wise." The implied contrast in this prayer is probably between the self-designated wise, the Pharisees and other opponents of Jesus, and a band of disciples who were drawn from less scholarly segments of first-century CE society. They were infants in the eyes of the self-designated wise.

The verse that follows, to judge by its content and phrasing, would be more at home in the Gospel of John than in Matthew. Jesus says, "All things have been handed over to me by my Father, and no one knows the Son except the Father, nor does anyone know the Father except the Son and those to whom the Son chooses to reveal him" (11:27). The gospel-of-John phrasing is another good clue that Matthew's three Little Wisdom chapters include materials from a sectarian wisdom source. John's gospel, as we will see later, is a direct portal into one branch of the wisdom tradition.

When Jesus goes on in this Matthew passage to invite listeners "who labor and are burdened" to "come to me" for rest (11:28), he echoes the call of Wisdom to those who want to learn. We hear this call, for example, in Sirach 24:19–21 ("Come to me, those who long for me, and satisfy yourself with my fruits . . . . Those who eat me no longer hunger and those who drink me no longer thirst.") and in Proverbs 9:5 (Wisdom says, "Come, eat my bread and drink of the wine that I have mixed."). Jesus then issues a second invitation that is linked to the wisdom tradition. He says, "Take my yoke upon you and learn from me, because I am meek and lowly in heart and you will find rest for your souls, for my yoke is kind[32] and my burden is light" (11:29–30). The comparison between a yoke placed on a draft ox so that it can pull a load and the responsibility assumed by a student who submits to the instructional program of a teacher was a well-known analogy in early Jewish literature. The rabbis spoke of "the yoke of the Torah" worn by its students. But the analogy is also found earlier, in the wisdom literature. Ben Sira wrote, "Draw near to me, you uneducated, and lodge in my house of instruction . . . . Put your neck under the yoke and let your soul receive instruction . . . . See with your own eyes that I have labored little and found for myself much

---

32. The Greek word *chrestos* is almost universally translated as "easy" in Matthew 11:30, but elsewhere it is translated as "good" or "kind" or "better," all of which come closer to the essential idea behind *chrestos*. For a discussion, see Mitchell, "The Yoke Is Easy."

rest" (Sir 51:23–27). In offering these invitations at the end of Matthew 11, Jesus takes on the role of a wisdom instructor, perhaps even the role of Wisdom itself.

The controversy that immediately follows (12:1–8) confirms that Wisdom, with its kinder and better yoke, is now present. The Pharisees catch the disciples of Jesus gleaning and eating grain from the field on the Sabbath, a violation of the law against unnecessary work. Jesus engages the Pharisees in a legal argument, maintaining that higher necessity can override sabbath regulations. He cites two examples from the Tanak, both involving a sanctuary, and quotes a saying about temple sacrifices from one of the prophets. During the arguments, Jesus says that "something greater than the temple is here" (12:6). He then caps off the chain of arguments with the claim that "the son of man is lord of the Sabbath" (12:8).[33] It is difficult for us, in a society where Sunday blue laws are so widely deprecated, to appreciate the force of this claim on Jesus's hearers. The Sabbath was a pillar of Jewish faith. Jesus was not undermining this pillar. He was just placing it in a wider context. The ordinary person is not licensed to annul Sabbath law. Jesus himself, though, is not ordinary, and the arguments are meant to lead us to this conclusion. Only Wisdom, God's creation companion, could be above the Sabbath and more than the temple. This is a form of argument that we will find multiple times in the Gospel of John.

When Jesus heals a man with a withered arm, doing it both on the Sabbath and in a synagogue (12:9–14), the conflict with the Pharisees reaches an apex. They "took counsel against him, how they might get rid of him."[34] Jesus, aware of this, moves to a new location. A crowd follows him, however, and brings to him people who are suffering. Jesus heals them and tries—without much success—to establish a cordon of secrecy around his ministry (12:15–16). Matthew connects this clandestine

33. This conflict story is unusual in Matthew's Little Wisdom section because there is a Marcan parallel to Luke and Matthew. Luke follows Matthew, leaving out, as might be expected, some of the more arcane Jewish details. Mark follows Luke's omissions but adds a line before the final summary about the Son of Man being lord of the Sabbath that says, "the Sabbath came about for people, not people for the sabbath" (Mark 2:27). This addition, which is consistent with the law-free approach of Mark, introduces an inconsistency into the line of reasoning found in Matthew, since it implies that Sabbath laws can be suspended by anyone. Jesus's logic in the Matthean text does not depend on reducing the force of the Sabbath laws but on recognizing that something greater than these laws (Wisdom, God's intimate child) is at work.

34. On why this should not be translated (as it is in most versions) "kill/destroy him," see Förster, "Translating from Greek."

ministry with a passage from Isaiah 42:1–4 (quoted in Matt 12:18–21—the gospel's longest quotation from the Tanak). In the Isaiah passage, God speaks about "my servant." The servant, who is God's "delight," is given a task. "I will put my spirit on him," God says, "and he will announce judgment to the nations." The announcement, though, will not be a noisy one. God's servant "will not quarrel or cry out, no one will hear his voice in the streets." In the context of Isaiah, the servant in the quoted verses is the nation of Israel. These servant passages in Isaiah, however, were understood by the early church to be prophecies about Jesus. It is possible, however, that Matthew is not retrojecting a later, novel Christian interpretation here. He may have picked this Isaiah quotation from a pre-Christian wisdom source in which the servant prophecies in Isaiah were transposed into a messianic framework.[35]

Following this quotation from Isaiah, Matthew narrates Jesus's healing of a blind and dumb demoniac (12:22–32). After the healing, the demoniac could both see and speak. The response of the people witnessing this event was, "Could this be the son of David?" Again, "son of David" may be a Solomonic reference, given that the name of Solomon was intimately associated with exorcisms. The response of the Pharisees to this healing was more negative than that of the crowds. The Pharisees accuse Jesus of using the power of Satan to perform the exorcisms. The logic behind this response—demons casting out demons—makes little sense, and Jesus brings down the full weight of this contradiction on his opponents. At one point, he says, "if I cast out demons by the Spirit of God, then the reign of God has come upon you." In identifying Jesus's healing ministry with the "Spirit of God," Matthew may be referring to the Isaiah passage he has just quoted ("I will put my spirit on him"). But he may also be invoking the close association between Wisdom and the Spirit of God in the later wisdom literature.

The connection between Person Wisdom and the Spirit of God in this Matthean passage throws some light on an enigmatic teaching at the end of this healing story. Jesus says, "The one who is not with me is against me, and the one not gathering with me scatters. I say to you, therefore, that every sin and blasphemy will be forgiven people, but blasphemy against the Holy Spirit will not be forgiven. Whoever speaks a word against the Son of Man will be forgiven, but whoever speaks against the Holy Spirit will never be forgiven, neither in this age or in the one to

---

35. See the section in the Appendixes on "The Nazorean Suffering Servant."

come" (12:30–32). This is the infamous unpardonable sin. Evangelicals, I recall, were quite exercised over what this sin might be. At Moody, a couple of my companions worried—in private—that they might have inadvertently fallen into it. The approach usually taken by their Bible teachers identified the unpardonable sin as failing to believe in Jesus as a personal Savior. In the context of Matthew's Little Wisdom section, however, the unpardonable sin is declining the invitation of Wisdom to be part of the light rather than the darkness. It is coming down on the wrong side of the two ways, choosing the way of death rather than the way of life. Jesus says that what people think about him is negotiable, a fault that can be forgiven. You may think that he is the Messiah, or you may not. You may think that he is divine, or you may not. What is not negotiable, however, is taking on the lifestyle and attitudes that are condemned in the wisdom literature. If you can read the description of the way of death in the first and second chapters of the Wisdom of Solomon and say, "That's me," then you have probably committed the unpardonable sin. The author of the Wisdom of Solomon points out that Wisdom, even though it is "a benevolent spirit," will "not forgive a blasphemer because God is witness to his inner thoughts, an overseer of his heart, and a listener to the tongue" (1:6). Jesus knew about this wisdom doctrine of an all-hearing God listening in on thoughts. A few verses later in the Little Wisdom section, he says, "At the day of judgment, people shall give account for every careless word that they speak. By your words you will be justified and by your words you will be condemned" (12:36–37).

Near the end of Matthew's chapter 12, the wisdom theme emerges again. In the story related in 12:38–42, the scribes and Pharisees press Jesus for some tangible sign (*sēmeion*) of his authority. They may not have asked this in good faith. Josephus tells us that several first-century Palestinian figures who promised provocative signs were punished by the Roman authorities for their audacity.[36] Perhaps the Pharisees were hoping to goad Jesus into making a prediction that would attract official attention. Jesus escapes the trap they have laid by directing his opponents to two signs from the Tanak. These were not, of course, the signs the Pharisees were asking for, but the word "sign" is ambiguous. The Greek word can refer to a demonstrative event, but it can also refer to an omen. The Tanak figures cited by Jesus are signs in the sense that they are omens

---

36. Josephus's descriptions of Theudas, of the Egyptian, and of other false deliverers are in Josephus, *Ant.* 20.

about what it would mean to not recognize the authority of Jesus. Like a good sage, Jesus knows how to play on ambiguity.

The first sign/omen that Jesus cites is the story of Jonah, who was swallowed by a fish while trying to escape the task God had sent him to do. Jesus tells about how Jonah survived his time in the fish and how his preaching caused the Ninevites to repent. "The men of Nineveh," he says, "will rise in the judgment with this generation and condemn it, because they repented under the preaching of Jonah, and behold, something greater than Jonah is here" (12:41). The second sign is the queen of the South, who "came from the ends of the earth to listen to the wisdom of Solomon." She will also condemn this generation at the judgment because "something greater than Solomon is here" (12:42).

Jesus, we note, has selected two wisdom characters as omens/signs. Solomon is the figurehead of the OT wisdom books. The curriculum in Jesus's wisdom school, we can be sure, included stories about him. The curriculum probably included discussions about the meaning of Jonah as well. Even though the book about him is found in the collection of the minor prophets, Jonah was widely understood to be a sage.[37] In calling these stories about Solomon and Jonah "signs," Jesus invites the Pharisees to bring wisdom tradition perspectives into their own interpretation of the Tanak.

Not only does Jesus cite the two wisdom figures as portents. He also tells the Pharisees that something "greater than Jonah" and "greater than Solomon" is present. Earlier in the chapter, Jesus used the same figure of speech when he said that something "greater than the temple is here" (12:6). This rhetorical device, the argument from the lesser to the greater, is widely used in wisdom rhetoric.

Evidence has been mounting throughout Matthew's Little Wisdom section that Jesus was a sage and that he had organized a wisdom school. Hanging in the background, however, has been the issue of Person Wisdom itself. As we have seen in the previous chapter, the personification of Wisdom was a major theme in the wisdom literature. By the time we reach the period when Jesus lived, Person Wisdom was more than a metaphor. It had become a companion of God, present at creation, even equated with the Spirit of God. The question that must be posed, then, is

---

37. The book of Jonah, with its wondrous plant and animal, provided opportunities for early exegetes to launch wisdom-like discussions about the marvels of creation. See the summary of connections between Jonah and wisdom literature in McLaughlin, *An Introduction*, 165–6.

whether Jesus identified himself with Person Wisdom. The full answer to this will have to wait until we look more closely at the Gospel of John. A case could be made, though, that the biographical materials in the Little Wisdom section of Matthew identify Jesus with Person Wisdom. What does Jesus mean, for example, when he claims to be greater than Solomon? A "greater than Solomon" could only be Wisdom itself, the source of Solomon's fame.

The author of Matthew wraps up the story of Jesus's interaction with the Pharisees with an analogy (12:43–45). Much of the controversy has been about exorcisms, so Jesus relates the story of a demon, an "unclean spirit," that has been cast out of a person. The demon "travels through waterless places seeking rest and does not find it." The demon decides to go back to its old house, the person he has left. When it returns, the demon finds the house "vacant, swept out, and tidied up." Finding plenty of room, it invites "seven other spirits more evil than itself," and they all set up housekeeping in the former victim. The result is that "the final state of that person is worse than the initial state." This story may be drawn from a wisdom teaching on the two ways. It illustrates the central problem with the way of death. Local solutions to problems encountered in the way of death won't work—small steps in the right direction presage larger failures. Only a complete conversion to the way of life can save a person.

PARABLES

The Little Wisdom section wraps up with Matthew's third package of Jesus's teaching. Matthew 13 contains seven parables, two of which are privately explained to the disciples. These are not the only place that parables are found in Matthew—the gospel contains, by traditional counting methods, about two dozen parables. This final part of Little Wisdom is, however, the largest clumping of parables in the gospel. Most of the parables in this chapter start off with a phrase similar to "the reign of heaven is like," and most of them have parallels in Mark or Luke or both.

Jesus's parables are broad analogies that depict scenes from the natural and social world and extract spiritual truth from these scenes. Some of the stories are meant, allegory-like, to have detailed, point-by-point mappings onto their analogues. Others have looser mappings, often just making a single point. Scholars have tried to isolate the special characteristics of Jesus's parables that make them different from the analogies used by other writers and speakers, but most of these attempts—in my opinion—fail. We can find stories in the Tanak, for example, that can be compared to certain NT parables, such as Nathan's accusation against King David's adultery in 2 Samuel 12.[38] And even when we believe that we have found a specific pattern in the parables of Jesus, we usually arrive at this conclusion by not including all of his analogies in our list of parables. You won't find Jesus's lily comparison in the Sermon on the Mount—the one that begins, "consider how the lilies/flowers of the field grow"—in typical lists of Jesus's parables, but reasons for leaving it out seem artificial. If we include it, then we need to expand what we call a parable.

A better approach is to think of Jesus employing many types of symbolic discourse that lie along a spectrum of analogy. If we want to hive off certain pieces of the spectrum and restrict the word "parable" to just those pieces, we can do this—so long as we don't forget the assumptions we have made. This point may seem trivial, but I don't think it is. Attempts to make Jesus's analogies fit a specific pattern can hide from us his broader connections to the wisdom tradition. The first chapter of Proverbs, as we noted earlier, charges the wise with learning the meanings of "sayings, wise words, enigmas, and riddles" (Proverbs 1:6). The student devoted to the study of the Torah in Ben Sira's school "seeks out the wisdom of all the ancients, . . . preserves the sayings of the men of renown, and enters into the twists of analogies;[39] he seeks out the hidden meanings of proverbs and is conversant with the obscurities of analogies" (Sirach 39:1–3). What we find in the parable discourse at the conclusion of the Matthew's Little Wisdom section, then, is a small cross-section of the kinds of symbols and analogies that Jesus used in his teaching. As a good sage, he also teaches his students how to use and interpret these symbols. This is probably why Matthew's sources have preserved—and Matthew has repeated for us in chapter 13—two examples of Jesus explaining to his disciples the meanings of his parables.

I won't discuss these parables here. What is of interest, though, are two of Matthew's three detours in this chapter into why Jesus employed parables. The first detour is in 13:10–17. The disciples ask Jesus about

38. Other Tanak parables might include the wise woman of Tekoa's deception of David (2 Sam 14:1–20), the anonymous prophet's pretense before Ahab (1 Kgs 20:35–43), the song of the vineyard in Isaiah (5:1–7), and Jotham's analogy about the trees (Judg 9:7–15).

39. The word in Sirach that I have translated as "analogies" is *parabolē*. In Ben Sira's context, it probably refers to a wide range of symbolic vehicles, perhaps not so wide as the Hebrew *mashal* but much wider than the English "parable."

his use of parables, and he tells them that "it has been given to you to understand the mysteries of the reign of heaven, but to others, it has not been given." He speaks to the crowd in parables, he says, because "seeing they do not see and hearing they do not hear or perceive." He then quotes a passage from Isaiah 6:9–10 that makes the same point, following it up with the macarism, "Blessed are *your* eyes because they see and *your* ears because they hear." Many prophets and righteous people, Jesus adds, "desired to see what you see and did not see and to hear what you hear and did not hear." In this last statement, Jesus is not making the obvious point that these prophets died before they could experience the events that were happening to the disciples. It is trivially true of any people at any time that things will happen after they die. His point, rather, is that they *did* foresee these things but lacked the skills to interpret the symbolism—skills that Jesus was teaching his disciples to use. Symbolic interpretation was a tool that they could apply to the writings left behind by these prophets and righteous souls. This is the essence of sectarian *pesher*. By introducing symbols and interpretations to his disciples, Jesus was teaching them how to restring the pearls of the Tanak.

The last detour into the meaning of symbolic discourse (13:51–52) is found at the end of the parables section. Jesus asks the disciples if they have understood his interpreted and uninterpreted parables. They answer, "Yes." Jesus then comments, "Every scribe becoming a discile to the reign of heaven is like a householder bringing out of their stores both things that are new and things that are old." Professional scribes were a fixture of the social scene. Matthew often refers to them, sometimes linking them with the Pharisees as "scribes and Pharisees." Here, though, Jesus is probably not referring to this social caste. Jesus is referring instead to the broader concept of a scribe as a person who has been trained in wisdom. In Sirach 38, Ben Sira contrasts the lifestyle of the student of wisdom and the lifestyle of the common laborer. "The wisdom of the scribe depends on the opportunity for leisure," he says. "Only the person cutting back on business can become wise" (Sir 38:24). A disciple of Jesus was this sort of wisdom scribe, and Jesus compares this scribe to a household manager making use both of tried-and-tested tools and of new tools. Jesus is advising his students to open themselves up to new ways—his way—of understanding the meaning of the Tanak.

The Little Wisdom section ends, appropriately enough, with a crowd once again marvelling at what was happening in this new wisdom school (13:53–58). Jesus and his disciples decamp to his home territory, his *patris*, and the people there say, "From where is this person getting this wisdom and these miracles?" We have heard this refrain from the crowds before, but now it is heightened by the contrast between the words and actions of the adult Jesus and what the people know who watched him grow up. "Is this not the son of the carpenter?" they say. "Is his mother not called Mary and are his brothers not James and Joseph and Simon and Judas? Are not all his sisters among us?" Just a few verses ago, Jesus was challenging his disciples, his wisdom scribes, not to limit themselves to the old tools, the ones that they had acquired before becoming part of the school of Jesus. Now Jesus himself is struggling to prove that his new teaching can exist beside his old life. "A prophet is not without honor," he replies, "except in his own *patris*."

THE SECOND HALF OF MATTHEW

For some reason, Matthew chooses to depend less on his wisdom sources after the Little Wisdom section in chapters 11–13. There is, however, one exception to this. An important wisdom text occurs at the end of chapter 23, a chapter given over to accusations (woes) against the scribes and Pharisees.

The last accusation Jesus makes against the Pharisees and scribes in chapter 23 is that they claim—falsely—that they are not guilty of shedding the blood of the martyred prophets (23:29–36). In the middle of this passage there is a break in the flow. The chapter has been a steady stream of second-person accusations—"Woe to *you*," "Woe to *you*." In a sudden switch, Jesus flips into first person and says, "*I* am sending you prophets." It feels like Matthew has turned to a new source. Possibly the theme of martyrdom in the final accusation has brought this new source to mind.

The inserted text reads, "Behold, I send to you prophets and wise people and scribes. Some of them you kill and crucify, and some of them you scourge in your synagogues and pursue from town to town." Because of the way the Jewish people have treated God's messengers, "all the blood of the righteous that has been poured out on the earth will come upon you, from the blood of the righteous Abel to the blood of Zechariah son of Berechiah, whom you murdered between the temple and the altar. Truly, I say to you that all these things will happen to this generation." Then comes Jesus's famous lament, "O Jerusalem, Jerusalem, killing the prophets and stoning those sent to you. How often have I desired to gather your children, just as a hen gathers her brood under her wings, and you did not want it. Behold, your house is left desolate. For I say to you that you will not see me again until you say, 'Blessed is the one who comes in the name of the Lord.'"

This insertion at the end of chapter 23, perhaps drawn from a wisdom source, seems like it is not being quoted verbatim. It bears marks of revision. I detect four of these marks. First, the indignities suffered by the prophets and wise people and scribes include crucifyings and synagogue scourgings. Matthew's addition of crucifixion, not a method of death employed in the Tanak, may have been an alteration of his source to point forward to Jesus's own passion, which the author is about to narrate. Second, when Jesus goes on to mention specific martyrs—Adam and Eve's son Abel, killed by his brother Cain (Gen 4:1–16), and Zechariah, a prophesying priest killed by King Joash (2 Chr 24:20–22)[40]—the author of Matthew adds that Zechariah was the son of Berechiah. The Zechariah whose father was Berechiah, however, was the post-exilic prophet (Zech 1:1) of that name. The martyred pre-exilic Zechariah was the son of the priest Jehoiada. The addition of Berechiah as the father appears to be a mistake introduced by Matthew during his revision of the source. Third, the line "Truly, I say to you that all these things will happen to this generation" seems like it might have been added in anticipation of a similar line in the Little Apocalypse of the next chapter, which reads, "Truly I say to you that this generation will not pass away until all of these things have happened" (24:34). Finally, in the lament over Jerusalem, Matthew adds that "your house" (presumably the Jewish temple) will be "abandoned and desolate"[41] and that Jerusalem will not see Jesus again until its people say, "Blessed is the one who comes in the name of the Lord." Both of these anticipate events in the next chapters of Matthew—the abomination of

---

40. These two martyrs seem to represent a sort of A to Z of martyrs. But not because their names start with the first and last letters of the alphabet—the letters nearest to the sound of the English letter "Z" are not the last letters of either the Greek alphabet or the Hebrew alphabet. The most common theory is that Abel and Zechariah represent all martyrs because their deaths bookend the martyrs of the Tanak—Abel was the first to die, and Zechariah the son of Jehoiada is the last martyr. But that's assuming that 2 Chronicles, where Zechariah's death is mentioned, is regarded as the final book of the Tanak. This was an ordering of Tanak books, however, that was only fixed in recent centuries. Interpreters in the early centuries of the church had other theories about why Abel and Zechariah could stand for the whole range of martyrs. For a discussion, see Gallagher, "The Blood."

41. Some NT manuscripts do not have "and desolate," but most textual critics believe that it was in the original text.

desolation and the Palm Sunday chant—and may have been added to the wisdom source by the author of Matthew.

I mention the marks of revision in this inserted passage because, by subtracting these revisions, we come up with a text that looks like it comes from a wisdom source. Reinforcing this conclusion is an unexpected difference between the parallel texts in Matthew and Luke. At the very beginning of this insertion, Matthew has Jesus say, "I send you prophets and wise people and scribes." In Luke's passage (11:47–51), however, the phrase reads, "the *Wisdom of God* said, I will send to them prophets and apostles." Where did this "Wisdom of God" in the Lukan version come from?[42] The most plausible explanation, in my opinion, is that Luke had access—somehow—to the wisdom oracle that Matthew draws on. He inserts part of it here and part of it (the "Jerusalem, Jerusalem" passage) two chapters later, at Luke 13:34–35.[43]

When we remove the parts of the Matthean passage that hint at authorial revisions, we come up with the wisdom text that both Matthew and Luke had access to. The oracle may have read something like this, with Wisdom speaking:

> I will send to you prophets and wise people and scribes, some of whom you will kill, so that all the blood of the prophets that has been poured out since the foundation of the earth will come upon you, from the blood of Abel to the blood of Zechariah, whom you murdered between the temple and the altar. O Jerusalem, Jerusalem, killing the prophets and stoning those sent to

42. Some redaction critics argue that the wisdom passage in Matthew 23, which is found in both Matthew and Luke, is drawn from the lost Q source. They suggest that the Q source is largely a wisdom document and that Luke, in prefacing the passage with "the Wisdom of God said," has retained the original Q reading. Matthew, because he identified Jesus with Person Wisdom, felt licensed to change the Q source by omitting "the Wisdom of God said" and letting readers think that Jesus was the speaker. The redaction critics that argue this point seem to rely on the pioneering work of Jack Suggs in Suggs, *Wisdom, Christology, and Law*. The two-source hypothesis of the redaction critics, of course, is not needed to argue for Lukan access to wisdom sources. For the double tradition material—the places in the Synoptics where Luke and Matthew, but not Mark, are in rough agreement—the two-gospel hypothesis also allows for alternate Lukan sources. "In all such cases where the author of Luke has had access to sayings of Jesus in his special source material which have parallels in Matthew, he was in a position to preserve these sayings in a form which plausibly could be closer to the original than the same sayings as found in Matthew" (Farmer, "A Fresh Approach," 42).

43. The authors of Luke and Matthew share a single goal: they both want to make Jesus the speaker of Wisdom's "Jerusalem, Jerusalem" lament. Matthew does it by making Jesus the speaker of the "I sent you prophets" line before the lament. Luke does it by transposing the lament to a later position where Jesus is the speaker.

you. How often have I desired to gather your children, just as a
hen gathers her brood under her wings, and you did not want it.

The fact that Wisdom laments "how often" she longed to gather in
her children is a further indication that Matthew has lifted this from a
wisdom source. In Matthew and the other Synoptic Gospels, Jesus visits
Judea only twice as an adult, once when he is baptized by John and once
when he goes there for Passover and is crucified. Putting the words "how
often" in the mouth of Jesus seems out of place. Wisdom, in contrast, has
worked tirelessly since the day of creation to bring the children of God
to their Father. The lamentation adapted by Matthew may expand on the
sad passage about Person Wisdom in the Similitudes of Enoch (*Enoch*
42:2) that I mentioned earlier: "Then Wisdom went out to dwell with
the children of the people, but she found no dwelling place. So Wisdom
returned to her place, and she settled permanently among the angels."[44]

MATTHEW AND APOCALYPTIC

In this chapter, I have surveyed the wisdom context of the first two-thirds
of the Gospel of Matthew. We will pass over the final five chapters of
the gospel. These chapters include, in addition to the Passion, the Little
Apocalypse (chapter 24) with its parables of judgment and the discourse
on the second coming (chapter 25).

The inclusion of an apocalypse in Matthew and the other Synoptic
Gospels, however, deserves some attention. I reviewed in chapter 3 the
wide influence that apocalypticism and new views of the afterlife had on
Judaism. Apocalyptic ideas attracted some segments of Jewish society more
than others. We see its strongest imprint on sectarian movements, such as
the Essenes and Christian Judaism. In contrast, the few apocalyptic themes
that we find in the Mishnah and Tosefta seem muted. The apocalyptic is
not so much exorcized from the Mishnah as it is sanitized, confined to a
few safe talking points. We hear about the joys waiting for the righteous in
the life of the world to come and about the final destruction of the wicked,
but details are scant. If we accept that the Mishnaic tractates throw light on
the two centuries surrounding the birth of Jesus, we might even speak of a
fundamental distrust of the apocalyptic in core Judaism.

The Little Apocalypse of Matthew, coming as it does on the heels of
a gospel that is dotted with wisdom themes, stands out. It reminds us that

44. Translation from Isaac, *1 (Ethiopic Apocalypse of) Enoch*, 33.

the merger of sapiential and apocalyptic thought that we find in the Wisdom of Solomon and in the NT, as strange as the marriage might seem in the abstract, was real. Nor should we imagine that either side—the wisdom focus of Jesus's teaching or the apocalyptic framework of his mission—was an overlay of the later church on Jesus's message and ministry. Elements of *both* trace to the historical Jesus. It was Albert Schweitzer's 1906 book,[45] translated into English as the *Quest of the Historical Jesus* in 1910, that first brought the apocalyptic side of Jesus's own worldview into wide discussion. Schweitzer's view of Jesus as an apocalyptic prophet quickly colonized NT critical studies. His arguments convinced me when I read the *Quest*. The influence of the newly discovered apocalyptic perspective on Jesus became so strong in the first half of the twentieth century that the picture of him as a teacher in the wisdom tradition struggled to find a foothold, gaining momentum only in the 1970s.

The convergence of these vectors of scholarship—the apocalyptic and the sapiential—has left me, and many others in the twenty-first century, in a quandary. The historical Jesus that emerges from studies is a first century Jewish sage gripped by an apocalyptic perspective. As a sage, he speaks in a symbolic language that plumbs the depths of the mystical union between God and creation. His wisdom teachings feel as timeless as any truth available to us. At the same time, however, his words are embedded in an archaic cosmology that current readers can find baffling.

For me, this quandary is not just intellectual. It has played itself out in my own journey. In the years when I was an evangelical, I read Matthew's Little Apocalypse in a way that is no longer available to me. There was, at that time in my life, little difference between the signs in Matthew 24 that Jesus says will precede his return and the stories I heard on the nightly news. In entering this apocalyptic view of reality, populated with angels, demons, translated saints, final judgments, heavenly assizes, and militant messiahs, I gave up the way I once understood the modern world. I was all-in, as gamblers say, and the commitments I made shifted my perspective. Readers having personal experience with American Evangelicalism will know what I'm talking about. You may even attach some specialized vocabulary to it, using words such as "rapture" and "premillennial dispensationalism." Today, though, even those without this background have some inkling what it might mean to look at the world in this way. One of my classmates at Moody, Jerry Jenkins, coauthored the bestselling novel

45. Schweitzer, *Reimarus*.

Left Behind (1995)[46] and all its dozen-plus sequels and prequels. The books have become the basis for several film series, video games, and other spin-offs. The vocabulary of the end times has entered the public domain.

When I first stepped into this modern apocalyptic, I entered without the understanding that I now have of the line of wisdom that links me, binds me, to the Person Wisdom and its teachings. And now that I have the wisdom connection, I have, ironically, lost my place in the apocalypse. It is both easier and harder for me than it might be for other students of Jewish and Christian Scriptures to perform the gymnastics needed to stand inside a Jesus movement that includes the apocalyptic. Easier because I have been there. Harder because my own spiritual identity is defined by *not* being there.

MATTHEW AND WISDOM

The Gospel of Matthew, though not given its current shape as a comprehensive life of Jesus until perhaps thirty years after the crucifixion, contains within it the oldest strata of the collected teachings of Jesus and the stories about what Jesus did. Most of these stories and teachings were probably remembered and transmitted—and some perhaps even recorded—by participants in the school that Jesus had established and taught. The milieu in which this documentation came together was the Jewish sect of Christians that flourished in Jerusalem and Galilee in the mid-first century CE.

In the Matthean stories and teachings, we find evidence that the first generation of Christian Jews were shaped by a wisdom tradition. The belief that Jesus himself was the incarnation of Person Wisdom may have played a role in how these wisdom traditions developed. By the time the Gospel of Matthew took on its final form, however, the wisdom traditions were not as front and center as they were in the early movement. The hands that put together Matthew's gospel had more than one agenda. In our review of the text, we found that only certain passages retain the wisdom watermark. To round out our understanding of what the wisdom tradition meant for the early Christian church, we need to look at two other documents, the Epistle of James and the Gospel of John. When we look at these, we will see more—and better—evidence for a wisdom sect behind Christian Judaism.

46. Jenkins and LeHaye, *Left Behind*.

5

Brother James

WHEN YOU TAKE AWAY the four gospels, the history book of Acts, and the Apocalypse of John from the twenty-seven books of the NT, the twenty-one remaining books are all epistles. Or, to use a less formal term, letters. Thirteen of these letters cite Paul as the author. One of them is anonymous (Hebrews). The other seven, the Catholic (i.e., general) Epistles, claim to have been written by four significant figures of the early church: Peter, James, John, and Jude.

That NT authority should be carried on the shoulders of epistles should elicit some surprise. None of the works in the Tanak have this format. The deuterocanonical additions to the Tanak include only one letter (the Letter of Jeremiah). This dearth of OT epistles is not because letters were unfamiliar to writers and readers when the OT came together—letters were in common use among literate people in the ancient Middle East throughout the Second Temple period. They are absent from the OT because letters were considered too pedestrian, too workaday, to convey the high ideas of religion. In Hellenistic cultures, however, letters began to take on a more literary quality.[1] Writers of novels, essays, and poetry began to adapt their genres to epistolary formats. By the time the NT was being assembled, any concern about conveying literary and abstract ideas in letters had vanished. Only a few of the NT letters, we note, limit themselves to the chatty and personal content we would associate with a personal letter (e.g., Philemon, 2 John, 3 John). Most of them incorporate

---

1. On the many roles of letters in Hellenistic societies, see the collections in Rosenmeyer, *Ancient Greek Literary Letters*.

content that could have originated in other genres, such as creeds, sermons, commentaries, liturgies, and theological essays. This is perhaps why we persist in referring to the NT letters "epistles." If you are away at school and your mom writes you a letter, you look forward to reading it. If she writes you an epistle, you're in trouble.

Historians are thankful for the ascendency of the letter format in the Hellenistic mind. Letters tend to be signed, which connects them to an author and sometimes provides a time and a place of composition. Works in other genres, in contrast, can be notoriously hard to pin down to specific authors, times, and places—the books of the Tanak being exhibit number one.

Letters, though, can present their own problems. They may not be anonymous, but they can be pseudonymous, not actually written by the person they claim to be from. Over the years, students of the NT have challenged the authorial claims of most of the NT epistles. Only about half of Paul's letters, for example, are currently thought to come from his hand. Paul became so widely acknowledged as an authority on the new Christian faith that writers borrowed his name, hoping to find recognition for their ideas by attributing their words—via forged letters—to the famous apostle. Fortunately for us, and unfortunately for the forgers, we have enough of Paul's letters to see, or at least think we see, the difference between the real deal and the forgeries. We are not so fortunate with the catholic epistles. Did the famous persons who signed these epistles really write them? We have few tools for determining this. We can, of course, compare the content of these letters with what we know about their alleged authors from other sources. We can also check whether the ideas in these letters correspond to the stage of theological development in the purported contexts of the letters.

THE EPISTLE OF JAMES

Among the catholic epistles, the letter of James stands out. It checks more of the authenticity boxes than any of the other six Catholic Epistles. Its reputed author, a person with deep connections to the Jesus movement and the early church, models a version of the same law-observant Christian Judaism that we find in the earliest strata of Jesus's teaching, the themes that we found in the Gospel of Matthew.

But checking the right boxes is only definitive when there are enough boxes to check, and for the Epistle of James and the other catholic epistles we don't have enough boxes. This opens them up to all sorts of academic speculation. A recent critical commentary on the Epistle of James, for example, takes the extreme position that it is an early second-century forgery.[2] Nor is it just the odd modern critic raising questions about the epistle. In the two thousand years since its composition, the letter has fallen under more than one cloud of suspicion. The church father Jerome, writing at the end of the fourth century CE, summed up the opinion of the ancient church when he observed that the Epistle of James was "claimed by some to have been published by some one else under his name, and gradually, as time went on, to have gained authority."[3] The epistle fared slightly better in the Middle Ages, thanks to a boost from St. Augustine, but took another hit in the Reformation. Martin Luther, a fan of Paul's law-free approach to the Christian message, found that the Epistle of James focused too much on law and not enough on grace. In his 1522 German translation of the Bible, Luther consigned the epistle to an appendix. He complained in the preface to his Bible that James was "a very straw-like letter" compared to other parts of the NT.[4]

Did I pick up some of this Protestant ambiguity about the Epistle of James when I first grappled with the text in my days at Moody? If I did, I don't remember it. Indeed, the evangelical certainty that all (and only) the books contained in the Protestant Bible were inspired and that each book had a purpose in the canon became the overriding rule of interpretation. It was impossible, by evangelical standards, for inspired books to be at cross-purposes.

To keep the messages in their NT books consistent, evangelicals reading the Epistle of James must resolve three potential conflicts between James and the other NT books. First, the author of James has little to say about Jesus. The writer doesn't seem to be aware of the theological framework taking shape around Jesus's life, death, and resurrection. Second, James rejects any attempt to imagine a stage of belief that precedes and is separate from works. In making this point, James seems to contradict specific Pauline teachings about the relationship between faith and

2. Allison, *James.*

3. Jerome, *Theodoret, Jerome, Vir. ill.* 2.

4. The phrase is "ein rechte stroern Epistel." Presumably the contrast is between books that are the true bread of the word, made from kernels of wheat, and those that are made from the less nourishing parts of the wheat, the chaff.

works. The Epistle of James draws a conclusion about the ordering of faith and works from the life of Abraham, for example, that opposes the lesson that Paul gleans from the same story (Jas 2:20–24 and Gal 3:6–14). Third, God's judgment of individuals in James seems to be based on their works rather than their beliefs. For the people I knew at Moody, the solution to these awkward problems was to position the books of the NT along a timeline of personal experience. We should read Paul, they said, in order to come to belief in Christ. James was for those who had already believed and who wanted to know whether they had acquired saving faith.

A timeline is involved, but it is not the one my evangelical instructors applied. It would not have occurred to them that the Epistle of James and the letters of Paul may represent stages, not in the outlook of believers, but in the development of the Christian faith itself. The approach I will take in this chapter is that the Epistle of James reflects early Palestinian Christian Judaism at a time before it became a predominately gentile faith. To the author of the epistle, the Jesus movement was still a Jewish sect—the gentile hegemony that would arrive in the last decades of the first century was not even on the horizon. This developmental timeline, which positions the faith content of the Epistle of James *before* that of most other NT materials, reverses the sequence based on personal experience that I learned at Moody. James comes first, not last. Paul's emphasis on faith and belief is a later development, a repackaging to address the status of gentiles within the Jesus movement.

ASSUMPTIONS

As was the case with the Gospel of Matthew, I will be making some assumptions about the Epistle of James. The first is that the letter was written by James, the brother of Jesus. The letter does not explicitly claim this. It begins with the simple salutation "James, servant of God and of the Lord Jesus Christ" (1:1). James ("Jacobus" in Greek, in Hebrew "Jacob") was a common name in first-century Jewish circles. There are two men with this name in the synoptic lists of the twelve apostles. One is James the son of Zebedee and brother of the apostle John. The other is James the son of Alphaeus. Three other Jameses are also mentioned in the gospels. Two of them are minor figures. The third is the brother of Jesus. We only hear about this last James in one place in the Gospel of Matthew, at 13:55–56 (with a parallel in Mark at 6:3), a passage we looked at in the previous chapter. The reference to Jesus's brother James comes about when Jesus returns, in the rounds of his public ministry, to his *patris*, the place where he grew up. He teaches in one of the synagogues and the locals are astounded, in the light of what they knew about his early life, at the wisdom and miracles of the mature Jesus. They ask one another, "Is his mother not called Mary and are his brothers not James and Joseph and Simon and Judas? Are not all his sisters among us?"

In the gospels, then, James is just one of four brothers and (at least) two sisters of Jesus, but we hear more about him in the book of Acts. He cuts an imposing figure in the early Jerusalem church. At the church council in Acts 15, when the issue of how gentile believers should relate to Jewish law is discussed, James seems to have the last word on the council's decision. When Paul makes his final visit to Jerusalem, the one in which he is arrested by the Romans, he seeks out James and finds him in the company of the other elders of the Jerusalem church (Acts 21:18). James may have been—later writers will assume this—the head of the Jerusalem contingent of believers.

James is also mentioned in Paul's letters. In the Book of Galatians, Paul informs us that he met with James, the Lord's brother, on his first visit to Jerusalem after joining the Christian sect (1:19). In Paul's later visit to Jerusalem, which may correspond to the council in Acts 15, he talks about meeting with "James and Cephas and John, who were acknowledged pillars [of the Jerusalem body of believers]" (2:9). Paul mentions that the brothers who persuaded Peter to cease table fellowship with Antioch gentiles were "certain men from James" (2:12). Paul also records in 1 Corinthians that Jesus appeared to James after the resurrection (15:7). After this, the NT falls silent about the brother of Jesus. The Jewish historian Josephus provides us with an ending to the story. James, he says, was tried by the Jewish Sanhedrin and stoned to death during a short gap in the Roman administration of Jerusalem. The timing of James's death is hard to work out in Josephus's texts, but it would have been somewhere in the 60s CE.[5] In these biblical and extra-biblical narrations, James comes across as an authority figure with a special attachment to Christians who were still following the Jewish religious laws. Later Christian writers would emphasize his piety and life of prayer.

5. Josephus, *Ant.* 20.9.1. For an argument that Josephus is not referring to James the brother of Jesus, see List, "Death of James." List, however, still places the death of this brother of Jesus in the period before the fall of Jerusalem.

Though there have been attempts throughout the history of the church to link the Epistle of James to one of the other people named James in the NT, the consensus, at least since the third century, has been that the James in the salutation of the Epistle of James is either the James who is the brother of Jesus or someone pretending to be him. I would agree. I also think that there is good reason to believe that the letter is not pseudonymous. The lack of any strong claim in the epistle to the identity of the writer is in itself a minor bit of evidence that Jesus's brother was the author. A later writer would have wanted to resolve any ambiguity regarding authorship—as the author of another Catholic Epistle, Jude, does in the salutation to his letter when he calls himself "the brother of James" (1:1). The strongest evidence, though, that the author was not a later writer borrowing the name of James lies in what we will look at in the rest of this chapter—the letter's participation in the wisdom traditions of the Christian Jewish sect. The case for Jesus's brother James being the author would have been strengthened if the letter reflected the specific personal situations—places and times and associates—of the author or of the persons addressed, but details such as these are almost entirely missing from the letter. The high level of generality in the letter has caused it to be compared to an encyclical.

The second assumption I will make in this chapter is that the context for the teachings reflected in the Epistle of James is the Judean and Galilean churches in the two to three decades following the death of Jesus. The near end of the dating window is constrained by my previous assumption that the author was James, the brother of Jesus. Since this James died in the sixties CE, the letter must have been composed and sent before this. The far end of the letter's date range is harder to peg. As I will argue shortly, James has a distinct wisdom orientation, one that bears some similarity to the earliest levels of tradition in the Gospel of Matthew, so a date in the 40s CE is not impossible. Some scholars have supposed that the passage on faith and works in James (2:14–26) is a refutation of Pauline theology. If it is a reaction to Paul, then the epistle would probably be set in the 50s CE or later. The faith and works passage in James, however, does not have to be read in this way.[6]

---

6. Even those who read it in this way believe that Paul and James are talking past each other, misunderstanding basic points about each other's views of faith and works. If this is the case, then the assumption that they are independent of each other is just as valid as one that says they are codependent. Nicholas List makes this point in the form of a syllogism in List, "Problematising Dependency," 385.

The place of the epistle's composition is uncertain. There is a small hint that the author may be residing in the Jewish heartland by the way the recipients of the letter are named. The letter is addressed to "the twelve tribes of the diaspora" (1:1). Unless we read this as some kind of metaphor, the intended recipients would have been Jewish people living outside of Judea, suggesting (weakly) that the writer may have been in Judea at the time of composition. The assumption that the brother of Jesus is the one who wrote the letter also bears on the place of composition. In Paul's letter to the Galatians, we have evidence of James living in Jerusalem and sending emissaries, but we have no NT account of James traveling outside of his Jewish homeland. A Judean venue also fits with Jerusalem being, as we see in Acts, the center of authority for Palestinian believers. An encyclical letter would carry the most weight if it were issued by an authoritative person residing in an authoritative location.

THE WISDOM OF JAMES

The Epistle of James is a wisdom text—as much a wisdom text as the wisdom books of the OT. It contains explicit references to the word "wisdom" in two of its passages. The first is at the beginning of the letter. After the salutation, the author begins his instruction by recalling the trials experienced by the letter's recipients. He follows this by saying, "if anyone lacks wisdom, let that person ask from the God who gives to all single-mindedly and without reproaching and it shall be given to him" (1:5). Coming so near the beginning of the epistle, this admonition establishes a wisdom context for the rest of the letter. Acquiring the wisdom that James says his readers should pray for means, among other things, taking to heart the teachings found in the letter.

The second mention of wisdom is found in a passage in the middle of the book (3:13–17). The writer begins this section by asking, "Who is the wise and understanding person among you?" Such a sage, he goes on to say, is someone whose life is characterized by "the gentleness of wisdom" rather than by "jealousy and ambition." This wisdom-driven person is "irenic, moderate, pliable, and full of mercy and good works." Twice in this passage, wisdom is described as "coming down from above." While the most parsimonious reading of this phrase is that this wisdom is a gift from God above, we may have an allusion here to the Person Wisdom narratives found in the wisdom tradition. This Wisdom, living in the presence of God and descending to serve as the intermediary between God and creation, comes down from above.

The wisdom context of the Epistle of James shows itself throughout the text, however, and not just in passages that use the word "wisdom." Even the organization of the book—or rather the lack of it—defines it as a wisdom text. Efforts by students of the Bible to detect a logical sequence of topics in the book come to nothing. Like most of the wisdom texts we looked at in the OT, the instructions in James are a roiling cloud of topics interspersed with sharp adages. There is no more linkage from topic to topic than what we find in Proverbs or Sirach or the Sermon on the Mount. The author of the epistle wanders through discussions of partiality, faith and works, the effect of an untamed tongue, doublemindedness, obsession with business deals, patience, over-elaborate oaths, healing prayer, and restoring backsliders.

Wisdom discourse, as we have seen, is characterized by several of the rhetorical devices lumped under the difficult-to-translate name *mashal*. We looked at several of the *meshalim* in our earlier discussion of Proverbs. The Epistle of James employs, like the Matthean teachings of Jesus, some of these wisdom vehicles. We find, for example, the macarisms that are typical of wisdom discourse (1:12, "Blessed is the person who endures trials.") There are also proverbial sayings expressed in antithetical couplets (4:7–8, "Resist the devil and he will flee from you, draw near to God, and God will draw near to you.") and synonymous couplets (4:8, "Cleanse your hands, you sinners, and sanctify your hearts, you doubleminded."). Worth noting, too, is the way that the text of James is sprinkled, like other wisdom literature, with homely illustrations taken from nature, images such as waves tossed by wind (1:6), a hot sun blasting the beauty of plants (1:11), horses being led about by small bits (3:3), forests set ablaze by little fires (3:5), springs gushing with fresh water (3:11), mists that appear and vanish (4:14), moths that eat fabric (5:2), and farmers waiting for early and late rains (5:7). We also find sequence sayings in James, passages in which one behaviour leads to a second and the second to a third. The book begins with one of these (1:3–4, testing of faith –> steady patience –> a perfect person). Another is found at 1:15 (desire –> sin –> death).

Like Proverbs, almost every topic covered in the Epistle of James contains memorable adages. Some of these pithy sayings include:

Let every person be quick in hearing, slow in speaking (1:19).

For judgment is without mercy for the one not showing mercy (2:13).

For just as the body without the spirit is dead, so also faith without works is dead (2:26).

For where there is jealousy and strife, there is disturbance and every base practice (3:16).

Friendship with the world is enmity with God (4:4).

Knowing a good thing to do and not doing it is sin (4:17).

The one who turns a sinner from the error of his way saves his soul from death (5:20).

Finally, we find a few extended comparisons in the Epistle of James that look like small parables. These may be a connecting link between the similes found in traditional wisdom literature and the more developed stories in the synoptic parables of Jesus. One of these is found at the beginning of the third chapter, in a discourse on the problems of taming the tongue (3:1–12). The smallness of the tongue is related to the size of its effects by means of cascading comparisons—a bit and bridle on a horse, a rudder on a ship, and a small flame that leads to a forest fire. Another parable-like passage is at the end of the first chapter (1:22–25), where a person who doesn't transform a truth heard into a truth done is compared to someone who looks briefly in a mirror, sees something that needs attention, doesn't take care of it, and then forgets about it.

James does not quote a lot of Scripture. His letter has about one-fifth as many quotations per page, for example, as Paul's epistle to the Romans. In this respect, James is following the pattern of Sirach. Ben Sira captured the essence of the Proverbs wisdom tradition without quoting the sayings in Proverbs. He preferred to rephrase the ideas of the sages in his own words, and James does the same.[7] A lack of explicit citations, however, does not mean lack of dependence on other wisdom authorities. The teachings in the Epistle of James embody the wisdom teachings of Jesus that we observed in the Sermon on the Mount. There are about twenty places in the letter that echo sayings from the sermon. James achieves

7. James does mention, in 2:8, the "royal law" of loving one's neighbor as oneself, referencing Leviticus 19:18, and three verses later he quotes two of the Ten Commandments. While talking about Abraham, he quotes the line from Genesis 15:6 about Abraham's righteousness coming from his trust in God (2:23). In chapter four, James quotes as Scripture a line that is not in the OT (4:5, "The spirit which God established in us longs with envy."), and in the next verse he cites the Septuagint version of Proverbs 3:34 (4:6, "God opposes the proud but gives grace to the humble."). But these citations are the only ones in the epistle—the rest of the wisdom teachings in the book seem to come directly from the mouth of James.

this dense cross-referencing, however, without a word-for-word quoting of any of Jesus's Matthean teachings. The nearest James comes to an explicit quote is when he advises his readers, "Do not make oaths, either by heaven or by earth" (5:12). This looks like what Jesus says in Matthew 5:34–35, "I say to you, do not make any oaths, neither on heaven, because it is the throne of God, nor on the earth, because it is the stool for God's feet." James goes on to say, just as Jesus does (but in slightly different words), "Let your 'Yes' be yes and your 'No' be no." The rest of the parallel passages to the Matthean sermon are looser allusions. Both James and Jesus tell us to rejoice in our trials (Jas 1:2, Matt 5:11–12), to ask God without hesitation for what we need (Jas 1:5, Matt 7:7), to be both hearers and doers of the word (Jas 1:22, Matt 7:24), to avoid the dilemma of serving both God and the world (Jas 4:4, Matt 6:24), to refrain from investing our lives in moth- and rust-prone treasures (Jas 5:2–3, Matt 6:19–21), and to follow the example of the prophets when facing persecution (Jas 5:10, Matt 5:11–12). When James asks in 2:5, "Has not God chosen the poor in the world to be rich in faith and heirs of the reign that God has promised?," the background to his question seems to be the two macarisms in Matthew about the reign of heaven belonging to the poor and the meek inheriting the earth. (Matt 5:3,5). Richard Bauckham sums up these wisdom parallels between the Epistle of James and the teachings of Jesus: "We can see James as a sage who has made the wisdom of Jesus his own. He does not repeat it; he is inspired by it. He creates his own wise sayings, sometimes as equivalents of the specific sayings of Jesus, sometimes inspired by several sayings, sometimes incapsulating the theme of many sayings, sometimes based on points of contact between Jesus' sayings and other Jewish wisdom."[8]

Bauckham also mentions the negative image of these parallels between the Epistle of James and the Sermon on the Mount—the *absence* in both documents of certain themes and topics found in other wisdom literature. Neither text, for example, dwells on such typical wisdom topics as how to avoid suffering, why we should work hard and earn our own livings, what the difference is between good and bad wives, how we should bring up children properly and manage marriageable daughters, or why we should treat slaves fairly.

---

8. Bauckham, *James*, 82–3.

THE FAMILY OF JESUS

James was the brother of Jesus—along with, as we noted earlier, Joseph, Simon, and Judas. But what does "brother" mean? Discussions about the meaning of this word are often steered by theologies. Some interpreters argue that these were Jesus's full brothers, the sons of Mary and Joseph. The view found most often in the critical literature is that James and the other brothers were sons of Joseph by a previous marriage and not physical sons of Mary. Since even this popular position can create theological static, some scholars have suggested that "brother" means "cousin" in the context of the Gospel of Matthew. Each of these positions has pros and cons. I'll assume in this book the middle position, that Jesus's brothers were his half brothers, but I don't have a strong preference. Anything I say based this assumption could easily be recast to fit other assumptions about the family relationship between James and Jesus.

James was not the only relative of Jesus linked to the churches in Judea and Galilee. After James died in the 60s, leadership of the Jerusalem church devolved, according to the fourth-century church historian Eusebius, to Simeon/Symeon, the son of Clopas. This Clopas, according to Eusebius's source, the second-century writer Hegesippus, was a brother of Joseph, making Simeon a first cousin of James.[9] Simeon remained head of the church in Jerusalem for thirty years or more, finally dying a martyr's death under the emperor Trajan. Another Hegesippus passage, also reported by Eusebius, mentions more relatives of Jesus. The grandchildren of Jesus's brother Judas, he says, were haled before the Emperor Domitian, who examined them and let them go, judging them to be simple farmers and no threat to his rule. After the release of these grandchildren, says Hegesippus, they "ruled the church,"[10] presumably assuming authority after the death of Simeon. This could take us up to the Bar Kokhba revolt of 132 CE, which would mean that relatives of Jesus may have guided the Jerusalem church for almost a century.

Simeon the cousin and Judas's grandchildren are known from Eusebius, an extra-biblical source, but other relatives of Jesus appear in the gospels. Besides Mary and Joseph, we hear about a sister of Mary. She is mentioned in the Gospel of John in a list of women standing near the cross during Jesus's crucifixion (19:25). We could also include in the wider family of Jesus both John the Baptist and his mother Elizabeth—in

9. Eusebius, *Hist.* 3.11.
10. Eusebius, *Hist.* 3.20.

birth narratives of Luke, the angel who announces Jesus's miraculous conception to his mother Mary says that John the Baptist's mother, Elizabeth, was Mary's kin (1:36). There are also relatives of Jesus named in the two genealogies of Jesus in Matthew and Luke. Some of Jesus's relatives, though, are mentioned but unnamed in the gospels. When the twelve-year-old Jesus was left behind in Jerusalem after his parents started home, Mary and Joseph, says Luke, "looked for him among their kin" who were traveling with them (2:44). Another relative of Jesus may be the person who was married in the village of Cana when Jesus turned the water into wine in the Gospel of John (2:1–12). The evangelist says that Mary was at the wedding—she seems to have had some administrative role in the wedding feast—and that Jesus and his disciples had also been invited. Scholars have speculated that the bridegroom may have been one of Jesus's four brothers.

Outside of the gospels, in the other documents of the NT, we find a few more references to Jesus's kin. Acts says that after the ascension of Jesus, the eleven remaining disciples returned to the "upstairs chambers" where they were staying and devoted themselves to prayer, along with Mary and the other women followers of Jesus "and with his brothers" (1:14). In 1 Corinthians, Paul argues for the right of an apostle to have a Christian sister as wife, just like "the rest of the apostles and the brothers of the Lord" (9:5). A clutch of Jesus's brothers and perhaps other close relations, it would appear, remained a definable group long after the crucifixion. It was from this group that the Judean churches sought leaders.

We should also note that the short letter of Jude claims to have been penned by "Jude, a servant of Jesus Christ and brother of James" (1:1). Whether this letter was really written by a brother of Christ has been widely debated. Unlike the Epistle of James, the Epistle of Jude is not a wisdom document. The person who wrote it had an apocalyptic bent and strong connections to the wider Essene traditions that took inspiration from the *Book of Enoch*. There is, however, reason to believe that the relatives of Jesus were part of a group with an eschatological orientation (more on this later), so it is at least possible that the Epistle of Jude is another family-of-Jesus document.

A few decades ago, scholars of the Bible competed to find kinship connections between Jesus and other people mentioned in the NT. Well over a hundred named characters play roles in the NT and perhaps twenty of these have been proposed, at one time or another, as relatives of Jesus. Several of the twelve disciples, for example, have been included among his relatives, mostly by linkage through a string of similar names. Again, this topic is too tenuous and complex to pursue here.

Families can have family quarrels, and there are indications in the gospels of some friction between the mature Jesus and his close relatives. One incident, recorded in all three Synoptic Gospels, has Jesus's mother and brothers standing outside of a crowd gathered around Jesus.[11] When Jesus hears that his family wants to speak with him, he says to the crowd, "Who is my mother and who are my brothers?" He sweeps his hand over his disciples and says, "Behold my mother and my brothers. For whoever does the will of my heavenly Father, that one is my brother and sister and mother" (Matt 12:48–50).

In another family incident reported in John 7:1–10, Jesus travels around Galilee, avoiding Judea because authorities there were plotting to kill him. The Feast of Tabernacles arrives, a time when Jesus's family would normally make the pilgrimage from Galilee to Jerusalem. Jesus decides not to make the trip. His brothers encourage him to join them. To shame him into going, they accuse him of inconsistency, of wanting to play the public figure but not being willing to expose himself to the public. In an aside, the evangelist adds, "not even his brothers always believed in him."[12] In the reply to his brothers, Jesus contrasts his situation with theirs. They could safely travel to Judea because people didn't hate them, but his case was different. The religious authorities in Judea hated him because he spoke to them about their sins (implying, of course, that his brothers were *not* speaking the truth to power in the same way that he was). He would not, Jesus told them, be going to Jerusalem for the feast. After his family left for the pilgrimage, however, Jesus, perhaps stung by his family's criticism, went to the celebration in Jerusalem. And, as he had feared, the authorities there attempted to arrest him.

The behavior of Jesus's family after his death and resurrection contrasts with their earlier expressions of distance and distrust. The brothers become part of the movement that Jesus had launched and take on leadership roles in the new community. We should perhaps not read too much into his family's about-face. The same thing, after all, happens to

---

11. Mark expands this discourse, adding a house for the family to stand outside of and making the house so crowded that his family was moved to say, "He is out of his mind" (Mark 3:20–21, 31–35). Luke's version of the incident softens the sting of Jesus's response by leaving out Jesus's lead-in question about who his true family is (Luke 8:19–21).

12. I'm translating the imperfect of *pisteuō* as a habitual imperfect.

Jesus's disciples. Peter and the other disciples may have made earlier and stronger professions of belief in Jesus than his family did, but when put to the test at Jesus's trial and execution, the reactions of the disciples revealed a hidden ambivalence. For both his family and his followers, the post-resurrection appearances would shore up their wavering faith.[13]

13. Paul reports that the resurrected Jesus, after appearing to the twelve disciples, revealed himself to "more than five hundred brothers and sisters at once." Next, he "was observed by James, then all the apostles" (1 Cor 15:6–7). In the abbreviated post-resurrection passages that we find in Matthew, Jesus appears to only Mary Magdalene and one other woman on the day of resurrection. He instructs them to tell the disciples to go to Galilee, where they will see him (28:10). It seems possible, then, that many of these "five hundred" mentioned by Paul were Galileans and would have included, besides James, many members of Jesus's extended family and clan.

6

Nazoreans and Therapeutae

Discovering wisdom themes in the early layers of the Gospel of Matthew and in the Epistle of James, as we did in the previous two chapters, shows that rivulets of the wisdom traditions in the Tanak and the deuterocanonical writings flowed into Christian Judaism. Jesus, I have suggested, envisioned aspects of his own ministry in sapiential terms. He set up a wisdom school and gathered students to learn and distribute its wisdom principles. Jesus's understanding of his own role was probably influenced by his identification with Person Wisdom—a topic we will take up in more detail the next chapter.

This immersion in the wisdom tradition could have been an innovation introduced by Jesus, based on his own study of wisdom teachings. Finding wisdom content in the Epistle of James, however, makes us reconsider the sources of wisdom in Christian Judaism. Might Jesus have grown up in a family with a connection to wisdom traditions?

Sunday school lessons tend to present Joseph, Jesus's father, as a simple builder in wood and stone. It seems unlikely, though, that most of the sons of a rural rustic would end up playing roles in public ministry. Was Joseph's occupation really the focus of his life? As Bryan Wilson once noted, members of sects are typically identified by their sect allegiance—it becomes "the most important thing" about them.[1] Building a picture of Joseph from his occupation perhaps represents a bias of secular, capitalist societies—what you do for a living becomes who you are. In Joseph's own

---

1. Wilson, *Religious Sects*, 29.

eyes, his religious and sectarian allegiances could have been a large part of his self-identification.

Philo tells us that some groups of Essenes, in order to maintain their sectarian values, chose to live in small villages, avoiding larger population centers.[2] Some of these rural Essenes were farmers, others were artisans. They practiced a kind of voluntary poverty, bringing their wages into a common coffer and treating much of what they owned as communal property. These laboring Essenes must have moved into remote areas of Judea and Galilee together, since they met regularly on the sabbath for reading and discussion. We could envision Joseph belonging to a society of this sort. Not an Essene group, but one that, like the Essenes, fed on discontent with centralized authority and sought refuge in the smaller villages of Judea and Galilee. Unlike the Essenes, Joseph's group may have had a strong focus on historical wisdom traditions, but in other respects, his group may not have been all that different. The apocalyptic doctrines that captivated the Essenes, for example, may have been part of the mix. Joseph would have trained his family, including his son Jesus, in the customs and beliefs of his group. The most fundamental vectors of Jesus's life and ministry may have been shaped by his father's sect.

In the rest of this book, I will trace this underlying community, sketching the sect (fourth web) and exploring how divisions within it might underlie differences found in historical documents (fifth web). This is perhaps a good time to emphasize that the imaginative component of historiography comes into full play here. The earlier webs, while part of the overall project, may not have seemed to depend as much on imagination—the ideas in them are similar to discussions that can be found in some branches of Jesus research. In these last webs, though, the dial of imagination is turned up. I present a framework that rethinks the meaning of certain NT and pseudepigraphic documents, and the way to do this, it seems to me, is to indulge in a speculative scenario around the life and ministry of Jesus that ties together the topics in the five webs. The best response I could hope for is that you will at least agree that it *could have happened* in the way I describe.

---

2. Philo, *Good Person* 12.75–87.

NAZOREANS

We may know a name—perhaps even three or four names—for the group that Joseph and his family belonged to. The phrase "Jesus of Nazareth" is found more than a dozen times in the gospels and Acts. Every evangelist makes use of it. Let's take one example—the story of Jesus's encounter with a blind man as he was entering Jericho. Luke 18 relates this healing miracle. The blind man, hearing the tumult of the crowd around Jesus, asks what is happening. The people tell him that "Jesus of Nazareth" is passing by (18:37). The expression in this passage that identifies Jesus is *Iēsous ho Nazōraios*. This could be rendered as "Jesus the Nazorean." *Nazōraios*, the adjective that occurs in almost all these examples of "Jesus of Nazareth," is formed by attaching a suffix to a proper noun. The Greek suffix can turn a place name into a modifier, similar to the way English uses the suffixes "an/ian" or "ite" to form "Chicagoan" from "Chicago" or "Seattleite" from "Seattle." If *Nazōraios* is built from a place name using this grammatical rule, then "Jesus of Nazareth" would not be a bad translation of the underlying phrase, and in some cases where the expression is used, the evangelists may have had exactly this in mind—that Jesus came from the city of Nazareth.

But was Jesus tagged with the name "Nazorean" in the days of his public ministry simply because he had once been a resident of Nazareth? While people in first-century Palestine with popular names were occasionally individuated with place-of-origin descriptors, the practice was far from common.[3] People were more typically differentiated by their family relationships ("son/daughter of," "wife of"). Setting apart Jesus from other persons named Jesus (Joshua) by attaching the name of a small town that few would have been familiar with seems like an odd choice. "Nazorean" may have some other meaning than "a person from Nazareth."

We find an example of "Nazorean" with a different meaning in Acts 24. In this chapter, Paul has been arrested by the Roman garrison

3. Two oft-cited examples of place-based names are the gospels' "Mary Magdalene" and Josephus's "John of Gischala." But these examples have problems. While Mary may have been from a town called "Magdala" and friends derived her name from it, this is far from certain. *Migdal* in Hebrew is a word for a tower—her name could have referred to any literal or metaphorical tower. See the discussion in Schrader and Taylor, "The Meaning of 'Magdalene.'" And John, though from the Galilean town of Gischala, is called "John from Gischala" only once in the text of Josephus, in Josephus, *Life* 44. Elsewhere in Josephus's works, he is known as the "son of Levi," as in Josephus, *Life* 10.

in Jerusalem to keep him from being murdered by a mob. He is sent to Felix, the Roman governor in Caesarea, for trial. Felix holds Paul until his accusers arrive, then begins the initial hearing. The accusers put forward a spokesperson—we might call him the public prosecutor—who indicts Paul for being an agitator and a "ringleader of the sect of the Nazoreans" (24:5). In this case, the prosecutor clearly does not mean that the whole sect is from Nazareth. The substantive "Nazorean" in this passage is shorthand for the name of a movement.[4]

There is a scenario that pulls together the "Nazorean" epithet with what we have noticed about the involvement of Jesus's family in the early church. Calling Jesus "the Nazorean" may have been a way of associating him, not with a town, but with a wisdom sect of Second Temple Judaism. I begin, now, to weave my fourth imaginative web—a picture of this Nazorean sect.

The Nazorean movement would have been relatively small, of course—no contemporary writer thought them worth discussing, at least under the name "Nazorean."[5] Suppose that certain members of this sect, like the Essenes, moved to places where they could live simple lives and gather to worship in their own synagogues. One center for this group might have been the area around the village of Nazareth. The name of the village, in fact, might have been borrowed from the name of the sect—we have no evidence that the name "Nazareth" was applied to the village before the days of Jesus.

4. Not only were the followers of Jesus widely known as "Nazoreans" in the earliest days of the movement, they would continue to be called this by non-Christian Jews and Arabs for many centuries. They are still called this, in certain contexts, by modern Arabic and Hebrew speakers. Long after Christianity became a gentile faith, a Palestinian sect of the church went on referring to themselves as "Nazoreans." Members of this group believed in Christ but continued to practice Jewish law. The sect would persist into the Middle Ages.

5. The fourth-century abbot Epiphanius, in his *Refutation of all Heresies* (the *Panarion*), has a lengthy discussion of Jewish and Christian factions. He mentions a Jewish group called the "Nasaraeans" (Epiphanius, *Pan.* 18). In his brief treatment of this Jewish group, Epiphanius says that they lived east of the Jordan River, did not accept all of the Mosaic legislation, and refused to eat meat or sacrifice it. He also mentions a Christian sect called the "Nazoraeans," which he seems to link with Philo's Therapeutae (Epiphanius, *Pan.* 29). How these two factions mentioned by Epiphanius are related to each other and how they are related to Mandaeans, a sect that persists to the current day in Iraq, has been a topic of extensive discussion. Epiphanius's uncritical use of sources makes it difficult to trust what he says. Because of this confusion, I won't attempt to connect the Nazoreans that I discuss in this book with Epiphanius's sects. The Mandaeans linkage presents the same problem—it is too laced with assumptions for a brief treatment.

We don't know where the name of the village or the sect might have come from, but speculation has centered on the significance of *netser*, a Hebrew word associated with Messianic belief. The textual source for this messianic theme is the section of Isaiah found in chapters 7–12. This section begins with the sign, promised by Isaiah to King Ahaz, about a young woman bearing a son and calling him *Immanu-el*, "God-with-us" (Isa 7:14–16). A bit later in the section, the prophet's attention turns to "the land of Zebulun and the land of Naphtali," the region that in the first century CE encompassed Galilee. "In the latter time," the writer of this section of Isaiah prophesies, God will "make glorious the way of the sea, the land beyond the Jordan, Galilee of the gentiles. The people who walked in darkness will see a great light; those who dwell in a land of shadows, light will shine on them" (9:1). A child is promised who will be a ruler and sit upon the throne of David, and the ruler's name will be "Wonderful Counsellor, Mighty God, Everlasting Father, the Prince of Peace" (9:6). Before his rule begins, however, destruction will come to these northern areas. The great trees of Lebanon will be cut down. Then, out of the destruction, "a shoot shall come out from the stem of Jesse, and a branch (*netser*) from its roots shall bear fruit" (11:1). The branch must refer to a messiah figure, since the text goes on to say, "And the spirit of the Lord will settle upon him, the spirit of wisdom (*hokhmah*) and understanding, the spirit of counsel and might, the spirit of knowledge and the fear of the lord" (11:2). This messianic figure will exercise authority, judging the poor with fairness. In the pursuit of this judgment, "he will strike the earth with the rod of his mouth and with the breath of his lips slay the wicked" (11:3–4).

We know that this section of Isaiah was significant in the early church. In Matthew 4, Jesus leaves Judea after his baptism and retreats to Galilee. This move happened, says the author of Matthew, "so that the word of Isaiah might be fulfilled." Matthew then quotes the Masoretic text of the Isaiah passage about light shining on the regions of Galilee (4:14–16). This fulfillment text is often treated as an after-the-fact application of a prophecy about Jesus, triggered by the rare mention of Jesus's native region in the Tanak prophets. But what if Jesus grew up in a community that handled this Isaiah passage in the same way that the Essene *pesher* commentaries treated Scripture? The Nazoreans might have read their own situation into the Isaiah prophecy. Part of the Nazorean sect might even have moved into Galilee in response to their interpretation of this prophecy and named their settlement "Nazareth" because they were the Nazoreans, the people of the branch, the *netser*.

This apocalyptic hope that the branch would appear in this Nazorean community could explain one of the more cryptic fulfillment statements in Matthew. In the birth narratives of this gospel, we hear nothing about Nazareth being the home of Joseph and Mary before Jesus was born. It is Luke's gospel that leaves us with the impression Joseph and Mary started out in Nazareth in Galilee, came to Bethlehem in Judea to take part in a census, then returned to Nazareth after Jesus was born. In Matthew's gospel, Joseph and Mary start out in Bethlehem. After Jesus's birth, the family takes to the road. They make a detour into Egypt to avoid Herod's pogrom. Once Herod is dead, the family returns from Egypt, but instead of settling in Bethlehem, they go to "the regions of Galilee." Joseph and his family, Matthew says, "went to dwell in a city called 'Nazareth' so that the word spoken through the prophets, 'He shall be called a Nazorean,' might be fulfilled" (2:22–23).

Spoken through the prophets? No verse in any of the OT prophets contains this sentence.[6] What, then, could Matthew be referring to when he mentions the prophecy that Jesus will be "called a Nazorean"? Many NT scholars suggest that the reference in Matthew is to a lost work. This seems to me the most likely explanation. If we couple this with the scenario that I have been developing about the Nazorean sect having its own *pesharim*, then the source of that statement might be a line in a commentary that the Nazoreans treated as Scripture. The line might be from an interpretation of the key Isaiah 7–12 passages that include the branch prophecy. This interpretation could have been recorded in more than one *pesher*. Note that Matthew says, "the word spoken through the prophets," in the plural. We are not just lacking one text that has this prophecy—we are lacking two, perhaps more. We don't know what these lost Nazorean

---

6. The nearest analogy to this prophecy, some maintain, is in Judges, in the story about the birth of Samson. Samson was born to a family who thought they could not have children. His birth was announced by an angel who says the child's head should never be shaved because "the boy will be a nazirite of God from the moment of birth" (Judg 13:5). Nazirites were people who took temporary vows to abstain from products of the vine and to not shave their hair. The process is outlined in the Mosaic code (Num 6:1–21) and expanded in the tractate *Nazir* of the Mishnah and Talmud. Samson was unusual in that he was assigned to be a *lifelong* nazirite. It is difficult to see how the Matthean prophecy, however, could be connected to this Samson story. In fact, the words *netser* and *nazir* do not even share all their consonants—the middle one is different, with a tsade in *netser* and a zayin in *nazir*. The gospels, moreover, never associate Jesus with nazirite vows.

pesharim might have said. The phrase, "He shall be called a Nazorean," however, could reflect the group's association of the branch prophecy with the references in this same section of Isaiah about a child who would become king. The Nazorean sect may have believed that God had chosen them as the vehicle to bring the future king into the world.

We perhaps have an echo of this sectarian expectation of the branch in John the Baptist's query to Jesus that we looked at earlier. John's disciples ask Jesus, "Are you 'the coming one,' or should we wait for someone else?" (11:3). The phrase used by John's disciples, "the coming one," may have been a sectarian shorthand for the branch, the Messiah predicted in the Nazorean interpretations of Isaiah 7–12. Readers of the NT sometimes assume that when people of that time and place used the word "Messiah," they tapped into a widely shared and specific concept, but this was not the case. There was no single job description for the Messiah—different groups expected different kinds of divine deliverers.[7] The impression that there was widespread agreement on what sort of Messiah was expected in first-century Israel has perhaps been skewed by the way that the specific messianic expectations of the Nazorean sect about the branch and the coming one worked their way into Christian texts.

John the Baptist's family lived in Judea (Luke 1:39–40). Jesus's family was in Judea when he was born. Members of the Nazorean movement, then, were probably not restricted to the Galilean villages around Nazareth. The Galilee contingent may even have been a group planted there to conform to their special interpretations of prophecy. When Joseph brought Mary and Jesus to Nazareth, he may have been joining or rejoining this planted community. First, though, Joseph and his family may have gone to Egypt. The author of Matthew seems to have been aware of Joseph's Egyptian sojourn and worked it into his narrative as a response to the political situation in Judea. Because Matthew also connects this information to a prophecy (Matt 2:14–15, "I have called my son from Egypt."), and because a trip all the way to Egypt seems like an implausible journey for a rural Jewish family, interpreters have tended to see this Egyptian stay as an invention, a trip fabricated to make a prophecy work.

---

7. "Literature produced by the Judean scribal elite rarely mentions a messiah. This is in sharp contrast to previous Christian understanding, according to which the Jews were eagerly expecting the Messiah to lead them against foreign rule. But as scholars finally began to recognize about forty years ago, there was no such job description just waiting for Jesus to fulfill" (Horsley, "Jesus Movements," 28).

As I noted earlier, though, connecting Israel's Egyptian sojourn with the prophecies about Jesus, as Matthew does, requires a special type of allegorical reading, and *pesharim* such as the ones found in Qumran have these symbolic interpretations. What kind of Nazorean *pesher*, though, would bring together Egypt and the birth of the expected Nazorean Messiah? One explanation for this might be an active Nazorean community in Egypt seeking to tie its existence into the Hebrew scriptures. The presence of a Nazorean group there makes it more plausible that Joseph would take his new family all the way to Egypt. If they had family or some kind of faith community (or both) in Egypt, Joseph and Mary might have sought refuge there from Herod's schemes.

PHILO'S THERAPEUTAE

We know of no Jewish community in Egypt calling itself "Nazorean." There is, however, a group that might be linked to this sect. Jews had a strong presence in Egypt during the Second Temple period. The Alexandrian Philo, the Jewish philosopher that we looked at earlier in connection with Essenes and with the development of the Person Wisdom mythology, estimates there may have been a million Jews there in the first century CE. And they had been there for some time—evidence of a Jewish settlement in Egypt goes back to the sixth century BCE. After the Egyptian city of Alexandria was founded in the wake of Alexander the Great's invasions, a large number of Jews settled in it. They became important players in Egyptian social and political life in the Hellenistic period. Synagogues were established in several of the districts of Northern Egypt and a Jewish temple was built in the Nile Delta that survived, Josephus tells us, for more than 200 years.[8] Political unrest in Judea in the first centuries BCE and CE also brought an influx of Jewish immigrants to Egypt.[9] Life for the Jews of Alexandria became difficult in the first century CE, however. Under Roman rule, which began in 30 BCE when Octavian defeated Mark Anthony, many Jews were stripped of their rights and lands. Some were murdered by mobs. Historians have referred to these events as "the first Holocaust."

8. The Egyptian temple is discussed in Josephus, *Ant.* 13:3.

9. "From the time of Philo onward through the first century, the unrest and disasters in Palestine influenced many Palestinians to make their way to Alexandria and Egypt for various reasons" (Kraft, "Multiform Jewish Heritage," 195). For evidence, Kraft points to documents in Tcherikover and Fuks, *Corpus Papyrorum Judaicarum*.

Philo was drawn into the political struggles of the first-century Egyptian colonies. Many of his writings were defenses of Jewish customs. This is probably the case with his passages on the Essenes. Philo held up this Palestinian society as an example of an *active* philosophical life among the Jewish people. For an example of what Philo called the *contemplative* philosophical life, Philo picked a Jewish group in his home city of Alexandria. He called them "Therapeutae."[10]

Philo is, unfortunately, our only contemporary source about this remarkable group. What he says has been filtered through his own agenda, and, as we can see with his account of the Essenes—for whom we do have other contemporary sources—Philo's filters can be distorting. Still, we can extract some items from his description of the Therapeutae that seem like they might have a basis in fact. While his reports on the Essenes may have been largely second-hand, what he says about the Therapeutae could be—judging from the detail of his account—first-hand reporting.

Communities of Therapeutae, says Philo, can be found "in many parts of the inhabited world,"[11] but the ones in Egypt were "superabundant," especially around Alexandria. The specific group that Philo describes occupied a low hill just above Lake Mareotis, a body of water near Alexandria and close to the Mediterranean Sea. The Therapeutae did not have communal quarters—each lived in a small, simply constructed house. Each house had a sacred room, a kind of hermitage, where the inhabitant went to meditate on "laws, oracles declared through prophets, hymns, and other [writings] which increase and perfect understanding and piety."[12] Those who had joined the group gave up their worldly

10. Philo's discussion of the Therapeutae is found in his *Contempl. Life*. Quotations in this section are taken from the translation of Joan Taylor in Taylor, *Jewish Women Philosophers*, 349–59. Her translation is based on the Greek text of Francis Henry Colson that was published in Loeb Classical Library 363:112–71. Philo uses the Greek terms *therapeutai* and *therapeutrides* for the male and female members of the group and *therapeutai* as the collective term. The word "Therapeutae," with the Latin "-ae" ending, has by long usage become the collective term in English, so I will employ that here. For the adjective, I use "Therapeutan."

11. The Philo passage about the geographic distribution of the Therapeutae can have more than one reading. I have understood it as saying that cells of this group were found in other places. Others interpret Philo to be saying that *like-minded* groups were found in other places. This is the point of view, for example, in Simon, *Jewish Sects*, 121–2. Later in his book, however, Simon talks about the Lake Mareotis settlement as the "mother house" and raises the possibility that branches of this foundation existed (Simon, *Jewish Sects*, 123).

12. The description of these writings may correspond to the three divisions of the Jewish Bible, the Torah, the Nevi'im, and the Ketuvim. To these received Scriptures, the

wealth, transferring it either to family or friends. In joining the community, they sought solitude, having left behind "brothers/sisters, children, wives, parents, numerous relations, friendly companions." The Therapeutan membership included both men and women. The women were for the most part "elderly virgins."

The members of the Therapeutae "pray twice every day, at sunrise and at sunset." During the day they "philosophize by reading the sacred writings and interpreting allegorically the ancestral philosophy." Some of them may have engaged in home-based trades.[13] They dedicated themselves in their study to "the understanding and contemplation of the facts of Nature, according to the sacred instructions of the prophet Moses." The literal texts, they believed, were symbols from which an underlying meaning could be extracted. Their sacred texts, Philo notes, also included writings by the founders of the group. These founder texts were "models used [by the group] in order to imitate the methods of the practice [of allegorical interpretation]." Members also sang and composed "psalms and hymns to God in all kinds of metres and melodies."

This solitary study and prayer in their separate houses went on for six days of the week. On the seventh day, the Therapeutae met as a group, each person taking their assigned spots in the assembly and assuming prescribed postures. At this assembly, the senior members addressed the group with quiet, unornamented voices about the teachings of the society. Both men and women members attended the assemblies, separated by a wall left open at the top so that everyone in attendance could hear the speakers.

The Therapeutae were an ascetic sect and practiced strict self-control. During the day, Josephus claims, they did not eat or drink. Some of them, to focus on the teachings "supplied by Wisdom," took on three-day and even six-day fasts. When they did eat, the food was simple, plain bread seasoned with salt and sometimes with hyssop, and their drink was water. They took only enough food and water at their meals to satisfy

---

Therapeutae added "other" writings, probably their own inspired *pesharim*.

13. Philo explains how the Essenes worked at menial trades and brought their incomes together. He does not emphasize this in his description of the Therapeutae, perhaps because the Essenes were examples of the active life and the Therapeutae were his examples of the contemplative life. However, it is hard to see how the Therapeutae could have acquired the means of life unless some of them worked. Philo seems to admit this practical element at the end of his description of this group when he says that after their all-night celebration on the fiftieth day (or on Pentecost), they would go back to their own residences, "again to ply their trade and cultivate the use of philosophy."

their immediate hunger or thirst. Their clothing was also basic—a wool cloak in the winter and linen for the summer.

Philo describes at length a celebration—perhaps he attended one—that the Therapeutae held either every fiftieth day, on the sabbath of sabbaths, or at the annual Feast of Weeks (Pentecost).[14] The senior members wore white and reclined on rough couches, the men on one side and the women on the other. Those who were going to serve—not slaves or servants, but junior members of the society—stood at the ready behind the couches. The leading member of the group proceeded to interpret the sacred books of the group, speaking to both the diners and servers. The audience responded with scripted head and hand motions to indicate their assent and understanding. Everyone then applauded, and they moved into the musical phase of the celebration. Various members led out in songs, and the whole group joined on the choruses. The junior members then brought out the meal of bread, salt, and hyssop. After the sacred meal, everyone stood, and they formed themselves into two choirs, one of men and the other of women, each choir with its own leader. They sang hymns together, antiphonally and in harmony, men in the lower registers and women in the upper, "tapping time with hands and feet, engaging in procession, . . . and in the turns and counter-turns of choral dancing." The two choirs eventually merged. The festival went on until dawn, ending with a prayer while facing the rising sun.

The liturgy of the Therapeutae, Philo hints, had a focus on light and truth. In their daily morning prayers, he says, they asked for a "'fine day,' the 'fine day' being [that] their minds will be filled with a heavenly light." They also prayed that their souls would "follow the way of truth." In the overnight celebration that happened on the fiftieth day (or on Pentecost), they would face the rising sun in the morning and "pray for a 'bright day' and truth and clearness of reasoning."

Who, then, are these Therapeutae? Philo, in his attempt to reach a broad range of readers, strips them of many typically Jewish elements

14. The text of Philo can be understood in more than one way. The group may have had an assembly every fiftieth day, on the week of weeks, but the ceremony Philo describes is said to be on "the eve of the great special day which the number fifty has been assigned," so it may have been part of an annual Jewish feast. If so, we can guess which feast it was—the number fifty is associated with the Jewish festival of Shavuot, the Feast of Weeks, which occurred fifty days after Passover. It was often called "Pentecost" in Greek, using a cognate of the Greek word for "fifty." Possibly the Nazoreans/Therapeutae celebrated the Feast of Weeks, not Passover, as their most important annual event. The Essenes also seem to have centered their liturgical year around a covenant renewal ceremony at or near Pentecost (Wacholder, *The New Damascus Document*, 316-7).

and turns them into ethereal philosophers. It seems likely, though, that they were a Jewish sect and that they adhered to several Jewish customs and laws. One possibility is that the Therapeutae were a contemplative offshoot—near or distant—of the Essenes. Philo emphasizes, for example, that they read the scriptures "allegorically," the same description he attaches to Essene practices. They also, like the Essenes, included in their revered writings some of their own sectarian works. But Philo emphasizes the importance of wisdom to this group and de-emphasizes some of the communal aspects that he attributes to the Essenes. He also places them in different locales, the Essenes in Judea and Galilee, the Therapeutae in Egypt.

One popular theory about the identity of the Therapeutae can be ruled out. A tradition developed in the Christian churches of the second, third, and fourth centuries CE that the Egyptian group described by Philo was an early Christian group. The church historian Eusebius, who summarizes much of Philo's account of the Therapeutae in his history of the church, discovers many elements in the practices of the group—such as sacred meals, music, allegorical interpretation, and ascetic habits—that he associated with the church.[15] The timing, however, makes the Christian interpretation of the group impossible. The community Philo writes about was living in Egypt probably no later than the 40s CE, and the people in the community that he describes were not the founders of the society. Philo, who was a contemporary of Jesus and Paul and probably died by the early 50s CE, perhaps even earlier, shows no awareness in any of his other writings of John the Baptist, Jesus, or the early Christian Jewish sect.

It is possible that some link may exist between Philo's Therapeutae and the last of the OT wisdom books, the Wisdom of Solomon. This deuterocanonical text is generally thought to have been produced in Alexandria in the first century BCE, which puts it at the right place and time. Even if not composed by members of the Therapeutan community, it could have formed part of their curriculum of study. Certain phrasings and ideas in the Wisdom of Solomon stand in rough agreement with Therapeutan ideals outlined by Philo.[16]

---

15. Eusebius, *Hist.* 2.17.

16. In the initial chapters of the Wisdom of Solomon, the author singles out for a blessing "the barren woman, the undefiled" and the eunuch "whose hands have done no lawless deeds" (3:13–14). These sound like the two parts of the Therapeutan group that Philo mentions, the "elderly virgins" and the men who have left all family connections.

THE THERAPEUTAE AS NAZOREANS

In the last chapter, I set the stage for my fourth web of imaginative construction by assuming that the most wisdom-oriented book of the NT,
the Epistle of James, was written by a relative of Jesus. This suggested
that the wisdom themes we find in the Jesus stories, especially those in
the Gospel of Matthew, might have been derived—in part, at least—from
Jesus's home context. I then theorized that the unusual epithet applied
to Jesus in the gospels, "Jesus the Nazorean," might have pointed at his
family's connection to a Nazorean movement that had a presence in Galilee. One of the groups belonging to this movement was located in and
around the town of Nazareth, a village that may have taken its name from
its Nazorean founders. Nazoreans would have embodied, judging from
the Epistle of James and what the gospels say about Jesus, a first-century
wisdom tradition with a prophetic/apocalyptic focus. Like the Essenes,
the Nazoreans might have had their own inspired *pesharim*, writings that
linked Tanak prophecies to their community's immediate experiences. In
particular, they may have understood Isaiah 7–12 as the promise that a
messiah-like figure would be born in Galilee to one of their members. The
prophecy in Isaiah 11 about a branch, a *netser*, arising out of the stem of
Jesse might have been the source of their self-designation as Nazoreans.
Finally, I raised the possibility that the Nazorean community might have
had cells, not just in Nazareth, but also in Judea and—based on Joseph's
Egyptian detour on the way from Judea to Nazareth—in Egypt.

And now the last strand in this gossamer fourth web—I wonder if
the Therapeutae described by the Alexandrian philosopher Philo might
have been an Egyptian cell of the Nazoreans. I base this guess on three
observations, the first about the name "Therapeutae," the second about
certain aspects of the Therapeutan beliefs and practices described by

---

The author of the Wisdom of Solomon says that the experience of the Israelites with the
desert manna teaches that "it is necessary to rise before the sun to give God thanks and
to pray to God at the dawning of the light" (16:28)—a practice of the Therapeutae. The
personified Wisdom in later chapters of the Wisdom of Solomon "teaches self-control"
(8:7), a key virtue of the Therapeutae. The phrase, "I shall find rest with Wisdom when I
enter my house" (8:16) would have resonated with group members. The image of light,
important to the Therapeutae, is invoked several times in the Wisdom of Solomon. And
the retelling of Pentateuch stories in the second half of the Wisdom of Solomon could
count as the allegorical interpretation that Philo attributes to the Therapeutan community. These are tenuous parallels, but they do raise the possibility of some connection
between the deuterocanonical book and the Therapeutae.

Philo, and the third on a passage in Acts that hints at an Alexandrian Jewish community.

Scholars have long puzzled over the name "Therapeutae." The word appears to derive from the Greek verb *therapeuō*, which has two meaning loci. One locus is medical. The verb means to heal or to treat for disease. We are familiar with this meaning of *therapeuō* because English has derived words such as "therapy" and "therapeutic" from it. The word *therapeuō* with this meaning can be found in the texts of many of the NT healings performed by Jesus. The other meaning of *therapeuō* is cultic. It refers to providing service to a god. The NT uses this meaning for the verb *therapeuō* in only one place, in Acts 17:25. Paul is at the Areopagus in Athens, speaking to Athenians about Jesus, and when he says that God "is not served by human hands," the verb is an inflection of *therapeuō*. The cultic sense of *therapeuō*, so rare in the NT, was much more familiar to Philo—he uses it numerous times in his writings. At the beginning of his discussion of the Therapeutae, Philo himself puzzles over which of the two meaning loci lie behind the group's name. They may be called "Therapeutae," he says, "because they possess medical skill." Their skill to heal, though, was not a power over physical ailments, but a power over spiritual diseases such as pleasures, griefs, and fears. Or they may be called "Therapeutae," he says, because they "attend [as cultic servants] the Being who is better than Good, purer than a One, and older than a Monad."

The most likely source of the name "Therapeutae" is the Alexandria group's self-perceived role as servants of God. If this sense lies behind the group's name, then we have a possible connection to the Nazoreans. The members of the Jewish group may have referred to themselves as "Nazoreans," but they were in Egypt, living in a Greek-speaking community, and a Hebrew-derived name would not have meant anything to the people around them. The background of the Semitic "Nazorean," however, might have led them to adopt the Hellenistic name "Therapeutae" when they were in Alexandria. The prophecy about the branch, the *netser*, that would arise from the cut-off stem of Jesse, is found in the messianic prophecies of Isaiah 7–12 that refer to a coming child. Later in Isaiah, we find another clump of messianic passages, the Servant Songs, called this because the messianic figure in the songs is referred to as "my servant." One of these Servant Songs, the one that begins at Isaiah 52:13 ("See, my servant will act wisely"), is the one we looked at earlier as a possible wisdom passage. In the servant song of Isaiah 52–53, the prophet invokes an image that is like the one found in the *netser* passage. The servant, the song says, "grew like a shoot" in the presence of God, and "like a root from dry ground" (53:2).[17] Immediately following this servant song, Isaiah announces the gathering of the scattered children of Israel, their restitution to God's favor, and the failure of Israel's enemies. The passage ends, "This is the inheritance of the servants of the Lord" (54:17). The Septuagint (which is, recall, an Alexandrian initiative) changes the Hebrew noun "servants" into a verb and renders the line as "This is the inheritance of those who serve the Lord." The root verb of "those who serve the Lord" is *therapeuō*. For anyone reading the Hebrew scriptures in Hellenistic Greek, this verse would stand out, since *therapeuō* is not a common verb in the Septuagint—the word is used only twice in the medical sense (in the history books) and a half-dozen times in the cultic sense. An Alexandrian plantation of Nazoreans, living in a Greek city and thinking about themselves as the servants of God who would welcome the messianic figure of the Servant Songs, might have seized on *therapeuō*, being a servant of God, as the best word to describe their group. It defined not only their role as devotees, but also their eschatological role in ushering in a messiah that God called "my servant." They were the Therapeutae, both the servants of God and source of God's servant.[18]

Philo's description of the beliefs and practices of the Therapeutae also resonates with aspects of the surmised Nazorean movement. I'll review eight of these possible connections.

First, the Therapeutae operate in a *wisdom context*. Philo uses the word "wisdom" several times in his description of the Therapeutae. Members of the group practiced meditation and sought to understand "the facts of Nature." This chimes with the wisdom emphasis that we have associated with the Nazoreans.

The Nazoreans, however, seem to have had an apocalyptic overlay to their wisdom beliefs. If this overlay was part of Therapeutan beliefs, Philo does not tell us. I can think of two reasons why we hear nothing about Therapeutan apocalypticism. The first is that this was an important element of Therapeutan belief, but it was intentionally omitted by Philo. In his description of the Essenes, for example, Philo also overlooks the apocalyptic framework that we found in Essenes *pesharim* and elsewhere.

---

17. The word "shoot" in Isaiah 53:2 is not *netser* but a Hebrew synonym, *yoneq*.

18. See the section in the Appendixes on "The Nazorean Suffering Servant."

Commenting on Philo's treatment of the Essenes, the French theologian Jean Daniélou says that, while Philo "is not unaware of the notion of an eschatological judgment," it is "foreign to his thought: his ideal is inner." As a result, Philo "deliberately sets aside the whole eschatological component" of Essene belief, retaining "only its moral characteristics."[19] He may have censored his treatment of the Therapeutae in the same way. A second reason that Philo does not mention this aspect of Therapeutan belief may be that the Therapeutan group he encountered did not have a strong apocalyptic orientation. In the next chapter, I look more closely at the issue of whether there might have been different kinds of Nazorean sectarians.

Second, the Therapeutae and the Nazoreans were both *ascetic communities*. The Therapeutae included in their ascetic portfolio such practices as hermetic isolation, fasting, vigils, and assigned times for prayer and meditation on their Scriptures. They rejected physical comforts and abstained from wine, from fancy dishes, from luxurious clothes, and probably from meat. They renounced family ties and created bonds within their countercultural community. This strong strain of asceticism in the Therapeutae helped to persuade Eusebius that they were a Christian group—Christians in Eusebius's day were caught up in the fourth-century CE waves of ascetic monasticism.

The three figures we can most easily associate with the Nazoreans—Jesus, James, and John the Baptist—were also notable ascetics. John the Baptist, says Matthew, "had a garment made from the hair of a camel and a belt made from leather around his waist, and his food was locusts and wild honey" (3:4). He carried out his ministry in a semi-desert area and may even have spent part of his early life there (Luke 1:80). James, the brother of Jesus, gives advice in his epistle that could flow from ascetic habits. He warns against seeking too much luxury, discriminating based on apparel, and accumulating wealth. Traditions of the second century CE emphasized James's ascetic habits.[20] They tell us that James abjured alcohol and meat, refused to cut his hair, would not wear wool, and seldom bathed. He spent so much time kneeling in prayer that his knees became as calloused as those of a camel.

Jesus, like his brother James, was also an ascetic.[21] He renounced wealth and asked his disciples to do the same. They kept the money they

---

19. Daniélou, *Philo of Alexandria*, 34.

20. Reported by Hegesippus, as cited in Eusebius, *Hist.* 2.23.

21. See the arguments for this in Joseph, "The Ascetic Jesus."

were given in a common pot. Jesus valued his community of faith over those of blood and family and spent regular periods in meditation and prayer. When he sent his disciples out on ministries, Jesus told them to take only a single garment, not to carry purses and staffs, and to beg food as they went (Matt 10:9–10). These are features of ascetic movements. Jesus's asceticism is sometimes questioned because he did not encourage strict fasting. He shows up at several banquets, for example, and sometimes provides abundant food to his audiences. The disciples of John questioned Jesus's lax attitudes on this topic (Matt 9:14). This criticism, however, whether coming from modern critics or from Jesus's contemporaries, says little about Jesus as an ascetic. It assumes—wrongly—that every ascetic followed an essential subset of ascetic practices. John's disciples were not asking why Jesus was not an ascetic. They were asking why their two ascetic groups, Jesus's disciples and John's disciples, did not share the same portfolio of practices. And Jesus's answer to John's disciples, that his own role as the chosen one, the bridegroom, suspended the rules of fasting for his followers (Matt 9:15), was the exception that proves the rule—Jesus would not have had to explain his innovations unless there was a standard practice that was being changed. It seems likely that the main body of Nazoreans did include severe fasting in their ascetic portfolio, just as the Therapeutae did.

Third, the *themes of light and truth* that Philo associates with the prayers of the Therapeutae are found in the key Isaiah section that includes the *netser* prophecy of the Nazoreans. As noted earlier, Isaiah says that the people of Galilee "will see a great light; those who dwell in a land of shadows, light will shine on them" (9:1). This prophecy and the *pesher* teachings about it could have given rise to the light imagery that Philo notes in the Therapeutae prayers. This same imagery—light shining on those living in the shadow of death—occurs in the Benedictus, the prophecy attributed to the father of the Nazorean John the Baptist (Luke 1:67–79). Both hymns in Luke 1, the Magnificat and Benedictus, could be hymns that the author of Luke assembled from Nazorean sources.[22]

---

22. Philo reports that the Therapeutae composed "psalms and hymns to God in all kinds of metres and melodies." This was also a custom among the Essenes, as we can see from the *Hodayot*, the collection of Essene psalms. Judging from syntax and style, the Benedictus and Magnificat in Luke derive from Hebrew/Aramaic sources. (See, for example, the study of Magnificat passages in Méndez, "Semitic Poetic Techniques.") The similarity between the Aramaic Apocalypse (4Q246) from Qumran and some phrases in the Magnificat has also been widely noted.

Truth is also mentioned in the branch passages. The *netser* prophecy in Isaiah 11 goes on to say about the expected branch that "the spirit of the lord will rest upon him, the spirit of wisdom (*hokhmah*) and understanding, the spirit of counsel and might, the spirit of knowledge and the fear of the lord" (11:2). The branch will not make decisions based on outward show but will push beneath this to the truth, allowing him to "judge with fairness the poor of the earth" (11:4).

Fourth, the fact that the Therapeutae community *included both men and women* as full members is notable. Groups such as the Essenes may have had a few women, but what we know about them suggests that the Essenes were mostly monastic communities of men. In the late Second Temple period, there are almost no examples from the eastern Mediterranean area of groups that had roles for women that included study, prayer, or participation in the life of the mind. The Therapeutae and the Jesus movement stand out in this regard. As has been often noted, women appear to have had important roles among the followers of Jesus. They listen to his teaching and participate in aspects of the ministry. We hear little about group worship and prayer in the Jesus movement, but it isn't hard to imagine the women in Jesus's entourage being present at these times.[23]

The phrase "elderly virgins" in the Therapeutan community reminds us that women (widows, usually) and prayer are conjoined in the gospel stories, especially in the Gospel of Luke. There is, for example, the widow Anna who prays in the temple day and night and recognizes the importance of the child Jesus (Luke 2:36–38). Perhaps she and the elderly Simeon who was in the temple at the same time were members of the Nazorean sect.[24] In a later part of Luke, we find the parable of Jesus about a widow who pesters the judge until she finally gets his attention. This story is an example, says the gospel, of "the chosen ones" who cry to God

23. At the last supper, says Matthew in 26:30, those present "sang a hymn." Did the women disciples who were present carry the high parts when the community sang together on that last night of Jesus's life?

24. Simeon is said to be "righteous and pious, awaiting the consolation of Israel" (Luke 2:25), which may be a way of associating him with the lifestyle and the messianic prophecies of the Nazoreans. We tend to think of Anna and Simeon as accidently encountering the baby Jesus and his parents in the temple precincts, but Joseph and Mary may have sought out Jerusalem members of their sect on their visit. Anna's words to the baby are not quoted, but Simeon's blessing is revealing. He refers to himself as a "servant," and "servants" is a possible meaning of "Therapeutae." He also calls the child "a light" of revelation (2:32), picking up the light theme included in Therapeutan prayers and perhaps echoing the key Nazorean section of Isaiah about the Messiah being a light to the gentiles.

"day and night" (18:7). Perhaps Jesus was thinking about the important role of Nazorean widows in their community worship when he told this parable.

Fifth, the Therapeutae, like the Essenes, employed what Philo called an *"allegorical" interpretation of Scripture.* I have noted several times the way that the early Christian authors applied analogical readings to OT texts to make them relevant to the community. This was probably a feature of Nazorean hermeneutics that was taken up by the NT authors. We see in the teachings of Jesus a persistent attempt to push behind literal text and extract a symbolic meaning relevant to the lives of his followers and hearers.

Sixth, Philo discusses at length the way that the members of the Therapeutae, on entering the community, *abandon their wealth.* Jesus speaks often about how his own disciples must leave behind their concern for wealth and status to become part of his community. Acts mentions that in the early post-Pentecost church, "the multitude of those who believed were one in heart and soul and no one was claiming that anything of what they possessed was their own but that everything was held in common" (Acts 4:32).

Seventh, the Therapeutae, Philo says, had *a room dedicated to prayer* in each of their modest houses. Jesus says in the Sermon on the Mount that when you pray, you should not do it in public places. Instead, "you should go into your inner room and shut your door to pray to your Father" (Matt 6:6). Was Jesus passing along one of the Nazorean rules of life when he said this?

Eighth, Philo says that *cells of the Therapeutae could be found throughout the "inhabited world,"* probably meaning the countries around the eastern end of the Mediterranean. They were most abundant in Egypt, he says, but this may represent his Egyptian perspective. As we will see in upcoming chapters, Nazorean cells were not just located in Galilee—members of the sect had carried their message and lifestyle to other parts of the Roman Empire.

Of these eight parallels between Philo's Therapeutae and the Nazorean community, none are, taken alone, proof that Philo had encountered an Alexandrian cell of the Nazoreans. Taken together, though, they are suggestive. It is possible that Philo has given us a first-person (but slanted) record of the small Jewish sect that gave rise to Christian Judaism.

Finally, we find a possible linkage between Nazoreans and the Therapeutae in a passage from the Acts of the Apostles. The author of Acts, after describing Paul's second missionary journey, inserts a non-Pauline story: "A Jew named Apollos, a native Alexandrian and a learned person, arrived at Ephesus. He excelled in the Scriptures. This man had been instructed in the way of the Lord and was fervent in spirit. He was speaking and teaching accurately about what concerned Jesus, even though he was acquainted with only the baptism of John (18:25)." When Apollos was speaking in the Ephesian synagogue, Priscilla and Aquila, a missionary couple who had been part of Paul's team, heard him lecturing. They "took him in and explained to him the way of God more accurately" (18:26).

Apollos, Acts says, was from Alexandria and had been instructed in the "way of the Lord," presumably in Alexandria.[25] But what does "way of the Lord" refer to in this context? It can't be the Christian Jewish way—Apollos was acquainted with the teachings of John the Baptist, not those of Jesus. If we assume that Apollos was a member of the Therapeutan sect, and if we assume that the Therapeutae were Greek-speaking Nazoreans based in Alexandria, then that could explain how Apollos could have known about the exploits of John. As a Nazorean, Apollos would have been grounded in the messianic interpretations of the group. He might have known about John the Baptist's Judean mission to prepare the way for the Nazorean messiah. Apollos could then have had an "accurate" knowledge of what concerned the Messiah, as the author of Acts says, without having heard about Jesus. What Priscilla and Aquila would have communicated to Apollos was that the Messiah he was teaching about, the Messiah described in the Nazorean interpretations of Isaiah's prophecies, had already appeared. Apollos then goes to Achaia, says Acts, where he "forcefully and publicly refuted the Jews, demonstrating through the Scriptures that Jesus was the Messiah" (18:28).

In the next chapter of Acts, the author returns to Paul's peregrinations and mentions that Paul encountered about a dozen disciples in Ephesus that had been baptized with only John's baptism. They had not received (or even heard of) the work of the Holy Spirit in the Christian Jewish community (Acts 19:1–7). It is possible that these followers of John were a small cell of Nazoreans who had settled in Ephesus. Apollo may have been in Ephesus either as part of this settlement or as a visitor to this settlement.

25. The name "Apollos" was uncommon in the northern Mediterranean area because it was not a Greek name. It is Egyptian. (van de Weghe, "Name Recall," 98.)

THE NAZOREAN MESSAGE

I have placed the Jesus of the NT into context that will be new to some readers. In the web that I have woven, we see him growing up in a family with strong attachments to a sectarian form of Second Temple Judaism. His extended family has perhaps been a part of this movement for several generations. As the founding families of the Nazoreans multiplied and branched out, cells of this group could have been found in several of the villages and cities of Judea and Galilee by the beginning of the first century CE. Some Nazoreans perhaps emigrated to the Jewish diaspora, to Alexandria in the Nile Delta and to Ephesus in Asia Minor.

Jesus, born into one of the families of this sect, identifies with the beliefs and practices of this group. In his early years, he would not have drawn a hard line between his family and the group to which his family belonged. By the time that he reaches his early teens, however, he begins to interact as an individual with the group's beliefs. If, as some think, he was the youngest of Joseph's offspring, he may have been pulled into adult discussions of faith earlier than most of his cohorts. Luke tells us that when the twelve-year-old Jesus got lost on a family visit to the Jerusalem temple, Jesus spent his time interacting with experts on the Jewish faith. When his parents found him and complained about his insensitivity to their worries, he replied, "Did you not know that I had to be dealing with matters of my Father?" (2:49). Luke wants us to think that Jesus was taken up in the business of his heavenly Father—but these may also have been matters of interest to his human father.

As Jesus enters adulthood, he sorts out his relationship to the wider Jewish context. He explores how his own group relates to other Jewish groups, such as the Sadducees, Pharisees, and Essenes. The Nazorean theology and halakhah, at one time accepted by him as simple givens, start to merge in his mind into a larger system, one that defines itself against alternatives. Many details of this sectarian world view that Jesus inherited are lost to us, but we can guess at a few of the customs. The members of this movement would have interpreted standard Jewish practices through their wisdom-oriented filters. The cell that Jesus belonged was one that observed the major Jewish holidays, and its members made pilgrimages to the temple. At the same time, however, the group may have considered the temple culture corrupt and in need of overhaul.

Members of Jesus's sectarian group would have read the Jewish Scriptures in a way that made texts speak to their immediate conditions.

The movement's founders probably recorded some of these *pesher*-like interpretations, and their writings and oral traditions became patterns for further interpretations. Because of their attachment to Tanak prophecies and their conviction that they were living in the times when these prophecies were coming true, members of the group believed that they would have a special part in bringing about the promised Day of the Lord. They anticipated the appearance of a messiah figure, the branch, and may have believed that the branch would be born to one of the Nazorean families.

Did current events in Judea persuade some of the Nazorean groups in Judah that the Day of the Lord was at hand and that their Messiah would soon appear and start his reign? One of these Nazoreans, John the son of Zechariah, turned his belief into action. He started gathering around him people who wanted to be part of this new reign of God on earth and asked them to affirm their commitment through baptism and repentance. The physical rite of baptism that John employed, the source of which has long been a puzzle, may have been adapted from lustrations practiced by Judean Nazorean cells. John's moral demand for repentance could have been an extension of the Nazorean ethical and political outlook. John's way of wisdom, derived from his Nazorean upbringing, offered hope to people forced to the margin by other interpretations of Jewish halakhah.

People of all sorts were drawn to John. The crowds of people gathering around his Nazorean message caught the attention of Herod Antipas, the Tetrarch of the region where the Baptist's ministry was centered. Herod, fearing that John's followers might form the nucleus of a political uprising, had John arrested and imprisoned in the nearby fortress of Machaerus. Before John's arrest, however, another member of his sect, this one from a cell in Nazareth, visited John.

To understand how Jesus fits into this imaginative picture of the Nazoreans, however, we first need to visit the Gospel of John.

7

John the Nazorean

WE FOUND A PRIMITIVE Christian wisdom tradition scattered through the Gospel of Matthew. A similar wisdom tradition inspires the Epistle of James. Wisdom traditions, however, do not live in abstract spaces. They are halakhoth, not theologies. When we discussed the OT wisdom traditions in chapter 3, we searched for communities behind the ideas. The same impetus has led us, in our review of NT wisdom, to another community—a wisdom-oriented sect of Judaism shaping the ministry and message of Jesus.

Our final imaginative web will bring the Gospel of John into the wisdom picture. I do this with some trepidation. The placement of this gospel in the rise and spread of Christianity may be the most controversial topic in NT studies. The problems with the gospel began early. The lack of clear citations of the gospel in the late second century CE and the use of the gospel by one of the gnostic sects have convinced some scholars that the gospel had an uphill climb to the exalted position it finally attained in the doctrinal codifications of the fourth century CE.[1] In later church history, the Gospel of John settled into a supportive role, filling out—but not usually correcting—the story told in the Synoptics. In the nineteenth century, however, critical studies began to focus on the differences between John and the Synoptics.[2] Scholars came down hard

1. The devaluation of John in the second century, though widely assumed, rests on weak foundations. See the discussion in Hill, *The Johannine Corpus*.

2. Lists of these differences can be found in most commentaries on John. See, for example, the catalog of these differences in Puskas and Robbins, *The Conceptual Worlds*, 19–23.

on John. They banned it from studies of the early church and booted its composition into the second century CE. Only the Synoptic Gospels, it was believed, offered any hope (and that not much) of recovering the beliefs and practices of the first Christians. In recent decades, however, John has fared better.[3] We'll look, in a bit, at reasons why John has regained the trust of some of the critics.

JOHN FIRST?

When I was young and thinking about becoming an evangelical, I asked the pastor of the local evangelical church what parts of the Bible I should be reading. He suggested that I begin with the Gospel of John. Once I was introduced to the wider world of NT scholarship, I wondered why I had been directed to the Gospel of John as a starting point. Sending early inquirers into the Gospel of John seemed a bit like handing the *Republic* instead of the *Apology* to someone who wanted to get to know Plato. Or pointing a theological neophyte to the *Summa* of St. Thomas rather than to the *Confessions* of St. Augustine. John's controversial status and its weighty theological content argue for postponing its encounter to later in the Christian journey. While its vocabulary and sentence structure can make it feel like a simpler gospel—first-year courses in NT Greek often make use of John's texts—under the surface of the text lies an unplumbed depth. In his commentary on John, R.H. Lightfoot pointed out that the gospel was "hardly a book for children in the sense in which the Synoptic Gospels are suitable for, and can be largely understood by, the young." The apparent simplicity of the Gospel of John "may easily hide its maturity, profundity, and subtlety of thought."[4]

I found when I got to Moody that I was not alone in my early encounter with the Gospel of John. The advice to begin with this gospel was widespread in evangelical circles. As it still is—a few minutes on internet sites will show that nothing has changed since the sixties. What is it, then, that makes the Gospel of John, despite its inherent problems, a place for evangelicals to send inquirers and new Christians? I can think of two reasons for this practice. First, Evangelicalism places more emphasis on

3. See, for example, Charlesworth and Pruszinski, *Jesus Research*, which tries to sum up the work of the John, Jesus, and History Project at the Society of Biblical Literature meetings. The work of this project was published in the three volumes of Anderson, *John, Jesus, and History*.

4. Lightfoot, *St. John's Gospel*, 3–4.

believing that Jesus is divine. While almost all Christian groups recognize the divinity of Jesus in some form or fashion, evangelicals have turned personal belief in this doctrine into a rite of initiation, and the Gospel of John, more than any of the other gospels, draws attention to the divine nature of Jesus. His human side is pushed into the background. The Jesus that we see in the Gospel of John is aware of what people are thinking before they say it, knows exactly what is going to happen to him, and seems always to be in control. He has a philosophical certainty that he has come from God and is going to return to God.[5] If the goal is to see Jesus as God, the Gospel of John gets you there faster than the other gospels.

The second reason for recommending John may be the appeal of story. For the last two or three centuries, readers have been nourished on a banquet of written fiction, a trend that has been compounded by the turn toward visual media. When we are young, certain types of fiction appeal more than others. We like stories where the bad people lose, and the good ones win. But they must win for a reason—it isn't enough for the good ones to prevail by accident. They need to have some special power that gives them an edge. This longing for meaningful victory partly accounts, I think, for the appeal of superhero fiction to young minds. Any of the gospels could be read in this way, but John has—more than the other gospels—the feel of modern superhero fiction. In the Gospel of John, Jesus shows up at strategic times and bests his enemies in a series of complex engagements. In addition, the Gospel of John contains the strong narrative lines we find in fiction—the individual stories in the gospel are fewer in number than those in a Synoptic Gospel and are more developed, allowing us to enter more deeply into the lives of the characters.[6] The dramatic pacing of the gospel can at times have the lean of a good novel—we find ourselves anticipating, when John's stories begin, how Jesus's superpowers, his wisdom and insight, will turn the tables on his adversaries. In an age when the greatest sin a writer can commit is boring the reader, the author of John's gospel gets higher marks than other NT authors. If the cost of this engagement is a later suspicion that the gospel might be *only* fiction, it is a price that evangelicals are willing to pay.

5. Jesus's "sense of certitude in going back to the Father which pervades John's narrative might be compared to that of the philosophers who know that a part of them cannot be touched by death" (Doran, "Narratives of Noble Death," 387).

6. "It is not anachronistic to compare John's storytelling with twenty-first century fiction. . . . John's story enlists some of the tactics we see in contemporary fiction" (Stibbe, "Protagonist," 144).

ASSUMPTIONS AND OBJECTIONS

As always, you should be aware of the assumptions I'm making in this chapter. The main one is that *the Gospel of John is an eyewitness testimony to the life of Jesus.* The gospels of Mark and Luke are not eyewitness accounts—the authors are one or two steps removed from the first followers of Jesus. The Gospel of Matthew bears the name of a disciple and could be an eyewitness account. The disciple Matthew, though, was probably not the person who put the gospel into its final form, and we don't know what bits he may have contributed to what we know as the Gospel of Matthew. The Gospel of John, then, stands as our only eyewitness testimony. In this gospel, we hear the voice of a person with an intimate knowledge of the pre-resurrection Jesus.

Or we seem to. The gospel could, of course, be pseudepigraphy, a text written by someone pretending to be an immediate disciple of Jesus. And many scholars believe that this is exactly the case—that the gospel was composed not by an eyewitness, but by an author (or authors) who lived sixty or more years after the death of Jesus. This move effectively makes the gospel "off-limits for the historical quests for Jesus."[7]

While scholars have more than one reason for positing a late date, their conviction tends to be motivated by a single issue, and that issue is the high Christology of the gospel.[8] The Jesus of the Synoptics claims to have a unique relationship to God, but the claim is often made in an offhand manner. His divinity does not distort his humanity. Jesus's representation of his relationship to God in the Gospel of John, however, is insistent and unqualified. He says, for example, that "I and the Father are one" and that "the one who has seen me has seen the Father" (10:30 and 14:9).

This difference in the way the gospels represent Jesus's divinity is thought to be relevant to the dating of the texts. Social movements are often compared to the growth of individual minds. We start off as children dealing with a world of concrete objects and applying literal language to them. As we get older, we learn to handle abstract concepts and become more skilled at symbol and metaphor. Transferring this analogy to the rise of Christianity, we would expect to find less of this adult sophistication in early texts, more in later writings. And to some extent, this is true.

---

7. Anderson, "Prologue," 1.

8. "The Jesus who talks Christology is not the Jesus of Nazareth." The Synoptics "more faithfully represent the historical figure of Jesus as he was" (Smith, "John: A Source," 178).

Theological ideas can often be arranged along a sequence of sophistication and complexity. It is credible, for example, that Peter might have
confessed, "You are the Messiah, the Son of the living God" (Matt 16:16).
It would be startling, though, to hear on Peter's lips the words of the
fourth-century CE Nicene Creed, "We believe in one Lord Jesus Christ,
the Son of God, light of light, very God of very God, begotten not made,
consubstantial with the Father."

But does this analogy about the development of thought apply to
the dating of John? I don't think it does. Critics sometimes bring to the
study of NT documents a Galilean-peasant model of Jesus. They assume
that he was a rural rustic and that his movement started from scratch. As
we have seen in previous chapters, this was probably not the case. Jesus
may have inherited from his family and community a Jewish sectarian
point of view with a complex and sophisticated theology.[9] In the rest of
this chapter, I'll be looking at the Gospel of John from this perspective.
Whatever criteria we apply to the dating of this gospel, the level of theological development in the text does not offer much guidance.[10]

Critics have other reasons for doubting that the Gospel of John is
what it appears to be. Once theological development is taken off the table,
these other reasons don't seem very compelling. But they should be given
some weight. Let's consider two of the most common reasons: the issue of
narrative inconsistencies in John and the problem of John's relationship
to the Synoptics.

9. Daniel Boyarin rejects the idea that "low Christologies are 'Jewish' ones, while
high Christologies have come into Christianity from the Greek thought world." Instead,
the earliest versions of high Christology are best viewed as "emerging within a Jewish
religious context" (Daniel Boyarin, *The Jewish Gospels*, 54–5). For a systematic study of
how high Christological concepts were available to Jesus and his followers, see Bühner,
Messianic High Christology. Bühner points out that Second Temple messianism is "the
primary context even for the high Christologies found in the New Testament" (Bühner, *Messianic High Christology*, 5). As a result, we can no longer regard "the depiction
of Christ as divine" as "a 'Christian' innovation" (Bühner, *Messianic High Christology*,
200). The same sort of argument applies to the development of institutional complexity. We don't need to assume that Jesus and his followers developed a structure for the
young church from scratch. Jesus would have borrowed a way to organize his movement from his Nazorean background. John Bergsma comments, "The fact that many of
Jesus' followers were familiar with, or had been part of, 'new covenant communities' at
Qumran *or elsewhere* made possible the very rapid formation of the external structures
and practices of the early Church that we see reflected in Acts, the Epistles, and the
Apostolic Fathers" (Bergsma, *Jesus*, 204, emphasis mine).

10. For a review of how the perceived theological content in John shifted the esti-
mation of the gospel's historical worth, see James Charlesworth, "The Historical Jesus."

John's gospel contains several inconsistencies in the narrative line. These narrative breaks argue against the gospel being an eyewitness account. The prologue to the gospel introduces Jesus as the Logos (1:1), but the designation is dropped in the rest of the gospel. Passages in the text seem to be repeated, such as Jesus's claim to be the bread from heaven (6:35–50 and 6:51–58). The "second sign" in Galilee (4:54) is separated from the "first sign" (2:11), the changing of water into wine at Cana, by other events that are also called "signs" (2:23). Jesus is in Jerusalem throughout chapter 5 of John's gospel, but the beginning of chapter 6 has him crossing "to the other side of the Sea of Galilee" (6:1). At the end of the last supper, Jesus wraps up his remarks and says, "rise, let us go from here" (14:31), but he follows this command with three chapters of dialogue and discourse that seem to occur in the same setting. At this last supper, Jesus makes opaque remarks to the disciples about going away (dying), and Peter asks Jesus, "Where are you going?" (13:36), but in the same discourse, Jesus complains that "none of you ask me 'Where are you going?'" (16:5). Jesus's brothers encourage him to go to Judea and show his disciples there the miracles he has been performing in Galilee (7:3), but Jesus, by the time the brothers say this, has already been to Judea and performed miracles. In the third chapter of the gospel, John the Baptist's disciples seem to know nothing about Jesus's mission (3:25–26), even though the Baptist has already related to his disciples, in the first chapter (1:29–37), the essence of Jesus's mission. At the raising of Lazarus in chapter 11, Lazarus's sister Mary is described as the one who poured perfume on Jesus and wiped his feet with her hair (11:2), as though the story had already been told—but John doesn't get to the story until chapter 12. The Gospel of John appears to end at chapter 20 with a statement about the purpose of the gospel (20:30–31), but the text continues with another chapter that hints at the author's death (21:23).

Those wanting to retain a pure eyewitness narration for the Gospel of John have proposed explanations for each of these problems, and many of these scholars make good points, so it is hard to know just how seriously these breaks should be taken. Most scholars, however, solve these problems another way—they insert a not-overly-meticulous redactor (or redactors) into the composition process. I find myself leaning in this direction. But it is not necessary to thrust the gospel's composition to the end of the first century and remove all eyewitness value from it when admitting redaction. There are what might be called "heavy redaction" and "light redaction" approaches. Heavy redaction approaches ruled the

academic literature in the last decades of the twentieth century. Encouraged by the success of redaction criticism in the Synoptic Gospels, commentators began to describe detailed histories behind the text of John.
The problem with such reworkings, of course, is that we have no source
documents for these histories—all of them have to be reconstructed
from the text of John. These complex historiographic processes, moreover, lead to a final product that has a remarkable consistency in style
and vocabulary for a pieced-together document. The Johannine scholar
Pierson Parker commented, a bit tongue in cheek, "It looks as though,
if the author of the Fourth Gospel used documentary sources, he wrote
them all himself."[11] With the increasing influence of NT literary criticism,
which downplays the textual history of documents, efforts to describe the
construction of John's text seem to have fallen out of favor.[12]

I'll be taking a light redaction approach to the gospel. I think that,
except for the odd verse, the whole gospel was composed by the follower
of Jesus who refers to himself as "the disciple whom Jesus loved." This
authorship is documented in a signature line at the end of the gospel. The
writer of the line—either the beloved disciple or a redactor—says, "This
is the disciple who is testifying about these things and who wrote these
things" (21:24).[13] If the final verse of the gospel, which points out that
there are many things that Jesus did which could not be included (21:25),
came from the pen of the redactor, then we may have a clue how the narrative breaks occurred. The beloved disciple could have dictated or written, over a long life, many scrolls of stories about Jesus. After the death of
the evangelist, the task of the redactor was to select which of these stories
would fit on a single scroll. In selecting these, the redactor was hesitant
to make any changes to the text, with the result that the narrative breaks
introduced by the redactor's selection process were not smoothed over.[14]

11. Parker, "Two Editions of John," 304.

12. By 2009, one Johannine scholar could say, "Unending authorship theories together with attempts to isolate units of original source materials . . . have all but run into
dead ends" (Appold, "Jesus' Bethsaida Disciples," 28).

13. Since I think the touch of the redactor is light, I will take the liberty in this book
of using use the phrase "author of John" and "evangelist" to refer to the beloved disciple.
Other writers reserve these terms for the redactor.

14. Ben Witherington comments that the narrative breaks in John are "more easily
explained if a cautious editor who was not an eyewitness of these events was attempting
to put together in some sort of coherent order a collection of written . . . Johannine traditions . . . shortly after the death of the Beloved Disciple—an editor conservative enough
to leave in some of these small things without attempting to smooth out all the rough or
unexplained spots in the source material" (Witherington, John's Wisdom, 17–8).

Those who want to withhold eyewitness authority from the gospel lodge a further objection. The author of John, they maintain, seems to be having a conversation with the Synoptic Gospels and writes in response to them, both agreeing with them and disagreeing with them. This awareness of the Synoptics places the conversation at a later stage than what we find in the earliest synoptic passages.

What does it mean, though, that the author of John was aware of the Synoptics? Until the middle of the twentieth century, it was widely believed that John made literary use of the Synoptics. Scholarly opinion on this has since shifted, in small steps, to the view that the text of John, even in passages where the author narrates the same events chronicled in the Synoptics, is independent of the Synoptic line of textual transmission. "It is sufficient," the Johannine scholar Oscar Cullmann says, "to assume that the author knew the tradition underlying the Synoptic Gospels, without referring to the documents themselves." The author of the Gospel of John "will have known on the one hand a tradition common to all branches of early Christianity and made familiar to us through the Synoptic Gospels, and on the other a separate tradition, of special interest to us, which came down to him in the particular circle to which he belonged."[15]

I side with Cullmann and those who reject a direct literary dependence of John on the Synoptic Gospels. Recognizing the independence of John's account, however, does not make the author of John an eyewitness. If John's point of view on the Jesus traditions is still a reaction to what the synoptic authors published, even if no direct copying is involved, then the Gospel of John could still be late and derivative. Cullman, for example, though he rejects literary dependence, pushes the date of John to the end of the first century CE.[16]

So where on the transition timeline from Judaism to Christianity should we place the conversation between John and the Synoptics, assuming that there is one? It is easy enough to imagine, as critics do, the conversation taking place in the late first century CE. The Johannine circle would have had time to evolve an independent view of the events

15. Cullmann, *The Johannine Circle*, 6–7. Cullman's emphases omitted.

16. The problem with John being *both* late and derivative, of course, is that an author writing toward the end of the first century would almost certainly be aware of the Synoptic tradition. Such an ignorance, Craig Keener points out, "would be well-nigh impossible among late first century Christians" (Keener, "Historical Tradition," 155). If the redactor completed work on the Gospel of John at this late date, only a narrow focus on a single source—the scrolls left behind by the beloved disciple—could explain this lack of Synoptic awareness.

that had happened earlier in the first century. Less attention would have been focused, at a later date, on what Jesus said and did, more attention would have been given to what this meant for the existential problems faced by the Johannine circle. But what if the Johannine circle was, in a sense, pre-evolved? What if some of the differences between it and the other Christian traditions that led to the synoptic texts were borrowed from earlier sectarian differences? In this case, the conversation could have taken place much earlier—even, perhaps, before the Synoptic Gospels took their final shape. In the rest of this chapter, I'll be developing a point of view on John that takes this approach.

My goal here is to make you aware of my assumptions, not to argue for them. But let me mention three lines of evidence in favor of placing the conversation between John and Synoptics earlier than commonly thought. First, I have always puzzled why, if John were as late as some critics say, there is no clear indication that John knew any of the gospels as written sources. Not only do we fail to find explicit citations, we don't even see the author of John emphasizing disagreements with the Synoptics. His points of difference around the temple cleansing, the day of the crucifixion, the events at the last supper, and the trial (or lack of it) before the Sanhedrin would all have been a good excuse for soapbox rhetoric. We do not find such arguments in John.[17] Nor do we find arguments in the Synoptics against specific Johannine points. John and the progenitors of the Synoptic gospels, it seems to me, must have emerged from the same cauldron of events at about the same time. Which means than any argument drawing one of the Synoptics into an earlier time slot also pulls John with it.

Second, the Gospel of John, if written later than the Synoptics and after the destruction of Jerusalem in 70 CE, should contain fewer and less reliable details about the Jewish setting around the ministry of Jesus. Instead, we find *more* of these details in John. There are "more archaeological, topographical, and apparently historical materials in John," says Paul Anderson, "than in any other Gospel or even in all three combined."[18] And the details appear to be consistent with eyewitness reporting. We

---

17. "John seems to show little sign of a consistent anti-Synoptic agenda" (Matson, "Reviving," 141).

18. Anderson, "Aspects of Historicity," 587. Urban C. von Wahlde points out that there are thirteen topographical references unique to John and another seven references for which John provides information not found in the Synoptics (von Wahlde, "Archaeology").

can't confirm all of John's details, of course—for some we have no outside source—but those we can confirm appear to be accurate. What John says about the pool of Bethesda/Bethzatha (5:2–9) corresponds to archeological data.[19] John's Pool of Siloam (9:7), Portico of Solomon (10:23), and Jacob's Well (4:5–6) were real places. The information the author provides about the worship of the Samaritans (4:19–20) and the Feast of the Tabernacles (chapters 7 and 8) agree with what we find in other sources from the period. John's knowledge of the use of stone vessels to maintain cultic purity (2:6) is an offhand addition that a non-eyewitness could easily have got wrong.

Third, the tenor of the message in John is similar to that of the Synoptics. Critics who place John at the end of the first century CE tend to see it as an expression of a community that, as Michael Gorman notes, was "turned in on itself, a sect in survival mode, at odds with 'the world'—whether that world was non-believing Jews, and/or other Christians, and/or everyone." He formulates the message of the gospel, when seen in this perspective, as "Believe in Jesus so that you can have a personal encounter with God and join our sweet, holy huddle."[20] As Gorman notes, the message actually conveyed by the gospel does not fit well with this kind of social hunkering. Throughout the gospel, the author pictures the Son being sent from the Father and the Son in turn sending his disciples into the world (John 20:21, for example). The overall thrust is outward, inviting, and mission oriented. This is more consistent with an expansive stage in the community's development, not with a late-stage withdrawal into a sectarian shell.

THE AUTHOR OF THE GOSPEL.

If the Gospel of John is from the hand of an eyewitness and disciple, who is this eyewitness? The author does not give us a name—the self-description "the beloved disciple" is all that the text supplies. The earliest point of view was that the gospel's author was the John who was one of the original twelve disciples. The Synoptic Gospels have quite a bit to

19. "Bethzatha" is the preferred reading. On the meaning of the word, see Charlesworth, "Can Archaeology," 171–3.

20. Gorman, *Abide*, 31. Paul Anderson classifies this as a "two-level, history-and-theology approach" (Anderson, "Why the Gospel," 13, Anderson's emphasis removed). In this approach, the historical setting of the Johannine author and community at the time the gospel was written override the putative history in the story.

say about this John and his brother and fellow-disciple James. They were impetuous fellows—Jesus nicknamed them "sons of thunder."[21] Modern NT criticism, however, has favored other authorship candidates, and lots of them. In his book on the identity of the beloved disciple, James H. Charlesworth reviews more than a dozen credible authorial candidates.[22] Whoever he or she was, the beloved disciple was not, it seems to me, one of the twelve disciples. Beyond this, however, I'll hazard no guess. For the purposes of this book, it doesn't matter who the author was, as long as we accept that it was a disciple who knew Jesus.

The places where this unnamed disciple appears in the Gospel of John's narrative provide us with a sketchy biography of the author of the gospel. The first time we hear about this disciple is when Jesus comes to John the Baptist for baptism. A part of this passage (1:35–42) tells us that the Baptist, in the presence of two of his disciples, calls Jesus "the Lamb of God." The two disciples then follow Jesus and lodge with him. One of the two who switched from John to Jesus, says the passage, was Andrew, the brother of Simon Peter. The other, we can assume, was the beloved disciple.[23]

The subsequent stories about Jesus's ministry and miracles do not mention this disciple. The next place the disciple shows up in the gospel is the passion narrative. At the Last Supper, in the middle of Holy Week, the beloved disciple reclines next to Jesus at the table, a position that is a place of honor. When Jesus announces that someone at the table will betray him, Simon Peter passes a message to the beloved disciple to ask whom Jesus is talking about (13:21–30). The beloved disciple leans back against Jesus and poses the question privately. Jesus reveals who is the betrayer by using a table sign that only the questioner would understand. We do not learn whether Jesus's answer ever got passed back to Peter— the beloved disciple may have been the only one at the meal, besides

21. The picture of John the son of Zebedee developed in the Synoptic Gospels is at odds with his authorship of the Gospel of John. "How could the son of Zebedee . . . have omitted the calling of the Twelve, the transfiguration, the words of the institution, and the anguish of Jesus at Gethsemane, if he were indeed both present at those events *and* the traditional source of the Fourth Gospel?" (Paul N. Anderson, "Why This Study," 19, emphasis Anderson's).

22. Charlesworth, *The Beloved Disciple*, 225–87.

23. The first of these plausible self-references in the Gospel of John does not refer to the anonymous follower of John and Jesus as "the disciple that Jesus loved," perhaps because the claim would have been out of place at the disciple's initial encounter with Jesus.

Jesus and Judas, who knew which person at the table was the betrayer. The next time we see the beloved disciple may be later that night, at the start of Peter's three denials (18:15–16). We learn in this passage that the beloved disciple, if this is the one referred to in the text as "another" disciple,[24] travelled in the same circles as the high priest. The disciple's social connections allowed Peter to enter the compound where Jesus was being held. The beloved disciple next appears at the cross with Jesus's mother Mary and two or three other women. The dying Jesus hands his mother over to the care of the beloved disciple (19:25–27). After Jesus utters his last words and dies, the disciple, watching the Roman soldiers pierce Jesus's side with a spear, sees a flow of both blood and water from the wound.[25]

The beloved disciple puts in a final appearance in the resurrection and post-resurrection narratives. On the day of the resurrection, Mary Magdalene finds the tomb empty and hurries to tell Simon Peter and the beloved disciple. The two disciples run to the tomb. The beloved disciple arrives first, looks inside, sees the burial clothes, but does not enter the tomb. When Simon arrives, he enters the tomb. The beloved disciple then enters the tomb and "sees and believes" (20:1–9). In the last chapter of the gospel, the beloved disciple makes a final appearance. A group of seven disciples, including Simon Peter, Thomas, Nathanael, the brothers James and John, and two others, are fishing from a boat on the Sea of Galilee. Jesus arrives on the shore, but the disciples do not recognize him. He calls out to them and tells them where to cast their nets. When they end up with a great haul of fish, the beloved disciple realizes that it is Jesus on the shore. The disciple tells Peter, who rushes to meet Jesus. The others follow. In the ensuing dialogue between Jesus and his disciples, Jesus compels Simon Peter to relive the painful memories of his threefold denial by drawing out a threefold affirmation of Peter's love. This interaction ends with Jesus's prediction of Peter's martyrdom. Peter then asks about the beloved disciple and Jesus says, "if I desire this person to remain until I come, what is that to you?" (21:22). The last three verses, probably added

24. In John 20:2, the disciple "whom Jesus loved" is referred to as "the other disciple," using the same phrase as in 18:15 for the disciple who was known to the high priest. Both citations include the definite article.

25. At this point the text addresses the reader directly, saying, "And the one beholding this has borne witness and his witness is true, and that one knows that he tells the truth, so that you may believe" (19:35). I suspect that this is the voice of the redactor, but some argue that it is the voice of the author.

by the redactor, report a false rumor that the beloved disciple would not die before Jesus returned.

From these self-references in the text, we learn—and can surmise—some details about the author of the gospel.[26] The author was an early associate of John the Baptist, had connections in the highest circles of Jerusalem society, and was based in Judea rather than Galilee. The disciple was a follower of Jesus from the beginning to the end of the ministry, but probably not one of the twelve disciples mentioned in the Synoptics. Since the beloved disciple was the sort of person that could be entrusted with a mother who was going to lose both her son and perhaps her means of support, the author may have come from a family with significant wealth,[27] perhaps one with connections to Mary's family. Simon Peter, we notice, is almost always a part of the context whenever the beloved disciple is in view. Since Peter plays a secondary role in these encounters, the author of the Gospel of John claims an authority at least equal to that of Peter.

A TEACHER SENT FROM GOD

We can compile biographical details about the author of John from self-references in the text. By looking at what the beloved disciple writes about Jesus, we can gather ideas about the author's beliefs. The writer was a sage, an interpreter of a wisdom perspective, and he paints a picture of Jesus that reflects this. We see the reflection most clearly in two ways: how the author represents the teaching of Jesus and how the depicted Jesus assumes the role of incarnate Wisdom.

The teachings attributed to Jesus in Matthew, as we noted in chapter 4, place him in the line of Jewish wisdom instructors. The synoptic Jesus hands out practical ethical and religious advice to his followers. These

26. "The internal evidence suggests that the testimony enshrined in the Fourth Gospel is that of the Beloved Disciple, a Judean disciple who was an eyewitness of at least some of the ministry of Jesus, including at least the occasions when Jesus was in or near Jerusalem, especially during the closing weeks of Jesus' life. It is also very possible, but not certain, that this same disciple was originally a follower of John the Baptist" (Witherington, *John's Wisdom*, 16).

27. If the beloved disciple owned the house where the Last Supper took place, as I will later suggest, this is also an argument in favor of some measure of personal wealth. We could also imagine, however, that the beloved disciple, rather than being personally wealthy, may have been a member of a community that could command these resources.

admonitions resemble in content and form what we find in Proverbs and Sirach. To deliver this content, Jesus packages it in parables and other *mashal*-like devices. The purpose of Jesus's wisdom teaching, as we find it in the Synoptics, is to bring listeners into a right relationship with God and with each other. He prepares his listeners to be participants in a reign of heaven that is both a configuration of current society and a future intervention from a heavenly realm.

John's Jesus also traffics in wisdom-like aphorisms, but the settings of these aphorisms in John are quite different from the synoptic settings. His instruction in the Gospel of John, notes Sandra Schneiders, "is rife with techniques designed to destabilize the reader's conventional religious knowledge and commitments: double meanings, literal misunderstandings, irony, paradox, and dialectical tensions."[28] Jesus employs these destabilizing devices not so much to lead people to the God of the Tanak as to get people to see who *he* is. He brings to his listeners what he calls "eternal life." This expression, which fills the semantic slot of the Synoptics' "reign of heaven" (Matthew) and "reign of God" (Mark and Luke), feels more personal, less corporate. The author of John draws more heavily on themes in the OT wisdom books of Job, Ecclesiastes, and the Wisdom of Solomon[29] than on the Proverbs, Sirach, and Song of Songs[30] tradition favored by the Synoptics.

The Gospel of John, as we noted in the chapter on Matthew, contains almost nothing that we would call a synoptic parable. What the author of the gospel gives us in place of parables are vivid dialogues.[31] The

28. Schneiders, *Written*, 29.

29. A comparison between the Gospel of John and the Wisdom of Solomon can be found in Witherington, *Jesus the Sage*, 370–80. John and the Wisdom of Solomon have in common not only the Person Wisdom perspective in the first half of the deuterocanonical book but also the view of a Wisdom/Spirit presence in the story of Israel. For a comparison of the Gospel of John to Ecclesiastes, see Kashow, "Traces." The Gospel of John shares an epistemic tradition with Ecclesiastes, even though it comes to different conclusions about where this quest leads.

30. The Song of Songs may have been used by both the Johannine and Synoptic traditions. It is not directly quoted by anyone, but there are allusions to the book's vocabulary in the gospels, especially in the Synoptics. See the discussion in Tomson, "The Song of Songs."

31. While the contrast in teaching modalities between the Synoptics and John is stark, both are grounded in symbols and aphorisms. The appeal to aphorisms, tight packages of truth, is part of the sapiential tradition that lies behind all the Nazoreans. For a discussion of Jesus as aphorist, see Parsenios, "How and in What Ways," 89–90, the list of twenty-six aphorisms in Bridges, "The Aphorisms of Jesus," and the list of the hundred-plus aphorisms the appendix section of Aune, "Oral Tradition," 242–65.

dialogues follow a pattern. They begin with Jesus launching a metaphorical bolide. It explodes far over the heads of his interlocutors, who take
his symbolic language too literally. The ensuing dialogue makes use of
the tension between literal and metaphorical meanings to convey Jesus's
message. In the end, the person he is speaking to responds. In some of
the dialogues, people receive revelation and believe, in others they reject
his claims. This pattern occurs several times during the ministry of Jesus
described in the first half of John.

To see how this wisdom technique works, consider an early example
of the Johannine dialogue pattern, Jesus's encounter with Nicodemus. The
passage begins with the Pharisee Nicodemus coming to Jesus by night
(3:1–2).[32] Nicodemus starts the conversation by acknowledging Jesus's
miracles and his teaching role. Jesus pushes back against this attempt to
pigeonhole him as miracle worker and rabbi. He wants a different response, one that recognizes his role as God's representative. Only people
who are born "from above," Jesus tells Nicodemus, can hope to see the
reign of God. The word translated "from above" can also have the figura-
tive meaning, "anew, again." Nicodemus latches onto this latter sense and
asks, "How can a man who is old be born? He can't enter a second time
into his mother's womb and be born, can he?" (3:4). Nicodemus's confusion provides an opportunity for Jesus to discourse on the two orders of
existence, the order of the flesh and the order of the spirit, that provide
the tension in the metaphor (3:6). Jesus then adds a new metaphor, taken
perhaps from Ecclesiastes,[33] to explain how the order of the spirit can
exist alongside the order of the flesh and allow a person to be both old
and newly born. He employs a word, *pneuma*, which can mean either
"breath/wind" or "spirit," and says that "the *pneuma* blows where it wants
to, and you hear its sound, but you do not know where it comes from or
where it goes" (3:8). Nicodemus still doesn't get it, so Jesus turns to irony,
saying to him, "You are a teacher of Israel and don't know about these

32. Nicodemus is a Greek name that means "ruler of the people." But this is probably not a made-up name to indicate that Nicodemus could be any person of power.
The name Nicodemus was given to members of the first-century Gurions, a lay aristo-
cratic family of some renown. See the discussion in Bauckham, "Nicodemus."

33. The wind is cited by Qohelet at the beginning of Ecclesiastes as an example of
the continual cycles of nature. It goes where it wants. "Blowing to the south and turning around to the north, blowing round and round, the wind returns in its rounds"
(1:6). People cannot steer it. "No person has mastery over the wind, to control it" (8:8).
The author of Ecclesiastes uses *ruach*, the Hebrew equivalent of *pneuma*, to mean both
"wind" and "spirit."

things?" (3:10). He then draws the sort of analogy from the Tanak that he thinks Nicodemus, as an authority on the Jewish Scriptures, should have had in his own conceptual kit. "Just as Moses lifted up the serpent standard in the desert," Jesus says, "so it is necessary for the Son of Man to be lifted up, so that everyone who believes in him may have eternal life" (3:14–15).

Up to this point, the dialogue in John 3 has been pursued at a highly symbolic level. Jesus now eases up on the metaphors and describes the context in which the discussion has been taking place. God loved the world and sent the Son, Jesus tells Nicodemus, so that people might have eternal life (3:16). To enjoy this love and enter this life, people need to believe that Jesus is the source of this eternal life. Those who do not arrive at this conclusion are often deflected, Jesus points out, because they want to retain secrets that the light might reveal (3:19–21). The conversation ends here, with no response from Nicodemus, who was perhaps carrying secrets that he did not want to come out. Later in the gospel, we hear more about Nicodemus. When the Pharisees and chief priests are trying to arrest Jesus, Nicodemus pleas for a fair hearing (7:50–51). At the crucifixion, he helps Joseph of Arimathea, another undercover disciple from Jerusalem's ruling elite, to bury the body of Jesus. Nicodemus contributes a king's ransom in embalming spices and ointments (19:38–42). We can presume, then, that Nicodemus did finally number himself among those who believed Jesus was sent from God.

The dialogic pattern we see in Jesus's interaction with Nicodemus is reproduced several more times in the Gospel of John. It happens with the Samaritan woman at Jacob's Well (chapter 4), with the Jewish authorities who complain about Jesus healing on the Sabbath (chapter 5), with the people who are fed the loaves and fishes (chapter 6), in an argument with the Pharisees (chapter 8), in the case of the man born blind (chapter 10), and at the raising of Lazarus (chapter 11). If we step back and look at the flow of these individual dialogues, we see a *mashal* pattern that is just as distinctive as the parables in the Synoptics. Jesus plays the role of the teaching sage, and his interlocutors are the students. In struggling to follow the symbols laid out before them, they are knocked out of their comfortable world and become ready to hear—and accept or reject—the message of Jesus.

WISDOM INCARNATE

The second linkage between the author of John and the wisdom tradition is found in the way that Jesus is presented as Person Wisdom. We found a few hints of this in the Gospel of Matthew. We couldn't be certain, though, whether the author of that gospel fully grasped the identity between Person Wisdom and Jesus. In the Gospel of John, this identity is no longer in doubt. It infuses the gospel from beginning to end.[34] We find abundant evidence for it in the prologue to the gospel and in the teaching ministry of the Johannine Jesus.

In the initial verses of John's prologue (1:1–18), the author of the gospel uses the term "Logos" for Person Wisdom and equates this Logos with Jesus.[35] Wisdom/Logos, the first verse says, was present "in the beginning," was a companion "oriented toward God," and was "God-like." This triplet of attributes echoes what the OT wisdom books said about Person Wisdom. God brought Wisdom into existence "at the beginning . . . before his works of old" (Prov 8:22–23). Person Wisdom was also face to face with God, "near to the Lord, as dear child, and delighting day by day, always playing in front of the Lord" (Prov 8:30). Wisdom is also God-like. The author of the Wisdom of Solomon piles attribute on attribute in his encomium to Wisdom, bringing Person Wisdom as near to God as possible without identifying it with God. Wisdom, he says, is "a flawless mirror of the working of God" and "a pure emanation of the glory of the Almighty" (7:25–26). The Wisdom of Solomon also applies the unusual word *monogenēs* (unique, only-born) to Person Wisdom (7:22), a term that the prologue will later use to describe Jesus (1:14, 1:18).

The prologue goes on, after its initial verse, to assign to Wisdom/Logos a specific role in creation. "Through him all things came to be—not even one thing came to be without him" (1:3). The Person Wisdom tradition agrees. Wisdom is the "artificer of all things" (Wis 7:22). Philo, another heir of the wisdom tradition and probably a contemporary of the

---

34. In his commentary on John, Ben Witherington says that "recognizing that Jesus is being portrayed as God's Wisdom, indeed Wisdom incarnate, in this Gospel is *the key* to understanding the presentation of the central character of the story" (Witherington, *John's Wisdom*, 20, emphasis Witherington's).

35. There is a voluminous literature on how the prologue relates to the rest of the Gospel of John. Many scholars separate it from the gospel and assign it to a redactor. I'll be treating it as an integral part of the gospel. See the arguments for this position in de Boer, "The Original Prologue." Mark Stibbe compares the prologue to the opening crawl of the first three *Star Wars* movies (Stibbe, "Protagonist," 144).

author of John, pictured Wisdom/Logos as a demiurge, an intermediary in the creation of the world.

The next few verses of the prologue connect Wisdom/Logos and light. "In him was life, and the life was the light of people." This light "shines in the darkness, and the darkness does not overcome it" (1:4–5). Jesus "is the true light that comes into the world to enlighten every person" (1:9). Later in the gospel, Jesus will call himself, just before he restores the sight to a man born blind, "the light of the world" (9:5). Wisdom as light is not a metaphor that the author of the gospel pulls out of a hat. It is employed in several places in the wisdom tradition. In the Wisdom of Solomon, for example, Person Wisdom is said to be "a refulgence of everlasting light" (7:26).

The identification of Wisdom/Logos and Jesus is made explicit at the end of the prologue. The *Book of Enoch*, as noted earlier, expands the picture of Wisdom as a being who dwelt with God, left the heavenly courts to make a home with people, and not finding a welcome, returned to dwell with the angels (*Enoch* 42:2). John tells a similar story about Jesus. We learn in the prologue that "the Logos became flesh and dwelt among us" (1:14). And that "he was in the world and the world came into existence through him and the world did not know him" (1:10). At the Last Supper, Jesus reveals to his disciples that he is returning to the Father: "I came forth from the Father and arrived in the world. I am leaving the world and going to the Father" (16:28).

The prologue is explicit about Jesus being Wisdom, but we also find considerable evidence for this in the ministry of Jesus.[36] We will consider some specific passages in a moment, but let's begin by looking at the larger landscape. There are many parallels between Person Wisdom and the ministry of the Johannine Jesus, but I'll mention just three.

First, we note that John's preferred term for the miracles of Jesus is "signs." These signs, like other symbols in the Gospel of John, point beyond the tangible act to a transcendent fact. Compare this to what we find in the second half of the Wisdom of Solomon. The writer traces the career of Wisdom through the events of Jewish history, seeking places where Wisdom is behind the scenes, looking on. He says that Wisdom entered the soul of Moses, the servant of the Lord, permitting Moses to oppose the Pharaoh of Egypt with "signs and wonders," guiding God's people "along a marvelous way" (10:16–17). For the author of the

---

36. A long list of these ministry parallels can be found in Brown, *An Introduction*, 261–3.

Wisdom of Solomon, miracles reveal, when they become signs, the presence of Person Wisdom. We can read a similar sense into the use of the word "signs" in the Gospel of John.

Second, the connection that Jesus makes in the Gospel of John between accepting his teaching and having eternal life reflects the mission of Person Wisdom. A principal role of Wisdom, we know, is to convey a knowledge of God. "Who knows your counsel," asks the author of the Wisdom of Solomon, "unless you yourself have given Wisdom and have sent your Holy Spirit from on high?" (9:17). This knowledge, when accepted, brings both life and immortality. "The one who finds me finds life," says Person Wisdom in Proverbs (8:35). Heeding the advice of Wisdom, the Wisdom of Solomon says, brings "the assurance of immortality" (6:18). All the instances of "eternal life" in the Gospel of John—some seventeen of them—can be read as pointers to the mission of Wisdom.

Third, many of the teaching symbols that Jesus employs in the Gospel of John are the symbols that Person Wisdom uses in its own instruction. The three impersonal symbols found most often in the gospel are light, bread, and water.[37] We have seen the emphasis in the prologue on Jesus as the *light* and the way that the light metaphor is worked into the dialogue with Nicodemus. Later in the gospel, Jesus will call himself "the light of the world" (8:12). He also refers to himself as "the *bread* of life" that "comes down from heaven and gives life to the world" (6:33–35). His words, he says, are heavenly *water*: "Whoever drinks the water that I shall give will never, ever thirst" because the water will become "a spring of water welling up to eternal life" (4:14). In a similar way, Person Wisdom in the OT is "a refulgence of everlasting *light*" (Wis 7:26). Wisdom invites those needing wisdom to "come, eat my *food* and drink the wine that I have mixed." Those who do will "walk in the way of understanding" (Prov 9:6). "God created Wisdom," says Ben Sira, and "*poured it out* on all his works" (1:9). A shared symbolic universe can reflect a shared tradition— John's Jesus speaks with the metaphors of wisdom because John identifies him with Person Wisdom.

We turn now to specific events from the ministry of the Johannine Jesus that display this identity. One of the first places in the gospel where we see what it means for Jesus to be Person Wisdom comes at the end of the third chapter. John the Baptist tells his disciples that he must decrease so that Jesus can increase (3:30). Following this is a six-verse description

---

37. Culpepper, *Anatomy*, 189.

of Jesus that seems, by its placement, to be coming from the mouth of the Baptist (3:31–36). Not every translation, however, puts this section inside the quotation marks with John the Baptist's testimony. The passage feels more like a voice-over spoken by the omniscient narrator of the prologue. Or by Jesus himself.[38] The Son, the verses say, comes from heaven to bear witness to what he has seen and heard there (3:32). God has sent him from heaven to utter the words of God, "for God does not measure out the Spirit [to him]; the Father loves the Son and has given everything into his hand" (3:34–35). The dependence of this description of Jesus's ministry on the Person Wisdom narrative is transparent. It is Wisdom who was with God before creation and basked in God's love, and Wisdom, often synonymized with God's Spirit, who was sent to reveal the counsels of God. This small section of the gospel ends with a promise and a warning. The one who believes in the Son "has eternal life." The one who does not "will not see life" and will experience "the wrath of God" (3:36). This two-pronged fate reminds the reader of the contrast in the first chapters of Proverbs—and many other places in the wisdom literature—between those who follow the way of foolishness and those who follow the way of wisdom.

In the next chapter, Jesus says to the woman of Samaria that he meets at Jacob's Well, "If you knew the gift of God and who is saying to you, 'Give me something to drink,' you could have asked him, and he would have given to you the water of life" (4:10). Wisdom may be the gift from God that Jesus is referring to ("The Lord gives wisdom," Prov 2:6). The water he mentions is used as a metaphor for the generous flow of wisdom from God to the world—in Sirach 24:21, Person Wisdom mentions those who "drink me." Person Wisdom, then, is like an ever-flowing, life-giving source of water. A few verses later, Jesus extends the metaphor, saying to the Samaritan woman that "whoever drinks of the water that I will give, that water will become in the person a spring that wells up to eternal life" (4:14). The artesian spring that was Person Wisdom is transferred to the one receiving the water, and that person in turn becomes a spring that wisdom can flow from, just as wisdom is passed from sage to student. Jesus will say something like this in a later chapter when he predicts that "rivers of living water" will flow from the heart of the person who believes in him (7:38).

---

38. Nothing in the text indicates that Jesus has resumed speaking. For an argument that this could be the case, though, see Parsenios, "How and in What Ways," 87–8.

The fifth chapter of John, which contains Jesus's dialogue with the man healed on the Sabbath and with the Jewish teachers who criticized Jesus for the man's untimely healing, also contains high-concept statements about Jesus and his relationship to the Father. Jesus says to his critics, "my Father is working up to now and I also am working" (5:17). The Sabbath restrictions on what could be done on the seventh day have their source in the Genesis creation narrative—God spends six days creating the world and rests on the seventh. In the record of the Sabbath restrictions in Exodus 31:12–17, God says to Moses that the Sabbath is an eternal symbol of God's relationship to Israel because "in six days the Lord made heaven and earth," but on the seventh day God "stopped work and took a breather." But could God really stop all activity? There are discussions in the early rabbinic literature about this problem. God could have stopped some of his activity, the rabbis noted, but not all of it. Philo also makes the point that God's rest on the Sabbath of creation cannot mean a cessation of all activity, since God by nature cannot stop doing what is good.[39] Jesus, it seems, is making a similar point. As Wisdom, Jesus shares the nature of God, and all that he does is part of the work of goodness that God cannot cease to do. His Sabbath healing work was a continuation of the same active force that God exercised after the six days of creation. His hearers understood his claim in this way—the text of John goes on to say that they renewed their efforts to kill him, not only because he broke the Sabbath, but "because he was also calling God his own Father, making himself equal to God" (5:18).

We hear this word "Father" on the lips of Jesus more than a hundred times in the Gospel of John, far more often than in any of the other three gospels, and Jesus names himself "Son" about thirty times. Many of these references to the father-son relationship between God and Jesus may allude to the role of Person Wisdom. The word *amon* in Proverbs 8:30, the word applied to the Wisdom that was "near to the Lord" and "delighting day by day, always playing in front of the Lord," can mean "child" and seems to have been understood in this way in later wisdom literature. That the father-to-son relationship of God and Jesus is an alternate metaphor for the God-to-Person-Wisdom relationship is further suggested by what comes next in the fifth chapter. "The Son," Jesus goes on to say, "is not able to do anything on his own unless he sees the Father doing it. For what God does, the Son is likewise doing. For the Father loves the Son

---

39. Philo, *Cherubim* 87. For the rabbinic discussion, see *Genesis Rabbah* 11:10.

and shows him everything" (5:19). A few verses later, Jesus underlines this connection to the Father by saying, "I can do nothing on my own. Just as I hear, I judge. And my judgment is just because I do not seek my own will but the will of the one who sent me" (5:30). If we think of Jesus as nothing more than a favored human, statements such as these make little sense—people sometimes do the will of God and sometimes don't. Only if Jesus saw himself as the intimate companion of God, the Person Wisdom who was with God before creation, could he make such claims as these.

Equally strong claims are made in chapter 6. After the feeding of the five thousand, Jesus engages his followers in a dialogue about bread. He says, "I am the bread of life. The one who comes to me will never hunger" (6:35). Most of the dialogue in this chapter plays on the tension between literal and metaphorical meanings of "bread." While exploring this metaphor, Jesus says, "I have come down from heaven" (6:37) and "No one has seen the Father except the one who is alongside the Father—this one has seen the Father" (6:46). Again, these statements of intimacy between Jesus and the Father evoke the image of Person Wisdom basking in the glory of God before creation. To understand what an incredible claim this must have been to his Jewish listeners, consider that not even Moses, the most important figure in mainline Judaism, was granted this privilege. Moses spoke with God "face to face, as a person might speak to his friend" (Exod 33:11), but when Moses asked to see God's glory, God told him, "You are not able to see my face, for no person can see my face and live" (Exod 33:20). As a concession, God arranges for Moses to see the divine back while God is walking away—but not the face (Exod 33:23). Jesus's hearers, both his opponents and his disciples, must have struggled with these claims of intimacy. His opponents in this chapter mention his parents, whom they seem to know, and wonder how Jesus could possibly say that he comes down from heaven. Even his disciples are perplexed by the claims. Their response is that "This is a hard teaching. Who can understand it?" (6:60). Many of these puzzled disciples, John reports, parted ways with Jesus after this exchange.

In John 8, Jesus's claims that he is the pre-existent Person Wisdom rise to a crescendo. In his dialogue with the Pharisees, Jesus says "You yourselves are from below, but I am from above. You yourselves are from this world, but I am not from this world" (8:23). "I do nothing on my own initiative, but I speak these things just as the Father has taught me" (8:28). "I speak about what I have beheld while with the Father" (8:38). "I came from God and arrived here. For I have not spoken on my own initiative, but that one sent me" (8:42). Jesus caps off these claims to be the Person Wisdom who was at God's side with a reference to his relationship to Abraham, the revered progenitor of the Jewish people. Jesus says that those who believe and follow him "will never, ever see death" (8:51). The Pharisees object. Since Abraham and the prophets all died, they say, Jesus was claiming to be greater than Abraham. Jesus does not deny this. In fact, he expands the claim: "Your father Abraham rejoiced that he could see my day . . . . Before Abraham existed, I am" (8:56, 58).

In John 10, while Jesus is in Jerusalem for the annual Hanukkah celebration, he resumes the earlier discussion he had been having with his opponents, saying that he would give his followers eternal life. "They will never, ever perish," he says, "and no one will be able to wrest them from my hand." They were given to him by God, and what God does, Jesus points out, humans cannot undo—taking them from Jesus would be like taking them from God "because I and the Father are one" (10:28–30). In the context of this passage, it isn't clear what this claim to be one with God means. The claim is somewhat clarified in the Johannine Last Supper discourse. There, Jesus tells his disciples that he is "the way, the truth, and the life," and that knowing and seeing him was equivalent to knowing and seeing the Father (14:6–7). One of his disciples insists on a more direct perception of the Father, and Jesus replies, "I am in the Father and the Father is in me" so that "the one who beholds me, beholds the Father" (14:9). This equality does not work on every level, however. Jesus also says, "the Father is greater than I" (14:28).

In the Last Supper discourse (John 14–17), the Gospel author introduces a new twist into the Person Wisdom story. Jesus reveals to his disciples that he is "leaving the world and going to the Father" (16:28). Sadness grips the disciples, but Jesus consoles them with a promise. It is to their advantage that he goes away, he says, because if he goes away, and only if he goes away, God will send to them "another companion." This will be someone Jesus calls "the Spirit of truth." This companion will be with them and live in them (14:16–17). Like Jesus, this new companion will speak with God's own authority. "All that the Father has is mine," Jesus says, and the Spirit "will receive what is mine and declare it to you" (16:15). Specific actions of this companion Spirit include reminding the disciples of what Jesus has taught (14:26), bearing witness to the person of Jesus through the preaching of the disciples (15:26–27), and preparing listeners to be receptive to the message (16:8–9). At the end of the

Gospel of John, the resurrected Jesus will fulfill this promise to send the Spirit by breathing on the disciples and saying, "Receive the Holy Spirit" (20:22). Because the concept of God's Spirit is closely linked with Person Wisdom in the OT wisdom literature, the Johannine development of the Holy Spirit as Jesus's replacement points us—again—to the identification between Jesus and Person Wisdom.[40]

SECTARIAN JOHN

In the previous chapter, I wove an imaginative web that depicted a sectarian background for Jesus and his movement. I connected the wisdom tradition represented by the Gospel of Matthew and the Epistle of James to sectarians who may have called themselves "Nazoreans." Identifying them with the group that Philo refers to as "Therapeutae," I suggested that the movement had several operating cells. One or more of the cells would have been in Galilee, in and around Nazareth. Other cells could have been in Egypt and Ephesus. If we add the Gospel of John to this Nazorean picture, we can also assume that Nazorean cells were active in Judea.

Treating John as an expression of Nazorean belief, however, requires that we recognize internal tensions among the Nazoreans. "There are traits that bind the Gospel of Matthew to one strain of first-century 'Judaism'" says the talmudic scholar Daniel Boyarin, "while other traits bind the Gospel of John to other strains."[41] The differences between the outlook we find in James and Matthew and what we find in John are usually attributed by NT scholars to later differences between Christian communities. They speak of a "Matthean community" as the source of the Gospel of Matthew and a "Johannine community" as the source of the Gospel of John and assign the differences in these gospels to disagreements in the underlying communities.[42] By pushing the publications of the gospels to late in the first century CE, scholars give these communities time to develop diverging outlooks. But if we assume that these two gospels were much earlier, perhaps with some of their initial drafts emerging in the 50s

40. "Because the author of the Wisdom of Solomon equated Wisdom with God's Spirit and the Fourth Evangelist seems to be drawing on his work, or perhaps sharing common late wisdom material," the ideas in the Gospel of John about the Spirit and the person of Christ "owe something to the sapiential corpus" (Witherington, *John's Wisdom*, 26).

41. Daniel Boyarin, *The Jewish Gospels*, 22.

42. See the section in the Appendixes on "The Communities Behind the Gospels."

and 60s CE, the differences between John and Matthew must either have developed rather quickly—in the span of thirty years, perhaps less—or the point of divergence between the communities must be sought in a Jewish context that existed *before* the ministry of Jesus.

This earlier divergence is, in fact, what I think happened. The Nazorean communities may have been in existence for many decades before Jesus was born. They were a sect following a wisdom tradition, but they had picked up—as every sectarian group did in the late Second Temple period—certain apocalyptic themes. As the Nazorean movement spread, groups within the sect began to evolve in different directions. The diverging groups may have acquired geographic associations.

To help keep these groups sorted, let me give them names. One group we might call "system Nazoreans." I'll refer to them as "s-Nazoreans."[43] They would have been centered in Galilee. They were poorer than other Nazorean communities. Almost all of them would have been farmers or tradespeople. Many of them would have been bilingual, speaking both Aramaic and Greek, but they would have employed Aramaic as the everyday language among members of the group. Families and kinship ties were important.[44]

43. The buzz around a recent article in the behavioral science community has influenced my choice of nicknames for these communities. Nick Chater and George Loewenstein of the Behavioural Science Group at UK's Warwick Business School discuss what they call "s-frame" and "i-frame" approaches to public policy issues (Chater and Loewenstein, "The i-Frame"). In choosing the term "frame," the authors draw from a long history of work in psychology on the *framing effect*—the way that people approach decision-making with inherent biases and frames of reference. I see this kind of framing in the approaches taken by the two Nazorean communities introduced in this chapter. The resemblance between Chater and Loewenstein's s-frame and i-frame and my Nazorean groups, however, probably goes no deeper than these borrowed nicknames and a shared interest in psychological framing. They apply their frames to analyzing the public policy effectiveness (mostly the lack of it) in recent attempts to replace systemic action with an appeal to the choices of individuals.

44. Using the English word "family," which often refers to a nuclear family of parents and their immediate children, can be misleading when applied to social structures in Second Temple Judaism. The family unit was a *household*. Households were "multigenerational and consisted of two or three families, related by kinship and marriage, who lived in a residential complex of two or three houses connected together" (Perdue, "The Israelite," 166). Second Temple households could also include debt servants and slaves and might embrace sojourners of various types. In addition to the people and their living quarters, the household, especially in rural areas, "included its fields, orchards, vineyards, pastures, livestock, and the tools and implements for living and working" (Perdue, "The Israelite," 175). The needs of these conjunctions of people and things "took precedence over those of individual members who formed its constituency" (Perdue, "The Israelite," 167).

Although they identified themselves in the world of Second Temple Judaism as an independent sect, the s-Nazoreans were oriented toward—and adapted to—multiple facets of the Jewish religious system. Many of these Nazoreans traveled to Jerusalem to observe the major Jewish festivals, and they observed the festivals in ways that were similar to the Jewish context in which they lived. They did not fully assimilate, however. One of the ways that the s-Nazoreans maintained a distinction between themselves and other Jewish sects and groups was by having unique interpretations of Scripture. Some of the early members of the Nazoreans, regarded as prophets, received what others believed were inspired interpretations. These revelations often included apocalyptic themes. Some of these interpretations became *pesharim*—they were written down and served as patterns for later interpretations. One focus of this group's sectarian apocalyptic was on a messiah who would usher in what they called "the reign of God."[45] Some in the group probably believed that they had been chosen as the vehicle to introduce this messiah to Israel.

Jesus's family, resident in Nazareth, would have been part of this s-Nazorean group. In the epistle of Jesus's brother James, we find an outline of the teachings they followed. They had a strong emphasis on practical ethics, believing in fairness in financial dealings, social justice, and compassion for the poor. They had a high regard for the book of Proverbs and perhaps for Sirach. Some of their members were probably healers and exorcists.

The other group I will call "individualistic Nazoreans," or "i-Nazoreans." Their communities centered around Judea, Alexandria, and Ephesus. They were, if you like, city mice to the s-Nazoreans' country mice. The i-Nazoreans would have focused on the more cosmopolitan, universal, and ecumenical aspects of their sectarian faith. Martha Himmelfarb, in her survey of Second Temple Jewish movements, emphasizes how sectarian movements, in order to draw boundaries, invoke either ancestry or merit.[46] While the Nazorean movement, as a whole, would be more merit-based than mainline Judaism, the i-Nazoreans would have placed less value than the s-Nazoreans on having Jewish ancestry

45. Biblical scholars struggle to overturn the assumption that the messianic role assumed by Jesus was constructed by Jesus or the early Christians out of a pastiche of prophecies that Jewish groups had not connected up to that time. In fact, "almost the entire story of the Christ" is present "in the religious ideas of some Jews who didn't even know about Jesus." Jesus "entered into a role that existed prior to his birth" (Boyarin, *The Jewish Gospels*, 72–3).

46. Himmelfarb, *A Kingdom of Priests*.

and more value on individual merit. The devaluation of Jewish ancestry probably allowed the i-Nazoreans to include in their communities Jewish sympathizers who were not ethnic Jews. The conditions under which the sympathizers were admitted would not have included the full set of Jewish boundary markers. The Jews and non-Jews gathered into i-Nazorean cells would have formed a "fictive kin group," a group realizing many of the community ideals that were traditionally "based on blood ties."[47]

Like all Nazoreans, the i-Nazoreans followed wisdom traditions, but they had a strong interest in the Person Wisdom angle. They would have conformed to basic Nazorean messianic beliefs, but they did not dwell on the apocalyptic details surrounding the messiah's coming. The i-Nazoreans probably had schools and synagogues where they met to study, meditate, and pray, but not all of them would have lived communally. As with the Therapeutae, women in i-Nazorean groups probably experienced a greater freedom to pursue spiritual goals and act in leadership positions. The i-Nazoreans, both men and women, would have shared a set of mystical practices and beliefs that shaped their worship.

Our main source of information about the i-Nazoreans is the Gospel of John. A secondary source is what Philo says about the Therapeutae. We have discussed the Therapeutae. Let's consider what the Gospel of John might tell us about this group of Nazoreans.

The author of John, the beloved disciple of the gospel, was probably a member of the i-Nazorean community in Jerusalem. The author was a person of influence having connections to high-priestly circles and perhaps belonging to a family with financial resources. The author would have subscribed to the Nazorean belief that the Messiah would soon appear. When John the Baptist, who was probably another Judean i-Nazorean,[48] took up his calling as the forerunner of the messiah, the author of the gospel accepted the legitimacy of the Baptist's prophetic role. The author followed closely the Baptist's ministry and believed that the Baptist's call to repentance was a message from God.

John's baptism site, toward the south end of the Jordan River, was not far from Jerusalem. The gospel author may have visited the site regularly and perhaps supported the ministry financially. The beloved disciple happened to be near the Baptist when the forerunner identified Jesus as the Lamb of God. The gospel author trusted John enough to follow Jesus

47. Bartchy, "Community of Goods," 313. For the term "fictive kin group," Bartchy borrows from work in the social sciences on pseudo-kinship.

48. See the section in the Appendixes on "Was John the Baptist an i-Nazorean?"

and see what he would do. When John was arrested, Jesus moved his ministry to Galilee. We shouldn't imagine that the future evangelist was part of the inner core of disciples during the Galilean phases of Jesus's ministry. The author of John probably remained at a base in Judea and kept track through friends (the disciple Andrew, for example) of what Jesus was doing. The death of the Baptist would have transferred the author's full attention to Jesus. The author probably met up with Jesus during times that Jesus and his disciples came to Jerusalem for the major festivals. When Jesus made his final, fateful pilgrimage to Jerusalem at the last Passover, the author of John would have been there to help organize the events. The beloved disciple may have hosted the Last Supper.[49] The author became a first-hand witness of the events that led up to the crucifixion and resurrection.

We don't know what happened to the author of John in the years following the end of Jesus's ministry. It seems likely that almost all the Nazoreans, both the groups in Galilee and in Judea, came to believe that Jesus was their prophesied Messiah. The Nazorean sect was transformed, in effect, into the earliest phase of what we have been calling the Christian Jewish sect. The few Nazoreans who did not make this transition died out. This may be why a significant body of pre-Christian Nazorean documents has not survived—parts of their writings and liturgy were assimilated into the growing Christian Jewish sect, and those that could not be adapted were mostly lost.[50] (The exception may be the *Psalms of Solomon* discussed in the next chapter.)

When the followers of Jesus ran afoul of the Jewish leadership in Jerusalem after the death of Jesus, the ones with s-Nazorean backgrounds, already tilted toward mainline Judaism, found ways to remain within the larger society of Jews. We know that a Christian Jewish community

49. If the beloved disciple organized and hosted the Last Supper, then the beloved disciple may have been the one that the Synoptic Gospels mention in the passages about the preparation for the Last Supper. In Matthew, Jesus sends the disciples "into the city, to so-and-so" (26:18) to announce that Jesus will keep the Passover at his house. Mark (14:13–16) and Luke (22:8–13) add a male servant to the picture—the servant, Jesus says, will be carrying a water jar, and the disciples are to follow the servant to find the "householder" who will host the feast. Do the Synoptic passages keep this hosting person anonymous—calling him "so-and-so" and "householder"—because the authors do not want to link themselves to the beloved disciple's exiled faction?

50. We have a parallel to this loss of documentation in the case of the Pharisees. Scholars struggle to attach the Pharisees to any writings from the Second Temple period. The assimilation of the Pharisees into Rabbinic Judaism may have discouraged the preservation of Pharisaic literature that could not be adapted to later perspectives.

under the leadership of James continued to operate in Jerusalem until the decade before the Romans destroyed the city. The i-Nazoreans, however, with their more universal and less ethnically Jewish perspectives, might not have been as welcome in the Holy City. Perhaps the author of the Gospel of John united with Christian Nazorean cells outside of Jerusalem in the years following the ministry of Jesus. The author may even have taken up residence with cells outside of Palestine. Early Christian writers associate the author of the Gospel of John with Ephesus, a city that, as I speculated earlier, could have been the site of a Nazorean cell.[51]

I-NAZOREANS IN THE GOSPEL OF JOHN.

We looked earlier for evidence in the Gospel of John that Jesus was Person Wisdom—and found it. This evidence also links the gospel to the Nazorean sect. It does not make John's gospel, however, a product of the i-Nazorean faction. All of the Nazorean groups would have made this connection to some extent. When we examined the Gospel of Matthew, for example, we found hints that Jesus was Person Wisdom.

I have sketched what the i-Nazorean group might have believed and how it differed from the s-Nazoreans. Let's now review elements in the Gospel of John that might indicate the gospel was a product of a Nazorean group with different beliefs and practices than what we find represented in Matthew and the Epistle of James. I'll consider these elements in the order that they occur in the Gospel of John.

The placement of the gospel's prologue (1:1–18) announces that we are in a different theological space than the Synoptic Gospels. Matthew begins with infancy narratives. This makes sense because the s-Nazoreans were immersed in family relationships. Jesus had to be positioned in a kinship structure, with both an immediate family and a family tree. John's gospel, in contrast, sets the opening scene, like Milton's *Paradise Lost*, in heaven. Jesus, as Logos and Wisdom, begins his life in the presence of God. We hear nothing about his earthly family. Members

---

51. Early associations of the author of John with Ephesus can be found in Irenaeus, *Haer.* 3.1.1 and Eusebius, *Hist.* 3.23.1–4. What the connection is between the author of John and the city of Ephesus depends on the complex question of who is identified as the beloved disciple. Richard Bauckham identifies the Ephesian-based John the Elder as the author of the gospel in Bauckham, *Testimony*. A balanced summary of the authorship issues and their relationship to the city of Ephesus can be found in Kok, *The Beloved Apostle*.

of the i-Nazorean group were probably more connected to each other by intergroup ties than family ties. Members may have entered the full fellowship of the group in the way that the Therapeutae did—by severing ties of kinship and establishing a relationship with a mystical, worshipping community.

Even before the prologue ends, the author of the Gospel of John introduces us to John the Baptist. All the gospels begin the story of Jesus's ministry with John the Baptist. John and the Synoptics, however, have significant differences in their treatment of the forerunner. First, the Gospel of John does not describe, as Matthew and Mark do, the Baptist's ascetic practices. In the Synoptics, the Baptist's brand of asceticism will set him apart from the asceticism of Jesus. Second, the Synoptics—Luke in the main—include examples of John's ethical instructions. The role of John the Baptist in the Gospel of John, in contrast, is stripped to its essentials—his job is to testify to who Jesus is, nothing more. This is reinforced in the Gospel of John's account of the descent of the Spirit on Jesus. The Synoptic Gospels turn it into a spectacle, with Jesus being baptized, the heavens opening, and an audible voice saying, "This is my Beloved Son." The Gospel of John does not even say that Jesus was baptized. The heavenly fireworks are replaced by John the Baptist's vision, narrated as a mystical experience. John says, "I saw the Spirit descending from heaven as a dove and it remained on him" (1:32). The word "remaining" in this verse, the same word (*menō*) that John will use in chapter 15 for the way he and his disciples will *abide* in each other, also ties John's vision to mystical experience. Third, John's gospel interweaves the ministries of Jesus and John the Baptist more than the Synoptics do. We see disciples shifting from one person to the other (1:37). Jesus and his followers have a Judean baptizing ministry, just as the Baptist does (3:22).[52] Fourth, John's gospel,

52. It appears that Jesus himself baptized his followers and listeners. John 3:22 says that while the Baptist was baptizing at Aenon, Jesus and his disciples "went into the Judean countryside" and that "he spent time with them there and baptized." In the next chapter, however, there is a parenthetical aside that seems to contradict this. People were reporting to the Pharisees that Jesus's baptizing ministry was surpassing that of John (4:1). To escape the attention of the Pharisees, Jesus transfers his ministry to Galilee (4:3). The gospel inserts: "although Jesus himself did not baptize, only his disciples did" (4:2). This insertion, which uses a vocabulary word for "although" that is not found anywhere else in John (or anywhere in the Greek Bible, for that matter), may be one of the rare additions of a later redactor into the text. Possibly the i-Nazoreans group linked to the Gospel of John did not baptize, and the editor wanted to distance Jesus from the practice. For a discussion of whether the account of Jesus baptizing in John can be trusted, see Lincoln, "'We Know,'" 187–91.

and only John's gospel, has the Baptist referring to Jesus as the "Lamb of God." The phrase recalls the Servant Song in Isaiah 53 where the prophet says that we, like wandering sheep, have gone astray, and that the Lord made our sins fall on his servant. The servant accepts our punishments without complaint and is silently "led to slaughter like a lamb" (53:6–7). In this "Lamb of God" reference in John—and its absence in the Synoptics—we may be hearing a difference between the s-Nazoreans and the i-Nazoreans. The Galilean branch of the Nazoreans had only minor quarrels with temple Judaism and its system of sacrifices. The Judean group, however, seems to have approached the temple system in a way similar to that of the Essenes—their own worship, they believed, stood as a valid alternative to temple sacrifices. The NT Book of Hebrews, a pseudo-Pauline letter, lines out this position in detail in chapters 6–10. The sacrifice of Jesus, the letter writer says, makes the daily temple sacrifices irrelevant. The physical temple where priests offer daily animal sacrifices is but a "copy and shadow" (8:5) of the "greater and more complete" sanctuary in heaven (9:11), where Jesus has offered a once-for-all sacrifice of himself, making the old arrangements "obsolete" (8:13). The i-Nazoreans may also have taken this temple-optional approach, replacing the lambs for God with the Lamb of God. The Essenes, who also rejected the temple services and sacrifices, were banned from the temple precincts. In the political hothouse of the last decades before the destruction of Jerusalem, i-Nazorean groups may also have found themselves unwelcome in the temple precincts.

An i-Nazorean perspective may also underlie the curious passage in the Gospel of John about the calling of Nathanael (1:43–51).[53] In this passage, Jesus has just invited Philip, one of the twelve disciples, to follow him. Philip seeks out Nathanael and tells him that "we have found the one that Moses wrote about in the law and the prophets, Jesus of Nazareth, the son of Joseph" (1:45).[54] Nathanael responds to Philip's testimony with what appears to be, in all translations and commentaries that I have ever seen, a skeptical question. The question is usually rendered, "Can

53. Nathanael is not cited as one of the twelve disciples in the lists in the Synoptics and Acts. Some scholars, however, believe that Nathanael is an alternate name for the Bartholomew who appears in the lists.

54. In John's post-resurrection narrative, we learn that this Nathanael was from Cana in Galilee (21:2), a place associated with Jesus's natal family (2:1–12). Philip perhaps assumed that Nathanael knew Jesus's family. This may be why John uses the phrase "Jesus from Nazareth" (not, as in most other references, "Jesus the Nazorean") and refers to Jesus as "the son of Joseph."

anything good come out of Nazareth?" (1:46). Philip's response to this
is the challenging "Come and see." Nathanael's response, however, can
be read as a statement instead of a question. He may have said, "Something good might come out of Nazareth," and Philip's reply may have
been an invitation for Nathanael to explore his surmise.[55] If Nathanael is
not, as we have always thought, a skeptic about a Messiah from Nazareth
but instead has reason to think that something good might arise from
Nazareth, Nathanael may have been a Nazorean. Earlier, we considered
the passage from Matthew that says Joseph, on his return from Egypt,
"went to dwell in a city called 'Nazareth' so that the word spoken through
the prophets, 'He shall be called a Nazorean,' might be fulfilled," and we
linked this prophecy with Nazorean *pesharim*. Nathanael, hearing from
Philip about the new prophet and the place he came from, might have
made a connection with these sectarian scriptures, prompting him to
remark that something good could indeed come from this small place.

Jesus, when he sees Nathanael coming, says, "Behold, truly an Israelite in whom is no deceit" (1:47). Nathanael asks how Jesus knows
him, and Jesus ends the exchange by revealing something that surprises
Nathanael, saying, "Before Philip called you, when you were under the
fig tree, I saw you" (1:48).[56] Nathanael's reaction to this cryptic comment
is over the top. He immediately proclaims Jesus "Son of God" and "King
of Israel" (1:49). Jesus, also thinking that the reaction of Nathanael was
out of proportion, says, "Because I said to you that I saw you under the
fig tree, do you believe? You will see greater things than these." Jesus adds
that Nathanael "will see heaven opened and the angels of God ascending
and descending on the Son of Man." This final statement alludes to an
OT story. After Jacob stole his brother's birthright, Jacob's father, perhaps
to get Jacob away from the angry Esau, sent him to a distant city to take
a wife from among his mother's kin. Jacob stops along the way at a place
called Bethel and has a dream (Gen 28:10–17). In this dream, he sees a
ladder with its bottom on the earth and its top in the heavens. God is at
the top of the ladder and the angels of God are ascending and descending on the ladder. In the Jacob story, the angels in the vision ascend and
descend on the land of Israel. More specifically, they make their visits to

---

55. See the section in the Appendixes on "Did Nathanael Ask a Question?"

56. Speculation about what Nathanael might have been doing under the fig tree has
been endless. The line of thought we've been following suggests yet another answer. If
Nathanael was a Nazorean, he might have had times of regular meditation, and, in the
absence of an inner room, a fig tree may have been his private meditation spot.

the temple of God—Bethel, which means "house of God," seems to have functioned as a place of worship in Israel's the pre-monarchical period. In Jesus's version of the vision, the bottom of the ladder terminates on "the Son of Man," not on the temple. This appears to be another of John's identifications between Jesus with the nation of Israel.

After the calling of the disciples, we have the first of the miraculous signs recorded in the Gospel of John. Jesus turns some water in stone jars into wine—a lot of wine—to provision a wedding feast. One feature of this account that catches our attention is Jesus's treatment of his mother. When his mother asks Jesus to perform the miracle, Jesus says, "What do you and I have in common?" (2:4) The idiom he uses is harsh. It is the same phrase, for example, that is used by a demon-possessed man in Mark. When Jesus exorcizes the demon, the possessed fellow screams out, "What do you and I have in common?" and asks Jesus not to torment him (Mark 5:7).

I can think of two reasons that the author of the gospel might have included Jesus's strong reaction to Mary's request. One is that the author has in mind the i-Nazorean practice of separating from kin in order to pursue one's true calling, the practice that Philo noted in the Therapeutae. Jesus could be objecting to his mother's attempt to pull him back into the fold of family and kinship. A second possibility is that that John believes that Jesus, like the Therapeutae, had renounced alcohol. Jesus in this case might be objecting to his mother asking him to provide inebriants. (We'll pick up this topic of water versus wine later, when we come to John's account of the Last Supper.)

A second feature of the Cana passage may also derive from John's sectarian standpoint. When the steward of the feast tastes the wine that Jesus has made, he tells the bridegroom that instead of serving the lower-quality wine at the end of the feast, when the people are tipsy and can no longer discern the good from the bad, he has saved the good wine for last (2:10). This may be the sectarian author of John saying, by way of metaphor, that an interpretation of Judaism does not have to be served first to be good. The i-Nazorean sectarian faith, though novel from the standpoint of mainline second-temple Judaism, can still be what is best and true. The way that it restrings the pearls of the Tanak can be more correct than the interpretations of the Jerusalem priesthood.

The miracle at the Cana wedding is followed in the gospel text by the cleansing of the temple (2:13–22), an event also reported in the Synoptics. In the Gospel of John, the episode occurs at the beginning of

Jesus's ministry. In the Synoptics, it occurs during Jesus's last week. The timeline placement is significant—a protest against temple malpractice at the start of Jesus ministry may be a way of fronting the differences between Jesus and the temple system. But more than just a time shift is involved. The cleansing of the temple in John is also more violent than the ones recorded in the Synoptics. John's Jesus weaponizes his protest by making a whip out of cords, and he uses the whip to drive out, not just the moneychangers, but also their animals. And only John, of all the gospels, observes that Jesus, when he cleared out the vendors, was consumed by angry zeal. Another subtle difference in wording between John and the Synoptics may also be significant. In the Synoptics, Jesus complains that the moneychangers have turned the temple precincts into a "den of thieves," as though the problem had to do with unethical business practices. John puts a broader complaint in Jesus's mouth. The moneychangers have made the temple a "house of business," suggesting that any mixing of money and worship is a problem (2:16). Since the temple system of animal sacrifices would have been unworkable without business dealings, condemning all temple transactions raises questions about whether temple worship was valid. The report of this event in the Gospel of John, we also note, is the only one that follows the temple cleansing with Jesus's paradoxical comparison of his body and the temple. "Destroy this temple," Jesus says to the Jews, "and in three days I will raise it up." It was the sacrifice of Jesus that was important, not the stones of the temple. Halakhic difference between the i-Nazoreans and the s-Nazoreans probably lie behind these differences in the temple cleansing passages.

Note that Jesus names his interlocutors in this post-cleansing discussion "the Jews." This broad term for Jesus's opponents in the Gospel of John has been one of the thorniest problems in Johannine studies. The Gospel of Matthew knows about a large and diverse group of opponents, referring to them as Herodians, elders of the people, Pharisees, Sadducees, scribes, and chief priests. Only once (28:15) does Matthew resort to calling opponents "the Jews." John, in contrast, has a much smaller set of names for his opponents and frequently covers them with the blanket term, "the Jews."

The terms "Jews" and "Jewish" occur more than sixty times in the Gospel of John, and about half of these instances are negative references. Some of the negative ones are markedly negative. John's Jesus says that "the Jews" do not believe their own Scriptures and authorities (5:45–47) and that they judge by appearances (7:24). "The Jews" will die in their sins

(8:24), do not belong to God (8:47), and are spiritually blind and guilty (9:41). He calls them "liars" and "the devil's children" (8:55 and 8:44). If we are looking to excuse the author of John for this careless stereotyping, we can find reasons—Jesus himself was, after all, a Jew, and he was talking about people who were calling him names and trying to put him to death. We also know that sectarian rhetoric in the Second Temple period could be vitriolic. In a day and age, however, when we have become aware of the tragic consequences of negative descriptions of the Jewish people, the excuses seem to come up short. The Gospel of John feels at best insensitive, at worst inciting. The most famous Johannine scholar of my generation has advised that homilists, when they interpret John for their congregations, "be careful to caution hearers that John's passages cannot be used to justify any ongoing hostility to Jewish people."[57]

Some students of the gospel seek to take the hard edge off John's vocabulary by replacing "the Jews" with more specific terms, such as "Jewish authorities/leaders." Or they try to make "the Jews" a metaphor for people in general.[58] Moves like this, however, can distance us from John's mindset. We need to ask *why* John chose to use the terms he did. This means putting the Gospel of John into a context that explains this word choice. Scholars who imagine a late first-century CE setting for the gospel describe a Johannine community that had been written out of synagogues and cursed, a community that saw itself as minimally Jewish and who viewed the early rabbinic community as their most immediate threat. In the scenario that I have been developing, however, a different context comes into view. The writer of John is a member of the i-Nazorean faction, and members of this group identify with a cosmopolitan wisdom tradition that defines their relationship to God in terms of individual mystical ascent. They do not usually participate in the Jewish festivals. Instead, they apply alternate and metaphorical interpretations to Jewish rites and transfer this meaning to their own liturgies. This sectarian group was already on the fringes of mainline Judaism, even before it accepted the prophetic messages of John the Baptist and Jesus. The death of their messiah—at the hands of the Romans but with the collusion of the Jewish

---

57. Brown, *An Introduction*, 168. Amen to that suggestion.

58. The best work to consult for the range of opinion on John's use of "the Jews" may be Bieringer, *Anti-Judaism*. Ruth Sheridan makes a good suggestion. See proposes retaining the translation "the Jews" but putting quotations marks around it. Her point is that we need to retain—even while distancing ourselves from it—the "putative historical identity" that "the Jews" had in the context in which John was written (Sheridan, "Issues in the Translation," 695).

authorities in Jerusalem—would have driven them even further away. I'll present evidence in the next chapter that they were expelled from Jerusalem. When the author of John came to tell the story of Jesus, the writer viewed Jesus and his opponents through an i-Nazorean lens. John can see a continuity between the i-Nazoreans and the s-Nazoreans, even though disagreeing with the way the s-Nazoreans have assimilated to traditional Jewish practices. The Jews pulling the author's s-Nazorean compatriots away from the mystical practices of the i-Nazoreans, however, have become enemies. Standing at the distance of a rejected sect, the author of John's gospel finds it easy to label opponents with an ironical term.

In the encounter between Jesus and Nicodemus in chapter 3, which we looked at earlier, we also find sectarian themes. Jesus applies to himself a Tanak story, the one about the serpent standard being used to stop a plague. Here—and throughout the Gospel of John—stories from the Hebrew Scriptures are read as though their meaning was found in the life of Jesus. The author of the gospel, putting the ancient writings and prophecies side by side with contemporary events, creates a sectarian *pesher* that transfers the reference of Tanak stories to a contemporary reality. A metaphorical reading of this type may be an example of the allegorical method that Philo found in the Therapeutan interpretations.

The first three chapters of John, taken as a whole, can be read as a sectarian symbol for entrance of candidates into i-Nazorean groups. Mary Coloe develops a scenario for these chapters around bridegrooms, marriages, and birth.[59] We know that the bridal metaphor, which was employed in the Tanak to describe God's relationship to Israel (Hos 1–2; Jer 2:2, 32; Isa 61:10, 62:5), was picked up by the church to explain Jesus's relationship to believers (2 Cor 11:2; Eph 5:25–33; Rev 22:17). The extended analogy of this bridal relationship in the Gospel of John begins with the Baptist taking on the role of witness and deputy (1:19–34), negotiating the contractual arrangement between the families of the bride and bridegroom. He introduces his own disciples, as brides, to Jesus the bridegroom (1:35–51). This is followed by the wedding at Cana where "his disciples believed in him" (2:11) when he unveiled his powers. The wedding is followed by a bridal procession of disciples and family to the bridegroom's house (2:12). In the next passage, the dialogue with Nicodemus, we learn about the birth of children (being "born anew/from above"). At the end of the sequence, John says that "the one who has

59. Coloe, "John as Witness."

the bride is the bridegroom; the friend of the bridegroom, attending and listening, rejoices with great joy at the voice of the bridegroom. This my joy is complete" (3:29).

Another passage that may reflect the theology of the i-Nazoreans appears in John 4, in the dialogue between Jesus and the Samaritan woman. The Samaritan woman raises the question of whether the holiest religious site was on Mount Gerizim (as the Samaritans believed) or on the Temple Mount in Jerusalem (as the Jews believed). Jesus, though coming down on the Jewish side in this argument, downplays the difference. "The hour is coming, and now is here," he says, "when the true worshippers will worship the Father in spirit and in truth, for the Father seeks such to worship him. God is spirit, and those worshipping him must worship in spirit and truth" (4:23–24). The reality of faith, according to the Johannine Jesus, does not lie in temple rites and sites. It resides in an interior space expressed in the context of a spirit-led community. Ideas such as these are probably core i-Nazorean beliefs.

When Jesus reveals to the Samaritan woman that he is the Messiah, she delivers this message to the people in her Samaritan town, and many of them come to believe in Jesus. He stays in Samaria for two days, teaching the people, and more of the Samaritans confess that Jesus is "the Savior of the world" (4:42). The disciples, meanwhile, have their own discussion with Jesus. He tells them that "the fields are white for harvest," perhaps referring to the Samaritan people, and that "both the sower and the reaper will rejoice together" when the harvest is gathered (4:35–36). In this case, the disciples are playing the role of reapers, not sowers. "I have sent you to reap what you have not labored over," says Jesus. "Others have labored, and you have entered into their labor" (4:38). Who, though, are these "others" that did the sowing? The i-Nazoreans, it appears, may have had an outreach work among the Samaritans in the years before Jesus's public ministry.[60] The Book of Acts describes active missions among the Samaritans in the years following Pentecost—perhaps these were continuations of earlier i-Nazorean projects.[61]

60. The dialogue between Jesus and the Samaritan woman "probably does hint at a Christian mission in Samaria which had been important in the birth of the Johannine movement" (Meeks, "'Am I a Jew?," 178). The ministry of John the Baptist seems to have skirted the edges of Samaritan territory. See Robinson, *Twelve*, 63–6, and the expansion of this argument in Keener, "Historical Tradition," 160.

61. In the middle decades of the twentieth century, several Johannine scholars tried to locate the source of John's gospel in Samaritan factions of the Jesus movement. See the summary in Scobie, "The Origins."

A Nazorean presence in Samaria would have been controversial. Jews and Samaritans in the late Second Temple period, even though they shared many of the same Scriptures and claimed to worship the same God, were more enemies than friends. On occasion, their disagreements escalated into armed conflict. The Nazoreans, however, believing that true faith was found in a spiritual dimension, would not necessarily have followed the party line on Jewish-Samaritan differences. This may have led to tensions between them and the Jewish authorities in Jerusalem. In one of the Johannine conflict dialogues, "the Jews" accuse Jesus of being a Samaritan (8:48). Perhaps his opponents, aware of the controversial attempts by the Nazorean sect to reach out to the Samaritans, were using Samaritan-baiting to undercut Jesus's message. The stories in Luke of the good Samaritan (10:25–37) and the Samaritan leper who was more thankful than others who were healed (17:11–17) may also reflect Nazorean sympathy for a despised religious group. They show both compassion and gratefulness in persons who should have been enemies of Israel.

The feeding of the five thousand in John 6:1–15 can also be read in the light of i-Nazorean ambivalence about Jewish rites and sacrifices. This episode is one of the few found in both John and the Synoptics, and we find significant differences between the accounts. The miracle in the Synoptics is triggered by a crowd that follows Jesus to a deserted area. The crowd has no place to acquire food, so Jesus feeds them. In John, however, this motivating event for the miracle is missing. Jesus goes up a mountain and sits down to teach his disciples. A crowd follows them. John, but not the Synoptics, notes that "Passover was at hand." Jesus has a short dialogue with Philip, asking the disciple a question "to test him." Then he has the people sit down in the grass, he gives thanks for the bread (but not the fish, as in the Synoptic accounts), and the people eat their fill. The leftovers are collected, twelve baskets. The people seeing this miracle call Jesus "the prophet, the one coming into the world." Jesus perceives that they want to make him king, so he withdraws alone into the surrounding hills.

The author of John seems to be transforming a received story about the feeding of the five thousand into an alternate Passover. He provides several clues that this is his intent. First, he tells us that the miracle happened at the time of Passover. Second, the people who are present sit together and partake of a ritual food.[62] Third, at this alternate Seder, as at the sanctioned Seder, a test question is employed to elicit a teaching.[63] Fourth, bread is blessed and distributed. Finally, Jesus is proclaimed "prophet." Moses, who both participated in the first Passover and gave the people the Passover ritual, was known as "*the* prophet," and God had promised to raise up a prophet like Moses (Deut 18:18).

The section in John 5–10, as commentators note, places the ministry of Jesus in the context of the major Jewish feasts. In addition to the Passover reference at 6:4, John also anchors this section on an unnamed feast (5:1, possibly the Feast of Pentecost), the Feast of Tabernacles (7:2, 37), and Hanukkah (10:22). The various metaphors employed by Jesus in these chapters may be based on the themes of these four feasts. Some have interpreted this as an attempt by the author of John to provide a replacement liturgy. "Just as the Pharisees under Yohanan ben Zakkai respond to the destruction of the temple by adapting its liturgical feasts to the synagogue, so does John respond to the loss of the synagogue by reinterpreting the Jewish liturgical calendar in the light of the person Jesus."[64] The invocations of these feasts are more likely, from the point of view I have adopted, to reflect i-Nazorean symbolic codings of the Jewish festivals. The i-Nazorean communities would have sought ways to celebrate these festivals within their mystical and temple-optional framework. Interpreting the details of these codings is difficult, however, because we know so little about i-Nazorean liturgy and also because what we know about the meanings of festival celebrations in mainline first-century CE Judaism is limited.[65]

Assuming an i-Nazorean context for the Gospel of John also helps to explain the text's focus on the toxic relationship between Jesus's followers and the mainline synagogues. Nicodemus came to Jesus by night, perhaps not wanting his colleagues to know about his interest. He and

---

62. A food (fish) that did not require the sacrificial slaughter of animals, as the standard Passover ritual did.

63. One problem in drawing parallels between John's feeding of the five thousand and any aspect of the Jewish Seder, such as the Four Questions asked by the youngest reader at the table, is that we don't know what parts of the Seder ritual, the Haggadah, emerged during the Second Temple period. For a discussion of the issues, see Kulp, "The Origins," and Marcus, "Passover."

64. Yee, *Jewish Feasts*, 27. For a review of various attempts by Yee and others to correlate Jesus's Johannine teachings with the Jewish feasts, see Daise, *Feasts in John*, 31–103.

65. See Johnson, "The Jewish Feasts."

Joseph of Arimathea became secret followers of Jesus (19:38–42). The author of John explains in several places why part of Jesus's following was penumbral. One of these explanations is in John 9. Jesus heals a blind beggar, and the healing comes to the attention of the Pharisees. They question the former blind man and urge him to play down the event, but he insists that what happened to him was a real miracle and that Jesus was a true prophet. The beggar's parents get pulled into the controversy, but they refuse to commit to their son's point of view. The author of John explains that the parents "feared the Jews, for the Jews had already resolved that if anyone professed Christ, they would be put out of the synagogue" (9:22). Their once-blind son persists in his belief and is indeed "cast out" (9:34). The same theme emerges in the twelfth chapter, when John explains why Jewish leaders were not accepting Jesus's message. God, he says, had "blinded their hearts." Some of the Jewish authorities did accept the message, but they did not admit this publicly so that "they would not be put out of the synagogue." John's conclusion is that "they loved praise from people more than praise from God" (12:42–43). A third installment of this excommunication drama comes in a prediction that Jesus makes in chapter sixteen. He tells his disciples that "they will put you out of the synagogue." Even worse, "the hour is coming when everyone who kills will think that they are offering service to God" (16:2). In all three passages, being "put out of the synagogue" is just one word in Greek, *aposynagōgos*. The word may have been an official term in Jewish circles for a formal ban that would result in a loss of community and religious status.[66] While it is possible that Jesus's followers experienced this penalty in the short years of his public ministry, most commentators find this hard to believe. They maintain that this legal process was experienced by Christian Jews many decades *after* the ministry of Jesus, closer to the time when Christianity and Judaism split. The web I'm weaving here nudges the beginning of this process into an earlier period. Some of the Nazorean groups, the s-Nazoreans, made peace—or at least came to a truce—with Jerusalem's religious authorities in the years following the death of their Messiah. The i-Nazoreans, living closer to the boundaries that circumscribed Jewish belief and practice, slipped outside the circle.

66. See the extensive treatment of *aposynagōgos* as a form of excommunication in Martyn, *History and Theology*, 17–41. Martyn places the experience of *aposynagōgos* in a late first-century CE setting. For a critique of Martyn that locates the experience in the first decades of the Jesus movement, see Jonathan Bernier, *Aposynagōgos*, and Klink, "The Overrealized Expulsion." The thesis that *aposynagōgos* may have been a formal legal act may also be an assumption (Cirafesi, "Rethinking John").

The i-Nazorean cells were declared *aposynagōgos* and turned out of the synagogues.[67] The Gospel of John, penned in these alienated cells, attaches this liminality to the ministry of Jesus.[68]

Finally, let's consider the role of women in the Gospel of John and what this might mean for a specific i-Nazorean point of view. We have looked at Jesus's encounter with his mother in chapter 2 and the Samaritan woman in chapter 4. The other two passages in the gospel that feature women are his interactions with Mary and Martha (chapter 11 and the beginning of 12) and Mary Magdalene (at the cross in 19:25 and in the post-resurrection narrative of chapter 20).

To judge from the positive references to women in both the Synoptics and John, the Nazorean wisdom sect had a more inclusive and less patriarchal view of women than the Near Eastern cultures in which they were embedded. Luke in particular is given high marks for the way he parallels male and female actors in his gospel. His touching portraits of Mary, Elizabeth, and Anna in the gospel's birth narratives have impressed generations of readers. The rise of feminist theology in the late twentieth century, however, has helped us to see that more is going on behind the scenes than a casual reading might suggest. The Synoptics, including Luke, draw androcentric boundaries around the roles of women in the young church.[69] By the end of the first century CE, this agenda would become more explicit. The injunction put in the mouth of Paul, "Let a woman learn in silence with all subjection. I do not permit a woman to teach or exercise authority over a man" (1 Tim 2:11–12), became the standard Christian perspective over the next few centuries.

Against this background, the Gospel of John stands out. Five women in the gospel have strong, decisive characters and are given roles

67. The anonymity of the author of John may be connected to this loss of community status and fellowship. If i-Nazorean communities had been disfellowshipped and the beloved disciple had become a pariah, the author of John may have been concerned that a message about Jesus, if attached to the author's name, would have been rejected out of hand. The name "beloved disciple" both conceals the author's name and emphasizes that the rejection experienced by the author and his group did not come from the Messiah.

68. In the next chapter, I will use the first part of Acts to propose a more explicit timeline for this exclusion.

69. For a range of views on the handling of women in Luke, see Levine and Blickenstaff, *A Feminist Companion*. Compare also a 1996 book by Barbara Reid (Reid, *Choosing*), which emphasized Luke's suppression of women as leaders, with Reid's revisionist approach in her presidential address to the Catholic Biblical Association of America in 2015 (Reid, "The Gospel of Luke").

associated with leadership. Mary, Jesus's mother, has perhaps the least significant role of the five. Still, we see her in chapter 2 with an important office at the marriage in Cana. When Mary asks Jesus to intervene in the wedding's wine problem, Jesus protests, but in the end, he takes directions from her, performing the only miracle-by-order in the gospels. The portrait of the young Mary in Luke's birth narratives, in contrast, has her in an entirely passive role. She is a servant who "ponders in her heart" (2:19) and says, "Let it be to me according to your word" (Luke 1:38).

The Samaritan woman is the recipient of two firsts in the gospel. She is the first to hear Jesus's famous "I am" (4:26, often left out of the usual list of seven "I am" statements) and the first to whom Jesus reveals that he is the Messiah (4:25–26). When she goes to tell other Samaritans about Jesus, she takes on the mission of an apostle, the same mission that the Synoptics assign to the Twelve. And her mission is successful—because of her, many believe in Jesus (4:39). The dialogue that she has with Jesus in chapter 4, which shows openness and perception, contrasts with the befuddlement of the male Nicodemus in the previous chapter. The Samaritan woman is "the most theologically oriented interlocutor of Jesus in the Fourth Gospel."[70]

At the events surrounding the raising of Lazarus, it is Martha and Mary, not their brother Lazarus, who enter into dialogue with Jesus. When Jesus asks Martha if she believes, the question evokes from her the confession, "I believe that you are the Christ, the Son of God who comes into the world" (11:27). Martha's words remind the reader of the confession of Peter in Matthew—Jesus asks who Peter thinks he is and receives the reply, "You are the Christ, the Son of the living God" (Matt 16:16). In Peter's case, the confession becomes the doorway into the leadership of the Twelve and the post-resurrection church. Martha's equally impressive confession could also be interpreted as a badge of church leadership.

Martha's sister Mary is also cast in a leadership role. Six days before Passover, Martha and Mary and their brother Lazarus help to host a dinner for Jesus in Bethany (12:1–8). Since John's Passover falls on a Sabbath (19:31), subtracting six days means that the dinner event happened on Sunday, the day that Christians would select, in honor of the resurrection, for their weekly meetings. The gospel's Bethany meal thus becomes a model for Christian worship. Martha, the text tells us, served at this Sunday meal. Mary anointed the feet of Jesus with nard and dried them

---

70. Schneiders, "Because," 532.

with her hair, performing a double act—the first act, anointing Jesus for his upcoming burial, the second one, cleaning Jesus's feet, a ritual similar to one that Jesus will commend to his disciples a few days later at the Last Supper. In the texts of all four gospels, men object to this extravagant female gesture and are rebuked by Jesus. Mary of Bethany models, in this early pattern of a Christian rite, the role of a worship leader.

At Jesus's Friday death, Mary Magdalene joins the women at the foot of the cross. On Sunday, she is the first to encounter the risen Christ (20:1–18). Mary goes to the tomb before daybreak and finds the tomb open, the door stone removed. She runs to tell Peter and the beloved disciple. The two come to investigate, find the tomb empty, and leave. In the meantime, Mary, who was now weeping outside the tomb, sees a pair of angels. They talk to her. She then turns around and sees Jesus, mistaking him at first for a gardener. When Jesus speaks her name, Mary recognizes him and calls him "rabboni," a word meaning "my teacher," a designation that highlights Mary's role as a student and disciple. Jesus reveals to Mary that he has risen from the dead and charges her with the task of telling his brothers and sisters that he is leaving to meet with God. As commanded, she relates the story to the disciples, saying "I have seen the Lord." Later that day, in the evening, Jesus certifies Mary's witness by also appearing to his disciples (20:19–23). Mary Magdalene thus becomes the first witness to the resurrection and the first to announce the Easter message of the risen Lord. Comparing John's account with the Synoptic Gospels brings John's favorable treatment of Mary into high relief. Of the three Synoptic Gospels, only Matthew mentions Mary by name in the post-resurrection accounts. In Matthew's version (28:1–10), however, Mary loses her exclusive role by being paired with another woman. Her dramatic first-person witness to the brothers and sisters about Jesus's resurrection and heavenly journey is reduced to a message about Jesus seeing his disciples later, in Galilee—the sort of conveyance that might be relegated to a household servant.

The community from which the Gospel of John arose, to judge by the significant roles attached to these five female figures, had a view of women in worship and leadership that was not shared across all the Nazorean communities. Sandra Schneiders sums up this difference: "Not only are an extraordinary number of John's main characters women, but these women are assigned the very community-founding roles and functions, namely Christological confession, missionary witness, and paschal proclamation, that are assigned to Peter and the Twelve in the

Synoptics."[71] The i-Nazoreans and s-Nazoreans, it is likely, differed over
the roles women could play in their communities. The i-Nazoreans admitted women as equals to men in their society and ceremonies and accepted them into leadership positions.[72]

DIFFERENCES THAT MATTER

By projecting from parts of the Jesus story found in the Gospel of John,
I have derived a few details about the i-Nazoreans. But what about the
parts of the story that are in the Synoptics but missing from John? These
might also indicate differences in the communities of origin, some even
going back before the events they describe. Let's look at John-Synoptic
disparities on four points: handling of the disciples, differences in apocalyptic expectations, inclusion of detailed ethical norms, and matters of
geography and chronology.

First, John and the Synoptics do not handle the *identity of the disciples*
in the same way. Jesus had twelve primary disciples, and Acts and all three
of the Synoptic Gospels have lists of these Twelve. With a little tweaking,
we could argue that the Synoptics and Acts agree on their names. The
Gospel of John, however, has no such list. The author of John is aware of
them, though—in several Johannine verses "the Twelve" are mentioned,
and at various places in the text of John, about half of the synoptic Twelve
are referred to by name. We also have several persons in the Gospel of John
that, if we didn't have lists of the Twelve from the Synoptics, we would be
tempted to assign to this exclusive male cadre. There is Nathanael, whom
we looked at above. He is grouped with other disciples in John 21:1–2.
And Lazarus, the friend that Jesus raised from the dead. The beloved disciple, the author of the gospel, would be another candidate.

Individual disciples in the synoptic Twelve do not get the same
treatment in John. Peter claims about the same amount of space, but

71. Schneiders, "Because," 518.

72. You may have noticed that I have not employed the unpaired masculine pronoun for the author of John that I used for the authors of Matthew and Luke. Some
scholars believe that the extensive female perspective in the Gospel of John is an argument for female involvement in the authorship of the gospel. This is possible, and I
don't want to exclude it. But the motivation behind such arguments seems to be that
androcentrism was so pervasive in this time and place that only a woman's hand could
account for the strong female perspective. This does not take into account the thesis I'm
developing in this chapter—that there was a group of Christian Jews actively seeking to
reduce the significance of gender roles in the search for God.

several disciples who have speaking roles in the Synoptics have lower
profiles in John. The brothers James and John, for example, are prominent in the Synoptics but only appear in the Gospel of John once, as "the
sons of Zebedee" (21:2). A few of the Twelve, in contrast, get much larger
roles in John than in the Synoptics. Three of these—Philip, Andrew, and
Thomas—receive an unusual amount of attention in the text.

Philip, Andrew, and Thomas, we might speculate, were given larger
roles in the Gospel of John because they had some association with the
author or the author's community. One possibility is that they may have
had i-Nazorean backgrounds or have been received into a community
with other i-Nazoreans. In support of this, consider that members of the
i-Nazorean group were probably more cosmopolitan and literate than
their s-Nazorean counterparts. Chances are that most of the i-Nazoreans
would have been fluent in Greek. For some it would have been their main
language. Interestingly, of the twelve disciples listed in the Synoptics,
only Philip and Andrew have names of unquestionable Greek origin.[73] It
seems likely that these two came from homes where Greek was a primary
language.

We have some further evidence of Philip and Andrew's Greek background in the text of John. During Holy Week, just after Jesus's triumphal
entry into Jerusalem, some "Greeks" (Greek Jews, we can assume) came
to Jerusalem and sought out Philip. They told him they wanted to see Jesus. Philip reports this to Andrew, and the two of them take the message
of these Greeks to Jesus (12:20–22). Jesus responds with a speech about
his impending glorification, a reference to his death. He prays to the Father to "glorify your name," and the response is a voice from heaven that
says, "I have glorified it, and I will glorify it again" (12:23–30). As I will

73. The original name of the disciple that Jesus rechristened as "Peter" (in Greek) or
"Cephas" (in Aramaic) is given in most textual traditions as "Simon," a name occasionally given to males in Greek cultures. But the Greek "Simon" has a close equivalent,
"*Shim'on*" (sometimes transliterated as "Simeon" or "Symeon"), in Hebrew/Aramaic.
It seems likely that, in spite of the Greek-influenced NT spelling "Simon," many of the
first-century Jews with this moniker thought of themselves as having a Hebrew/Ara-
maic name. The popularity of the name "Simon" in first-century Palestine argues for
this—it was the most common male name among Greco-Roman Palestinian Jews in
this period according to Ilan, *Lexicon*, 226. While Hebrew literature often preserved
the distinction between "Simon" and "Simeon," for Josephus and some Septuagint authors, Ilan notes, "there really was no difference" (Ilan, *Lexicon*, 227). Still, the fact that
Simon Peter and the Greek-named Andrew were brothers and presumably grew up in
the same household leaves open the possibility that Simon Peter's parents may have
bestowed on him what they thought of as a Greek name.

point out below, "glory" is probably a code term in i-Nazorean communities. What we may be dealing with in this passage is an i-Nazorean group reaching out to Jesus through two members of the faction who belonged to Jesus's inner circle. But why did they ask for a meeting? Consider that when Jesus had entered Jerusalem at the beginning of Holy Week, he had been acclaimed with palm branches and shouts that he was the "King of Israel" (12:13).[74] Setting up an immediate messianic reign through political revolution would not have been part of the i-Nazorean agenda. The members of this delegation of Greeks were probably concerned about this turn of events. Perhaps they were seeking reassurance from Jesus that he would continue to follow the path laid out in their spiritual framework. He was the Wisdom/Logos who comes from God and returns to God, not an earthly potentate. They are assured, not only by Jesus, but also by a heavenly voice, that glory—both coming from it and returning to it—was still the agenda.

The third disciple to get special treatment in the Gospel of John, Thomas, may not have had the same background as Philip and Andrew. His name—which means "twin"—is Semitic, not Greek. Possibly Thomas came from an s-Nazorean background but later associated himself with those who had roots in i-Nazorean communities. If that is the case, it throws some light on his role as doubting Thomas in the Johannine post-resurrection narrative (20:24–29). Unlike the more mystical i-Nazoreans, Thomas, at the time when Jesus rose from the dead, had little experience in believing what he could not see and handle. His insistence that he needed physical proof to believe that Jesus had risen from the dead provides the Johannine Jesus with the opportunity to commend to him—and through him to everyone—a mystical journey to God. "Blessed are those who have not seen," says Jesus, "and yet believe" (20:29). Thomas, we might assume, eventually adopted the mystical path and united with the i-Nazorean faction. This would explain his prominence in the Gospel of John. It also might explain why, of the seven times that his name is mentioned in the Gospel of John, in three of them he is said to also be "known as Didymus," a Greek word for "twin." Switching language communities can mean changing names.

A second difference that reflects the sectarian split between the Gospel of John and the Synoptics is *the way that the gospels treat apocalyptic themes.* Matthew, Mark, and Luke have chapters that script the end times.

---

74. Only the Gospel of John records that the crowd acclaimed Jesus as king. The Synoptic Gospels are less specific.

Several of the synoptic parables convey messages about how to respond during these last events. John omits such materials. The gospel does, though, provide two small snapshots of the future. The first is about the final judgment. In John 5, Jesus says that "the hour is coming—and now is—when the dead will hear the voice of the Son of Man, and those who hear will live." Those who have died will come forth from their graves, "the ones who have done good things to the resurrection of life, but the ones who have done evil to the resurrection of judgment" (5:25–29). In the next chapter of John, Jesus says three times that he will "raise up" the ones who believe in him "on the last day" (6:40, 44, 54). The second snapshot in the Gospel of John may be about Jesus's second coming. At the beginning of the Last Supper discourse, Jesus says that he is going to the Father to prepare a place for his disciples, and that he will "come again and receive you to myself, so that you will be where I am" (14:3). Whether this really refers to the second coming of Christ, however, is far from clear. It could be a preview of what comes next in the discourse, the gift of the Spirit. These two small glances are all John gives us of end times. There is no detailed scripting, no signs of the second coming, no abomination of desolation, no wars and rumors of wars.

Not only are these apocalyptic themes missing from John, they may also be criticized in the gospel. In chapter 11 of John, in the scenes around the raising of Lazarus, Martha intercepts Jesus on the way to the house that she and Mary shared with their brother Lazarus. She complains that Jesus had come too late. "If you had been here," she says, "my brother would not have died." Jesus assures her, "Your brother will rise again." Martha, misunderstanding what Jesus is predicting, utters the line, "I know that he will rise again in the resurrection at the last day." In Martha's somewhat dismissive response, we may be hearing the lack of interest in John's community about the end times. The last judgment, though certain and final, does not merit a lot of thought. Unless, of course, the judgment can be given an immediate and mystical meaning. Which is just what Jesus does in his next words to Martha. "*I* am the resurrection and the life," he says. "The one who lives and believes in me shall never die" (11:21–26). We can see the same anti-apocalyptic dismissal played out in 1 John, a letter widely believed to originate in the group that gave rise to the Gospel of John. The writer says, "you have heard the antichrist is coming." The letter's readers would have heard this, of course, from end-times scripts, such as the ones in the Synoptic Gospels, that were circulating in the churches. The author's response, that "many antichrists have come," seems like it is intended to discredit these scripts.[75] The epistle goes on to identify these antichrists as those who had separated themselves from the community—a far less threatening foe than the armies of evil imagined in apocalyptic texts (2:18–22).

The s-Nazoreans, to judge by the Synoptic Gospels, adopted several elements of the apocalyptic approach that had captivated the imaginations of many Jewish sects in the late Second Temple period. The i-Nazoreans, however, seem to have held the apocalyptic dimension at arm's length. They sought a mystical union with God that was more real than any future intervention in history. Jesus had promised his disciples that, through the Spirit he would send, they would know "that I am in my Father and you in me and I in you" (14:20). Those who experience the mystical reality of Christ's presence don't have to wait for his bodily return to be in the presence of God.

A third disparity between the Synoptics and the Gospel of John is in the *attention they give to ethical rules*. As we noted in our earlier discussion of Matthew's gospel and the Epistle of James, the followers of Jesus replaced the detailed legal framework of the Pharisees with a new set of laws. There was, to be sure, a unifying theme behind these moral imperatives, which Jesus summarized as loving God and loving one's neighbor (Matt 22:36–40). But focusing on these core principles did not do away with the need for more specific imperatives. The Sermon on the Mount contains many of these detailed commands, and the Epistle of James is a broad compendium of the new law. The adage-oriented wisdom tradition of Proverbs and Sirach is on full display in the s-Nazorean side of Christian Judaism. The Gospel of John, in contrast, lacks these detailed rules. Like Matthew, John invokes a core ethical imperative: "A new commandment I give to you, that you love one another" (13:34). But unlike Matthew, the Gospel of John does not unpack this core principle into more detailed directives. The ethical perspective in John is more implied than explicit.[76] These two ways of dealing with ethical norms may reflect a

---

75. Later in the development of the church, remarks Bryan Wilson, the institution "had ready-made enemies in the figures of devils and Anti-Christ, who could clearly be made to symbolise sectaries" (Wilson, *Religious Sects*, 18). Perhaps the term "antichrist" had already become an overused term in apocalyptic discourse at the time 1 John was written.

76. The recognition of an implied or implicit ethics in the Gospel of John has generated a number of recent studies. For a review of these, see Skinner, "Ethics." Ethics in John, Skinner observes, "must be discussed in ways that depart from the outdated indicative-imperative approach" (Skinner, "Ethics," 285).

difference between i-Nazorean and s-Nazorean halakhah. The Gospel of John arises from an i-Nazorean community that is committed to a mystical understanding of life, one that values inner attitudes over an external conformity to norms. For mystics, spelling out duty to God in a rulebook can seem more of a loss than a gain. It takes eyes off the real prize. We might compare this difference in how rules are handled to the modern trend to do prenups before marriage. Prenups make a lot of sense, but fewer than 10% of marriages use them. Recording the meaning of love on a piece of paper can feel like it devalues the love that leads people into marriage. If our goal is union with God, laying out the path to the goal as a set of rules makes us feel like we don't trust our own intentions, that we are afraid the Holy Spirit will not provide enough guidance.

The author of John may, in fact, have explained to us the absence of detailed rules in the gospel. The Johannine Jesus says to some of his less devoted disciples that if they continue to follow him, "you will know the truth and the truth will make you free." The disciples are offended by the implication that they are not free, saying that "we are the seed of Abraham and have never been in subjection to anyone." On a physical level, the statement is patently false. Israel had been in subjection to many nations—Egypt, Babylon, Persia, Syria, and most recently Rome. But Jesus doesn't respond on this level. He is talking about a different kind of freedom, an inner autonomy that allows us to love and be loved. "Everyone who commits sin is a slave to sin," Jesus points out, and slaves do not have the same relationship to their masters that children have to their parents (8:31–38). Detailed rules are more consistent with master-slave scenarios. The free and intense love between a parent and child reaches a better goal with fewer rules. Those in i-Nazorean circles sought to perform the works of servants while using the motivation of loving children.

The last difference between the Gospel of John and the Synoptics that I would like to highlight is the *issue of geography and chronology.* In Matthew and Mark, the ministry of Jesus is a Galilean phenomenon. He grows up in Nazareth and he travels to Judea only twice as an adult, first to be baptized and then to die. The Gospel of John, however, has Jesus making multiple trips between Galilee and Judea, with miracles and signs occurring in both places. The author of the Gospel of John, who probably called Judea home during the years of Jesus's ministry, wants to make sure readers know that Jesus, though he grew up in Nazareth, spent time in both Galilee and Judea.[77] John is making the point, I believe, that Jesus belongs to *all* the Nazorean groups, not just to the s-Nazoreans living around Nazareth. The Gospel of Matthew, reflecting the perspective of the s-Nazoreans, is happy to leave us with the impression that the ministry of Jesus was a Galilean project.

This two-locus emphasis comes out in a difference between Synoptics and John about Jesus's *patris*, his home territory. In Matthew's narrative, we find Jesus stopping off at his *patris* during his travels around Galilee. This would have been Nazareth (though only Luke names the place). The people in his home territory struggle to connect this famous miracle worker to the person they had known as a child. Jesus reminds the people of the adage, "a prophet is not without honor, except in his own *patris*" (Matt 13:53–58). Jesus's *patris* according to the Synoptics, then, is in Galilee. The author of John gives us a different setting for this same saying. In chapter 4, Jesus "departed again to Galilee" after a controversial baptizing ministry in Judea (4:3). He pauses in Samaria for a short stop then continues on his way to Galilee. At this point, John adds the comment: "For Jesus himself bore witness that a prophet has no honor in his *patris*." The gospel goes on to relate that "when he came to Galilee, the Galileans welcomed him" (4:44–45). The natural assumption of anyone reading this passage would be that Jesus invoked the dishonored prophet adage about his home territory of *Judea*.[78] So where was Jesus's *patris*— Judea or Galilee? Possibly the s-Nazorean and the i-Nazorean groups had different views on this topic.

One of the most serious chronological differences between the Gospel of John and the Synoptics concerns the dating of events in the last week of Jesus's life. John and the Synoptics report many of the same details in their Holy Week stories. Both assume that Jesus shared a Last

77. The setting for about four-fifths of the verses in John is Judea.

78. Later in the Gospel of John, during the interaction between Jesus and the crowd at the Feast of Tabernacles, the people say that they know that Jesus is from Galilee, not from Judea (7:41–42,52), a supposition that Jesus does not contradict. This makes it less likely that the author would have left the impression in chapter 4 that Galilee was not Jesus's *patris*. I can think of two ways of interpreting 4:44 that could avoid the assumption that Galilee was not Jesus's *patris*. The first is to read the linking particle, which in most translations is rendered as "for," as introducing, not a reason in favor, but a reason against, as though it meant "yet" or "even though." This would constitute, however, an extremely rare sense of the particle. The second tactic is to understand 4:44 as the work of a careless redactor. The statement in 4:44 about prophets and their *patris* does in fact look like it could be an editorial interjection. Some translators even put parentheses around it.

Supper with his disciples on Thursday,[79] died on a Friday, and rose from the dead on a Sunday. Both tell us that the events took place at the beginning of Passover, the most important of the Jewish festivals. What they don't agree on is how the days of Holy Week map onto the Jewish religious calendar. The calendar employed by the Jerusalem priesthood for the timing of religious festivals was not in sync with the weekly cycles. The day before Passover (the Day of Preparation) and Passover itself could have been either a Thursday-Friday or a Friday-Saturday in the year of Jesus's death. John assumes that Friday was the Day of Preparation and Saturday was Passover. The Johannine Jesus, then, would have died on the afternoon of the Day of Preparation, when the lambs were slaughtered at the temple for the upcoming Passover Seder in the evening. This means that John's Thursday night Last Supper, occurring at the evening beginning of the Day of Preparation, would not have been a Passover Seder. The Synoptics, however, opt for a Thursday-Friday mapping. They say the Friday when Jesus died was the day of Passover, making the Last Supper, which took place the evening before his death, a celebration of the Passover Seder.

I can't pause to look into the details here—many books have been written to reconcile or to divide the gospel authors on this timeline question. I'm more interested in how these differences reflect underlying points of view. From the synoptic perspective—and probably from the perspective of the s-Nazoreans centered in Galilee—it would have been appropriate for Jesus to enter into the full ritual of this highest of Jewish holidays. By instituting the Eucharistic meal at Passover, the Christian Jewish sect acquired a symbolic meal that both reflected and transcended the Passover meal. Passover celebrates the deliverance of the Jewish people from Egyptian bondage. In the Eucharist, Jesus delivers his people from the bondage of sin. For the author of John, Jesus is the Lamb of God. He comes from the Father, sacrifices himself for the world, and returns to the Father. The most appropriate mapping of his death, then, is to the Day of Preparation, at the time when the Passover lambs were slaughtered. At the Johannine Last Supper, Jesus and the disciples share a meal, but there are no indications that it is either a Seder or a Eucharist. Students of the NT are perplexed by the absence of the core Christian sacrament,

79. Strong arguments have been made that the Last Supper may have been on a Wednesday rather than a Thursday. See, for example, Humphreys, *The Mystery*. This perspective depends on a synthesizing approach to the events of Passion Week, where each gospel reveals only a part of a complex series of events.

the Eucharist, from John's gospel. Some argue that John gives us a reinterpreted Eucharist in the "I am the bread of heaven" sequence in John 6.
Even if they are right, however, the problem does not go away—John still
does not show Jesus initiating the Eucharistic rite in the context of his
passion. This suggests that either John's community did not celebrate the
Eucharist described in the Synoptics, or that it did, but the author wanted
to minimize the significance of the Eucharist.

This discrepancy over what happens at the Last Supper in John and
in the Synoptics also hints that the s-Nazoreans and the i-Nazoreans may
have had different ways of observing Passover. The s-Nazoreans families
seem to have been open to the full Jewish Passover ritual, with many of
them making the pilgrimage to Jerusalem to celebrate the festival with
a temple-slaughtered lamb. The i-Nazorean "families," which may have
been mostly fictive kin groups than actual blood relatives, may have
replaced the Passover Seder with a ceremony that did not involve the
slaughter of an animal.[80]

The i-Nazoreans may also have omitted wine from their Passover
rite. Bread appears to have been part of the meal at John's Last Supper—
Jesus quotes a line from one of the Psalms about his betrayer sharing
bread with him (13:18, quoting Ps 41:9). But no cup is mentioned. Jesus,
John says, dips a morsel of bread in something, but it is not clear whether
he dips it in a food dish or a drink. And if it was a drink, it may have
been water rather than wine. We are reminded of the Therapeutan rituals
described by Philo. They seem to have had no meat at their sacred meals,
and the bread and herbs (hyssop) were served with water.[81]

If the Passover rite of the i-Nazoreans did not include slaughter-
ing lambs or drinking cups of wine, what did it include? The Johannine

80. The author of John may reflect s-Nazorean and i-Nazorean differences about
Passover when he described Jesus's first attendance at the Jerusalem Passover festival
in chapter 2. Rather than saying "the Passover" was at hand, the text says that "the
Passover of the Jews" (2:13) was coming, as though its particular rites were not shared
by the author. In a similar way, the author describes, earlier in the same chapter, stone
jars that were set aside "according to the purification customs of the Jews," also suggesting that John's community did not practice the same rites. John 2 is not an isolated
example—John uses the phrases "feast of the Jews" and "Passover of the Jews" three
more times (5:1, 6:4, 11:55).

81. John does not mention Jesus's drinking habits. Matthew, however, does—he says
that the opponents of Jesus called him a "drunkard and a glutton" (Matt 11:19). It is
possible that the evangelists had conflicting agendas on this issue, with John representing a community that wanted to downplay Jesus's use of wine and Matthew speaking
for a community in which drinking wine not only was not an issue, but even had a
liturgical and symbolic role.

account of the Last Supper suggests that foot washing may have been part of their observation. Washing the feet of guests at meals was a common ritual and could easily have been worked into the i-Nazorean's formal celebrations, not only at the Passover but at the other times when they came together as a community. The strange dialogue between Jesus and Peter at the Johannine Last Supper may reflect differences in how the two Nazorean groups observed community rituals. The dialogue starts off with Peter refusing to have his feet washed. Jesus lays down an ulti-matum: either he washes Peter's feet or Peter loses his relationship with Jesus. Peter, overreacting, asks Jesus to perform a more thorough wash-ing, but Jesus refuses, saying, "The one who has bathed needs only to have his feet washed to be completely clean. You are clean." Jesus then adds, "but not all of you [are clean]," referring to Judas (13:6–11). We don't have much information about what was included in first century CE Jewish festivals, but full immersions in *mikvoth* were common dur-ing this era—more than 300 of these stepped, plastered baths have been found in Judea and Galilee.[82] In this dialogue with Peter, the Johannine Jesus may be defending the foot-washing ceremony of the i-Nazoreans. If the participants in a ceremony, following the way of life rather than the way of death, are spiritually clean and not harbouring the evil plans of a Judas, then the standard guest service of foot washing is ritually adequate. The more extreme lustrations employed by the non-sectarian Jews—and perhaps accepted as valid by the s-Nazoreans—conveyed the wrong symbolic message. Such extreme rites, John seems to be saying, symbolize that a person can live in a morally unclean state and then have this magically removed by a ritual bath. The person following the way of wisdom lives in a state of grace. To enter into full communal worship, the person needs only the dust of the road, a symbol of the distractions of daily life, removed.

The introduction of a water rite in John's Last Supper and the failure to mention wine at the meal may be connected to another passage in John. The beloved disciple, witnessing the crucifixion, testified that both water and blood came out of the side of Jesus when the Roman guard pierced

82. Reed, "Archaeological Contributions," 52. One explanation for Jesus's puzzling statement in John 13 about bathing and foot-washing is that visitors to Jerusalem, mak-ing use of one of the *mikvoth* in the villages surrounding the city to ensure that they entered Jerusalem in a ritually pure state, still picked up foot dust on the short trip into the city and needed foot-washing to remind them of the effects of their immersion. This explanation, however, overlooks the symbolic frame that Jesus casts around the discourse when he refers to Judas not being clean.

him with a spear (19:34–35). There has been much speculation about what John meant by including this passage and why it is connected in the text to giving "true testimony." Most commonly, interpreters reference the event to baptism (water) and the eucharist (blood). But what if the author of John has in mind the difference in s-Nazorean and i-Nazorean practices? The i-Nazoreans may not have used blood-like wine at their communal celebrations. They seem to have replaced it with rites, such as foot-washing, that were based around water. Many of the i-Nazoreans, if the experience of the Therapeutae is applicable, may have drunk only water. The solemn affirmation by the author (or redactor) about the beloved disciple's observation of both blood and water may be symbolically connected to the fractured Nazorean communities. John could be saying, in essence, that both substances and both factions belong to the Jesus movement. Another Johannine passage with wide-ranging interpretations may also be relevant here. In the good shepherd allegory of John 10, Jesus says that he has "other sheep that are not from this sheepfold" that need to be included. He will call them, and they will hear his voice and become "one shepherd, one flock" (10:16). Though usually understood as a joining of gentiles and Jews, the author could be symbolizing the coming together of the two main branches of the Nazoreans.

SECTARIAN VOCABULARY

Let me wrap up this chapter on the Gospel of John with a few thoughts about the vocabulary of the i-Nazoreans. Up to this point, I've been dealing with the relationship between John and the i-Nazoreans in terms of concepts and rituals. I'd like to drop to a lower level and ask if preferred terms and phrasings might be part of the i-Nazorean package. My own journey through several branches of modern Christianity has made me aware how important the choice of words can be. We can often locate a person in a certain movement or denomination or spiritual orientation by the way they speak. If you're suffering, and I tell you to "offer it up," then you can assume that I'm a Catholic, probably a cradle Catholic. If I see you hanging out with the wrong crowd and warn you about "fellow-shipping with unbelievers" and I sprinkle my speech with words such as "pretrib rapture" and "saved," you know that I'm an evangelical.

Before we consult specific terms in John, we should think a moment about what can be learned from the overall style employed in the Gospel of John. We looked earlier at some wisdom devices in the gospel—irony, dialogues, ambiguity, abstractions. These are part of the Johannine style. But the author's way of stringing words together also sets John apart. The sentences in this gospel are usually shorter and the verbs simpler than what we find in the Synoptics. Contiguous clauses are frequently joined with coordinating rather than subordinating conjunctions. Words and phrases from one sentence are repeated in the next. The narrative line is not arranged in argument form. Instead, the author circles back to topics, inserting them into new contexts. (You don't need to read the gospel in Greek, by the way, to notice this unique style—a reasonably literal translation will do.)

In the nineteenth and early twentieth century, these curious Johannine stylisms were often put down to the gospel being either a translation from a Semitic language or written by someone whose first language was a Semitic tongue. This theory has fallen out of favor. The Gospel of John is good Greek, and the writer has the language command of a native speaker. We need another explanation for the differences in style between John and other Greek writers. I don't know what this explanation is—the answer is no doubt complex—but I do have one idea to toss into the mix. We may be looking at a prose style that arose in a mystical community. In my readings of the mystics, I have noticed the way that language can bend under the sense of an indwelling spirit. Examples that come to mind are the journals of Quaker divines, such as the *Journal of John Woolman*. Or Julian of Norwich and the fourteenth century English mystics. Without a more extensive body of texts from the Johannine community, however, we have no way of knowing what aspects of John's style derive from the author's own affectations and what might be due to a community style. I just put forward, as a mere possibility, that we may be dealing with a mystagogic prosody. Its purpose is not only to tell a story but also to guide the reader into a state of mind that is receptive to mystical experience. The goal is not just to inform, but to transform.

The same warning about the lack of other texts applies to vocabulary choices—we can only hypothesize that the terms I will mention below represent the vocabulary of a sectarian community and not just the idiosyncrasies of an author. Here, though, are five terms that catch my eye when I read through the Gospel of John.

The first is the word "glory," a word often associated with God. The Hebrew word most often translated as the English "glory" is *kavod*. We find this noun or its verb form about 200 times in the Tanak, about half of which are in the Psalms and Isaiah. Commentators point out that *kavod* is closely associated with the Shekinah, the presence of God that was manifested in the pillar of fire that led the Israelites out of Egypt and across the desert. The usual Greek translation of the Hebrew word for "glory" is *doxa*. *Doxa* is at least as common in the NT as *kavod* is in the Tanak.

While the words for "glory" are part of the general religious vocabulary of both Judaism and Christianity, the Gospel of John stands out from this background. It has more instances of *doxa* than any of the Synoptics, and it has ways of using this term that expand the boundaries of its meaning. Many of John's most idiomatic uses of *doxa* occur in chapter 17, in the prayer that Jesus speaks at the end of the Last Supper. He asks the Father to glorify the Son so that the Son can glorify the Father (17:1). Jesus associates glory with his pre-incarnation state, asking the Father to "glorify me alongside yourself with the glory I had alongside you before the world came into existence" (17:5). He imparts this heavenly glory to the disciples (17:22), with the result that he is "glorified in them" (17:10). He tells the Father that he wants his disciples to be with him some day and to "see my glory," the glory that God gave to him because God loved him "before the foundation of the world" (17:24). In the mind of the author of John, "glory" becomes a code term for the splendor of God's presence, the Shekinah. We can imagine this word popping up in the meditations and prayers of the i-Nazoreans, taking on a symbolic role that goes beyond the everyday sense of the word. "Glory," in fact, may have been a staple of i-Nazorean worship long before John placed the word in Jesus's mouth. The Simeon who blessed the baby Jesus in the temple and who may be, as I speculated earlier, a Nazorean sectarian, called Jesus "a light of revelation for the gentiles and the *doxa* of Israel" (Luke 2:32). Simeon has drawn his statement about Jesus being a light for the gentiles from the messianic prophecy in Isaiah 9. That prophecy begins with the claim that God will "make glorious [the verb form of *kavod*] . . . the Galilee of the gentiles" (Isa 9:1–2).

A second Johannine phrase that may have gained a more restricted sectarian meaning among the i-Nazoreans is "eternal life" (*zoē aōinios*). The Gospel of John uses this phrase 17 times. We hear it a few times in the Synoptics, but in these gospels, it is simply one term among many. John raises it to a new level. "Eternal life," in its most basic sense, is a phrase that looks toward a future state. We see the focus on the future, for example, when Jesus says that it is the will of his Father that everyone who believes "will have eternal life, and I will raise him up on the last

day" (6:40). Every example of the phrase in the text of John is compatible
with this future-oriented meaning. But "eternal life" may also refer to a
quality of life, something possible in the present. In the fifth chapter of
John, for example, Jesus says, "the one who hears my word and believes
in the one who sent me has eternal life and does not come into judgment
but is passed over from death into life" (5:24). The tenses in this verse,
the present and the perfect, lead us to think that eternal life is a current
possession of Jesus's followers.[83] The phrase "eternal life" was probably
layered with mystical meaning for the i-Nazoreans.

The third term that has a strong metaphorical role in the Gospel of
John is "light." Light's literal opposite, "darkness," is also merged into the
metaphor, as is "truth" (3:21). The prologue of John evokes this image
of light. Jesus is the "true light that comes into the world to enlighten
every person" (1:9). Later in the gospel, Jesus is called "the light of the
world" (8:12, 9:5), and as long as Jesus is around, the darkness is held
at bay (12:35). Those who believe in him become "the children of light"
(12:36). The frequent use of the light metaphor in John—over a dozen
times—suggests that it was part of the i-Nazorean vocabulary. The Therapeutae, as Philo explains, also invoked metaphors of light and truth. The
members prayed that their minds would be "filled with a heavenly light"
and that their souls would "follow the way of truth." When the Dead Sea
Scrolls were published, scholars discovered that the Johannine community held no patent on this group of metaphors—the Essenes also made
regular use of "light" and "darkness."[84] In the case of light and its metaphors, we are probably dealing with important elements in the liturgical
and conceptual universe of the i-Nazoreans.

Because "glory," "eternal life," and "light" occur at high frequen-
cies in the Gospel of John, the metaphors that they mark out seem like
plausible candidates for sectarian language. But words without these fre-
quencies may also be part of the i-Nazorean vocabulary. The term "gatekeeper," which the Gospel of John places in the mouth of Jesus only once
(10:3), could be part of the sectarian argot. In the tenth chapter of the
Gospel of John, Jesus unpacks a series of related analogies. (In 10:6, John

83. They could, though, be examples of present and perfect tenses used to create
a sense of vividness.

84. The overlap at the metaphorical level, however, may be superficial—the Essene
images arise from a dualistic framework that is not part of the NT backstory. For more
on the comparison between Essene dualism and that in the Gospel of John, see Brown,
"The Qumran Scrolls and John."

calls this type of speech *paroimia*, an equivalent of the Hebrew *mashal* or some subset of it.) Jesus begins by talking about the difference between a shepherd and a sheep thief. The thief tries to break into the sheepfold by a back way. The shepherd goes in at the door of the fold, which the door-keeper (*thyrōros*) opens (10:1–6). In this analogy, Jesus is the shepherd. The disciples don't seem to understand this image, though, so Jesus starts another analogy, one in which Jesus is the door (*thyra*), and the sheep enter through him to find pasture (10:7–10). Could *thyrōros*, I wonder, be the name that members of the i-Nazoreans applied to leaders of the groups? Jesus is the door, *thyra*, and no leader would pre-empt that role, but "doorkeeper" could apply to someone who guided people to the door. The mixed metaphors—Jesus being in one analogy the shepherd and in another the door—may be reflections of multiple explanations in the i-Nazorean communities about the symbolic roles of their doorkeepers, their leaders. And some of these leaders, as I noted earlier, were probably women.[85]

Another term of interest is "branch." In the fifteenth chapter of the Gospel of John, Jesus begins an extended analogy by saying, "I am the true vine, my Father is the gardener." The disciples in this analogy are pictured as branches on the vine. The relationship of the branches to the vine is called "abiding," and when the branches are in this state, they bear fruit. The branches are also pruned so that they bear more fruit. If they don't bear fruit, the branches are lopped off and burned (15:1–8). The Nazorean sect, I speculated earlier, took their name from the word "branch" in Isaiah 11:1, where the prophet says that "a shoot shall come out from the stem of Jesse, and a branch (*netser*) from its roots shall bear fruit." If we make a connection between "branch" in this gospel passage and the name of the sect, we come up with a reading that may relate to divisions within the Nazoreans. All the Nazorean groups and all their members are branches. But only the ones following the mystical practice of abiding are the ones who bear fruit. The others—the s-Nazoreans— must submit to pruning, to take them closer to the true vine, or they will be permanently separated from the vine.[86]

85. See the section in the Appendixes on "I-Nazorean Doorkeepers."

86. The Gospel of John has many "I am" metaphors. The classic seven are all fol-lowed by predicate nominatives: "I am the bread of life" (6:35), "I am the door" (10:9), and so on. The "I am" of John 15:1, "I am the true vine," is the only one of these seven sayings that qualifies the predicate noun with the adjective "true." This suggests that there is a vine that is *not* true. Most casual readers probably understand this "true" as a marker for a metaphor, a role the word plays elsewhere in John (e.g., in 1:9 and 6:32,

JOHN AND MATTHEW

In this chapter, I have used the Gospel of John to explore a rift in the sectarian Judaism that merged with Christian Judaism. I contrasted the Gospel of John with the Synoptics, treating the gospels as representatives of two subgroups of the Nazorean sect. A topical question occurs at this point. Which of the two is closer to the Jesus they each claim to represent? Should we put more trust in the Gospel of John or in the Gospel of Matthew?

For myself, I find the question clouded with personal bias. On the one hand, it is difficult for me to set aside my early exposure to the synoptic stories. I tend to measure everything I have read against them.[87] On the other hand, the mystical John resonates with my own journey, and I believe that John's account, even if slanted, includes events at which the author was an eyewitness. In the imaginative webs I have been weaving in the last two chapters—the story of a sectarian wisdom tradition and the fractured Nazoreans—I detect a slight preference for the synoptic accounts. As I close out the story of this last web, however, I would like to shift back to a more balanced point of view. I do not think that either Matthew or John can claim sole ownership of the historical Jesus.

But how can they both be right? To answer this question, let me unroll a short scenario that might explain how the two perspectives, that of Matthew's s-Nazoreans and that of John's i-Nazoreans, could have lodged in the life and ministry of Jesus. I'll do this by returning to my imaginative narrative and projecting the later differences between the two groups of Nazoreans back into the family of Jesus.

Joseph, Jesus's father, seems to me a solid s-Nazorean. Let's assume that he lived in an s-Nazorean community around Nazareth, married an s-Nazorean wife, and had a large family. Joseph's wife dies, and Joseph, perhaps on one of his festival trips to Jerusalem, contracts for a young

---

"true light" and "true bread from heaven"). But one wonders why this is the only "I am" saying to be marked this way—they are all metaphors and unlikely to be understood in any other way. It is possible that the author of John is not flagging a metaphor by using the word "true" but emphasizing how important it is that the s-Nazoreans, who call themselves "branch" people, do not forget that the true vine is Jesus and not the communities that the people belong to.

87. Most current Jesus research also has this bias. "If we will ever be able to determine the language of the historical Jesus, it will be much closer to the style of the Synoptic sayings than to the Johannine dialogues and discourses" (Frey, "Kingdom of God," 443).

wife from a more urbanized i-Nazorean family living in the Judean hills around Jerusalem.

In Matthew's birth narratives, which I will follow here, we do not learn where Mary was at the time of the Annunciation. She was pledged to Joseph, but she may have been living at her home in Judea, perhaps in Bethlehem, when the vision of the angel came. She becomes pregnant, and Joseph, having returned to Galilee after arranging the contract, hears about her pregnancy. After some thought and prayer—and a vision—he decides to honor the marriage contract.

Hoping to minimize the fallout from the untimely pregnancy, Joseph decides not to bring Mary to Nazareth right away. He will go to her home and stay for a while. He leaves his younger children from his first marriage with kin/sect members in Nazareth, hands his business over to the oldest sons, and makes the journey to Bethlehem to marry his betrothed. Their son Jesus is born. Herod, hearing about the Nazorean prophecy and the birth, takes an unhealthy interest the child. To protect the baby, Joseph, Mary, and Jesus leave Bethlehem. Galilee would not have put them out of the reach of Herod's long arm, so they travel to Egypt and take refuge with i-Nazoreans connected to the family of Mary. When Herod dies, the family tries to return. Hearing that the Romans have given Herod's son Archelaus the crown, they bypass Judea and go to Joseph's home in Nazareth.[88]

Jesus grows up in Nazareth, surrounded by older stepsiblings. Through his mother, he keeps an attachment to the i-Nazorean communities around Jerusalem, picking up from his mother and her family a subset of i-Nazorean teachings. He is especially drawn to their ideas about Person Wisdom and Wisdom's unity with God. From his father's family, he takes up ideals about practical wisdom, and he adopts the

---

88. To construct the speculative scenario on these pages, I've drawn on material from the Gospel of John and the Matthean birth narratives. Luke also has a birth narrative, but I find it difficult to reconcile Luke's version with Matthew's. I believe that Luke has sources that are omitted by Matthew, but in his zeal to stitch these sources into a compelling narrative, Luke has made some questionable assumptions. Among these assumptions are that Joseph and Mary were both from Nazareth and that the Annunciation happened there. Luke knows that Jesus was born in Bethlehem, though, so he has to find some way to get Joseph and Mary there. The plot device that Luke employs for this is a Roman census that forces people to return to their tribal homelands—something no Roman census ever did. The census Luke cites, moreover, is that of Quirinius, which was, according to information about it in Josephus, about ten years *after* the birth of Jesus. Luke's mistakes about the census suggest that the author is trying too hard to turn some scattered Nazorean stories into a connected historical narrative.

voluntary poverty of their s-Nazorean lifestyle. Joseph dies—we don't know when—and Mary, always considered somewhat of an outsider, starts to feel more estranged from the community in Nazareth.

When Jesus is about thirty, an associate of his mother's i-Nazorean community launches a renewal movement in Judea. John the Baptist attracts large crowds to his baptismal site across the Jordan from Jerusalem. He predicts the coming of the Nazorean Messiah. Jesus, by now certain that he is this Messiah, the embodiment of Person Wisdom, visits John. Inspired by what John has accomplished, he starts his own public ministry in Judea, eventually transferring it to Galilee. The Nazorean sect members in his Nazareth community, however, do not rally behind him. The i-Nazorean concepts and practices that Jesus has picked up from his mother's side of the family seem strange to them. They do not trust the proclamations of the i-Nazorean Baptist.

Mary continues to play whatever role she can in the Nazareth group, but her stepsons gradually take over the leadership of the large family. The last Galilean appearance of Mary is when she organizes food at the marriage in Cana, perhaps for one of her stepchildren or in-laws, and travels with her family to Capernaum. Unlike the Galilean s-Nazoreans, the i-Nazorean cells in Judea have begun to rally around Jesus, believing that he is the sect's promised Messiah. Mary starts spending more time in Judea, perhaps returning to Galilee now and then to follow her son on his itinerant missions of preaching and healing. Through his mother, Jesus maintains active connections with i-Nazorean sect members. On his trips to Jerusalem, he lodges with them. Lazarus and his sisters, resident in Bethany, are probably part of this Judean network.[89]

Mary's i-Nazorean family also has connections to the i-Nazorean cell of the beloved disciple. At the crucifixion, Jesus entrusts the welfare of his mother to her i-Nazorean community rather than to her s-Nazorean stepchildren, making her a fictive mother in an i-Nazorean cell. To do this, he uses what appears to be a ritual (John 19:25–27),

89. In developing a scenario of Essene poor houses scattered through most of the villages of Judea, Brian Capper pictures Lazarus, Mary, and Martha as supporting members of the Essene poor house in Bethany. See Capper, "Essene Community Houses." (The name "Bethany," Capper speculates, derives from a Hebrew phrase for "house of the poor.") While Capper's scenario assumes more commonality between the Nazoreans and the Essenes than I am comfortable with, the notion of a Judean network of sectarian settlements as the matrix of the Jesus movement dovetails with the thesis of this book.

telling the mother-adoptee, "Behold, your son," and the other party, "Behold, your mother."[90]

After Jesus's death, his disciples take over leadership of the movement. The s-Nazoreans, in the face of mounting evidence for Jesus's claims to be the Nazorean messiah—his miracles, the post-resurrection appearances—become part of the new movement. The disciples, whose outlooks have been formed by Jesus's teaching, have adopted both s-Nazorean and i-Nazorean beliefs. Some are pulled one way, some the other.

The falling out between Jesus and the Jerusalem authorities, which has resulted in his death, renders the position of the disciples precarious. At this crucial point, Jesus's brothers begin to assert more authority. The family of Jesus, s-Nazoreans who have a long history of adapting themselves to mainline Judaism, step in and find a way to pacify the authorities' opposition. Those who come from an i-Nazorean background, or who adhere closely to i-Nazorean theology (including, probably, many of the Greek-speaking Jews), find it convenient to leave areas that are under control of the Jerusalem authorities. Since Peter and other leaders among the disciples continue to treat Jerusalem and Galilee as the center of Christian Judaism, they are drawn into closer alliance with s-Nazorean factions. In the years to come, s-Nazorean influence on Christian Judaism in Judea will increase, and that of the i-Nazoreans will decline.

The i-Nazorean author of the Gospel of John, effectively exiled from Jerusalem, finds control of the Jesus movement—a movement that once regarded the author as a leader—slipping away. Worried that the spirituality of the i-Nazoreans is about to be overwhelmed by the evangelistic expansion of s-Nazorean spirituality, the author of John pens his or her thoughts, narrating the story of Jesus from the i-Nazorean perspective. Peter and his s-Nazorean influencers, the author of the Gospel of John argues, have no monopoly on the meaning of Jesus's life. Jesus had accepted i-Nazorean teachings about Person Wisdom. He had identified himself as Wisdom and encouraged his followers to enter into a mystical union with himself, God, and the Spirit of God.

We know now, of course, that John's worries about an s-Nazorean takeover were not misplaced. Before the century was out, the author's group of Nazoreans would lose what little influence they had on the

90. The passage that follows, John 19:28–30, may also be part of an i-Nazorean liturgy, with Jesus saying, "I thirst" being given vinegar on sponge mounted on a sprig of hyssop, then saying, "It is finished." Hyssop was an important part of Therapeutan ceremonial meals.

expanding church. But John's written gospel, an attempt to reclaim the i-Nazorean aspects of the Jesus they had known, would survive. In the church councils of the fourth and fifth centuries CE, the gospel's vision of Jesus as Person Wisdom would be lifted from its i-Nazorean and wisdom matrix and used to shape the theology of the Christian Trinity.

8

Psalms of Solomon and Acts

THE FOURTH IMAGINATIVE WEB described the Nazorean movement. For the fifth web, I split the Nazorean movement into two factions. In weaving these final webs, I constructed, where I could, an imaginative narrative about how the stories in the gospels might be read against this Nazorean background. There were many gaps in the imagined story because much of what we would like to know—or guess—about the Nazoreans remains elusive. But we haven't exhausted all of the sources. In this chapter, I will touch on two sources that will help us to round out the narrative, one from the pseudepigraphal writings, the other from the NT.

PSALMS OF SOLOMON

The *Psalms of Solomon*, a collection of eighteen psalms from the first century BCE, was known to the early church, though perhaps not widely used in liturgies. The document appears to have been included in the Codex Alexandrinus, a fifth-century parchment Bible, but the section of the codex containing this document is now lost.

The *Psalms of Solomon* came to the attention of Western scholars in the seventeenth century in the form of several medieval Greek and Syriac manuscripts. Over the last two hundred years, the text of the *Psalms of Solomon* has been studied and translated, and critical editions have been published.[1] Scholars assume that the work was originally composed in

---

1. Quotations in this section are translated from the critical edition of Robert Wright (Wright, *The Psalms of Solomon*).

Hebrew or Aramaic, but no portion of the work in either of these languages has ever turned up, and the question about whether the Greek text is original (a minority of scholars) or a translation (the majority of scholars) is still debated.

Although superscriptions in the psalm manuscripts refer to the figure of King Solomon, nothing in the psalms themselves suggests that the speaker is Solomon. Scholars speculate that the similarity between the picture of the Messiah in the canonical Psalm 72, which in the Tanak is called "a song of Solomon," and the messianic visions in parts of the *Psalms of Solomon* may account for the attribution. I'll offer another explanation below.

In the nineteenth century, scholars often assigned the *Psalms of Solomon* to a community of Pharisees. The conjecture was driven in large part by the need to find *some* Pharisaic work from the Second Temple literature. When the Dead Sea Scrolls began to be published in the middle of the twentieth century, the sectarian character of the community described in the *Psalms of Solomon* made the Essenes seem like a better source. But the Essenes also fell out of favor—no fragments of the *Psalms of Solomon* have been found in the scroll pieces from the Dead Sea caves, nor has the special vocabulary we associate with the Essene sectarians been detected in the *Psalms of Solomon*. Over the last three decades, a number of scholars have switched to the view that the *Psalms of Solomon* text came from a Jewish sectarian community unknown to Second Temple scholarship.[2]

The picture of this mysterious sectarian community that emerges from the psalms is drawn in subtle strokes. Events and people mentioned in the text are often described in an elusive and indirect manner. The interpretation of certain words and phrases is contentious. Without entering into the fray of these discussions, let me summarize for you what I believe, based on the imaginative webs developed in this book, to be the community context of these psalms.[3]

2. Robert Hann's comment is an example of this new position: "The sect which composed the Psalms of Solomon was a later generation of an original movement of disenfranchised priests" (Hann, "The Community," 170). He speculates that the sect was a variety of early Essenism that kept itself separate from the main body of Essenes. See also Kenneth Atkinson's comment: "Our present corpus of *Psalms of Solomon* document the worship practices and beliefs of an unknown Jewish sectarian community that resided in Jerusalem" (Atkinson, *I Cried to the Lord*, 1).

3. My interpretation of the *Psalms of Solomon* context corresponds closely to that of Kenneth Atkinson's early articles. See, for example, Atkinson, "Herod the Great." In

HISTORICAL CONTEXT

To understand the social context of the *Psalms of Solomon*, we first need to look at the political setting. Israel in the first century BCE, according to Josephus, was a hotbed of minor intrigues. A regional power vacuum in the middle of the second century BCE, brought on by the partial withdrawal of Persian, Egyptian, and Syrian influences, allowed local Jewish leadership to assert control over Israel and some of the surrounding territories. The Hasmonean rulers of this period came to power under Mattathias ben Johanan and his sons. The dynasty was launched by the Maccabean Revolt, an event still celebrated by Jews at Hanukkah.

The deuterocanonical book of 1 Maccabees tells the story of this family and their wars. The path to political power took the Hasmoneans through the Jewish high priesthood. Later in the dynasty, they also assumed the title and power of kings. For some Jews, the Hasmonean adoption of these roles was a problem. Although the Hasmoneans were a priestly line, descendants of Aaron, they were not from the line of Zadok, the high priest appointed by Solomon. A custom stretching back seven centuries and enshrined in the Tanak (Ezek 40:46) decreed that only Zadokites could occupy the office of high priest. In addition, the Jewish people had been accustomed, since their return from the Babylonian Captivity, to not having a Jewish royal family. Prophecies suggested that if the monarchy were ever reconstituted, the ruler would not come from the Levites or the descendants of Aaron. The ruler would be from the family of King David, a member of the tribe of Judah.

At the time the Hasmoneans were filling the offices of high priest and king, the Romans were beginning to expand their influence in the Middle East. Violent party politics in Israel, coupled with resentments arising from these acts of violence, ensured that no claimant could ascend to the high priesthood and the Hasmonean throne without military backing. The Romans took advantage of these internecine quarrels, playing off Jewish factions against each other. In 63 BCE, an army under the Roman general Pompey took control of Jerusalem. Pompey reorganized the Jewish government as a client state of Rome, permitting friendly Hasmonean allies to retain the high priesthood and remnants of political

---

his later book on the subject (Atkinson, *I Cried to the Lord*), however, he seems to have changed his mind about the Herodian setting of Psalm 17. For a review of research positions on the *Psalms of Solomon* in the two decades before Atkinson's articles, see Trafton, "The *Psalms of Solomon*."

power. This period, however, was the beginning of a turbulent time for the Roman Empire. Pompey was a member, along with Julius Caesar, of what historians used to call the "First Triumvirate." The arrangement collapsed, and the armies of Pompey and Caesar fought a civil war. Caesar won, but he was assassinated in 44 BCE, leading to the so-called "Second Triumvirate" and more war. The struggles ended with the collapse of the Roman Republic and the founding of the Roman Empire under Augustus. Roman attention to Israel wandered in this period, and the Jewish state devolved—once again—into clashing forces.

The Parthian Empire, which was based in Iran, took advantage of Roman inattention to send an army into Israel in 40 BCE and begin its own meddling. It installed the Hasmonean Antigonus II, the son of the previous Hasmonean king, on the Judean throne. This opened the door for the Idumeans, the nation just south of Israel, to further their own interests in Judea. The Idumean ruler Herod, continuing the policies of his father Antipater, aligned with the Romans and against the Parthians and became a claimant to the Judean throne. Herod besieged and conquered Jerusalem in 37 BCE, backed by Roman legions.[4] The siege lasted several months and led to an extensive famine. When the city was finally taken, Roman soldiers went on a rampage, killing not only the city's defenders, but Jewish women, children, and the aged. Herod had to bribe the soldiers and their leaders to leave Jerusalem. He ousted the Hasmonean king and sent him off to exile and execution. Once he was in full control of the Jewish state, Herod began to eliminate other Hasmonean contenders for the throne. He would go on to rule Israel for more than thirty years, setting up his own royal dynasty.

THE DEVOUT

The earliest dateable event reflected in *Psalms of Solomon* is the takeover of Jerusalem by the Roman general Pompey in 63 BCE. Though Pompey is not referred to by name in the texts, descriptions of the events in two of the psalms make the identification almost certain. Psalm 2 tells about the struggle for Jerusalem and about Pompey's eventual assassination in 48 BCE. Psalm 8 mentions that some of the Jerusalem leaders welcomed Pompey and opened the gates for him (8:16–17).[5]

4. Josephus, *Ant.* 14.16.

5. Josephus, *Ant.* 14.4.2.

Psalm 2, written from a Jewish perspective, does not have kind words for the Gentile armies. Another party, however, also comes under fire in the psalm. Pompey's armies, says the psalmist, dealt with the leaders of Jerusalem "according to their sins" (2:7), repaying them for their transgressions of the law. The author focuses mostly on the sins of sexual promiscuity and prostitution among the Jewish leaders. In Psalm 8, theft from the temple and defilement of temple practices are added to the charges (8:9–12). In Psalm 17, the leaders are blamed for supporting a non-Davidic monarchy (17:4–6).

Not everyone in Israel, however, either merited or received punishment at the hands of the Romans. For those who remained righteous and under the Lord's protection, God "acted with mercy" (2:36) during this time of change. In Psalm 2 and later psalms, this protected group is called "*hoi Hosioi*," the devout ones. To have experienced the bittersweet revenge that Pompey inflicted on the sinning Jewish leaders, the *Hosioi*—presumably the community that produced the *Psalms of Solomon*—must have been a well-established sect at the time of Pompey's invasion. We don't hear anything in the psalms about a leader or leaders who might have broken with the Jewish leadership and established this sectarian community. It would be reasonable to assume that in 63 BCE the *Hosioi* had been part of the Jewish social mix for a generation or more.

The next psalm in the collection is a paean of praise to God for the way the righteous are protected. "Sin upon sin does not make its home in the house of the righteous," says Psalm 3, because the righteous person continually examines the house "to remove injustice and transgression" (3:6–7). "House" in this and succeeding psalms may be a code word for the individual cells of the *Hosioi.*[6] The cells, Psalm 3 seems to be saying, maintained enough internal discipline to weed out from their congregations the secret sins displayed by the Jewish leadership. To cover sins of ignorance, a task usually relegated to the sacrificial system of the temple, the cells practiced "fasting and humbling of the soul" (3:8).[7] The fate of sinners is to be destroyed and forgotten, the psalmist concludes, but "those who fear the Lord shall rise up to eternal life. Their life is in the light of the Lord and will never end" (3:12).

---

6. The word "houses," here and in Psalm 12, probably refers to "local units of the cult like those which existed among the Pharisees and the Essenes" (Hann, "The Community," 171).

7. For a comparison between the halakhah of community behind the Psalms and that of the temple priesthood, see Atkinson, "Perceptions."

Psalm 4 is a song of curses. The target of the curses is the hypo-crite who "sits in the council of the *Hosioi*" but whose heart is secretly set on sin. The hypocrite, condemning with fluent speech the very sins that he practices, enters into the cells ("the houses"), cheerfully pretend-ing innocence (4:2–5). The psalmist prays that God will reveal the true works of these hypocrites. The *Hosioi* will then certify God's judgment on the hypocrites by removing them "from the presence of the righteous" (4:7–8). What we seem to have in Psalm 4 is a community racked by internal heresies. A community with this problem is probably one that has been around for some time—another hint that the *Hosioi* were firmly established in the Jerusalem social scene.

The most extensive allusions to the community that created the *Psalms of Solomon* are in Psalm 17, which also contains, outside of the NT, the longest messianic prophecy of the late Second Temple period. This psalm is sometimes thought by scholars to describe the same events as Psalm 2 and Psalm 8, the 63 BCE incursion of Pompey and its aftermath. Psalm 17, however, may refer to events from a later period. The psalmist begins by recognizing that God chose David and his descendants to be the royal line of Israel (17:4). Rejecting this divine directive, "sinners" (the Jewish authorities) set up their own royal house and vacated the throne of David (17:6). The psalmist predicts—after the fact, presum-ably—that God will reject the choice of the sinners and "remove from the earth" the descendants of the royal line. God's tool for this removal is "a person alien to our race" (17:7). Employing this tool, God "sought out their descendants and did not let one of them escape" (17:9). But the destruction did not fall only on the ersatz royal line. "The lawless one laid waste our land," complains the psalmist, and made it uninhabitable. "He did away with young and old, together with their children" (17:11). He brought into Jerusalem gentile practices from other cities and influenced Jews in the diaspora to follow his customs (17:14–15). These events in Psalm 17 are similar to those surrounding the capture of Jerusalem by Herod the Great in 37 BCE.

Unlike the events of 63 BCE, the events of the 30s BCE had direct and dire consequences for the *Hosioi*. "Those who loved the synagogues of the *Hosioi* fled, as sparrows fledge from their nests. They wandered in wildernesses to save their souls from evil" (17:16–17). They were "scat-tered over the whole land by the lawless one." The dispersal was accom-panied by a severe drought (17:18–19). Some of the psalms, such as 7, 10,

13, and 16, focus on God's purifying acts of discipline. Sections of these psalms may derive from the upheaval of these times.

In the second half of Psalm 17, the writer foresees the coming of a "king, a son of David" who will "rule over your servant Israel" (17:21). He will both "cleanse Jerusalem of its gentiles" and "drive out the sinners" (17:22–23). He will "judge peoples and nations in the wisdom of his righteousness" (17:29). This future king, called "Lord Messiah,"[8] will be "free from sin" and "taught by God." He will rule over a land in which "everyone will be holy" (17:32–36). Metaphors of violence are associated with the coming of this Messiah—he will "break up all the possessions" of sinners with a "rod of iron" and "smash the arrogance of the sinner like a potter's vessel" (17:23–24). His overall policy, however, will be peaceful— "He will not put his hope in horse or rider or bow" and will not depend on money or troops to achieve his ends (17:33). He will not grow weak during his regency because "God will make him strong with a holy spirit and wise (*sophos*) with the counsel of understanding" (17:37).

The last psalm in the collection, Psalm 18, continues the reflection on what it will be like to live in the days of the "Lord Messiah, in the fear of his God, in the wisdom of spirit and righteousness and strength" (18:7). The final three verses of the psalm take a sudden turn to traditional wisdom topics, extolling the God "who arranged the lights in their courses to mark off the seasons from day to day" (18:10) and who does not permit them "to turn aside from their paths" (18:12).

NAZOREAN BEGINNINGS

The *Hosioi* of the *Psalms of Solomon* may be the s-Nazoreans that I have been tracking in this book. Besides the obvious correlation—that both groups are Jewish sectarian movements at the right time and place—several other similarities also point in this direction. First, the two groups include apocalyptic elements in their theology, and the Messiah described in the *Psalms of Solomon* closely corresponds with the Messiah expected in early Christian Judaism. The expected Messiah, moreover,

---

8. This unusual appellation is found in all the manuscripts of the *Psalms of Solomon*. Most scholars prefer to amend the phrase to "the Messiah of the Lord." See the bibliographic discussion of the various positions in Kenneth Atkinson, "On the Herodian Origin," 440. The phrase also occurs in Psalm 18:7, but there the whole phrase is in the genitive, so it is easy to read it as "Messiah of the Lord." It is possible that "Lord Messiah" was an in-group title that the Nazoreans used when speaking about the Messiah.

is associated with the Holy Spirit and wisdom by both groups. Second, we find evidence in the two groups of a wisdom tradition. Attaching the name of Solomon to their community hymns may have been a way of underlining this heritage. Third, both traditions express disaffection with temple leadership and hint that the goals of temple service can be achieved through the halakhah of a believing community. Fourth, members of the Nazoreans and the *Hosioi* both wrote hymns and psalms as acts of devotion.

If we identify the community behind the *Psalms of Solomon* with the s-Nazoreans, then a few blank spaces in the Nazorean timeline begin to fill in. I suggested earlier that the Galilean s-Nazoreans were a transplanted community. This new assumption tells us where they came from and when they left. The Nazorean's original home was Jerusalem. In Jerusalem, they had high social status, perhaps as members of a Jerusalem scribal class.[9] But the community had an unhappy relationship with the Pharisees and Sadducees who ruled in Jerusalem and Judea. When war engulfed Jerusalem in the late 30s BCE, the s-Nazoreans fled the city. Many of them may have settled in communities in Galilee, perhaps motivated by a belief that the end times were at hand and the Messiah would arise in this northern area. In their flight, they abandoned most of their wealth. Their policy of voluntary poverty, at first a theoretical stance (5:16–17), became all too concrete. Several times in the *Psalms of Solomon* the writers refer to their group as "the poor."

Not all of the *Hosioi* left Jerusalem in the 30s BCE, however. The complaints about embedded hypocrites in Psalm 4 may point to Nazoreans who were at odds with the group that wrote the *Psalms of Solomon*. Could the i-Nazoreans be the target of these complaints? At the forefront of the charges against the hypocrites, we note, are sins relating to women. The eyes of the hypocrites "are upon all women, not making a distinction" (4:4). They "speak to all the women in their sordid gatherings" (4:5). The two groups of Nazoreans, as we have noted, disagreed about women's roles in worship and in the community. The s-Nazoreans may have viewed the male-female interactions of the i-Nazoreans as a form of sexual sin.

Other i-Nazorean signatures are found in the Psalm 4 complaints. Was the psalmist who wrote that the hypocrites in their midst "quote the Torah with guile" (4:8) and "destroy the *sophos* of others with words

9. Werline, "The Formation," 134–5.

that transgress the law" (4:9) thinking about the use of allegorical interpretation to undercut the literal prescriptions of the law? When the
writer says that the hypocrite "does not desist until he succeeds in scat-
tering [the *Hosioi*], making them like orphans" (4:10), was he perhaps
referring to differences in the constituencies of the two communities?
The i-Nazoreans stressed individuality, and the s-Nazoreans emphasized
family and kinship. From the perspective of the s-Nazoreans, a member
who had abandoned the family synagogue to meet with unrelated people
for mystical worship would have been a metaphorical orphan, a person
lacking a family.[10] Among the curses pronounced on the hypocrite in
the latter part of the psalm (4:14–22) is the wish that his old age will be
passed "in the solitude of childlessness" (4:18), a malediction appropriate
to men and women who had forsaken sexual relationships and family
ties.

The removal of the s-Nazorean groups to the Galilean hinterland
in the 30s BCE may have left behind some of the hypocrites, the ones
we have identified as i-Nazoreans. Cells of this urban group, focused
on mystical wisdom, could have had a Jerusalem presence for many decades after the s-Nazoreans left. Over this long residence, members of
the i-Nazoreans would have become deeply articulated—as the author
of the Gospel of John was—with the Jerusalem priestly caste. As priests
and scribes in a major urban center, the i-Nazoreans would have been
literate in Greek and may even have spoken Greek in their homes and
convocations.

The *Psalms of Solomon*, then, may point us to the 37 BCE takeover by
Herod as the time when internal disagreements within the Nazorean sect
led to an external division into s-Nazorean and i-Nazorean factions. In
spite of the strong internecine rhetoric in the *Psalms of Solomon*, however,
we should not assume that the split undermined all feelings of sectarian
unity. The two factions of Nazoreans shared a long heritage of sectarian
writings and sectarian beliefs. The even stronger alienation between the
Nazoreans and the Judean leadership would have been a continual coun-
terforce pressing the Nazorean factions together. A need to find spouses
within their sectarian milieu may also have led to continuing interaction.

10. In *Joseph and Aseneth* 11:13, in a story which seems to come from about the
same period as the *Psalms of Solomon*, we find a similar metaphorical use of "orphan."
The Egyptian gentile Aseneth marries Joseph and converts to her husband's faith. She
tells how her family, even her parents, come to hate her for rejecting their gods. She
prays that the God of Jacob, who is the father of orphans, will have compassion on her
orphaned state (Burchard, *Joseph and Asenath*, 217–8).

This fragile unity, however, would be tested in the years following the death of Jesus. We can see the outlines of this renewed division in the NT book of Acts.

HEBRAISTS AND HELLENISTS

The Acts of the Apostles, probably by the same author who penned the Gospel of Luke, adds further detail to the Nazorean backstory. Tracing Jewish sectarian differences through this material, however, is not easy. The author of Acts puts a positive spin on internal conflicts in the Jesus movement.[11] We should assume that Acts, insofar as it recognizes s-Nazorean and i-Nazorean differences, makes them less significant than they really were.

We see some evidence of these suppressed differences in the way that the author covers the disagreement between the Hellenists and the Hebraists in Acts 6–8. Reading the account of the clash between the disciples of Jesus and the Jewish leadership in Acts 2–5 leads the reader to expect that the death of Jesus would be followed in short order by the martyrdom of the disciples. Instead, the disagreements between the disciples and the Jerusalem authorities are suddenly muted. The author of Acts supplies the intervention of the famous Gamaliel (5:33–42) as the reason, but this may be the historian inventing connections. In any case, the conflict between the Jesus movement and the Jewish leadership soon returns. This time around, however, it does not affect all parts of the growing movement in the same way.

To explain this two-sided treatment of Christian Jews by the Jewish leaders, the author of Acts introduces us to a clash between two factions of the Jesus movement, the Hellenists and the Hebraists.[12] One of the

11. We can see the tendency to downplay conflicts, for example, in the Acts handling of the debate over Gentile believers and Jewish Law. If we did not have the letters of Paul, the coverage of this issue in Acts would not tell us how controversial this problem was in the decades following the death of Jesus.

12. The word used for "Hellenist," *hellēnistēs*, is derived from the verb *hellēnizō*. In its most undifferentiated sense, a "Hellenist" could simply be someone who was from Greece (*hellas*) or who spoke Greek. From the Jewish perspective, a "Hellenist" could be someone who was not Jewish (Acts 11:20). But the term "Hellenist" was often used—as it is in Acts 6—to designate a person who took on the manners, customs, or beliefs associated with Greek culture. The other party is designated as *hebraios*, Hebrews, using a word that can refer to any Jewish person—as it does in 2 Corinthians 11:22. In parallel with *hellēnistēs*, the word *hebraios* could refer to someone whose native language was Aramaic or Hebrew. But it could also, again in parallel with more differentiated

most fundamental points of difference between the groups seems to have concerned the role of women in the sect.[13] The outcome of the disagreement, described at the beginning of Acts 6, is the initiation of an order of leadership, the deaconate, that is composed of Greek-speaking male believers. In the last part of the chapter, the fury of the Jewish leadership is focused on Stephen, one of these deacons. Stephen is tried by the Sanhedrin (6:8–15). After an incendiary speech that challenged temple-based worship,[14] he is dragged out of the city and stoned to death. On that day, Luke reports, "a huge persecution arose against the Jerusalem church, and all were scattered through the regions of Judea and Samaria, *except the apostles*" (8:1).

The last three words, "except the apostles," is Luke's admission that the Jewish authorities recognized two distinct parties in the Jesus movement. These factions, I believe, correspond to the two groups of Nazoreans. There were, first, the Aramaic-speaking, law-keeping s-Nazoreans, called in Acts the "Hebraists." As we noted above in the discussion of the *Psalms of Solomon*, this group may have originated in Jerusalem. In the days of Jesus, however, their principal base was Galilee, where they had lived for perhaps six decades. Over the years of their exile from Jerusalem, the s-Nazoreans had become more conservative and law-observant. The apostles, many of whom came from Galilee, would have been lumped with these s-Nazoreans. And then there were the i-Nazoreans, who had always had a Jerusalem presence.[15] Their broad interpretations of Jewish

---

meanings of "Hellenist," designate someone who followed the religious practices and customs of the Jewish culture in Judea. Given the implied contrast in the passage with "Hellenist," I have chosen to translate *hebraios* as "Hebraist."

13. This issue, however, is obscured by translations of 6:1–3 that imply the disagreement was about something less significant—the unequal allocation of food. For the translation options, see the section in the Appendixes on "Rethinking the Translation of Acts 6:1–7."

14. Scholars have found evidence that the speech put in Stephen's mouth may have originated in a community with strong ties to Samaritan theology. See the summary of this research in Scobie, "The Origins," 390–400. Scobie comments that we could "envisage Stephen and his followers as representatives of some type of Palestinian sectarian Judaism." The sect had "little use for the Jerusalem cult" and would possibly have had "certain contacts with and sympathies for Samaritanism" (Scobie, "The Origins," 399). This sounds like the i-Nazoreans.

15. The Acts story about the Jerusalem believers in the period immediately following the crucifixion, how they shared their goods and lived as though they were one large household (2:42–47 and 4:32–35), suggests that the Hellenists and Hebraists, before the split, were open to the fictive kin group model of the i-Nazoreans who were in Jerusalem.

law and weak enforcement of Jewish boundary markers, as well as their acceptance of Greek language and culture,[16] pushed the i-Nazoreans to the periphery when the more nationalist elements dominated the Jerusalem leadership.

A disagreement about the role of the temple and temple service in Jewish life may also have been a point of difference between the Jewish leadership and the i-Nazoreans. The i-Nazoreans, as we noted in the chapter on the Gospel of John, seem to have questioned the efficacy of animal sacrifice. This led them to develop alternate rituals for some of the feasts—Passover in particular. We get a glimpse into i-Nazorean beliefs about temple sacrifice in Acts 6–7, the story of Stephen's martyrdom. The Hellenist Stephen debates with a group of non-Christian Jews and bests them. To get revenge, his opponents arrange for Stephen to be accused and tried before the Jewish Sanhedrin. The accusers contend that Stephen has spoken "words of blasphemy against Moses" and "against this holy place and the law." They link him to Jesus's prophecy about the destruction of the temple (Acts 6:8–15). The trial provides the opportunity for the author of Acts to put on record Stephen's defense before the Sanhedrin. It is a long defense, taking up most of Acts 7.

Putting crafted speeches to put into the mouths of dead persons was a common practice among the classical and Hellenistic Greek historians. The Book of Acts contains many of these speeches. We would not, under normal circumstances, expect that the author of Acts would have had special insight into Stephen's actual beliefs. The speech, however, is unusual when compared with the other speeches in Acts, and its oddness has convinced many NT scholars that the author of Acts tapped into some source of Hellenist theology when he constructed Stephen's speech to the Sanhedrin.[17]

16. The classic review of the roles of the four languages of Second Temple Palestine—Latin, Greek, Aramaic, and Hebrew—is found in Joseph Fitzmyer's presidential address to the Catholic Biblical Association of America (Fitzmyer, "The Languages of Palestine"). Fitzmyer, adopting the stance of C.F.D. Moule, understands the terms "Hebraists" and "Hellenists" in Acts 6 as reference to language preferences. "Hellenists," he says, "undoubtedly denotes Jerusalem Jews or Jewish Christians who habitually spoke Greek only" and who for that reason "were more affected by Hellenistic culture." The ones called "Hebraists," in contrast, "were those who also spoke a Semitic language" (Fitzmyer, "The Languages of Palestine," 515).

17. Compared to other synopses of the Christian message, says Marcel Simon, Stephen's speech is "aberrant." It has "a strongly antiritualistic trend, and a fierce hostility toward the Temple. . . ." It also "lacks any positively Christian message" (Simon, "Saint Stephen and the Jerusalem Temple," 127, 141). Because of these differences, we are

The speech of Stephen before the Sanhedrin seems to be, on the surface, a simple retelling of Tanak stories structured around the lives of Abraham, Jacob, Moses, and David. It ends with Stephen's prophet-like condemnation of his judges and accusers. The first few times I read Stephen's speech, this was all I saw—some potted history and a provocation. When I began to think about the speech as an expression of sectarian differences, however, a theological layer emerged that I hadn't noticed before. The long historical prologue in the speech is meant to show that "the God of glory" (7:2) cultivated a people with a special relationship to the divine, one that was different from the relationship that other nations had with their gods. God's centuries-long effort comes to a head during the forty years in the wilderness, at Sinai and the giving of the law. At this point, the path to the present forks. Moses, following God's detailed instructions, gives the people a tabernacle, a tent of meeting, to represent God's presence with them. The people, unsatisfied with this new system, attempt to return to the type of worship they had known in Egypt. Aaron helps them make a golden calf to replace the tabernacle.

Stephen then leaps forward in his narrative, to the time of David, where he finds the same dichotomy at work. David provided a *skēnōma*, an encampment in Jerusalem where God could dwell in a tabernacle. In this respect, David's actions resemble what the speech says about Moses. Solomon, in contrast to his father David, "built a house" for God, the first Jewish temple (7:46–47), putting himself in the same role as Aaron, who had provided the people with a golden calf. The problem with housing God in a building, Stephen says (quoting Isaiah 66:1–2 to underscore his point), is that God doesn't need a house—God is already housed in creation. Stephen wraps up his long retelling of Jewish history by saying that "the Most High does not dwell in temples made by

---

"entitled to admit" that Stephen's speech "expresses what can be called the Hellenist tradition of thought" (Simon, *St. Stephen and the Hellenists*, 40). The interpretation of Stephen's speech that I present on these pages has multiple lines of agreement with Marcel Simon's work on it. Simon has not developed a detailed picture of the group I call the "i-Nazoreans," but he does think that the Hellenists represented some kind of sectarian "reformed Judaism" that was already at odds with the orthodoxy of the Jerusalem establishment before it was taken up by the Hellenist followers of Jesus (Simon, "Saint Stephen and the Jerusalem Temple," 141). "We might be in the presence of a community of Jews from the Diaspora, settled in Jerusalem under circumstances to us unknown, with a synagogical organization of their own, and differentiated from the average type of Jerusalem Judaism by some specific features even before they were touched by the Christian message" (Simon, *St. Stephen and the Hellenists*, 8).

hands."[18] He then rounds on his accusers, calling them "stiff-necked and uncircumcised in heart and ears." He says that they are "always opposing the Holy Spirit," and he compares the killing of Jesus ("the righteous one") with the killing of the prophets (7:51–52). Marcel Simon sums up the main thrust of Stephen's speech like this: "Sacrifices, even if offered to Jahveh, a temple, even if built in Jerusalem, remain what they were in the beginning—works of idolatry."[19] If the speech of Stephen in Acts 7 is based on sources that derive from the i-Nazorean Hellenists, the author of Acts has given us another important difference between the i-Nazoreans and the Jewish religious establishment. It is a disagreement about the temple system of worship and animal sacrifices. The difference, in all likelihood, predates Jesus.[20]

These disagreements between the i-Nazoreans and the Jerusalem elite—the i-Nazoreans' broad interpretations of Jewish law, their openness to Greek cultural norms, and their failure to acknowledge the efficacy of the temple system—play a role when the Jesus movement begins to unravel along the seam defined by the differences between the i-Nazoreans and

18. It might seem that the tabernacle, the tent of presence, was also "made by hands." However, the phrase "made by hands," *cheiropoiētos*, is one that is used in the Septuagint to denote graven images. Stephen would have regarded the tabernacle as something made by God, since the exact plan for it was revealed to Moses. (It is described twice in great detail, in Exodus, 25–31 and 35–40.) Idols and other divine images, in contrast, are planned by human workers. (In Isaiah 44:9–20, the writer provides a humorous description of a craftsman who goes to the woods and cuts down a tree, using half of it to make an idol and half to cook his supper.) The builders of Solomon's temple did not have divine plans in hand, making it, like an idol, *cheiropoiētos*.

19. Simon, "Saint Stephen and the Jerusalem Temple," 138. Marcel Simon also says that, from the perspective of Stephen's speech, "the sacrificial cult first appeared among the Israelites as an act of idolatry and it is fundamentally nothing else; it can be intended only for false gods, and the very fact that the Israelites practise it is the proof that they are given up worshiping the host of heaven" (Simon, *St. Stephen and the Hellenists*, 49).

20. "Stephen's position on the matter," Marcel Simon says, probably "existed before he became a Christian." (Simon, "Saint Stephen and the Jerusalem Temple," 128.) We know that some Jewish Christian groups in the second and later centuries rejected animal sacrifices and may even have been vegetarians. Discussions around this point often center on the lost Gospel of the Ebionites. Epiphanius, in his book on cults, cites from this gospel in his chapter on the Ebionites: "I came to abolish sacrifices, and if you do not cease to sacrifice, wrath will not cease from you" (Epiphanius, *Pan.* 30.16.5). For a thorough review of the discussion around this ancient anti-sacrifice position, see Joseph, "'I Have Come.'" Joseph concludes, "The Gospel of the Ebionites . . . contains *non*-Synoptic traditions which represent a different discourse on Jesus' identity and his relationship to the Temple cult and the Mosaic Torah, raising questions still at the very center of contemporary discourse on the historical Jesus and the relationship between Early Judaism and nascent Christianity" (Joseph, "'I Have Come,'" 110, emphasis Joseph's).

the s-Nazoreans. This difference between the two groups of Nazoreans is concealed by the author of Acts when he describes the conflict between the Hellenists and Hebraists in Acts 6–8. The author seems to view the appointment of seven Hellenist deacons as a Spirit-led plan to cope with the complexities of expansion—as though the appointees were a kind of middle management acquired by a growing business. If the introduction of the deaconate had this goal, however, there would have been no need to restrict the appointment to seven Greeks. And we would have heard more details about the new role and its job description. Also, if the deaconate was about ministry to the Jerusalem believers, the deacons somehow didn't know it—they left Jerusalem and began to carry out the same evangelization that the apostles were reserving for themselves.

A more likely explanation for the events (mis)narrated in Acts 6 is that the followers of Jesus, faced with one of the periodic and violent pogroms of the Roman client leadership in Judea, decided to prune away the parts of the movement that were forcing them to the Jewish periphery. To give the lopped-off elements the best chance to survive, the community set up a shadow apostolate to guide the group. Appointing twelve new leaders would have suggested a definitive split, so another, smaller holy number of leaders were appointed. The apostles "prayed and laid hands" (6:6) on seven men, commissioning them to lead (and lead away) the ones that were being expelled from Jerusalem. The expulsion may have been the occasion for a formal excommunication by the Jewish leaders, the *aposynagōgos* discussed in the previous chapter. Once the objectionable Hellenistic cells of the Nazoreans were expelled, the Twelve presented themselves to the Jerusalem leadership as Sabbath-keeping, law-observing Jews.[21] What the Twelve and the s-Nazoreans did not foresee was that the dispersed i-Nazoreans, vested with their own leadership, would lay the foundation for a gentile church.[22]

21. See the argument developed in de Boer, "Expulsion." De Boer connects the *aposynagōgos* passages in the Gospel of John with disagreements between Jesus and the Pharisees about the Sabbath (de Boer, "Expulsion," 382–90). The differences between the Jewish leaders and the i-Nazoreans around this halakhah may have precipitated their expulsion, both from synagogues and from Jerusalem.

22. The question about when gentiles began to be admitted to the church without first becoming Jews has been widely debated. From the viewpoint of Acts, this happens in Acts 10, when Peter visits the house of the gentile Cornelius. Only after this, in Acts 11, do the expelled Hellenists approach gentiles with the Christian message. "The ones dispersed by the persecution that took place at [the death of] Stephen traveled to Phoenicia, Cyprus, and Antioch." At first, these dispersed Christians "preached the word only to Jews." Some of them, however, when they came to Antioch, "started

WHAT'S IN A NAME?

We began this trip through the five webs in search of a nameless sect that gave rise to Christian Judaism. We now have three candidate names. Factions were known as Nazoreans ("branch people"), Therapeutae ("cultic servants"), and *Hosioi* ("the devout ones"). Later we will add another possible name, "The Way." The proliferation of names for the sect should not surprise us. Essene groups had many names for themselves ("The Community," "The Poor," and "Sons of Light," for example).

The oldest of these names is probably *Hosioi*. Members of the sect seem to have called themselves this early in the first century CE, when they were a unified movement. The name "Nazorean," in contrast, was probably associated with the s-Nazorean cells in Galilee. We know "Therapeutae" as Philo's term for an i-Nazorean community that settled in Egypt, but it may have been in wider use by i-Nazorean cells located in the Greek-speaking Jewish diaspora.

By combining the data points from the *Psalms of Solomon* and the reinterpreted events in the first third of Acts, and by adding this to what we have learned from our wisdom review of NT documents, we can build a tentative picture of the Jewish sect behind the Christian church. The sect would have emerged no later than the first third of the first century CE. One of the strong influences on the sect was the OT wisdom tradition. While this wisdom focus may have differentiated them from other Jewish groups, it did not necessarily unite them. From its earliest days, members of the sect would have felt the tension inherent in combining a national covenantal theology with the universal themes of the wisdom tradition. A secondary influence on the sect in its early years was apocalypticism. This led to the development of messianic beliefs. Detailed apocalyptic

---

preaching to Greeks" about Jesus, with the result that "a large number of these [Greeks] believed and turned to the Lord" (Acts 11:19–21). A more likely scenario is that the Peter and Cornelius scenes have been inserted where they are to maintain the priority of Peter. In the sequence developed in this book, i-Nazorean cells of Hellenists outside of Judea would already have had gentiles in them who were observing a minimal set of Jewish boundary markers. When the Hellenists believing in Jesus were expelled from Judea, they encountered and evangelized these mixed cells. These conversions became the occasion for an influx of Christian gentiles. The Antioch location for the gentile conversions in Acts 11:20 is perhaps stressed by the author of Acts because that is the place where Paul and Barnabas had their set-to with the emissaries from the Judean church (Acts 15) and where Paul confronted Peter and the people from James (Galatians 2). In reality, gentile conversions probably happened wherever and whenever mixed i-Nazorean cells accepted the Christian message.

scenarios, however, appealed more to the sect members who emphasized covenantal theology.

Members of the sect probably belonged to a Jerusalem scribal class and served in positions that required literacy in both Hebrew/Aramaic and Greek. During the early decades of the sect's existence, authors from this group developed a body of writings—some of them interpretations of messianic prophecies—that acted as guiderails for the group's theological beliefs. In the later stages of the Hasmonean era, the sect began to put more distance between itself and the Jewish parties that were friendly with the centralized powers of the Jewish state. The sect's relationship to God became less attached to temple sacrifice, more expressed through its own community worship. During this period of withdrawal, they may have made common cause with Essene communities, exchanging literature and ideas.[23]

The sect made it through the Roman conquest of Jerusalem under Pompey without too much change. They even took some satisfaction in the discomfit that the Roman brought to Pharisees and Sadducees. When Herod assumed the reins of the Jewish state in 37 BCE and Jerusalem was devastated by war and famine, however, they did not escape persecution. A widening rift, stoked by disagreements between those who held to a broad-based, humanitarian wisdom tradition and those who adopted practical, Jewish-oriented wisdom beliefs, turned into a physical split. The ones more attuned to covenantal theology abandoned Jerusalem. Cooperating with the Hasmoneans had been a stretch, but at least the

23. Similarities between the Jesus movement and the Essenes, especially their mutual espousal of communitarian and ascetic values, have led scholars to speculate about possible sectarian linkages. In this study, I have suggested that the Nazoreans and the Essenes may have had, during the first century BCE to the mid-first century CE, a filial relationship, which may have included an exchange of ideas, halakhah, and even members. In thinking about what connections might have existed between the two movements, I have been inspired by the writings of Brian J. Capper. His many studies of the similarities and differences between the Jesus movement and the Essenes are summarized in Capper, "The Judaean cultural context." (This paper and the other papers in Capper's ongoing Judean cultural context series, both published and unpublished, can be found online in the Capper's Canterbury Christ Church University online repository.) Capper posits a more intimate connection between the Johannine group of Jesus's followers and the Essenes than what I have envisioned. In his scenario, the Johannine group was an Essene faction that remained behind in Jerusalem when most of the Jerusalem-based Essenes reoccupied the Qumran site in the years following the death of Herod. By the time John the Baptist began his ministry, more than two decades later, the "theological inheritance from Qumran" of the group still in Jerusalem may have "undergone some modification." The Johannine group "preserves a Christian version of that already modified inheritance" (Capper, "'With the Oldest Monks . . .,'" 48).

Hasmonean rulers and high priests stemmed from a priestly line of Jews. The notion of building a Jewish state under the Idumean Herod, however, was unthinkable. To sect members with apocalyptic beliefs, this must have seemed like the end times. Relinquishing their ancestral properties, family groups moved to rural areas, especially to Galilee, a region with messianic significance. They took up more practical professions, becoming artisans and farmers. People in these Galilean communities became known as Nazoreans. I have referred to them as s-Nazoreans.

Members of the sect who were more influenced by Hellenism and philosophical/mystical perspectives responded to the rise of Herod in a different way. Some of them left Jerusalem, perhaps in the exodus of the 30s BCE, and migrated to the Jewish diasporas in Samaria, Egypt, and Asia. Others remained in Jerusalem and its satellite villages. Some of those communities, when they were located in Greek contexts, became known as "Therapeutae." They continued to emphasize lives of personal holiness, and they formed voluntary ascetic communities around their special forms of worship. Both men and women became part of these fictive kin groups. These are the ones I have called i-Nazoreans.

In previous chapters, I imagined how Jesus and his family may have been connected to this sect. Joseph, I suggested, came from the Galilean s-Nazoreans, Mary from the Judean i-Nazoreans. Their son Jesus appears to have united in his person—and reflected in his teaching—the two factions of the Nazorean sect. During the years of his public ministry, Jesus drew followers from both camps. After his death, sect members from both factions accepted Jesus as the expected Nazorean Messiah. The rapid spread of the Jesus movement may have been due to preexisting sectarian cells, including the ones in Galilee founded by the s-Nazoreans and the ones in the diaspora established by i-Nazorean exiles. The believers from the two factions had different views, however, about the meaning of Jesus's messiahship and how this related to the wisdom tradition. The tensions between the two sides of the divided sect reemerged in the early church, leading to what we found in the first chapters of Acts—a Hellenized faction that downplayed Jewish boundary markers, rejected animal sacrifice, and actively associated with gentile Godfearers, and a Hebrew faction composed of law-observant Jews. The differences between these two groups, differences inherited from their parent sect, would dominate the first four decades of the young church. These differences would be put on display in the writing and distribution of the gospels. Matthew and the other synoptic writers emphasized the practical ethics and cultural

Jewishness of Jesus's s-Nazorean context. John painted Jesus as the Person Wisdom of the i-Nazoreans, bringing to both Jews and gentiles a law-free message about a mystical union with God.

I can now answer—or at least explain why I cannot answer—a question I left hanging in chapter 2. I tried there to slot Christian Judaism into one of Bryan Wilson's sect types. As should be now apparent, we are not dealing with a single sect type. The Nazorean universe was a multiverse. If the movement initiated by Jesus and John the Baptist seemed to be charismatic and conversionist in its earliest expressions, it took on new shapes when it merged into the Nazorean matrix that birthed it. The s-Nazorean faction, which had embraced an apocalyptic vision, moved the Jerusalem church in the direction of Wilson's adventist sect type. The i-Nazorean communities assimilated by the young church, in contrast, leaned toward Wilson's introversionist type, a type that Wilson modeled on the Quakers. All of these sectarian streams of Nazoreans and Christian Jews would flow, in the second century CE, into a single river, the Christian church. New sects would emerge that would define themselves over against an emerging mainline Christianity.

9

Nazoreans Elsewhere

ON THIS JOURNEY OF imagination, I have focused on parts of four NT documents—the Gospel of Matthew, the Epistle of James, the Gospel of John, and the Acts of the Apostles. We saw in these books how the ministry and message of Jesus was embedded in a sectarian wisdom community and how the fissures in the early church reflected divisions in this background community. Several other NT documents might, with further study, be connected to the imaginative webs I have developed. Among these documents are 1 John, Luke, Hebrews, Ephesians/Colossians, Philippians, the Corinthian letters, Revelation, and some of the gospel sections not considered in early chapters. Let me provide a few brief thoughts about how these other NT books might relate to ideas developed in the webs.

I mentioned the letter of *1 John* when we examined the Gospel of John. Scholars who have attempted to chart the course of the Johannine community make use of this sermon-like catholic epistle and the shorter personal letters of 2 John and 3 John. If we regard 1 John as a late addition to the NT corpus that was written by someone attempting to imitate themes in the Gospel of John—one recent study[1] of the letter does exactly this—then it has almost no relevance to discussions about a sectarian wisdom movement. But if we assume that 1 John was written by either the author of John, the redactor of John, or someone in the author's or redactor's community, passages in it could be relevant to i-Nazorean

---

1. Méndez, "Did the Johannine."

beliefs. About thirty-five theme texts in 1 John have echoes and allusions in the Gospel of John.[2]

I've referred to the Gospel of *Luke* several times in this study. The Benedictus and Magnificat found in the gospel's birth narratives could have been based, I noted, on Nazorean hymns. Luke's attribution of an oracle to Person Wisdom in Luke 12, discussed in chapter 4, also raised provocative questions. A larger view of Luke that looked at his relationship with the other gospels might find that Luke, in his role as a historian-evangelist, had access not only to Matthew's s-Nazorean gospel but also to documentary sources that derived from i-Nazorean communities. Some of the many similarities between the Gospel of Luke and the Gospel of John—widely discussed in the scholarly literature—could trace back to Luke's now-lost Nazorean sources.[3]

The Epistle to the *Hebrews*, an anonymous letter that was historically assigned to Paul, might come from the hand of someone with a wisdom background. At the beginning of the letter, the writer says that Jesus, who is the "refulgence of glory and the image of the person of God" and who "upholds all things by his word of power," sat down after his time on earth "at the right hand of the majesty on high" (1:3). This description reminds us of the encomium to Person Wisdom in the Wisdom of Solomon. The same unusual Greek word, the one translated "refulgence," is used in both Hebrews and Wisdom of Solomon 7:26. A closer study of the letter might connect several of the epistle's central points to Nazorean doctrines.

Many NT scholars believe that *Ephesians and Colossians* are pseudepigrapha attributed to Paul. The theological framework of the two letters seems to have Nazorean influences. In Ephesians 1:3–14, which is one long sentence of cascading clauses,[4] we have a synopsis of the i-Nazorean Christology that uses the key terms "wisdom," "glory," and "beloved." On the surface, the passage appears to be a statement about the

2. See the chart in Puskas and Robbins, *The Conceptual World*, 32–33.

3. The most significant compilation of similarities between the gospels of Luke and John may be Parker, "Luke." In a survey of points of contact between the two gospels, Parker notes that "we find the Fourth Gospel in contact 26 times with Matthew only, 19 with the Second Gospel only, and 23 with both of these against Luke. *But John sides 124 times with Luke only*" (Parker, "Luke," 331, emphasis Parker's). For a more recent updating of Luke/John similarities, see van de Weghe, "The Beloved Eyewitness." These similarities also extend to the Acts of the Apostles, presumably written by the author of Luke. For a discussion of these John-Acts similarities, see Parker, "The Kinship."

4. As I learned when assigned to parse the sentence for my first class in Greek syntax—I had to keep pasting together pieces of paper to hold the ever-descending diagram.

blessings bestowed on the Ephesian believers. All of these gifts, however, come through a metaphysical union with Christ—in the space of these verses, the author employs the phrases "in Christ," "in him," or "through Christ" about a dozen times. What is said about the believers—that they were "chosen before the foundation of the world" to be "holy and blameless" and that by "the good pleasure of the will of God" they were "predestined to adoption" for "the praise of the glory of God's grace"—are better read as descriptions of the Christ-as-Wisdom that believers possess because of their union with "the beloved." The "riches of God's grace," which have arrived "in all wisdom and insight," reveal to the Ephesians the mystery that "all things will be summed up in Christ." Later in the letter, the writer of the epistle will go on to explain that Jesus, now raised from the dead, sits at God's right hand "in heavenly places," (1:20) and that those who believe in Christ will also be raised from the death of sin and made to sit "in the heavenly places with Christ Jesus" (2:6). One long passage toward the end of Ephesians riffs on the wisdom metaphor of light and darkness (5:8–14). Colossians contains the same perspective. We learn in this epistle that Jesus is "the image of the invisible God, the firstborn of all creation" (1:15). All things were "created by him and for him" and he is "before all things and all things are held together by him" (1:16–17). In him, "all the treasures of wisdom and knowledge are hidden" (2:3). Phrasings such as these argue for a connection to Nazorean wisdom sources. Whether other themes in these letters represent Nazorean doctrines is a question that needs investigation.

Some of Paul's authentic letters may also throw light on the study in this book. Before considering these, however, we should think about how Paul's life might interlace with the story of the Nazoreans. Paul, who started out as a diaspora Pharisee (Phil 3:5), admits in one of his letters that he became a persecutor of the church (1 Cor 15:9) before shifting his allegiance to the followers of Christ. The fuller—and some scholars think less than reliable—story about Paul's transition from persecutor to believer is found in Acts, which relates Paul's road-to-Damascus experience no less than three times (in Acts 9, 22, and 26). The author of Acts also associates Paul with the stoning of the Hellenist Stephen (7:58) and the persecution of the Hellenists that arose at this time (8:1–3). As a person engaged by the Judean religious leaders to root out a sectarian threat, Paul may have focused his arrests, not on believers in Christ per se, but *on the i-Nazorean communities.*

We find hints that the i-Nazoreans might have been the object of Paul's attention in Acts 9:2. This verse says that the letters addressed to the Damascus synagogues, which Paul had obtained from the Jerusalem leadership, licensed him to seize both "men and women of [the group calling themselves] 'The Way.'" First, we have to wonder why, if Paul was targeting believers in Christ, he would head to Damascus. The ones who were scattered in the post-Stephen dispersion, some of whom would have made for Damascus, were probably the i-Nazorean Hellenists. Second, the fact that Paul was pursuing *both* men and women in these persecutions could reflect the important role that women played in the leadership of the i-Nazorean cells. Third, the name "The Way" points toward the i-Nazoreans. Scholars often cite it as an early Christian self-designation,[5] but it could originally have been an i-Nazorean endonym for their sectarian group. Note that the only other place where we find the designation "The Way" is in Acts 18–19, in conjunction with Ephesus, Apollo, and the presumed i-Nazorean cell there. Acts 9:13 is also suggestive. The Damascus disciple sent to cure Paul's blindness after his encounter with Christ, Ananias, says that he is aware of "how many bad things [Paul] has done to [God's] holy ones in Jerusalem." We tend to hear "any believers in Christ" when we read "holy ones," but the ones being most actively persecuted at this time were i-Nazoreans believers.

Paul's change from persecuting i-Nazoreans to becoming a believer in Christ did not necessarily mean that Paul acquired any strong allegiance to the i-Nazorean perspective of Christian Judaism. The letters of Paul that scholars believe may be from his own hand do not, at least as a group, lend themselves to a study of Nazorean issues. There are, however, three exceptions. The Epistle to the *Philippians* contains a famous kenotic passage in 2:6–11 that could have been lifted from a Nazorean hymn.[6] Jesus, the hymn says, was "in the form of God" but did not consider this equality with God "something to cling to." He "emptied himself" and took on the "form of a servant" and "human likeness." After his death, God "exalted him" to a place where he would be worshipped. We could imagine Paul quoting this old hymn, though, without importing the

---

5. The phrase was also used by the Qumran sectarians to designate their own group. See the discussion in Beers, *Followers*, 61–2.

6. While many students of Paul believe that this is an older hymn that has been inserted into Philippians, we have no way of knowing this. For a discussion of this problem, see Bühner, *Messianic High Christology*, 35–6.

whole Nazorean setting of Person Wisdom. But it does hint at some contact between Paul and those who had Nazorean backgrounds.

The *Corinthian letters* are also of interest, but more because they show opposition rather than allegiance to i-Nazorean ideas. Paul founded the church in Corinth, and after Paul left, his co-worker Apollos—the one I surmised in chapter 6 may have come from an i-Nazorean/Therapeutan community in Alexandria—made his way to Corinth and taught the new believers. In his letters to the Corinthians, Paul refers to factions that had taken root in the Corinthian church. Believers were aligning themselves with Paul or with Apollos (1 Cor 3:4–5). But what differences between Paul and Apollos led to these polarizations?

We may have evidence of these differences in some of the issues Paul raises in the Corinthian letters. In the initial chapters of 1 Corinthians, Paul diminishes the value of wisdom, contrasting it with his simple belief in the crucified Christ (1:18–31). The message he delivered to the Corinthians, he says, came to them "in weakness and in fear and in much trembling" and not in "persuasive words of wisdom," so that the faith of the Corinthians might not rest on "human wisdom" (2:3–5). Some of the Corinthian believers claimed to have become, at least on a spiritual level, rich royalty who were "wise in Christ" (4:8–10). In 1 Corinthians 7, Paul addresses problems caused by those who were leaving their marriages or refusing conjugal intimacies. In the next chapter he faults those who, puffed up by the knowledge that the pagan sacrificial system was a sham, injured weaker believers who did not share this knowledge. At the end of 2 Corinthians, Paul, hearing about mystical visions among his opponents, feels compelled to mention his own vision of being caught up to the third heaven, to paradise, and hearing "inexpressible words that a person is not allowed to speak" (12:4). Looking at this list of topics, a case might be made that Apollos had imported an i-Nazorean wisdom agenda into Paul's Corinthian church. The Apollonian agenda may have included, besides an emphasis on wisdom, the Therapeutan ideal of a celibate community whose members renounced conjugal and family relationships. Apollos's Corinthians followers, seeing themselves joined to a Johannine Logos, may have spoken about their own elevation as spiritual kings, their claim to divine riches, and their mystical visions. The i-Nazorean devaluation of the sacrificial system may have been carried over into their viewpoint on pagan offerings.

The struggle between Nazorean groups may also throw light on another group of NT documents. We have noted the presence of apocalyptic passages in the Synoptics and surmised that s-Nazoreans were more open to the late Second Temple apocalyptic shift than the i-Nazoreans. If they were, then we might assume that s-Nazoreans had some hand in the apocalyptic letters of Jude and II Peter. They might also have been the source of the most significant apocalyptic text in the NT, the Book of *Revelation.*

For much of my life, the scholarly consensus around Revelation has been that it was a late first-century—perhaps even early second-century—product of Christians who had broken with Judaism. This consensus no longer holds. Around the turn of the current millennium, several scholars made a strong case for a new perspective on Revelation.[7] They reassigned the book to sectarian Jewish sources and opened the possibility of an earlier date. One of the major reasons for this revision was a recognition of the importance of halakhic purity to the author of Revelation.

But which Jewish sect gave us the Book of Revelation? At the beginning of the book, before the long run of apocalyptic visions, the author (or an editor) has inserted a series of letters addressed to seven Christ-believing communities in Asia Minor. These letters draw sharp boundaries between the author's group and those who do not belong to the group. The author's opponents, the letters say, "maintain that they are apostles but are not" (2:2) and "call themselves Jews and are not" (2:9, see also 3:9). Instead, they are "a synagogue of Satan" that "holds to the teaching of Balaam" (2:14) and "the teaching of the Nicolaitans" (2:15, see also 2:6). They also "tolerate the woman Jezebel" (2:20). We don't know who the Nicolaitans were—possibly they had some connection to Nicholas, one of the seven Hellenist deacons appointed in Acts 6. Balaam and Jezebel, both figures from the Tanak, were non-Israelites whose association with the Jews led the people of Israel into sin. The sins noted in the letters in Revelation include eating what had been sacrificed to idols, committing fornication, and learning Satanic "deep things" (2:14, 20, 24). The opponents of the author also led the faithful to say, "I am rich, I have prospered and need nothing" (3:17).

John W. Marshall, pulling together the picture of John's opponents in these seven letters, suggests that they were "a mixture of Pagan Godfearers and comfortably Hellenizing Jews who welcome the God-fearers without requiring a substantial (in John's eyes) separation from

7. These were some of the same scholars who were part of the New Perspectives on Paul movement. A summary of this change in how we understand Revelation is in Frankfurter, "Jews," 402.

Greco-Roman culture."[8] Using the story developed in our imaginative webs, we can refine Marshall's summary. The author of Revelation
may have belonged to an apocalyptic s-Nazorean group that was worried about incursions of i-Nazorean beliefs and practices into the Asian
churches. The i-Nazoreans, I noted above, adhered less strictly to Jewish
customs. They did not practice animal sacrifice and taught their followers
that food was not improved or harmed by becoming a religious offering. They did not observe all the boundary markers of mainline Judaism, and they probably welcomed into their groups—and intermarried
with—gentiles. When the author of Revelation says that his opponents
"called themselves Jews" even though they weren't, he may have had in
mind these mixed i-Nazorean cells. From the author's perspective, the
i-Nazoreans, with their cavalier attitudes toward animal sacrifice and
their pursuit of a deeper symbolic understanding of Jewish rites, were
overstepping the bounds of acceptable behaviour. Their intermarriages
with gentiles would have amounted to what the letters call "fornication."
They probably had women in leadership roles—ones that the author of
the letters calls "Jezebels."

In addition to rethinking how these NT documents relate to a sectarian wisdom source for the Jesus movement, I find myself wondering
how this perspective might affect the way we view some of *the familiar
stories and teachings in the four gospels.* The passages I have looked at
in the gospels of Matthew and John are ones that provide the best evidence for the wisdom point of view. Once the point of view is accepted,
however, many other stories—ones with less evidential merit—might be
linked to Nazorean sources. I find myself asking, whenever I read one
of the direct sayings of Jesus, "Could Jesus have learned this from his
Nazorean upbringing, or did he add this to what he had been taught?"
The same question applies to what the gospels say about Jesus's actions.
Could some of these be sourced to his background?

A question I left hanging in an early chapter is related to this issue. When we covered Jesus's three temptations by Satan in chapter 4, I
suggested that the story arose from Jesus's sectarian context. Now that
we have drawn a more detailed picture of this context, I can provide a
guess about how this might have happened. The three temptations may
possibly have been a symbolic vehicle developed within the Nazorean

8. Marshall, *Parables of War*, 134.

communities.[9] The story may have been meant to explain, by way of an allegory, how a prototypical Nazorean might make use of sectarian interpretations of the Tanak to meet challenges that arose from other factions of Judaism. When Jesus became the point person in this factional struggle, the symbolism was adapted to his role. The temptations eventually became accepted by the synoptic authors as actual events that happened to Jesus during one of his solitary fasting retreats.

The gospel stories about the cleansing of the temple may also have Nazorean sources. As pointed out earlier, the Johannine and synoptic timelines, besides differing on the details of the event, have a major disagreement about when this is supposed to have occurred—the Gospel of John places it at the beginning of Jesus's ministry, but Matthew, Mark, and Luke assign it to Holy Week. The cleansing passages feel like they may have been adaptations of a free-floating story, picked out of the tradition to serve the literary goals of the evangelists.[10] Behind these adaptations may lie an earlier i-Nazorean departure from temple-based worship and a reinterpretation of festivals and sacrifices. We could imagine public demonstrations by the i-Nazoreans against the excesses of temple culture, with stories about these events being drawn, like the temptation legend, into the emerging description of what Jesus said and did. But we don't have to remove all literal elements from the cleansing passages. Perhaps Jesus and his disciples, on their several trips to Jerusalem, did participate in sectarian protests against the temple practices of mainline Jewish traditions.

Several other stories and teachings in the gospels might benefit from a similar analysis. The Transfiguration, for example, could have a Nazorean backstory—the suggestive parallels with Moses at Sinai[11] and the prioritization of Jesus over Moses and Elijah makes the Transfiguration narrative feel like it has some dependence on sectarian material.

9. The forty-day length of the fast and the Sinai-like desert setting remind us that we are more in the realm of symbol than biography.

10. Taking her cue from the public violence of Jesus's death at Roman hands and the lack of official interest in pursuing Jesus's followers, Paula Fredriksen develops a scenario for Holy Week that makes better sense if it does *not* include a violent act against the temple system. John's setting of the event, however, while more plausible, is more laden with symbolism. These problems, she argues, turn the temple cleansing passages into a "floating story" that can be "bracketed out" (Fredriksen, "The Historical Jesus," 270).

11. For a comparison between Moses at Sinai and the Transfiguration, see Moses, *Matthew's Transfiguration Story.*

Parables with agrarian and aquatic themes, or ones that involve banqueting and weddings, might also have had their origin in rural s-Nazorean communities. The many teachings that involve reversals (the last shall be first) might have their foundation in the losses and poverty of members of the Nazorean sect. These are all speculative thoughts, of course, but it is surprising how a shift in perspective can trigger novel interpretations of familiar stories.

10

Misapplied Metaphors

I BEGAN THESE FIVE imaginative webs with a probe of my own religious journey and with a discussion of Jewish sectarianism. Let me end with a brief return to these two points of departure. My way back will be through a pair of misused phrases. (Only "misused" in a schoolmarmish sense. They aren't semantic errors—just phrases that have departed from their etymological roots.)

The first of these adapted sayings is "ghost in the machine."[1] In a recent book, Claire Dederer applies this phrase to situations in which people, unaware of their own subjectivity, assume a false objectivity.[2] Their words proceed from a ghost that others can often see, but they can't. Dederer is concerned about the immaculate stance assumed by art and media critics. But the point she is making with her borrowed phrase applies equally well to biblical studies. When we write about Moses or Jesus, we often draw curtains around our own subjectivity, turning it into a ghost. When our self-identity intrudes—as it must[3]—we can fail to notice it.

1. "Ghost in the machine" was popularized by the English analytic philosopher Gilbert Ryle. In a famous 1949 book, Ryle used the phrase to describe the way the dualistic metaphysics of René Descartes handled the mind-body problem (Ryle, *The Concept of Mind*). Mind and body, in Descartes's view, were separate, but they operated in parallel. Since only the body is physical, mind becomes a sort of unseen ghost inhabiting the brain.

2. Dederer, *Monsters*.

3. "Interpretation," says the Johannine scholar Robert Kysar, "requires that interpreters know themselves. Every interpretation is really autobiographical" (Kysar, "What's the Meaning," 176).

I have spent a lifetime learning how to catch glimpses of this ghost. In some ways, this is what philosophy is all about, and it is probably what drew me, many years ago, to the study of philosophy. I don't imagine for a moment, of course, that I am more immune from hidden subjectivity than others who have chosen to study Christian history. I have agendas— some personal, some cultural—that I am not clever or brave enough to bring into the light. Writers about mystic spirituality often refer to these agendas as the "shadow self," an image popularized by Carl Jung. Exposing the shadow self, bringing it to the light, is the hardest personal work that anyone can undertake.

To reveal this ghost and its role in my five webs, I have tried to be as open in this book as I could about my own experiences with Christian faith. Whether this has made my shadow self more visible to me is uncertain. But openness at least makes it more likely that others will detect spectral outlines that are hidden from me. Discovering a teaching sage and a wisdom sect beneath the biblical stories, stories that others read in different ways, is probably the work of one of these ghosts. The involvement of a ghost does not mean, of course, that what it discovers is not there. But it does mean that I am, of all people, the person least likely to notice the ghost's mistakes.

The second maladapted saying, "thin red line,"[4] a theological phrase for the intimations of Christ in the OT, takes us back to the issue of sectarianism. The scholarly discussion around the distinction between church and sect, launched in the first half of the twentieth century by Max Weber and Ernst Troeltsch, is vast and complex.[5] Work on the topic was motivated by the search for a sociological framework—a typology— that might help to understand the post-Protestant fracture of the church. The typologies that have come out of this quest, however, have strayed from the land where they were born. They have been applied to earlier stages of church history and even to other religions.

At the heart of these typologies is the distinction between a dominant, successful religious culture (the church) and the religious groups that reject this religious synthesis (sects). In this book, I looked at this

---

4. The idiom "thin red line" is recycled from a military image. The thin red line was a battle line, an array of red-coated Highlanders in a conflict of the Crimean War. Rudyard Kipling popularized the idiom in his poem "Tommy": "It's 'Thin red line of 'eroes' when the drums begin to roll."

5. For a review of the sociological discussion around church and sect, see Dawson, "Church-Sect-Cult."

dichotomy in the first web, and I made use of it in the other webs to build a picture of what was happening in late Second Temple Judaism. We can map the Jewish religious establishment in Judea onto the church side of the church-sect typology. The religious movements that challenged this establishment we can treat as sects. In the last two imaginative webs, I assembled a picture of the Nazoreans, a Jewish wisdom sect that thrived in the decades surrounding the beginning of the first millennium. This sect was the cradle of the Jesus movement and the apostolic church.

The approach taken in this book, which claims that Christianity was a morph of sectarian Judaism, has not always been well received by those telling the story of the church. We find attempts to suppress this view, for example, in the earliest ecclesiastical histories. In his fourth-century history of the Christian church, Eusebius often relied on five books of memoranda written by the second-century Hegesippus, the author I mentioned in my earlier coverage of James and the relatives of Jesus. In one of Eusebius's extended quotations from these early memoranda, Hegesippus weighs in on the issue of sects, both in Christianity and Judaism.[6] When the church began to centralize its administration under bishops, identifying a single stream of theological thinking as orthodox, divergent versions of the Christian tradition were declared heterodox. Hegesippus looks back on a century of struggle between orthodox and heterodox movements and names some of the Christian sects. He also says that there were seven *Jewish* movements, factious groups with "differing opinions" from one another, that opposed "the tribe of Judah and the Christ." He names the Jewish movements as "Essenes, Galileans, Hemerobaptists, Masbotheans, Samaritans, Sadducees, and Pharisees."

Eusebius refers to these seven Jewish groups as "sects/heresies," using the same word that Hegesippus employed for the groups who had opposed orthodox Christianity.[7] This application of the meaning of "sect" should give us pause. Calling the deviant Christian groups "sects" makes some sense—they were peripheral branches of Christianity that did not follow the beliefs and behaviors propagated by the mainline church. But it makes no historical sense to refer to the seven Jewish groups as Christian sects. Named among the Jewish groups are the Pharisees and Sadducees

---

6. The citation of Hegesippus is found in Eusebius, *Hist.* 4.22.

7. Eusebius and Hegesippus use the term *hairesis* for "sect." The word can be a general term for a school of thought or a religious movement. It is used this way by Josephus. At the time Eusebius and Hegesippus were writing, however, *hairesis* had begun to take on the more technical meaning that we know from its English cognate, "heresy."

who were at the core of Second Temple Judaism. In our discussion, we mapped these two groups onto the church when we applied the church-sect typology.

Hegesippus seems to be aware of this inconsistency. He addresses the problem by placing a tradition of orthodoxy that he calls "the tribe of Judah and the Christ" at the center of Jewish life, in the position that would later be occupied by the church. While it strains the idea behind the church-sect typology to replace a mainline religious tradition—core Judaism—with a socially peripheral person and movement, Hegesippus has not abandoned the church-sect framework. From his perspective, the orthodox church that he belonged to was not absent from Second Temple Jewish culture. It was there all along, in ovo, in the person of Jesus. And not just in the person of Jesus—the church itself had existed since the days of Adam, hiding itself as a thin red line that traced through the faithful in every age.[8] This is probably what Hegesippus meant by adding "the tribe of Judah" to "the Christ." Both Jesus and the church that he would establish were present, in some mysterious way, in the prophecies that the Messiah would come from the tribe of Judah and from the royal dynasty of King David. Because God was carrying out the work of salvation through this hidden process, every other Jewish faction, including the Pharisees and Sadducees who were at the center of Jewish religious practice, could be lumped with the heterodox sects of Christianity.

Hegesippus's line of thought, odd as it may seem, has had its followers. Evangelicals often make use of it. I remember hearing sermons about "the thin red line" when I was at Moody. Just as women are born with all the eggs that they will ever need to produce children, Jesus, from this point of view, arrives on earth with the church inside him. His mission is to give birth to it. But even before he does, the church already exists—not in actuality, perhaps, but in some kind of virtuality. We could also say, using a different metaphor, that Jesus *invents* the church by using plans that had been drafted before the world existed. Bits of the plan leaked out before Jesus came, tracing through history the thin red line that leads to the church.

---

8. "Orthodox Christianity did not proceed from just any form of historic Judaism. No, it is seen as proceeding from that true religion as old as humanity itself, represented and practiced by Adam, Noah, the patriarchs, and the prophets. This true religion was unfolded in a continuous tradition throughout the course of biblical history; in the final analysis, it was already Christian" (Simon, *Jewish Sects*, 133).

The thin red line theology of the early church historians and of modern evangelicals devalues the Jewish social context of the Jesus movement. But so does much of the work of post-Enlightenment, modernist theologians. They don't have a thin red line in their theologies, but they do have an institution—the church—that invents itself. Some of these theologians picture Jesus as a religious genius.[9] Others, veering toward a Galilean peasant model for Jesus, relocate the genius factor in Jesus's followers. In either case, these theologians depict the church as an institution that comes to prominence by rejecting and surpassing its Jewish matrix. The Christian church manifests something entirely new. Over the last two-thirds of the first century CE, the church, they maintain, created a body of Scripture that expounded and explained this newness, laying a foundation for future growth. NT scholars dig through the layers of this Scripture, like archeologists excavating a tell, looking for evidence of this genius. When they reach a level in the mound that corresponds to what they think is original and unique, these scholars stop digging. They clean up their work site, put up a sign that says, "The Beginning of the Church," and start conducting tours through it. The layer where they stop digging, however, is not determined by the foundations and walls they uncover and the relics they dig up. It is decided by the assumptions they bring to the dig.

In the imaginative webs in this book, I have followed a way of thinking about the church that has become more popular in recent decades.[10] It does not start with the church-oriented viewpoints of Hegesippus, evangelicals, or classical modernists. This newer approach digs *through* the layers that have been labeled "The Beginning of the Church." The genius of the church goes much deeper. A large part of it resides, I have

9. Because my focus has been on the Nazorean communities, I have not engaged the long-standing debate about whether Jesus was a mystic. I would obviously agree, in this debate, with those who find evidence of a mystical perspective in Jesus's teachings and actions. But in taking this side in the debate, I feel some ambiguity. Scholars who emphasize the mystical elements in the Jesus story sometimes do this in service of a larger agenda that conflicts with my perspective. By describing Jesus as a mystic, they play down his dependence on a Jewish community with shared values. Jesus becomes a religious prodigy who anticipates the Western mystical tradition. This mysticism becomes the foundation on which the church is built, and the sources of his mysticism in Jewish sectarian thought are overlooked. This move is not necessary. "To identify the historical Jesus as a first-century Jewish mystic," Simon Joseph notes, "is not to dissociate him from his original cultural context with an anachronistic category. On the contrary, this identification serves to illuminate his distinctive role within the history of Judaism" (Joseph, "'I Shall Be Reckoned,'" 242).

10. See the section in the Appendixes on "Which Quest Are We in?"

proposed, in a Jewish sectarian movement with a wisdom orientation. During the first century BCE, the Nazoreans gave shape to the essential elements of what would become the church, bequeathing to it even the sect's internal conflicts. The cells and conventicles of this sect defined, through their OT interpretations and their own prophetic writings, the role that Jesus would step into. In the widely quoted statement of the Jewish scholar Daniel Boyarin, "All the ideas about Christ are old; the new is Jesus. There is nothing in the doctrine of the Christ that is new but only the declaration of *this* man as the Son of Man!"[11]

Siting the beginning of the church at a lower, earlier level leads to a rethinking of how the writings of the NT developed. Most of the space in this book has been given over to this task. Even so, the little I have done here has been too little. Those who find a productive framework in my imaginative webs will have work ahead of them. Those who don't will be challenged, I hope, to spin their own webs around the Jewish wisdom tradition and its impact on Christian Judaism and the church.

11. Boyarin, "Enoch," 353. Emphasis and punctuation are Boyarin's.

Appendix

THE PROBLEM WITH "OLD TESTAMENT"

The Hebrew Scriptures make up two thirds of the modern Christian Bible. This assimilation of Jewish text and tradition by the Christian church may be the single largest cultural appropriation in human history, surpassing even the massive steal of Greek culture by the Romans. The takeover is all the more glaring because the Jewish faith and culture from which Christians lifted their texts is still around, and Jews assign their own religious meanings to these documents.

Christians know the Hebrew Scriptures in their Bibles as the "Old Testament." This is a term I would prefer to avoid—hidden in the name is the subliminal message that this section of the Bible exists only to be superseded by something better, a *New* Testament. Some modern authors replace "Old Testament" with the less tendentious "First Testament." Another option, one often used by Jewish scholars, is replacing "Old Testament" with "Tanak" (or "Tanakh"), an acronym based on the traditional tripartite division of Hebrew holy books into the Law (*Torah*), the Prophets (*Nevi'im*), and the Writings (*Ketuvim*). This second option is the one I have selected.

But the new term doesn't solve all problems. The terms "Tanak" and "Old Testament" are not always synonymous. For Protestants, the terms have equivalent referents—the Protestant Old Testament includes just the books of the Tanak. These are books that have been transmitted to us in Hebrew and Aramaic. Roman Catholics, however, add to their Old Testament extra writings, texts that have come to us through Greek lines of transmission. Catholics often refer to these other writings as the "deuterocanonical books." Protestants tend to call them the "Apocrypha."

Other ancient Christian groups have extra books in their Old Testaments that have come down to us in other languages, such as Coptic.

We need, then, some word that can encompasses the Christian collection of Hebrew, Aramaic, and Greek-plus texts that have traditionally been called the "Old Testament." I experimented with alternatives when writing this book, but they seemed either too long and clunky or too novel. I decided, in the end, to use the abbreviation "OT," which could be understood as "Other Testament" or "Original Testament" as well as "Old Testament." Readers can mentally expand the abbreviation in the direction they choose. I use the term "Tanak" where I can, then, and "OT" when the focus is on the larger Christian canon derived from Second Temple Judaism. By the same logic, I have used "NT" instead of "New Testament," leaving room to understand it as "Next Testament."

THE NAZOREAN SUFFERING SERVANT

Four passages in Isaiah—42:1–4, 49:1–6, 50:4–11, and 52:13–53:12—are usually included in the Servant Songs. These passages all refer to "my servant" or "his servant." Because the Synoptic Gospels quote from/allude to these Servant Songs and apply them to Jesus, commentators have sometimes assumed that there was a widespread meme in the Second Temple period about a suffering servant with messiah-like qualities. Such an assumption—just as in the case of Second Temple messianic expectations—tends to read later Christian interpretations into the more diffuse Jewish matrix from which the church arose. The suffering servant defined by modern scholarship, says Leroy Huizenga, "was not a meaningful category within the ancient Jewish encyclopedia with which the Gospel of Matthew operates."[1]

Huizenga also doubts whether NT writers could have inherited an explicit theology that linked the Servant Songs to the suffering of Jesus. This position, however, has found less acceptance.[2] Martin Hengel and Daniel Bailey, summarizing references to Isaiah 53 in this period, conclude that "already in the pre-Christian period, traditions about suffering and atoning eschatological messianic figures were available in Palestinian

1. Huizenga, *The New Isaac*, 189. See his whole chapter on "The Suffering Servant and Matthean Christology" in 189–209.

2. See, for example, the critique in Brown, "Matthew's Christology." A chapter in Holly Beers's book on Jesus as the suffering servant surveys the variety of Second Temple uses of Isaiah's servant motif (Beers, *The Followers*, 49–84).

Judaism." Jesus and the early church "*could* have known and appealed to them."[3] Hengel and Bailey call attention to the way the sectarians of the Dead Sea Scrolls had already narrowed their understanding of the Isaiah's servant. The sect members understood their own group, not Israel in general, to be the subject of the Servant Songs.

The thesis developed in this book offers another slant on this much-discussed issue. I agree with the critics that there may not have been a generalized concept of an Isaianic servant in Second Temple Judaism. And I agree that most Jewish writers in this period interpreted the Servant Songs as references to the sufferings and restoration of Israel as a nation.[4] But it is possible that the Nazorean movement, seeing itself as a faithful remnant, an Israel within Israel, may have formulated—and expressed in pesher-like commentaries—an explicit theological framework around servanthood, one that inserted its own community experiences into the role of the servant in the Servant Songs. The long quotation of Isaiah's first servant song (42:1–4) in the middle of the Little Wisdom section of Matthew (12:18–21), a passage I discussed in chapter 4, could be an echo of this sectarian theology. The choice of the name "Therapeutae," the servants of God, may also have been motivated by a sectarian interpretation of the Servant Songs. When Jesus took on the role of the Nazorean "coming one," a transfer of the group's servant theology to his own mission and person would have been a natural move. It may not be anachronistic, then, to identify an explicit theology of a suffering servant behind references to it in the NT documents. The repeated designation of Jesus as God's servant in the early chapters of Acts (3:13, 3:26, 4:27, 4:30) may be remnants of this identification.

In addition to the four Servant Songs, two other Tanak passages may have been packaged into the Nazorean picture of the servant. One is Isaiah 61:1–2, which starts out "The spirit of the Lord God is upon me." While it does not refer to "my servant," the passage displays a "similarity in function between the servant of the songs and the figure"[5] described in the passage. Luke depicts Jesus reading this Isaiah passage in the Nazareth synagogue at the very beginning of his ministry (4:16–21). In the Lukan story, Jesus tells his listeners that "today this scripture has been fulfilled, as you heard [it read]." What Jesus may be linking himself to in

3. Hengel and Bailey, "The Effective History," 146. Emphasis in the source.

4. Passages in Isaiah surrounding the Servant Songs, such as 41:8 and 44:1–2, refer to "Israel/Jacob my servant."

5. Holly Beers, *Followers*, 45.

Luke 4 is a sectarian interpretation of the servant of God that included Isaiah 61:1–2 in its textual base. By positioning the event in Nazareth at the beginning of Jesus's ministry, Luke tightens the focus of Nazorean servant theology around Jesus. Luke makes Jesus say, in effect, that "you Nazoreans identify as the servant-of-God community; I am the completion of that identity, the servant as a person."

A second Tanak passage in the Nazorean servant package may have been Psalm 22, which begins "My God, my God, why have you forsaken me?" (Ps 22:1). The Psalm has lexical and thematic similarities to the last third of Isaiah.[6] We find multiple allusions to this Psalm and to the thematically similar Psalm 69 in the passion narratives. About half of the Tanak quotations in the passion narratives of the gospels, in fact, come from these two psalms. If they had already been integrated into the sectarian picture of a suffering servant, then making a connection between the sufferings described in the two psalms and the sufferings of Jesus could have been more than an invention of the evangelists. In his Psalms commentary, James Mays notes that the language of Psalm 22 "reflects a group who . . . are thinking and speaking about themselves and their relationship to God in a way that is beginning to redefine what it means to be Israel."[7]

DID NATHANAEL ASK A QUESTION?

What Nathanael says to Philip in John 1:46, literally and word for word, is "From Nazareth is able something good to be." This is usually read as a question: "Is something good able to come from Nazareth?" But is it a question? Hellenistic Greek manuscripts have no punctuation to differentiate questions from declarative sentences—only grammar and context can tell us when we should read a sentence as a question.

Grammar does not signal this as a question. John uses the verb *dunamai* in this sentence. This verb, which means "is able," is found about thirty-five times in John's gospel. Of these, ten of the instances are embedded in questions. Seven of these we know are questions because they are found in sentences with the interrogative pronouns "how," "who," or "why." The other three are negated verbs ("not able") and the questions start off with one of the two negative particles in Greek, *mē* or *ou*. This

6. See Lyons, "Psalm 22," for a comparison.

7. Mays, *Psalms*, 111–2.

grammatical trick, which is a common way of asking a question that assumes a positive answer (if *ou*) or a negative answer (if *mē*), also hints that these three sentences are questions. If Nathanael had asked a skeptical question that anticipated a negative answer, we would have expected the sentence to start off with the second negative particle, so that the question would have been, "Nothing good can come from Nazareth, can it?" What Nathanael says, however, has neither an interrogative pronoun nor a question-introducing negative. It could, then, be read as a declarative sentence. If so, it's meaning would be something like, "From Nazareth—something good is possible."

Does, however, the *context* suggest that it might be a question, even if the grammar does not point in this direction? Philip's reply to Nathanael to "come and see" might be thought of as an appropriate response to a question. Earlier in the same chapter, in fact, "come and see" is used in just this way. John the Baptist's disciples ask Jesus where he is staying and Jesus says, "Come and you will see" (1:39). But in this earlier case, the question that triggers the "come and see" is clearly a question—it has the interrogative pronoun "where." Nor is it a challenging question—the Baptist's disciples are not asking Jesus to prove anything. The "come and see" reply is merely an invitation to learn more. Nathanael's statement about something good possibly coming from Nazareth would also be the sort of utterance that might prompt the response to come and learn more about it.

I should also mention that the issue of whether there is an interrogative particle is not as open and shut as it might be. As the sentence is accented in Greek texts, it reads "something good," *ti agathon*. But it could be re-accented with *ti* as an interrogative adjective, making it read "what good?" and giving the sentence a question-signaling phrase. However, this would not be the usual way of reading this phrase. I have found no examples of this "what good?" in any Greek corpus. There are explicit examples, though, of "something good." In Xenophon's *Anabasis*, Xenophon addresses his troops and says, "Which of you have I hindered from saying something good (*ti agathon*), if anyone among you can?"[8]

In sum, I think the balance of evidence suggests that Nathanael's response is not a question. Nathanael knows about a prediction that the Messiah would be a Nazorean, and he wonders if Jesus being from Nazareth might connect with these promises.

8. Xenophon, *Anabasis*, 5.7.10.

I-NAZOREAN DOORKEEPERS

In the days of the First Temple, there appears to have been a formal order of temple servants whose members bore the title *shomer hasaph*, the
keeper of the threshold. Members of this society had rooms in the temple
compound (Jer 35:4) and a role in the management of temple treasures (2
Kgs 12:9, 23:4). In the early Second Temple period, we hear about doorkeepers, *sho'erim*, as part of the temple staff (Ezra 2:70, for example). The
sho'erim may have been later expressions of the earlier order.

The usual translation for *sho'erim* in the Septuagint is *pylōroi*, a cognate of the Greek word for "gate." In 1 Esdras, a Greek book dating from (we
think) the second century BCE, the term used for the temple doorkeepers
becomes *thyrōroi* (e.g., 1 Esdras 1:15), the same word for "door" employed
by Jesus in John 10. The i-Nazoreans, because they mirrored aspects of the
temple service in their own worship, may have adopted the name *thyrōroi*,
doorkeepers, to designate authorities in their own communities that they
thought had duties analogous to those serving in the temple.

Nazorean *thyrōroi* may have included women as well as men. There
are two interesting linkages between women and *thyrōroi*. One of these
connections is in the book of 1 Esdras. 1 Esdras is a close reworking
of the Hebrew Ezra, with extra chapters pulled from 2 Chronicles and
Nehemiah. In the middle of 1 Esdras, however, we find a story that is
missing from the Hebrew sources. It tells about a contest between the
bodyguards of King Darius. The bodyguards vie with each other to describe the strongest thing. One argues that wine is the strongest. A second opts for soldiers. The third maintains that it is women and truth.
This third bodyguard, who turns out to be the Jewish Zerubbabel, wins
the contest. As a reward, the king allows him to return to Jerusalem and
restore its temple. Recognition of the authority of women in a sapiential
context (truth) in this story from 1 Esdras calls to mind the i-Nazoreans.
If i-Nazorean elements were not actually behind the creation of this story
from 1 Esdras, they would certainly have been attracted to its message.

The second link between *thyrōros* and women is found in John's version of Peter's denials. All of the gospels agree that the first person to accuse Peter of being a follower of Jesus was a *paidiskē*, a female servant. In
the version found in the Gospel of John, however, she is also referred to as
hē thyrōros, a female doorkeeper (18:16–17). This is the only other use of
thyrōros in John. We could easily imagine that the author of John, enticed
by the irony of the image, depicted Peter failing in the most fundamental

way when confronted by a woman holding an office, doorkeeper, that was replicated in the i-Nazorean communities.

WAS JOHN THE BAPTIST AN I-NAZOREAN?

After the discovery of the Dead Sea Scrolls, NT scholars began to ask whether John the Baptist might have had a connection to the Qumran community. Nothing from either the NT or the Qumran scrolls provides a definitive answer to this, but the circumstantial evidence is impressive. There are a number of parallels. (1) John's presumed baptismal site was probably near the mouth of the Jordan, not far from Qumran. (2) Both John and the Essenes stressed water rituals that were connected to cleansing from sin. (3) Both were associated with the phrase from Isaiah 40:3 about a voice in the wilderness crying out "Prepare the way of the Lord." (4) Both spoke about the role of the Holy Spirit and referred to their enemies as "vipers." (5) Both adapted to the apocalyptic shift and believed in a coming judgment. (6) John's diet of food gathered from the wild (locusts and wild honey) corresponds to what a person who had taken Essene oaths and then been exiled from the Essene community might have been compelled to eat. (7) John was said to have "lived in the wilderness" (Luke 1:80) before his public ministry. (8) John condemned Herod for a sin explicitly named in the Qumran sectarian documents and not in the Torah—the marriage of an uncle to a niece. (9) Both John and the Essenes were concerned with community ranking. Raymond E. Brown observes that "almost every detail of [John the Baptist's] life and preaching has a *possible* Qumran affinity."[9]

But do these parallels mean that John was an Essene? The Nazoreans and the Essenes, both sects with a countercultural stance toward mainline Judaism, probably shared many beliefs and customs—what counts as evidence for one association may actually count for the other. Chances are that Nazorean groups had some type of exchange with Essene communities. The best analogy I can think of is the relationship between Mennonites, Amish, and German Baptist Brethren in the US from 1750 to 1900. Though coming from different European roots, all three were countercultural peace churches, and all three had Old Order members with peculiar practices and dress. At the denominational level, they maintained separate polity and institutions, but at the congregational level, they found

9. Brown, "The Qumran Scrolls and the Johannine Gospels," 207.

ways to interact. Young people, by moving from one group to another, could expand their options for spiritual growth. Spouses were sometimes selected from the other groups. The sects also cooperated against outside threats to their lifestyles.

The parallels between John the Baptist and the Essenes, then, instead of proving John had an Essene background, could be evidence of sectarian cooperation. Indeed, if John had been an Essene, one wonders why the evangelists would have avoided saying this—the Essenes were widely respected, and the linkage would have provided the basis for an evangelistic outreach to Essene communities. Jonathan Klawans, one of the many scholars who reject a close association between John and Qumran, argues that the evidence makes it more probable that John operated independently in his own Judean context and that he drew whatever he shared with Qumran "from larger, less-exclusive Essene or broader Jewish ascetic trends."[10]

If John the Baptist was a cradle Nazorean, was he an s-Nazorean or an i-Nazorean? Several small clues suggest that he was part of the i-Nazorean groups. The clues are in Luke's account of the Baptist's birth to Zechariah and Elizabeth in chapter 1. First, Luke tells us that John grew up in the Judean hill country, a location compatible with being i-Nazorean sectarians. Second, Zechariah was a priest. The i-Nazorean who wrote the Gospel of John also appears to have had some standing in the Jerusalem priestly establishment, and no s-Nazorean—that we know of—claimed priestly connections. Third, Zechariah and Elizabeth had some relationship to the i-Nazorean Mary. Luke says that Mary was a *syngenēs*, a relative, of Elizabeth (1:36). The meaning of *syngenēs*, however, can range from a close connection (a blood relative) to a loose connection (an in-law or even a member of the same tribe or nation), so it is difficult to know what Luke meant by this term. In any case, even if the relationship between Mary and Elizabeth was not one of blood, the families of John the Baptist and Jesus may have been socially close. Mary stayed with Elizabeth, Luke says, for three months toward the end of Elizabeth's pregnancy, presumably to serve in the kin birth cohort.[11] By juxtaposing and interweaving the two miraculous births, that of John the Baptist and that of Jesus, Luke further underlines the connections between these families.

10. Klawans, "Analogies," 30.

11. On Mary's reasons for staying with Elizabeth, see Mueller, "Helping." As Mueller points out, Mary traveled to Elizabeth not "with haste," as many translations of Luke 1:39 say, but "with a sense of duty."

Fourth, the angel who speaks to Zechariah in Luke says that John was not to drink wine or strong drink (1:15). This aligns him with the Therapeutan (and possible i-Nazorean) practice of drinking only water. Fifth, in Zechariah's song, the Benedictus (Luke 1:67–79), there are phrases that remind us of the Therapeutan devotion to the light. Zechariah refers to "the sunrise from on high." When it comes, he says, it will "shine on those sitting in darkness and the shadow of death," an echo of Isaiah's prophecy in chapter 9 about God's gift of a child to Galilee. Luke may have sourced his Benedictus from an i-Nazorean hymn.

When we turn to the picture of the adult John the Baptist, though, we find clues leading us in the opposite direction. There is nothing in the Gospel of John, of course, to make us think that John the Baptist was anything other than an i-Nazorean. The fact that the beloved disciple (as I have interpreted the unnamed disciple in John 1:35–42) began as a disciple of John the Baptist encourages us to think that the Baptist had i-Nazorean roots. Aspects of the Baptist's depiction in the Synoptics, however, could hint at s-Nazorean connections. In Luke's presentation of the Baptist at the beginning of chapter 3, we find the Baptist giving the sort of wisdom advice that Jesus gives in the Sermon on the Mount and that James provides in the Epistle of James. Also, the message that the Baptist delivers to the crowds makes use of apocalyptic themes. He refers to "the coming wrath" and axes ready to cut down trees that will be "thrown into the fire" (Luke 3:7–9). The Messiah, Matthew's John says, will "baptize with fire." The Messiah has his "winnowing tool in his hand," and when he separates the chaff from the wheat, he will "burn the chaff with unquenchable fire" (Matt 3:7–12). When we examined the interaction between John the Baptist's disciples and Jesus in the Little Wisdom section of the Gospel of Matthew, we observed a fundamental misunderstanding between John and Jesus about the role of the Messiah. Jesus thought of himself as the incarnation of Person Wisdom whose role was to die for the sins of the people, while John the Baptist hoped for an apocalyptic warrior. These synoptic associations of practical wisdom and apocalyptic visions with the Baptist are more consistent with s-Nazorean outlooks.

We must not fall into the trap, though, of imagining that the picture of the Baptist in the Gospel of John is slanted and the picture in the Synoptics isn't. Matthew could well have shifted his depiction of John in s-Nazorean directions and the other synoptic authors followed his reinterpretation. If we assume that the two biases found in the depiction of the adult John—that in the Gospel of John and that in the Synoptics—cancel each other out, then we are thrown back on what we can learn from Luke's birth narrative, and this point of view, as noted above, suggests that John the Baptist came from an i-Nazorean community.

RETHINKING THE TRANSLATION OF ACTS 6:1-7

Acts 6:1-3 is usually translated something like this: "A complaint of the Hellenist Jews against the Hebrew Jews arose because their *widows* were *being neglected* in the *daily distributions*. The Twelve called together the whole group of disciples and said, 'It's not right for us to leave the word of God to *serve tables*.'" They then asked the convened group to select "seven respected *men*" from their group who were "full of the Holy Spirit and wisdom" so that they could assign the task to them.

Five of the phrases in this passage, the ones highlighted by italics, are English terms selected from a range of possible English translations for the underlying Greek terms. Translators have chosen these meanings to produce a specific interpretation of this passage. Other meanings for these terms are possible, and the alternate meanings offer a different picture of what is happening. Let's consider each of these five phrases.

First, *widows*. This is the Greek *chēra*. Its basic meaning is "a woman who has a deceased husband and who is currently unmarried." There is evidence, however, that the term was used more broadly in pre-Christian and Christian circles to designate pious women who had some independence from the dominant patriarchal subcultures of the Mediterranean world. They accomplished this by living sexually continent lifestyles. The groups may have included, besides women who had dead husbands, unmarried women (virgins), divorced women, and married women who had chosen not to live with their husbands. The model for the order of widows in the early church may have been the "elderly virgins" of Philo's Therapeutae, the female leadership of the i-Nazorean faction.

A possible example of this kind of widows group is found in Acts 9:36-42. Peter, travelling in the area around modern Tel Aviv, was summoned to a community where one of their leaders had just died. In an upstairs room, the apostle found a group of "widows" who were weeping over their deceased companion, Dorcas. One of the group's ministries may have been making and repairing clothing for the poor—Dorcas's friends showed Peter clothing that Dorcas had made. Peter sent the grieving friends out of the room and resuscitated Dorcas. Calling back "the saints and widows," he presented the living Dorcas to her friends. The word "saints" in this text (*hagioi*, holy ones) is a nominalized adjective in the masculine gender. While the masculine form of the adjective could refer to both sexes, the fact that it is paired with a word designating women suggests that we should read the phrase as "the holy men and consecrated women." Dorcas and her friends, we might assume, were part of an i-Nazorean cell. Dorcas is even referred to as a "woman disciple" (9:36), the only example of the female form of the word for "disciple" in the NT. Perhaps she performed the same leadership role in her cell that the disciples did in the Jerusalem groups of Christian Jews.

These early Christian widow organizations might be in view in 1 Timothy 5. Written at a time when the church was moving into a more patriarchal phase, this chapter of 1 Timothy contains an extensive description (5:3–16) of who should be permitted to become part of these consecrated female groups and thus qualify for church subsidies. The passage begins with the phrase "honor widows who are truly widows" (5:3). This wording implies two kinds of widow groups, the groups that people call "widows" and the groups who, in the writer's opinion, are "truly widows." The author places four restrictions on membership in his true-widow groups. Members allowed to be enrolled in the group, he says, must be at least sixty years old, married only once, have no living relatives who can look after them, and be dedicated to good works. Such restrictions imply that some women's groups, ones that other Christians were calling "widows," did not fit all of the writer's restrictions. These more broadly conceived groups could, for example, have included unmarried, many-married, and under-60 women. The groups may also have utilized a variety of funding sources. And some may have focussed, like the virgins/widows of Philo's Therapeutae, on worship rather than good works. Detailed information on the order of widows within Nazorean and early church communities is hard to come by, however, because what we know about them usually comes from those trying to control them. In this 1 Timothy passage, we see early steps toward a circumscription of the role of widows, steps that would eventually lead to a more formal and regulated institutional role for them.[12] The freedom accorded to female i-Nazorean leaders, their "widows," would eventually be lost.

Second, the word *neglected*. The Greek verb *paratheōreō* usually means "to compare one thing to other things." It can take on, as it seems

---

12. See Thurston, *The Widows*. For a review of research on the office of widows in the first centuries of the church, see Methuen, "The 'Virgin Widow.'"

to do in this passage, the more specific meaning of setting aside one of the compared items, devaluing it. Outside of its use here in Acts, the only example of this more selective sense is a passage from Dionysius of Halicarnassus, a Greek historian writing during the reign of the Roman emperor Augustus. Dionysius compares the overall styles of two orators and says that "if anyone dismisses (*paratheōreō*) these [observations of mine about] styles as small and trivial, he can't be a competent critic."[13] The author of Acts is probably saying that the Greek widows, the consecrated women of the Hellenist believers, were not being passively overlooked but being actively set aside, discriminated against, by the Christian Jewish leaders.

Third, the *daily distributions*. This is the daily *diakonia* in Greek. The word *diakonia* can refer to a specific relief or benefit that comes about from someone's efforts. In Acts 11:29, for example, the word is used to describe the aid sent to the famine-oppressed people in Judea. Those who read Acts 6:1 as a "daily distribution of food" appeal to this sense. Even those interpreting it this way, however, are aware of the inconsistency between the minor issue of food distribution and the major problem it caused.[14] More commonly, *diakonia* means something like "ministry" or "divine appointment." Acts uses it this way, for example, in 20:24, where Paul tells the Ephesian elders that his goal is to complete "the *diakonia* that I received from the Lord Jesus to bear witness to the gospel of the grace of God." The "daily ministry" referred to in Acts 6:1, the occasion in which consecrated women were being pushed aside and devalued, was not necessarily something the women *received*, such as an allocation of food. It could have been something they *did*, such as a daily worship service, that was part of their ministry. If the daily worship included a eucharistic meal, the complaint voiced by the Greek community may have been that the women, who no doubt prepared the meal, were not permitted to conduct the ritual associated with it.

Fourth, *serve tables*. The word "serve" is *diakoneō*, the verb associated with *diakonia*, and it can take on the same range of meaning as *diakonia*. Paul uses the verb to describe the work of his own ministry (2 Cor 3:3). But what does *diakoneō* mean when it is conjoined to the word "tables"? To translate the phrase as "serve tables" or "serve at table" brings up the

13. Dionysius of Halicarnassus, *Commentaries on the Attic Orators* 3.18.

14. "It is hard to believe that a mere question of distribution of food should have been sufficient . . . to cause so great dissatisfaction among the Hellenists" (Simon, *St. Stephen and the Hellenists*, 5).

image of a waiter, as though the apostles were busy carting around plates of food. This is an unlikely scenario—women or slaves typically did this work in the first century CE. The word "table," we should note, can mean the food on the table and not just the furniture on which food is served, as it does in Acts 16:34 when the jailer "sets a table [i.e., a meal]" before Paul and Silas. This is the sense of "table" in the phrase "the Lord's table" (1 Cor 10:21) when it is used as a synonym for "Eucharist." It is "the Lord's meal"—the focus at the Eucharist is not on ecclesiastical furniture but on the holy food served on it. In Acts 6:2, Peter and the apostles were probably arguing that they should not be required to conduct daily worship and administer the Eucharist to the thousands of believers—they should instead be out preaching the gospel to those who had not yet believed. That this is the intent of the complaint is indicated by the outcome. Seven deacons were selected to do this job of daily ministry, and the qualifications for the job were that they should be "full of the Holy Spirit and wisdom." These are hardly prerequisites for bussing and waiting.

Finally, *men*. The seven chosen to replace the disciples are referred to as "males" (*anēr*), a term often used to contrast male and female, rather than the more generic word for "man" (*anthrōpos*). Peter and the apostles, it seems, were not ready to accept women as worship leaders. Their response to the complaint of the Greek believers was to create a new office, one that the church would eventually call the "diaconate," and populate it with the males from the Greek-speaking groups.

Putting these alternate meanings together, we come up with an interpretation for Acts 6:1–3 that differs from the one in the translation above. The verses could be saying something like this (my expansions in square brackets):

The Hellenistic groups [of the Nazoreans] complained to the Aramaic/Hebrew groups [of the Nazoreans] because the consecrated women [in the Hellenistic groups] were being discriminated against in the daily eucharistic meals [by not being allowed to conduct the liturgy]. The Twelve called together all the disciples [from both groups] and said, "We're not happy with neglecting the word of God to administer at [the Lord's] table [as we have been doing]. Brothers and sisters, [since we can't accept women replacing us in our liturgical roles] choose seven males who are full of the Spirit and wisdom to whom we can assign this task [of conducting the daily Eucharist for believers], and we will busy ourselves with prayer and the ministry of the word [to unbelievers]."

Understanding these verses in this way can also shape how we read a verse at the end of the passage. Peter and the apostles ordained seven men, who are named in the text (6:5–6). Then, reports Luke, "the word of God grew and the number of disciples in Jerusalem greatly multiplied. A great company of the priests submitted to the faith" (6:7). This verse is usually understood as a historical aside that is not closely connected to the events just narrated. But what if the sudden influx of priests was an *outcome* of the action of the apostles? The Jewish priests, whose ministry and experience of worship had always been in an all-male cadre, may have found the Greek Nazoreans and their countenance of women in worship leadership a stumbling block. Once the issue was resolved in favor of male leadership, the priests lost their objection to uniting with the s-Nazoreans.

WHICH QUEST ARE WE IN?

The approach I have taken in this book fits broadly within what N.T. Wright has dubbed the "Third Quest" for the historical Jesus.[15] One of the key features of this phase of Jesus research is "the placement of Jesus firmly within Second Temple Judaism."[16] There is also a distinctive methodological component—the Third Quest approaches the task of Jesus research by building coherent models around Jesus and his movement and testing these models against the data. The Third Quest, however, is vaguely delimited. It can be difficult to decide which studies fit within it and which do not.[17]

Some writers claim that scholars have been moving in recent years into a "Fourth Quest." Our uncertainty about the boundaries of the Third Quest underline the impossibility of detecting the start of a Fourth Quest. Designations of such large-scale phases, moreover, is the work of intellectual historians, and then only with a long retrospective. Still, some claims may end up being right. The Fourth Quest has been identified, for example, with the restoration of the Gospel of John as a historical witness to the life of Jesus.[18] The Fourth Quest has also been pegged to "dispensing with the myth of a rupture between Jesus and Christianity."[19] From

15. Wright, *The Contemporary Quest*, 29–92.

16. Massey, "The Quest," 76.

17. See, for example, the critique of the Third Quest in Anthony Le Donne, "The Quest."

18. Anderson, "Jesus in Johannine Perspective."

19. Bernier, *The Quest*, 162.

my perspective, the Fourth Quest would begin with positioning Jesus, not just against the Jewish background of the Third Quest, but inside the specific context of a late Second Temple Jewish sect.

THE COMMUNITIES BEHIND THE GOSPELS

The idea that the gospels arose out of distinct communities, that they reflect the agendas of these narrow groups, that we can reconstruct the beliefs of these communities, and that we can use these reconstructions to interpret the gospels—all this came under attack in the late nineties with the publication of Richard Bauckham's *The Gospels for All Christians*. In this book, Bauckham argues that the gospels are outward-facing texts written for a wide and diverse audience. He questions whether reading them as allegories of their communities is a legitimate hermeneutical move.

Bauckham's position elicited a vigorous response.[20] Bauckham's position seems to have had an effect on biblical scholarship. While in the last decades of the twentieth century it was common for putative histories of these communities to be written, "virtually no such histories have been produced" in the years following the publication of *The Gospel for All Christians*.[21]

I won't be taking sides on this issue. The debate about gospel audiences, though, has had a beneficial outcome for this book—it has underlined how the reconstruction of late-90s CE gospel communities is an exercise in imagination. The Johannine community in particular, notes Adele Reinhartz, "is a hypothetical entity." She argues that we should continue to "contemplate its existence and conjecture as to its contours," but we must "refrain from attaching historicity to our own constructions."[22]

In some ways, my reconstruction of the Nazoreans falls under Bauckham's censure since I am reading the NT and other texts as the products of different communities. I do not hesitate, however, to call my project a conjecture.

---

20. For a review of the history of this debate, see the articles in Klink, *Audience of the Gospels*.

21. Bernier, "Ben F. Meyer," 203.

22. Reinhartz, "Gospel Audiences," 144.

Bibliography

Allison Jr, Dale C. *James: A Critical and Exegetical Commentary*. London: Bloomsbury-T&T Clark, 2013.

Anderson, Paul N. "Aspects of Historicity in the Gospel of John: Implications for Investigations of Jesus and Archaeology." in *Jesus and Archaelology*, edited by James H. Charlesworth, 587–618. Grand Rapids: Eerdmans, 2006.

———. "Jesus in Johannine Perspective: Inviting a Fourth Quest for Jesus." *Conspectus* 32 (2021) 7–41.

———. "Prologue: Critical Views of John, Jesus, and History." In *John, Jesus, and History, Volume 1: Critical Appraisals of Critical Views*, edited by Paul N. Anderson et al., 1–6. Atlanta: SBL Press, 2007.

———. "Why the Gospel of John is Fundamental to Jesus Research." In *Jesus Research: The Gospel of John in Historical Inquiry*, edited by James H. Charlesworth and Jolyon G.R. Pruszinski, 7–46. London: T&T Clark, 2019.

———. "Why This Study Is Needed, and Why It Is Needed Now." In *John, Jesus, and History, Volume 1: Critical Appraisals of Critical Views*, edited by Paul N. Anderson et al., 13–73. Atlanta: SBL Press, 2007.

Anderson, Paul N., et al., eds., *John, Jesus, and History*. 3 vols. Atlanta: SBL Press, 2007, 2009, 2016.

Appold, Mark. "Jesus' Bethsaida Disciples: A Study in Johannine Origins." In *John, Jesus, and History, Volume 2: Aspects of Historicity in the Fourth Gospel*, edited by Paul N. Anderson, et al., 27–34. Atlanta: SBL Press, 2009.

Archer, Gleason L. and Gregory Chirichigno. *Old Testament Quotations in the New Testament*. Chicago: Moody, 1983.

Atkinson, Kenneth R. "Herod the Great, Sosius, and the Siege of Jerusalem (37 B.C.E.) in Psalm of Solomon 17." *NovT* 38 (1996) 313–22.

———. *I Cried to the Lord: A Study of the Psalms of Solomon's Historical Background and Social Setting*. Leiden: Brill, 2004.

———. "On the Herodian Origin of Militant Davidic Messianism at Qumran: New Light from Psalm of Solomon 17." *JBL* 118 (1999) 435–60.

———. "Perceptions of the Temple Priests in the Psalms of Solomon." In *The Psalms of Solomon: Language, Theology, History*, edited by Eberhard Bons and Patrick Pouchelle, 79–96. Atlanta: SBL Press, 2015.

Augustine. *The Confessions of Augustine*, edited by James J. O'Donnell. Oxford: Clarendon, 1992.

Aune, David E. "Oral Traditions and the Aphorisms of Jesus." In *Jesus and the Oral Gospel Tradition*, JSNT Supplement Series 64, edited by Henry Wansbrough, 211–65. Sheffield, UK: JSOT Press, 1991.

Barrier, Jeremy Wade. "Middle Platonism in the Wisdom of Solomon: A Comparison of Wisdom to Plutarch of Chaeroneia." *JSP* 32 (2023) 244–69.

Bartchy, S. Scott. "Community of Goods in Acts: Idealization or Social Reality." In *The Future of Early Christianity*, edited by Birger A. Pearson, 309–18. Minneapolis: Fortress, 1991.

Bauckham, Richard. *The Gospels for All Christians: Rethinking the Gospel Audiences.* Grand Rapids: Eerdmans, 1997.

———. *James: Wisdom of James, Disciple of Jesus the Sage.* London: Routledge, 1999.

———. *Jesus and the Eyewitnesses: The Gospels as Eyewitness Testimony.* Grand Rapids: Eerdmans, 2006.

———. "Nicodemus and the Gurion Family." *JTS* 47 (1996) 1–37.

———. *The Testimony of the Beloved Disciple: Narrative, History, and Theology in the Gospel of John.* Grand Rapids: Baker Academic, 2014.

Bauer, David R. *The Structure of Matthew's Gospel: A Study in Literary Design.* Sheffield, UK: Almond, 1988.

Beers, Holly. *The Followers of Jesus as the 'Servant.'* London: Bloomsbury–T&T Clark, 2015.

Bergsma, John. *Jesus and the Dead Sea Scrolls.* New York: Image, 2019.

Bernier, Jonathan. *Aposynagōgos and the Historical Jesus in John: Rethinking the Historicity of the Johannine Expulsion Passages.* Leiden: Brill, 2013.

———. "Ben F. Meyer and The Gospels for All Christians." In *Jesus and Christian Origins*, edited by Ben Wiebe, 201–23. Eugene, OR: Wipf & Stock, 2019.

———. *The Quest for the Historical Jesus after the Demise of Authenticity.* London: T&T Clark, 2016.

———. *Rethinking the Dates of the New Testament.* Grand Rapids: Baker Academic, 2022.

Bieringer, Reimund et al., eds. *Anti-Judaism and the Fourth Gospel.* Louisville, KY: Westminster John Knox, 2001.

Boyarin, Daniel. "Enoch, Ezra, and the Jewishness of 'High Christology.'" In *Fourth Ezra and Second Baruch: Reconstruction After the Fall*, edited by Matthias Henze and Gabriele Boccaccini, 337–61. Leiden: Brill, 2013.

———. *The Jewish Gospels: The Story of the Jewish Christ.* New York: The New Press, 2012.

Bridges, Linda McKinnish. "The Aphorisms of Jesus in the Fourth Gospel: A Look at John 4:35." In *John, Jesus, and History, Volume 3: Glimpses of Jesus through the Johannine Lens*, edited by Paul N. Anderson et al., 337–52. Atlanta: SBL Press, 2016.

Brown, Jeannine K. "Matthew's Christology and Isaiah's Servant: A Fresh Look at a Perennial Issue." In *Treasures New and Old*, edited by Carl S. Sweatman and Clifford B. Kvidahl, 93–106. Wilmore, KY: GlossaHouse, 2017.

Brown, Raymond E. *An Introduction to the Gospel of John*, edited by Francis J. Moloney. New York: Doubleday, 2003.

———. "The Qumran Scrolls and John: A Comparison in Thought and Expression." In *A Companion to John: Readings in Johannine Theology*, edited by Michael J. Taylor, 69–90. New York: Alba House, 1977.

_____. "The Qumran Scrolls and the Johannine Gospels and Epistles," In *The Scrolls and the New Testament*, edited by Krister Stendahl, 183–207. New York: Harper, 1957.

Browning, Robert. *The Poems of Browning*, edited by Daniel Karlin and John Woolford. London: Routledge, 2014.

Bühner, Ruben A. *Messianic High Christology: New Testament Variants of Second Temple Judaism.* Waco, TX: Baylor University Press, 2021.

Burchard, C., trans. *Joseph and Asenath*, in *The Old Testament Pseudepigrapha*, edited by James H. Charlesworth, 2:177–247. Garden City, NY: Doubleday and Company, 1983.

Campbell, Jonathon. "The Qumran sectarian writings." In *The Early Roman Period*, edited by William Horbury et al., 798–821. Volume 3 of *The Cambridge History of Judaism*, edited by W. D. Davies and L. Finkelstein. Cambridge: Cambridge University Press, 1990.

Capper, Brian J. Canterbury Christ Church University Research Space Repository. https://repository.canterbury.ac.uk/researcher/80qqz/dr-brian-capper.

_____. "Essene Community Houses and Jesus' Early Community." In *Jesus and Archaeology*, edited by James H. Charlesworth, 472–502. Grand Rapids: Eerdmans, 2006.

_____. "The Judaean cultural context of community of goods in the early Jesus movement, Part II." *Qumran Chronicle* 26 (2018) 1–30.

_____. "'With the Oldest Monks . . .' Light from the Essene History on the Career of the Beloved Disciple?" *JTS* 49 (1998) 1–55.

Charlesworth, James H. *The Beloved Disciple.* Harrisburg, PA: Morehouse, 2002.

_____. "Can Archaeology Help Us See Jesus' Shadows in the Gospel of John?" In *Jesus Research: The Gospel of John in Historical Inquiry*, edited by James H. Charlesworth and Jolyon G.R. Pruszinski, 168–186. London: T&T Clark, 2019.

_____. "The Historical Jesus in the Fourth Gospel: A Paradigm Shift?" *JSHJ* 8 (2010) 3–46.

Charlesworth, James H. and Jolyon G.R. Pruszinski, eds. *Jesus Research: The Gospel of John in Historical Inquiry.* London: T&T Clark, 2019.

Chater, Nick and George Loewenstein. "The i-Frame and the s-Frame: How Focusing on Individual-Level Solutions Has Led Behavioral Public Policy Astray." *BBS* 46 (2023) 1–60.

Chicago Statement on Biblical Inerrancy. https://www.etsjets.org/files/documents/Chicago_Statement.pdf.

Cirafesi, Wally V. "Rethinking John and 'the Synagogue' in Light of Expulsion from Public Assemblies in Antiquity." *JBL* 142 (2023) 677–97.

Collingwood, R.G. *The Idea of History.* New York: Oxford University Press, 1956.

Coloe, Mary L. "John as Witness and Friend." In *John, Jesus, and History, Volume 2: Aspects of Historicity in the Fourth Gospel*, edited by Paul N. Anderson et al., 45–62. Atlanta: SBL Press, 2009.

Crenshaw, James L. *Old Testament Wisdom: An Introduction.* Louisville, KY: Westminster John Knox, 1998.

Cullmann, Oscar. *The Johannine Circle.* London: SCM Press, 1976.

Culpepper, R. Alan. *Anatomy of the Fourth Gospel: a Study in Literary Design.* Philadelphia: Fortress, 1987.

Daise, Michael A. *Feasts in John: Jewish Festivals and Jesus' 'Hour' in the Fourth Gospel.* Vol. 229 of Wissenshaftliche Untersuchungen zum Neuen Testament, 2.Reihe, edited by Jörg Frey. Tübingen: Mohr Siebeck, 2007.

Daniélou, Jean. *Philo of Alexandria.* Translated by James G. Colbert. Cambridge: Lutterworth, 2014.

Dawson, Lorne L. "Church-Sect-Cult: Constructing Typologies of Religious Groups." In *The Oxford Handbook of the Sociology of Religion,* 525–44. Oxford: Oxford University Press, 2011.

de Boer, Martinus C. "Expulsion from the Synagogue: J.L. Martyn's History and Theology in the Fourth Gospel Revisited." *NTS* 66 (2020) 367–91.

———. "The Original Prologue to the Gospel of John." *NTS* 61 (2015) 448–67.

Dederer, Claire. *Monsters: A Fan's Dilemma.* New York: Knopf, 2023.

Doran, Robert M. "Narratives of Noble Death." In *The Historical Jesus in Context,* edited by Amy-Jill Levine et al., 385–99. Princeton, NJ: Princeton University Press, 2006.

Dunn, James D.G. *Jesus Remembered.* Grand Rapids: Eerdmans, 2003.

Epiphanius. *The Panarion of Epiphanius of Salamis: Book I (Sects 1–46).* Translated by Frank Williams. Leiden: Brill, 2009.

Epstein, Isidore and Judah J. Slotki. *The Babylonian Talmud.* Translated by H. Freedman. London: Soncino, 1961.

Erman, Adolf. "Eine ägyptische Quelle der 'Sprüche Salomos.'" *Sitzungsberichte der Preussischen Akademie der Wissenschaften, philologisch-historische Klasse* 15 (1924) 86–93.

Farmer, William R. "A Fresh Approach to Q." In *Christianity, Judaism and Other Greco-Roman Cults: Studies for Morton Smith at Sixty,* edited by Jacob Neusner, 1:39–50. Leiden: Brill, 1975.

Farrer, Austin. *The Revelation of St. John the Divine: Commentary on the English Text.* Oxford: Clarendon Press, 1964.

Fitzmyer, Joseph A. "The Languages of Palestine in the First Century A.D." *CBQ* 32 (1970) 501–31.

Fontaine, Carole R. "Wisdom in Proverbs." In *In Search of Wisdom,* edited by Leo G. Perdue et. al., 99–114. Louisville, KY: Westminster John Knox, 1993.

Förster, Hans. "Translating from Greek as Source Language? The Lasting Influence of Latin on New Testament Translation." *JSNT* 43 (2020) 88–92.

Frankfurter, David. "Jews or Not? Reconstructing the 'Other' in Rev 2:9 and 3:9." *HTR* 94 (2001) 403–25.

Fredriksen, Paula. "The Historical Jesus, the Scene in the Temple, and the Gospel of John." In *John, Jesus, and History, Volume 1: Critical Appraisals of Critical Views,* edited by Paul N. Anderson, et al., 249–76. Atlanta: SBL Press, 2007.

Freud, Sigmund and Karl Abraham, *Briefwechsel 1907–1925,* edited by Ernst Falzeder and Ludger M. Hermanns. Berlin: Turia und Kant, 2010.

Frey, Jörg. "From the 'Kingdom of God' to "Eternal Life.'" In *John, Jesus, and History, Volume 3: Glimpses of Jesus through the Johannine Lens,* edited by Paul N. Anderson et al., 439–58. Atlanta: SBL Press, 2016.

Gallagher, Edmon L. "The Blood from Abel to Zechariah in the History of Interpretation." *NTS* 60 (2014) 121–38.

Gorman, Michael. *Abide and Go.* Eugene, OR: Cascade, 2018.

Hagner, Donald A. "The *Sitz im Leben* of the Gospel of Matthew." In *Treasures New and Old: Recent Contribution to Matthean Studies*, edited by Carl S. Sweatman and Clifford B. Kvidahl, 27–48. Wilmore, KY: GlossaHouse, 2017.

Hann, Robert R. "The Community of the Pious: The Social Setting of the Psalms of Solomon." *SR* 17 (1988) 169–89.

Hays, Richard B. *Reading Backwards*. Waco, TX: Baylor University Press, 2016.

Hengel, Martin and Daniel P. Bailey. "The Effective History of Isaiah 53 in the Pre-Christian Period." In *The Suffering Servant: Isaiah 53 in Jewish and Christian Sources*, edited by Bernd Janowski and Peter Stuhlmacher, translated by Daniel P. Bailey, 75–146. Grand Rapids: Eerdmans, 2004.

Heisenberg, Werner. *Physics and Philosophy: the Revolution in Modern Science*. London: George Allen & Unwin, 1959.

Hill, Charles E. *The Johannine Corpus in the Early Church*. Oxford: Oxford University Press, 2004.

Himmelfarb, Martha. *A Kingdom of Priests*. Philadelphia: University of Pennsylvania Press, 2006.

Horsley, Richard A. "Jesus Movements and the Renewal of Israel." In *Christian Origins*, edited by Richard A. Horsley, 11–39. Minneapolis: Fortress, 2005.

Huizenga, Leroy A. *The New Isaac*. Leiden: Brill Academic, 2009.

Humphreys, Colin. *The Mystery of the Last Supper*. Cambridge: Cambridge University Press, 2011.

Huxley, Aldous. *The Perennial Philosophy*. New York: Harper, 1945.

Ilan, Tal. *Lexicon of Jewish Names in Late Antiquity: Part I, Palestine 330 BCE–200 CE*. Tübingen: Mohr Siebeck, 2002.

Isaac, E., trans. *1 (Ethiopic Apocalypse of) Enoch*, in *The Old Testament Pseudepigrapha*, edited by James H. Charlesworth, 1:5–89. Garden City, NY: Doubleday and Company, 1983.

Jenkins, Jerry B. and Tim LeHaye, *Left Behind* (Carol Stream, IL: Tyndale, 1995).

Jenkins, Philip. "The Crucible Era: 200 Years That Shaped Judaism, Jesus, and Us." *The Christian Century* 134 (2017) 38.

———. *Crucible of Faith: The Ancient Revolution That Made Our Modern Religious World*. New York: Basic Books, 2017.

Jerome. *Theodoret, Jerome, Gennadius, Rufinus: Historical writings, etc*, translated by Ernest Cushing Richardson. Vol. 3 of *On Illustrious Men, A Select library of Nicene and post-Nicene Fathers of the Christian Church*. 2nd series, edited by Philip Schaff and Henry Wace. Buffalo, NY: Christian Literature Publishing Co., 1892. https://www.newadvent.org/fathers/2708.htm.

Johnson, Brian D. "The Jewish Feasts and Questions of Historicity in John 5–12." In *John, Jesus, and History, Volume 2: Aspects of Historicity in the Fourth Gospel*, edited by Paul N. Anderson et al., 117–29. Atlanta: SBL Press, 2009.

Joseph, Simon J. "The Ascetic Jesus." *JSHJ* 8 (2010) 146–81.

———. "'I Have Come to Abolish Sacrifices' (Epiphanius, *Pan.* 30.16.5): Re-Examining a Jewish Christian Text and Tradition." *NTS* 63 (2017) 92–110.

———. "'I Shall Be Reckoned with the Gods." *JSHJ* 18 (2020) 242.

Josephus. Translated by H. St. J. Thackeray et al. 10 vols. Loeb Classical Library. Cambridge: Harvard University Press, 1926–1965.

Just, SJ, Felix. "The Catholic Lectionary Website." http://catholic-resources.org/Lectionary/Statistics.htm.

Kashow, Robert C. "Traces of Ecclesiastes in the Gospel of John: An overlooked Background and a Theological Dialectic." *Neot.* 46 (2012) 229–43.

Keener, Craig. "Historical Tradition in the Fourth Gospel's Depiction of the Baptist." In *Jesus Research: The Gospel of John in Historical Inquiry*, edited by James H. Charlesworth and Jolyon G.R. Pruszinski, 155–67. London: T&T Clark, 2019.

Klawans, Jonathan. "Analogies, Possibilities and Probabilities: Joel Marcus's John the Baptist." *JSHJ* 19 (2021) 27–38.

Klink III, Edward W., ed. *The Audience of the Gospels: The Origin and Function of the Gospels in Early Christianity*. London: Bloomsbury–T&T Clark, 2010.

———. "The Overrealized Expulsion in the Gospel of John." In *John, Jesus, and History, Volume 2: Aspects of Historicity in the Fourth Gospel*, edited by Paul N. Anderson et al., 175–84. Atlanta: SBL Press, 2009.

Koestler, Arthur. *The God that Failed: Six Studies in Communism*, edited by Richard Crossman. London: Hamish Hamilton, 1950.

Kok, Michael J. *The Beloved Apostle?* Eugene, OR: Cascade, 2017.

Kraft, Robert A. "The Multiform Jewish Heritage of Early Christianity." In *Christianity, Judaism and Other Greco-Roman Cults: Studies for Morton Smith at Sixty*, edited by Jacob Neusner, 3:174–99. Leiden: Brill, 1975.

Kugel, James L. *How to Read the Bible: A Guide to Scripture, Then and Now*. New York: Free Press, 2007.

Kulp, Joshua. "The Origins of the Seder and the Haggadah." *CBR* 4 (2005) 109–34.

Kysar, Robert. "What's the Meaning of This?" In *What We Have Heard from the Beginning: The Past, Present and Future of Johannine Studies*, edited by Tom Thatcher, 163–77. Waco, TX: Baylor University Press, 2007.

Lanier, Gregory R. "'As It Is Written' . . . Where? Examining Generic Citations of Scripture in the New Testament." *JSNT* 43 (2021) 570–604.

Larsen, Matthew D.C. "Accidental Publication, Unfinished Texts and the Traditional Goals of New Testament Textual Criticism." *JSNT* 39 (2017) 362–87.

———. *Gospels Before the Book*. Oxford: Oxford University Press, 2018.

Le Donne, Anthony. "The Quest of the Historical Jesus: A Revisionist History through the Lens of Jewish-Christian Relations." *JSHJ* 10 (2012) 63–86.

Levine, Amy-Jill and Marianne Blickenstaff. *A Feminist Companion to Luke*. London: Sheffield, 2002.

Lightfoot, R.H. *St. John's Gospel: A Commentary*, edited by C.F. Evans. Oxford: Oxford University Press, 1956.

Lincoln, Andrew T. "'We Know That His Testimony is True': Johannine Truth Claims and Historicity." In *John, Jesus, and History, Volume 1: Critical Appraisals of Critical Views*, edited by Paul N. Anderson et al., 179–98. Atlanta: SBL Press, 2007.

List, Nicholas. "The Death of James the Just Revisited. *JECS* 32 (2024) 17–44.

———. "Problematising Dependency: Soteriology and Vocabulary in James and Paul." *ET* 131 (2020) 383–91.

Lyons, Michael A. "Psalm 22 and the 'Servants' of Isaiah 54; 56–66." *CBQ* 77 (2015) 640–56.

MacDonald, Dennis R. "Imitations of Greek Epic in the Gospels." In *The Historical Jesus in Context*, edited by Amy-Jill Levine et al., 372–84. Princeton, NJ.: Princeton University Press, 2006.

McLaughlin, John L. *An Introduction to Israel's Wisdom Traditions*. Grand Rapids: Eerdmans, 2018.

Marcus, Joel. "The Enigma of the Antitheses." *NTS* 69 (2022) 121–37.

———. "Passover and Last Supper Revisited." *NTS* 59 (2013): 303–24.

Marshall, John W. *Parables of War: Reading John's Jewish Apocalypse*. Kitchener, ON: Wilfrid Laurier University Press, 2001.

Martyn, J. Louis. *History and Theology in the Fourth Gospel*. New York: Harper and Row, 1968.

Massey, Brandon. "The Quest for the Historical Jesus, 2000–2023." *JSHJ* 21 (2023) 75–161.

Matson, Mark A. "Reviving the Priority of John." In *Jesus and Christian Origins*, edited by Ben Wiebe, 128–66. Eugene, OR: Wipf & Stock, 2019.

Mays, James Luther. *Psalms*. Louisville, KY: Westminster John Knox, 1994.

Meeks, Wayne A. "'Am I a Jew?'—Johannine Christianity and Judaism." In *Christianity, Judaism and Other Greco-Roman Cults: Studies for Morton Smith at Sixty*, edited by Jacob Neusner, 1:163–86. Leiden: Brill, 1975.

Méndez, Hugo. "Did the Johannine Community Exist?" *JSNT* 42 (2020) 350–74.

———. "Semitic Poetic Techniques in the Magnificat: Luke 1:46–47, 55." *JBL* 135 (2016) 557–74.

Merton, Thomas. *The Seven Storey Mountain*. New York: Harcourt Brace, 1978.

Methuen, Charlotte. "The 'Virgin Widow': A Problematic Social Role for the Early Church?" *HTR* 90 (1997) 285–98.

Millay, Edna St. Vincent. *Collected Poems*. New York: Harper, 2011.

Mitchell, Matthew W. "The Yoke Is Easy, but What of Its Meaning?: A Methodological Reflection Masquerading as a Philological Discussion of Matthew 11:30." *JBL* 135 (2016) 321–40.

Moses, A.D.A. *Matthew's Transfiguration Story and Jewish-Christian Controversy*. Sheffield, UK: Sheffield Academic Press, 1996.

Mueller, Daniel P. "Helping the Expectant Mother Elizabeth: The Nature and Purpose of Mary's Travel in Luke 1:39." *CBQ* 85 (2023) 276–96.

Murphy, Roland. *The Tree of Life*. Grand Rapids: Eerdmans, 1996.

Musser, George. *Putting Ourselves Back in the Equation*. New York: Farrar, Straus and Giroux, 2023.

New English Translation of the Septuagint and the Other Greek Translations Traditionally Included Under that Title, edited by Albert Pietersma and Benjamin G. Wright. Oxford: Oxford University Press, 2009. https://ccat.sas.upenn.edu/nets/edition/.

Parker, Pierson. "Luke and the Fourth Evangelist." *NTS* 9 (1963) 317–36.

———. "The Kinship of John and Acts." On *Christianity, Judaism and Other Greco-Roman Cults: Studies for Morton Smith at Sixty*, edited by Jacob Neusner, 1:187–205. Leiden: Brill, 1975.

———. "Two Editions of John." *JBL* 75 (1956) 303–14.

Parsenios, George L. "How and in What Ways Does John's Rhetoric Reflect Jesus' Rhetoric." In *Jesus Research: The Gospel of John in Historical Inquiry*, edited by James H. Charlesworth and Jolyon G.R. Pruszinski, 85–95. London: T&T Clark, 2019.

Pascal, Blaise. *Pensées: Opuscules et lettres*, edited by Philippe Sellier and Laurence Plazenet. Paris: Classiques Garnier, 2010.

Perdue, Leo G. "The Israelite and Early Jewish Family: Summary and Conclusions." In *Families in Ancient Israel*, edited by Leo G. Perdue et al., 163–222. Louisville, KY: Westminster John Knox, 1997.

Philo. Translated by F.H. Colson et al. 10 vols. Loeb Classical Library. Cambridge: Harvard University Press, 1926–1965.

Puskas, Charles B. and C. Michael Robbins, eds. *The Conceptual Worlds of the Fourth Gospel: Intertextuality and Early Reception.* Eugene, OR: Cascade, 2021.

Rankin, Oliver Shaw. *Israel's Wisdom Literature.* New York: Schocken, 1936.

Reed, Jonathan L. "Archaeological Contributions to the Study of Jesus and the Gospels." In *The Historical Jesus in Context,* edited by Amy-Jill Levine, et al., 40–54. Princeton: Princeton University Press, 2007.

Regev, Eyal. *Sectarianism in Qumran: A Cross-Cultural Perspective.* Berlin: de Gruyter, 2007.

Reid, Barbara E. *Choosing the Better Part? Women in the Gospel of Luke.* Collegeville, MD: Liturgical, 1996.

———. "The Gospel of Luke: Friend or Foe of Women Proclaimers of the Word?" *CBQ* 78 (2016) 1–23.

Reinhartz, Adele. "Gospel Audiences: Variations on a Theme." In *The Audience of the Gospels: The Origin and Function of the Gospels in Early Christianity,* edited by Edward W. Klink III, 134–52. London: Bloomsbury-T&T Clark, 2010.

Rexroth, Kenneth. *With Eye and Ear.* New York: Herder & Herder, 1970.

Rezetko, Robert et al., "Introducing *Misusing Scripture.*" In *Misusing Scripture: What Are Evangelicals Doing with the Bible?,* edited by Mark Elliott, et al., 3–75. London: Routledge, 2023.

Robinson, John A.T., *Honest to God.* London: SCM Press, 1963.

———. *Redating the New Testament.* London: SCM Press, 1976.

———. *Twelve New Testament Studies.* Naperville, IL: Alec R. Allenson, 1962.

Rohr, Richard. *The Universal Christ.* New York: Convergent, 2019.

Rosenmeyer, Patricia A. *Ancient Greek Literary Letters: Selections in Translation.* London: Routledge, 2006.

Russell, David Syme. *The Method and Message of Jewish Apocalyptic.* Philadelphia: Westminster, 1964.

Ryan, Jordan J. "Jesus at the Crossroads of Inference and Imagination." *JSHJ* 13 (2015) 66–89.

Ryle, Gilbert. *The Concept of Mind.* UK: Hutchinson, 1949.

Schneiders, Sandra M. *Written That You May Believe: Encountering Jesus in the Fourth Gospel.* New York: Crossroads, 1999.

———. "'Because of the Woman's Testimony . . .': Reexamining the issue of Authorship in the Fourth Gospel." *NTS* 44 (1998) 513–35.

Schuller, Eileen M. *The Dead Sea Scrolls: What Have We Learned?* Louisville, KY: Westminster John Knox, 2006.

Schüssler Fiorenza, Elisabeth. *In Memory of Her.* New York: Crossroads, 1992.

Schrader, Elizabeth and Joan E. Taylor. "The Meaning of 'Magdalene': A Review of Literary Evidence." *JBL* 140 (2021) 751–73.

Schweitzer, Albert. *Von Reimarus zu Wrede: Eine Geschichte der Leben-Jesu-Forschung.* Tübingen: Mohr, 1906.

Scobie, Charles H.H. "The Origins and Development of Samaritan Christianity." *NTS* 19 (1973) 390–414.

Seland, Torrey. "Why and How to Study Philo." In *Reading Philo: A Handbook of Philo of Alexandria,* edited by Torrey Seland, 135–240. Grand Rapids: Eerdmans, 2014.

Skinner, Christopher W. "Ethics and the Gospel of John: Toward an Emerging New Consensus?" *CBR* 18 (2020) 280–304.

———. "Narrative Readings of the Religious Authorities in John: A Response to Urban C. von Wahlde." *CBQ* 82 (2020) 424–36.

Sheridan, Ruth. "Issues in the Translation of οἱ Ἰουδαῖοι in the Fourth Gospel." *JBL* 132 (2013) 671–95.

Simon, Marcel. *Jewish Sects in the Time of Jesus.* Translated by James H. Farley. Minneapolis: Fortress, 1967.

———. *St. Stephen and the Hellenists in the Primitive Church.* London: Longmans, Green, 1958.

———. "Saint Stephen and the Jerusalem Temple." *JEH* 2 (1951) 127–42.

Smend, Rudolf. "The Interpretation of Wisdom in Nineteenth-century Scholarship." In *Wisdom in Ancient Israel: Essays in Honour of J.A. Emerton,* edited by John Day et al., 257–68. Cambridge: Cambridge University Press, 1995.

Smith, D. Moody. "John: A Source for Jesus Research?" In *John, Jesus, and History, Volume 1: Critical Appraisals of Critical Views,* edited by Paul N. Anderson et al., 165–78. Atlanta: SBL Press, 2007.

Spender, Stephen. *The God that Failed: Six Studies in Communism,* edited by Richard Crossman. London: Hamish Hamilton, 1950.

Stassen, Glen H. "The Fourteen Triads of the Sermon on the Mount (Matthew 5.21–7.12)." *JBL* 122 (2003) 267–308.

Stibbe, Mark W.G. "Protagonist." In *How John Works: Storytelling in the Fourth Gospel,* edited by Douglas Estes and Ruth Sheridan, 133–50. Atlanta: SBL Press, 2016.

Suggs, M. Jack. *Wisdom, Christology, and Law in Matthew's Gospel.* Cambridge: Harvard University Press, 1970.

Talmud. Translated by William Davidson. https://www.sefaria.org/texts/Talmud.

Taylor, Joan E. *Jewish Women Philosophers of First-Century Alexandria: Philo's "Therapeutae" Reconsidered.* Oxford: Oxford University Press, 2003.

Tcherikover, Victor A. and Alexander Fuks, *Corpus Papyrorum Judaicarum.* Cambridge: Harvard University Press, 1957, 1960, 1964.

Thurston, Bonnie Bowman. *The Widows: A Women's Ministry in the Early Church.* Minneapolis: Fortress, 1989.

Tomson, Peter J. "The Song of Songs in the Teachings of Jesus and the Development of the Exposition on the Song." *NTS* 61 (2015) 429–47.

Torijano, Pablo A. "Solomon and Magic." In *The Figure of Solomon in Jewish, Christian and Islamic Tradition,* edited by Joseph Verheyden, 107–25. Leiden: Brill, 2013.

Trafton, Joseph L. "The *Psalms of Solomon* in Recent Research." *JSP* 6 (1994) 3–19.

van de Weghe, Luuk. "The Beloved Eyewitness." *NTS* 68 (2022) 351–7.

———. "Name Recall in the Synoptic Gospels." *NTS* 69 (2023) 95–109.

van den Dungen, Wim. "The Instruction of Amen-em-apt, son of Kanakht." https://www.maat.sofiatopia.org/amen_em_apt.htm.

von Wahlde, Urban C. "Archaeology and John's Gospel." 543–86 in *Jesus and Archaeology,* edited by James H. Charlesworth. Grand Rapids: Eerdmans, 2006.

Wacholder, Ben Zion. *The New Damascus Document: The Midrash on the Eschatological Torah of the Dead Sea Scrolls: Reconstruction, Translation and Commentary.* Studies on the Texts of the Desert of Judah, 56. Leiden: Brill, 2007.

Wenham, David. "Matthean Priority: You Must be Joking." In *Treasures New and Old: Essays in Honor of Donald A. Hagner*, 57–75, edited by Carl S. Sweatman and Clifford B. Kvidahl. Wilmore, KY: GlossaHouse, 2017.

Werline, Rodney A. "The Formation of the Pious Person in the Psalms of Solomon." In *The Psalms of Solomon: Language, Theology, History*, edited by Eberhard Bons and Patrick Pouchelle, 133–54. Atlanta: SBL Press, 2015.

Wilson, Bryan R. "An Analysis of Sect Development." *ASR* 24 (1959) 3–15.

———. *Religious Sects: A Sociological Study*. London: Weidenfeld and Nicolson, 1970.

Witherington III, Ben. *Jesus the Sage*. Minneapolis: Fortress, 1994.

———. *John's Wisdom: A Commentary on the Fourth Gospel*. Louisville, KY: Westminster John Knox, 1995.

Wright, N.T. *The Contemporary Quest for Jesus*. Minneapolis: Fortress, 2002.

Wright, Robert B. *The Psalms of Solomon: A Critical Edition of the Greek Text*. London: T&T Clark, 2007.

Yee, Gale A. *Jewish Feasts and the Gospel of John*. Eugene, OR: Wipf & Stock, 2007.

Name Index

(References include entries in the text and footnotes
but not the bibliography.)

Abel, 119–21
Abraham (patriarch), 32, 53–54, 73,
    90–91, 128, 133, 183, 209, 236
Abraham, Karl, 3
Adam, 67, 120, 255
Adams, Robert Merrihew, 21
Aesop, 94
Agee, James, 66
Ahaz, 143
Allison Jr, Dale C., 127
Alphaeus, 89, 128
Anderson Paul. N., 162, 164, 169–71,
    272
Andrew (disciple), 95, 103, 171, 188,
    205–6
Anna (widow), 156, 201
Antigonus II, 227
Antipater, 227
Appold, Mark, 167
Aquinas, St. Thomas, 162
Archer, Gleason, 45
Atkinson, Kenneth R., 225–26, 228, 230
Augustine of Hippo, 5–6, 82, 127, 162
Augustus, 227, 270
Aune, David E., 101, 174

Bailey, Daniel P., 43, 260–61
Banus, 93
Barrier, Jeremy Wade, 68
Bartchy, S. Scott, 187
Bathsheba, 41

Bauckham, Richard, 84, 134, 175, 189,
    273
Bauer, David R., 83
Beers, Holly, 246, 260–61
Ben Sira, 58, 65–67, 71, 105, 111, 117–
    18, 133, 179
Berechiah, 119–20
Bergsma, John, 165
Bernier, Jonathan, 87, 200, 272–73
Bieringer, Reimund, 195
Blickenstaff, Marianne, 201
Boyarin, Daniel, 165, 184, 186, 257
Bridges, Linda McKinnish, 174
Brown, Jeannine K., 260
Brown, Raymond E., 178, 195, 217, 265
Browning, Robert, 18
Bühner, Ruben A., 165, 246
Burchard, C., 232

Cain, 120
Campbell, Jonathon, 36
Capper, Brian J., 221, 240
Charlesworth, James H, 162, 165,
    170–71
Chater, Nick, 185
Chirichigno, Gregory, 45
Cirafesi, Wally V., 200
Clopas, 135
Collingwood, R.G., ix, 10
Coloe, Mary L., 196
Colson, Francis Henry, 147
Crenshaw, James L., 61

Cullmann, Oscar, 168
Culpepper, R. Alan, 179

Daise, Michael A., 199
Daniel, 66, 73–5, 86
Daniélou, Jean, 154
David (king), 41, 43, 48, 54, 56–57,
    90–91, 101, 113, 117, 143, 226,
    228–30, 236, 255
Dawson, Lorne L., 253
de Boer, Martinus C., 177, 238
Dederer, Claire, 252
Descartes, René, 252
Dionysius of Halicarnassus, 270
Domitian, 135
Doran, Robert M., 163
Dorcas, 268–9
Dungan, David L., 84
Dunn, James D.G., 84

Eddy, Mary Baker, 31
Elizabeth (wife of Zechariah), 135–6,
    201, 266
Enoch, 27–28, 73
Epiphanius, 142, 237
Epstein, Isodore, 54
Erman, Adolf, 59
Eusebius of Caesarea, 84–85, 135, 150,
    154, 254
Evans, Walker, 66
Eve, 120
Ezra (priest), 25, 73–74

Farmer, William R., 84, 121
Farrer, Austin, 85
Felix, 142
Fitzmyer, Joseph A., 235
Fontaine, Carole R., 63
Förster, Hans, 112
Frankfurter, David, 248
Fredriksen, Paula, 250
Freud, Sigmund, 3
Frey, Jörg, 219
Fuks, Alexander, 146

Gallagher, Edmon L., 120
Gorman, Michael, 170
Grimm (folklorist brothers), 94

Hagner, Donald A., 81
Hann, Robert R., 225, 228
Hays, Richard B., 42, 46
Hegel, G.W.F., 20, 21
Hegesippus, 135, 154, 254–56
Heisenberg, Werner, 22
Hengel, Martin, 43, 260–61
Herod Antipas, 90, 107, 160, 265
Herod the Great, 42, 144, 146, 220, 225,
    227, 229–30, 232, 240–41
Hill, Charles E., 161
Himmelfarb, Martha, 186
Horsley, Richard A., 145
Huizenga, Leroy A., 260
Humphreys, Colin, 211
Huxley, Aldous, 19

Ilan, Tal, 205
Isaac (patriarch), 32
Isaac, E., 122

Jacob (patriarch), 67, 73, 170, 176, 180,
    192, 232, 236, 261
James son of Zebedee, 95, 103, 128,
    171–72, 205, 254, 267
James, brother of Jesus, 119, 125, 128–
    29, 130–31, 133, 135–36, 138,
    154, 186, 189, 239
James, son of Alphaeus, 89, 128
Jenkins, Jerry B., 124
Jenkins, Philip, 72–73
Jerome, 127
Joash, 120
John of Gischala, 141
John the Baptist, 49, 90–91, 93, 95,
    106–10, 135–36, 145, 150, 154–
    55, 158, 166, 171, 173, 179–80,
    187, 190, 195, 197, 221, 240,
    242, 263, 265–68
John, son of Zebedee, 95, 103, 128,
    170–72, 205
Johnson, Brian D., 199
Joseph of Arimathea, 176, 200
Joseph, brother of Jesus, 119, 129, 135
Joseph, father of Jesus, 42, 90, 135, 139,
    140–41, 144–46, 156, 220–21
Joseph, Simon J., 154, 237, 256

Josephus, 26, 29, 33–35, 70, 91–93, 102,
    114, 129, 141, 146, 205, 220,
    226–27, 254
Judas Iscariot, 172, 213
Judas, brother of Jesus, 119, 129, 135
Jude, author of Epistle of Jude, 125,
    130, 136
Julian of Norwich, 215
Julius Caesar, 227
Jung, Carl, 253
Just SJ, Felix, 52

Kashow, Robert C., 174
Kastrup, Bernardo, 21
Keener, Craig S., 168, 197
Kipling, Rudyard, 253
Klawans, Jonathan, 266
Klink III, Edward W., 200, 273
Knibb, Michael A., 68
Koestler, Arthur, 5–6
Kok, Michael J., 189
Kraft, Robert A., 70, 146
Kugel, James, 8, 55, 77
Kulp, Joshua, 199
Kysar, Robert, 252

Lanier, Gregory R., 41
Larsen, Matthew, 83
Lazarus, 166, 176, 202, 204, 207, 221
Le Donne, Anthony, 272
LeHaye, Tim, 124
Levine, Amy-Jill, 201
Lewis, C.S., 14–15
Lightfoot, R.H., 162
Lincoln, Andrew T., 190
List, Nicholas, 129–30
Loewenstein, George, 185
Luther, Martin, 127
Lyons, Michael A., 262

MacDonald, Dennis R., 83
Marcus, Joel, 97, 199
Mark Anthony, 146
Marshall, John W., 248–49
Martha, 201–2, 207, 221
Martyn, J. Louis, 200
Mary Magdalene, 138, 141, 172, 201,
    203

Mary, mother of Jesus, 9, 90, 119, 129,
    135–36, 144–46, 156, 172–73,
    193, 201–2, 220–21, 241, 266
Mary, sister of Martha, 201–3, 207, 221
Massey, Brandon, 272
Matson, Mark A., 169
Matthew (apostle), 85, 89
Mays, James Luther, 262
McLaughlin, John L., 55, 115
Meeks, Wayne A., 197
Méndez, Hugo, 155, 243
Merton, Thomas, 18, 19
Methuen, Charlotte, 269
Millay, Edna St. Vincent, 20
Milton, John, 189
Mitchell, Matthew W., 111
Moses, 29, 32, 37, 47, 54, 66–67, 73, 77,
    92, 96, 148, 176, 178, 181–82,
    191, 199, 235–37, 250, 252
Moses, A.D.A., 250
Moule, C.F.D., 235
Mueller, Daniel P., 266
Murphy, Roland, 78
Musser, George, 21

Nathanael, 172, 191–92, 204
Newton, Isaac, 55
Nicodemus, 175–76, 179, 196, 199, 202
Noah (patriarch), 27–28, 73, 255

Octavian, 146
Orchard, Dom Bernard, 84
Origen, 91

Papias, 85
Parker, Pierson, 167, 244
Parsenios, George L., 174, 180
Pascal, Blaise, 3
Paul (apostle), 49, 63, 79–80, 96, 125–
    31, 133, 136, 138, 141–42, 150,
    152, 158, 191, 201, 233, 239,
    244–48, 270–71
Perdue, Leo G., 185
Peter (disciple), 47–48, 95, 103, 125,
    129, 138, 165–66, 171–73,
    202–5, 213, 222, 238–39, 264,
    268, 271–72

Philip (disciple), 191–92, 198, 205–6,
    262–63
Philo, 35, 69–71, 146–55, 157, 181, 187,
    193, 196, 217
Plato, 15, 68, 71, 105, 162
Plutarch, 68
Pompey, 226–29, 240
Pruszinski, Jolyon G.R., 162
Puskas, Charles B., 161, 244

Rankin. Oliver Shaw, 60
Reed, Jonathan L., 213
Regev, Eyal, 39
Reid, Barbara E., 201
Reinhartz, Adele, 273
Rexroth, Kenneth, 77
Rezetko, Robert, 9
Robbins, C. Michael, 161, 244
Robinson, John A.T., 4, 85, 197
Rohr, Richard, 19
Rosenmeyer, Patricia A., 125
Russell, David Syme, 74
Ryan, Jordan J., 10
Ryle, Gilbert, 252

Sanders, E.P., 80
Schneider, Susan, 21
Schneiders, Sandra M., 174, 202–4
Schrader, Elizabeth, 141
Schuller, Eileen, 39
Schüssler Fiorenza, Elisabeth, 1
Schweitzer, Albert, 1, 123
Scobie, Charles H.H., 197, 234
Seland, Torrey, 70
Sheridan, Ruth, 195
Simeon, 156, 216
Simeon, son of Clopas, 135
Simon, brother of Jesus, 119, 129, 135
Simon, Marcel, 147, 235–37, 255, 270
Skinner, Christopher W., 83–84, 208
Slotki, Judah J., 54
Smend, Rudolf, 53
Smith, D. Moody, 164
Socrates, 105

Solomon (king), 56–57, 62, 66–69,
    77, 101–3, 113, 115–16, 170,
    225–26, 231, 236
Spender, Stephen, 6
St. Francis, 19
Stassen, Glen H., 98–99
Stibbe, Mark W.G., 163, 177
Suggs, M. Jack, 121

Taylor, Joan E., 141, 147
Tcherikover, Victor A., 146
Thomas, 172, 205–6
Thurston, Bonnie Bowman, 269
Tomson, Peter J., 174
Torijano, Pablo A., 102
Trafton, Joseph L., 226
Troeltsch, Ernst, 253

Underhill, Evelyn, 19

van de Weghe, Luuk, 158, 244
van den Dungen, Wim, 59
von Wahlde, Urban C., 169

Wacholder, Ben Zion, 149
Weber, Max, 253
Weil, Simone, 19
Wenham, David, 84
Werline, Rodney A., 231
Wilson, Bryan R., 30–31, 39–40, 48–49,
    139, 208, 242
Witherington III, Ben, 76, 167, 173–74,
    177, 184
Woolman, John, 215
Wright, N.T., 272
Wright, Robert B., 224

Yee, Gale A., 199

Zebedee, 95, 128, 171, 205
Zechariah (prophet), 119–21
Zechariah (husband of Elizabeth), 160,
    266–267

Ancient Document Index

ANCIENT NEAR EASTERN DOCUMENTS

1 Enoch

42:2	69, 122, 178

Psalms of Solomon

2:7	228
2:36	228
3:6–7	228
3:8	228
3:12	228
4:2–5	229
4:4	231
4:5	231
4:7–8	229
4:8	231
4:9	232
4:10	232
4:14–22	232
4:18	232
5:16–17	231
8:9–12	228
8:16–17	227
17:4–6	228
17:4	229
17:6	229
17:7	229
17:9	229
17:11	229
17:14–15	229
17:18–19	229
17:21	230
17:22–23	230
17:23–24	230
17:29	230
17:32–36	230
17:33	230
17:37	230
18:7	230
18:10	230
18:12	230

OT DOCUMENTS

Genesis

1:1	64
4:1–16	120
5:21–25	27
6:1–7	28
15:6	133
28:10–17	192

Exodus

31:12–17	181
33:11	182
33:20	182
33:23	182

Leviticus

19:18	133

Numbers

6:1–21	144

Deuteronomy

6:13	93
6:16	93
8:3	92
18:18	199

Judges

9:7–15	117
13:5	144

2 Samuel

14:1–20	117

1 Kings

3:5–15	56
3:16–28	56
3:28	56
4:29–34	56
10:1–13	56
20:35–43	117

2 Kings

12:9	264
23:4	264

2 Chronicles

24:20–22	120

Nehemiah

9:6	53

Ezra

2:70	264

Job

4:7	61

Psalms

8:2	43
22:1	262
37:10	38
41:9	212
91:11–12	93

Proverbs

1:6	60, 117
1:9	179
2:6	180
3:34	133
6:6–8	60
6:18	179
8:22–24	64, 177
8:30–31	64, 177, 181
8:34	100
8:35–36	108, 179
9:5	111
9:6	179
11:20	61
11:24	61
15:11	61
15:17	61
22:20	59
26:17	61
30:18–19	61

Ecclesiastes

1:6	175
8:8	175
12:1–7	61
12:9–14	58

Isaiah

5:1–7	117
6:9–10	118
7:14–16	143
9:1–2	216
9:1	143, 155
9:6	143
11:1	143, 218
11:2	143, 156
11:3–4	143
11:4	156
29:13	44
40:3	265
41:8	261

42:1-4	113, 260-61
44:1-2	261
44:9-20	237
49:1-6	260
50:4-11	260
52:13—53:12	260
52:13	78, 152
53:2	153
53:6-7	191
53:11	78
54:17	153
61:1-2	261-62
61:10	196
62:5	196
66:1-2	236

Jeremiah

2:2	196
2:32	196
18:18	58
35:4	264

Ezekiel

| 40:46 | 226 |

Daniel

| 9:26-27 | 86 |
| 12:2 | 75 |

Habakkuk

| 1:5 | 38 |

Zechariah

| 1:1 | 120 |

Malachi

| 3:1 | 108 |

DEUTEROCANONICAL WRITINGS

1 Esdras

| 1:15 | 264 |

2 Esdras

| 14:42-47 | 74 |

Sirach

1:4	66
1:9	66
7:15-22	103
24:3-4	66
24:8	67
24:10-11	67
24:19-21	111
24:21	180
24:23	67
24:32-33	66
38:24	118
39:1-3	117
44:1	66
50:27	66
51:13-14	58
51:23-27	112
51:23	58
51:26	58

Wisdom of Solomon

1:6	114
3:13-14	150
5:15-16	76
5:17-23	76
6:12	68
6:16	68
6:22	68
7:17	68
7:22-23	68
7:22	68, 177
7:25-26	68, 177-79
7:27	68
8:7	151
8:16	151
9:17	69, 179
10:16-17	178
16:28	151

2 Maccabees

| 7:23 | 75 |

NT DOCUMENTS

Matthew

1:1–17	90
1:1	101
1:20	90
2:1–12	90
2:14–15	145
2:15	42, 45
2:22–23	144
3:1–17	90
3:4	154
3:7–12	267
3:11–12	107
3:17	90
4:1–11	91
4:3–4	92
4:6	93
4:7	93
4:10	93
4:14–16	143
4:17	96
5:3	134
5:5	134
5:11–12	134
5:17–20	97
5:20–48	98
5:21–26	98
5:34–35	134
6:6	157
6:19–21	134
6:24	93, 134
6:25–33	100
6:28–29	101
7:7	134
7:24	134
7:28–29	99
8:14–16	103
8:16	102
8:19–20	103
8:20	103
8:21–22	103
8:23–27	103, 106
9:9	89, 103
9:10–13	106
9:14	106, 155
9:15	155

9:35–37	104
10:1	104
10:5–6	104
10:9–10	155
10:40	106
11:1	107
11:2–19	107
11:3	107, 145
11:9–10	108
11:11	108
11:12–13	108
11:16–19	109
11:19	110, 212
11:25–30	110
11:27	111
11:28	111
11:29–30	111
12:6	112, 115
12:8	112
12:9–14	112
12:15–16	112
12:18–21	113, 261
12:22–32	113
12:30–32	114
12:36–37	114
12:38–42	114
12:41	115
12:42	101, 115
12:43–45	116
12:48–50	137
13:10–17	117
13:51–52	118
13:53–58	118, 210
13:55–56	128
14:13–21	103
14:22–33	103
15:32–39	103
16:16	165, 202
17:24–27	103
21:15–16	43
21:18–22	103
22:34–39	96
22:36–40	208
23:29–36	119
24:15	86
24:34	120
26:18	188
26:30	156

28:1–10	203	24:44–45	47
28:10	138		
28:15	194	**John**	
		1:1–18	177, 189
Mark		1:1	166
1:12–13	91	1:3	177
2:14	89	1:4–5	178
2:27	112	1:9	178, 217–18
3:20–21	137	1:10	178
3:31–35	137	1:14	177–78
5:7	193	1:18	177
6:3	128	1:19–34	196
7:5–8	44	1:29–37	166
7:7	44	1:32	190
14:13–16	188	1:35–51	196
		1:35–42	171, 267
Luke		1:37	190
		1:39	263
1:15	267	1:43–51	191
1:36	136, 266	1:45	191
1:38	202	1:46	192, 262
1:39–40	145	1:47	192
1:39	266	1:48	192
1:67–79	155, 267	1:49	192
1:80	154, 265	2:1–12	136, 191
2:19	202	2:4	193
2:25	156	2:6	170
2:32	156, 216	2:10	193
2:36–38	156	2:11	166, 196
2:41–51	92	2:12	196
2:44	136	2:13–22	193
2:49	159	2:13	212
3:7–9	267	2:16	194
4:1–12	91	2:23	166
4:16–21	261	3:1–2	175
5:27	89	3:4	175
6:17–49	106	3:6	175
7:18–35	110	3:8	175
8:19–21	137	3:10	176
10:25–37	198	3:14–15	176
11:47–51	121	3:16	176
13:34–35	121	3:19–21	176
17:11–17	198	3:21	217
18:7	157	3:22	190
18:37	141	3:25–26	166
22:8–13	188	3:29	197
24:13–27	47	3:30	179

John (continued)

3:31–36	180	7:24	194
3:32	180	7:37	199
3:34–35	180	7:38	180
3:36	180	7:41–42	210
4:1	190	7:50–51	176
4:2	190	7:52	210
4:3	190, 210	8:12	179, 217
4:5–6	170	8:23	182
4:10	180	8:24	195
4:14	179–80	8:28	182
4:19–20	170	8:31–38	209
4:23–24	197	8:38	182
4:25–26	202	8:42	183
4:26	202	8:44	195
4:35–36	197	8:47	195
4:38	197	8:48	198
4:39	202	8:51	183
4:42	197	8:55	195
4:44–45	210	8:56	183
4:54	166	8:58	183
5:1	199, 212	9:5	178, 217
5:2–9	170	9:7	170
5:17	181	9:22	200
5:18	181	9:34	200
5:19	182	9:41	195
5:24	217	10:1–6	218
5:25–29	207	10:3	217
5:30	182	10:6	217
5:45–47	194	10:7–10	218
6:1–15	198	10:9	218
6:1	166	10:16	214
6:4	199, 212	10:22	199
6:32	218	10:23	170
6:33–35	179	10:28–30	183
6:35–50	166	10:30	164
6:35	182, 218	11:2	166
6:37	182	11:21–26	207
6:40	207, 217	11:27	202
6:44	207	11:55	212
6:46	182	12:1–8	202
6:51–58	166	12:13	206
6:54	207	12:20–22	205
6:60	182	12:23–30	205
7:1–10	137	12:35	217
7:2	199	12:36	217
7:3	166	12:42–43	200
		13:6–11	213
		13:21–30	171

13:18	212
13:34	208
13:36	166
14:3	207
14:6–7	183
14:9	164, 183
14:16–17	183
14:20	208
14:26	183
14:28	183
14:31	166
15:1–8	218
15:26–27	183
16:2	200
16:5	166
16:8–9	183
16:15	183
16:28	178, 183
17:1	216
17:5	216
17:10	216
17:22	216
17:24	216
18:15–16	172
18:16–17	264
19:25–27	172, 221
19:25	135, 201
19:28–30	222
19:31	202
19:34–35	214
19:35	172
19:38–42	176, 200
20:1–18	203
20:1–9	172
20:2	172
20:19–23	203
20:21	170
20:22	184
20:24–29	206
20:29	206
20:30–31	166
21:1–2	204
21:2	191, 205
21:22	172
21:23	166
21:24	167
21:25	167

Acts

1:14	136
2:24	48
2:25–28	48
2:29	48
2:31–32	48
2:42–47	234
3:13	261
3:26	261
4:27	261
4:30	261
4:32–35	234
4:32	157
5:33–42	233
6:1–7	234, 268
6:1–3	234, 268, 271
6:1	270
6:2	271
6:5–6	272
6:6	238
6:7	272
6:8–15	234–35
7:2	236
7:46–47	236
7:51–52	237
7:58	245
8:1–3	245
8:1	234
9:2	246
9:13	246
9:36–42	268
9:36	269
11:19–21	239
11:20	233, 239
11:29	270
16:34	271
17:25	152
18:25	158
18:26	158
18:28	158
19:1–7	158
20:24	270
21:18	129
24:5	142

1 Corinthians

1:18–31	247

1 Corinthians (continued)

2:3–5	247
3:4–5	247
4:8–10	247
9:5	136
10:21	271
15:6–7	138
15:7	129
15:9	245

2 Corinthians

3:3	270
11:2	196
11:22	233
12:4	247

Galatians

1:19	129
2:9	129
2:12	129
3:6–14	128

Ephesians

1:3–14	244
1:20	245
2:6	245
5:8–14	245
5:25–33	196

Philippians

2:6–11	246
3:5	245

Colossians

1:15	245
1:16–17	245
2:3	245

1 Timothy

2:11–12	201
5:3–16	269
5:3	269

2 Timothy

4:10	63

Hebrews

1:3	244
8:5	191
8:13	191
9:11	191

James

1:1	128, 130–31
1:2	134
1:3–4	132
1:5	131, 134
1:6	132
1:11	132
1:12	132
1:15	132
1:19	132
1:22–25	133
1:22	134
2:5	134
2:8	133
2:13	132
2:14–26	130
2:20–24	128
2:23	133
2:26	133
3:1–12	133
3:3	132
3:5	132
3:11	132
3:13–17	131
3:16	133
4:4	133–34
4:5	133
4:6	133
4:7–8	132
4:8	132
4:14	132
4:17	133
5:2–3	134
5:2	132
5:7	132
5:10	134
5:12	134

5:20 133

Jude
1:1 136

1 John
2:18–22 208

Revelation
2:2 248
2:6 248
2:9 248
2:14 248
2:15 248
2:20 248
2:24 248
3:9 248
3:17 248
22:17 196

DEAD SEA SCROLLS

1QpHab
II, 1–9 38

1QS
V, 8–10 37
VI, 6–8 37
VIII, 15–16 38
IX, 4–5 39

4Q171
II, 7–8 38

CD–A
I, 5–11 37
I, 11 37
III, 14 37
VI, 3 37
VI, 7 37

CD–B
XX, 14–15 38

RABBINIC WRITINGS

Shabbat (Babylonian Talmud)
30b 54

Genesis Rabbah
11:10 181

Joseph and Asenath
11:13 232

GRECO-ROMAN
WRITINGS

Josephus

Ag. Ap.
1.8 26

Life
2 92–93
10 141
44 141

Ant.
8.45–6a 102
13.3 146
14.4.2 227
14.16 227
18.5.2 90
20 114
20.9.1 129

Philo

Contempl. Life
1–11 146–50

Cherubim
87 181

Philo (continued)

Drunkenness

30   71

Flight

52   63

Good Person

12.75–87   140
82   35

Xenophon

Anabasis

5.7.10   263

EARLY CHRISTIAN WRITINGS

Augustine

Confessions

9.1.1   25

Harmony of the Gospels

1.3   82

Dionysius of Halicarnassus

Commentaries on the Attic Orators

3.18   270

Epiphanius

Panarion

18   142
29   142
30.16.5   237

Eusebius

Hist.

2.17   150
2.23   154
3.11   135
3.20   135
3.23.1–4   189
3.39.16   85
4.22   254

Irenaeus

Haer.

3.1.1   189

Jerome

Vir. ill.

2   127

Origen

Orig. Princ.

4.16   91